In 'Vanity Fair'

An Encyclopedia
Thomas Gibson Bowles MP
Men of the Day No 986
19 October 1905
Spy

In 'Vanity Fair'

Roy T. Matthews and Peter Mellini

Scolar Press   London

University of California Press   Berkeley and Los Angeles

First published in Great Britain in 1982
by Scolar Press
James Price Publishing Ltd
90/91 Great Russell Street
London WC1B 3PY

Published simultaneously in the United States
by the University of California Press
Berkeley and Los Angeles

ISBN 0–85967–597–1 (UK edition)
ISBN 0–520–04300–6 (US edition)

British Library Cataloguing in Publication Data
Matthews, Roy T.
  In 'Vanity Fair'
  1. Caricatures and cartoons – England
  2. Vanity Fair
  I. Title   II. Mellini, Peter
  741.5'942   NC1478.V36

Library of Congress Catalog Card Number 81–52688

Designed by Alan Bartram
Typeset by Wilsted & Taylor Publishing Services
Printed in the United States of America
by Kingsport Press and Southeastern Printing

The authors and publishers are grateful to *Vanity Fair* Ltd. of
Cincinnati, Ohio, who permitted us to reproduce all the carica-
tures except: 'The Great Imperialist', Joseph Chamberlain,
(**36**), courtesy the National Portrait Gallery, London; Dr. T. R.
Allinson (**18**), George Alexander (**33**), 'Winnie', Winston
Churchill (**64**), and F. E. Smith, MP (**70**), courtesy the Peter
Mellini Collection.

Contents

To Lee Ann and Gisela

Preface

A comprehensive study of British caricature after the Georgian greats does not exist, though the topic has drawn perceptive comment from, among others, Max Beerbohm, Eileen Harris, Bevis Hillier, David Low, Bohun Lynch and Richard Ormond. Apart from a few exhibition catalogues, this is the first thorough overview of the trendsetting *Vanity Fair* caricatures, the chromolithographic portraits which have so shaped our notion of what many eminent Victorians and Edwardians looked like.

The book grew out of our long-standing interest in the caricatures. Roy T. Matthews has been concerned with the career of Spy (Sir Leslie Ward) and with the social and artistic impact of the cartoons, while Peter Mellini first encountered the series of portraits while researching his book on Sir Eldon Gorst. When we decided to collaborate on this project, we knew that information on *Vanity Fair* was both widely scattered and plagued by myth. The pages which follow have been constructed to serve the needs of scholar and collector as well as everyone fascinated by an intriguing piece of British social history, and our efforts to remove much of this myth will, we hope, serve to increase the enjoyment of all who encounter *Vanity Fair* cartoons.

In 'Vanity Fair' was a cooperative venture. The advice, assistance, support, hospitality and patience of a variety of individuals, institutions and organizations enabled and encouraged us to improve and to complete our book. The idea for the book developed out of discussions begun when we met in Denver, Colorado, at the 1974 Rocky Mountain Conference on British Studies. William Abrahams gave us pertinent suggestions on the initial form. Gordon Phillips, the archivist of *The Times* (London), directed us towards Scolar Press, where our editor, Sean Magee, shepherded manuscript and authors genially and carefully. He contributed the sketch on Lutteur III. Kathryn Hollingsworth also of Scolar kept us informed of developments, which we much appreciated. William J. McClung of the University of California Press welcomed *In 'Vanity Fair'* to the Press and has guided the book into print. Christine Taylor, of Wilsted and Taylor, applied herself to a complex manuscript. We are particularly happy with the sympathetic editing performed by Kath Davies and the handsome book design by Alan Bartram.

Research for the book took us beyond the libraries and archives which most historians frequent – to museums, art galleries, print dealers' shops and storerooms, publishers' offices, lawyers' chambers, hotels, restaurants, pubs, saloons, betting shops, private clubs and homes, wherever *Vanity Fair* cartoons are hung or bought and sold. We have spent days and nights talking to collectors, dealers and specialists knowledgeable in the print business. They have helped us bridge the gap between the abstractions of the historian and the realities of the market place. We are wiser for their advice, heartened by their cooperation, enriched by their friendship and delighted by their hospitality.

The professional staffs at several libraries in Britain and North America facilitated our research and made our tasks much more pleasurable. We are especially grateful to the library staff at Michigan State University, particularly those in the Art library, the Microforms library and interlibrary loan office. The scholarly resources of the University of California Libraries at Berkeley were also highly useful, and their staff has our thanks.

Richard Ormond, the Deputy Director at the National Portrait Gallery in London, was exceptionally cooperative. The staff of the Gallery, especially Miss Elspeth Evans, was always willing to let us see what we needed. We received full cooperation from the Victoria and Albert Museum, the University of London Library, the British Library in Bloomsbury and in Colindale, the Library of Congress, the New York Public Library, the Beinecke Rare Book and Manuscript Library of Yale University and the University of Michigan Library at Ann Arbor.

Dr Donald Lammers, chairman of the History Department at Michigan State University, read parts of the manuscript and made some useful suggestions. Carol Koch, with some assistance from Thomas Benjamin, assembled the caricature list with great care and attention to detail. Bevis Hillier gave us encouragement to finish the book. David Rose was most generous with his scholarly research and advice. Keith Wallace sagely advised us and warmly entertained us along the way, as did C. J. Carey.

We are especially indebted to Dr Eileen Harris and Richard Ormond whose work on Ape (Carlo Pellegrini) and *Vanity Fair* for the exhibition in 1976 at the National Portrait Gallery was a stimulus to us and a very useful source. Frank Miles of King's College School provided us with information on Thomas Gibson Bowles's schooling. Jane Abdy shared her knowledge of James Jacques Tissot's career.

Numerous print dealers were patient and informative. We fondly remember the late George J. Suckling of Cecil Court, who once locked one of the authors in his shop so that he could continue to research some albums of *Vanity Fair*. Mr Suckling's detailed memory of the London print trade in the twenties and thirties put us on the trail of David Weir and Paul and Ada Victorious and led us to Ron Chappel and Benjamin Weinreb. The latter two filled in some critical gaps in the clouded history of the stock of *Vanity Fair* cartoons between 1914 and 1973. Mr Chappel and Mr Weinreb frankly shared their recollections of those locust years. Mr Eugene O'Karma provided us with additional information on the cartoons and on Paul Victorious and graciously entertained one of us at Brobury House. Andrew Block corroborated much of what we had uncovered in our other interviews.

Thomas S. Benjamin, of *Vanity Fair* Ltd, of Cincinnati, Ohio, and Morton W. Olman, of the Old Golf Shop, also of Cincinnati, filled us in on the acquisition of Paul Victorious's stock of *Vanity Fair* cartoons. The majority of the caricatures in this book were provided by *Vanity Fair* Ltd. John Franks of London has amassed one of the most complete private collections of *Vanity Fair* cartoons. He has been most generous with his advice and help, as has Kenneth Taylor of La Belle Epoque, in Westwood, California.

The story of the cartoons, after the demise of *Vanity Fair* in 1914, was partially clarified by C. P. Allinson, son of Dr T. R. Allinson, the last proprietor of *Vanity Fair*, and by Mr and Mrs Frederick E. Goold and Mrs E. M. Harvey. Mrs Harvey and Mrs Goold are the daughters of David R. Weir, who acquired the remaining stock of cartoons in the 1920s.

We also wish to acknowledge the advice and interest of Robert J. Weir of Alfred Dunhill Ltd, A. 'Harry' Goss of Wildy & Sons, John Mason of Butterworth and Co Ltd, Dick Brennen of the Wig and Pen Club and Professor Peter Stansky of Stanford University.

Lucy Stevenson and Susan Studley typed the first part of the draft of the book manuscript, and Margaret Martin typed the last sections. Lia Olson and Maureen Cantor typed the caricature and artist lists swiftly and accurately. We wish to extend them our warm appreciation for their patience and high standards.

To the countless colleagues, book dealers, shop attendants, librarians and staff members not mentioned who helped us, we extend our heartfelt thanks. Last but most crucial we remain lucky to have such splendid spouses, who patiently endured the years necessary to produce *In 'Vanity Fair'*.

R. T. M.
P. M.

VANITY FAIR:

A Weekly Show of Political, Social, and Literary Wares.

" That which did not a little amuse the merchandisers was, that these pilgrims set very light
by all their wares."

THE GOVERNMENT.

THE one thing that is always said of a new Government as soon as it is formed is, that it " can't possibly last," and there are always good reasons by the dozen to give for the opinion. The fact that it has been said of the Gladstone administration is not, therefore, much of itself, but the reasons certainly appear stronger and better than is common, and the oft-repeated assertion is therefore so far the better worth examination.

There can be no doubt that the present Cabinet is grievously wanting in that cohesion which alone can give strength. The whole sense and meaning of a Cabinet is that the ministers composing it are prepared to agree upon a common course of action, and to support it, each and all of them, thoroughly and heartily. But in the present administration, every man seems determined to set up for himself, to back out of the common responsibility altogether, and to claim that he is responsible only for his own acts and opinions. The only two members of the Cabinet who are likely to let anything interfere with the interests of the party the ministry represents are Mr. Bright and Mr. Lowe. The former has already shown a disposition to detach himself from the newly effected alliance with the official leaders of the party. With very questionable taste he told the fishmongers at their dinner, that although he is the adviser *ex officio* of the Government, they will none of them take his advice—a declaration which probably occurred to him in a confused post-prandial moment as a method of protesting against the false position in which he now begins to feel that he has placed himself. In refusing to take a Secretaryship of State, and in falling back upon the Board of Trade, which is almost sacred to the memory of extinct Radicals, Mr. Bright appears to have thought that he escaped responsibility, and his fishmongers' speech was but a clumsy attempt to induce the outside world to share that opinion. But the administration is and must be regarded as a whole, and so long as any statesman remains in it he is fully responsible for every one of its acts, of whatever nature they may be. If he does not like any of its acts he may leave it, but so long as he remains he must be prepared to support honourably and heartily whatever line of policy it may pursue. Therefore, Mr. Bright's fishmongers' protest will not be of the slightest use to him. If he really thinks that the national taxation is greater by twenty millions than it ought to be, he is responsible to the nation, equally with every one of his colleagues, for the extravagance that necessitates the excess, and that whether the spending department will take his advice or not. There can indeed be no doubt that, although he may desire to avoid seeing it, he is quite aware of this fact, and combined as it is with the absence of any real controlling power, it is evidently making his position more distasteful to him every day.

On the other hand, if Mr. Bright is but little pleased with himself, Mr. Lowe is even less pleased with his colleagues. He is at no sort of pains to conceal the fact that he dislikes Mr. Bright just as much as ever, notwithstanding that a temporary arrangement has united them at the same council-board ; and it needs no great power of divination to understand that he is scarcely more devoted to the chief, in resisting whom he once declared that he placed his hopes of glory. When he said of Mr. Gladstone, a few days since, " If he has a fault, it is that he is too conscientious," possibly those who heard him took the remark for a compliment, but, coming from Mr. Lowe, it sounds to many very like a sneer. What may be in the bosom of the Future, or of any less abstract personage, cannot, of course, be known ; but if Mr. Lowe should ever become prime minister, to the exclusion of Mr. Gladstone, it could only be through the weakness of an excess of conscience on the one side, and the power derived from a deficiency of it on the other.

Added to these personal difficulties there are the difficulties inherent to the questions that will have to be dealt with by the Government. The Irish Church absolutely bristles with dangers, the greatest and worst of which have never yet been so much as looked at ; the Ballot, too, is much more perilous than at present it appears, and although it may be shelved for a time by a commission or a committee, it must be faced sooner or later ; and even the "diminished charge upon the country," which has been received as so pleasing a novelty in the Queen's Speech, will bring with it a host of those multitudinous and uncompromising enmities which must follow every Government that ventures to touch the most powerful of vested interests. Altogether, it is probable that we shall see strange things this year, but the strangest of all will be that the present Government should outlive the session.

JEHU JUNIOR.

"NAPOLEON IV."

A PAMPHLET with the above title has just been published in Paris, by the Comte G. de Ludre, who puts before his readers in a very forcible manner the dangers which lie ahead for the Napoleonic dynasty, and suggests a means of avoiding them, which he considers flows naturally from the situation.

The spectacle of an Imperial democracy, which we have in France, seems to many of us a strange and monstrous thing ; but, when examined from the French point of view, it will be seen to be but the natural consequence of that which preceded its establishment. From 1789 to 1848 the French tried every sort of government, based upon every sort of principle, and the revolution of the latter year found the middle classes almost despairing of the establishment of any permanent government at all. This despair soon gained the whole country, and the violence of the red republicans increased it till, in 1851, France was ready to throw itself into any strong arms that would deliver it from the Republic and the socialists. The arms that were held out were those of Louis Napoleon, and, in spite of the prejudice excited against him by the *coup d'état*, the country, by the vote for the empire, threw itself into them almost with one motion. "Aussi," says Count de Ludre, " la signification réelle du vote fut-elle " celle-ci ; la dictature de Louis Napoleon. Le pays abdiquait " en faveur du Prince." That is to say, it abdicated with this reservation, which is, indeed, inseparable from the vote in its favour, that the country alone was to be held to be the source of power, and this principle was accepted and embodied in the 5th Article of the Constitution, which declares that, " L'Empereur est responsable devant le peuple " français auquel il a toujours le droit de faire appel." It seems sufficient enough that the Sovereign should be responsible to the people, for that is the one principle on which every form of popular government rests ; but in the case of France, as the Comte de Ludre points out, the responsibility is really illusory. For who is to initiate its exercise by demanding the infliction of any penalty that may be required for evil-doing ? The Senate cannot do it, neither can the Corps Législatif, neither can the people. In fact, there is nobody at all to bell the cat, and as the responsibility is one which cannot be enforced, the Emperor, though not theoretically, is practically absolute and independent of the people from whom he derived his power in the first place, and subject to whom he professes to hold it.

But will the country, which has abdicated in favour of Napoleon III., be prepared to abdicate a second time in favour of Napoleon IV. ? Can the dynasty hope to continue to rule the French people on the same principles as those which now

INTRODUCTION

For nearly fifty years, from 1868 to 1914, *Vanity Fair* displayed its political, social and literary wares weekly for the nineteenth-century Pilgrim. Inviting its readers to recognize the vanities of human existence, the publication, through its original format, prose and coloured caricatures, became the envy and model of other Society magazines. The most successful Society magazine in the history of English journalism was the result of the guiding genius of its founder and editor, Thomas Gibson Bowles (1842–1922), set against a background of historical circumstances ranging from the more mundane – technological breakthroughs in printing and lithography – to the sublime, the British Empire at its height.

Written by and for the Victorian and Edwardian establishment, *Vanity Fair* was the magazine for those 'in the know'. Members of the Smart Set delighted in finding themselves caricatured in prose and picture. For them, *Vanity Fair* summarized each week the important events of their world. It reviewed the newest opening in the West End and the latest novel in the club's library; it aroused their curiosity and envy; it angered and amused them.

The news and Society columns, the book and play reviews, the serialized novels and word games and the colour lithograph caricatures give us a glimpse into the lives and reputations of the men and women who achieved either lasting or fleeting fame and fortune during the heyday of the British Empire. The caricatures, which have become the magazine's chief legacy, fascinate the scholar, the lay person and the collector for their historical and biographical value and their satirical and artistic quality. Although *Vanity Fair* is best remembered for these chromolithographic caricatures, the magazine was, at its zenith, recognized and respected in its totality – for its features, prose, advertising and format.

Format and Advertising

Vanity Fair's size and format was the brainchild of Bowles, whose past experience with Society publications convinced him of the need to make his magazine unique. His decision to publish in quarto dimensions of eight to ten pages per issue gave *Vanity Fair* instant identity. The grade of paper was above that of similar publications in order to reproduce the colour caricatures and to foster an image of a quality magazine. Profits were gleaned from subscriptions and advertisements. In 1869 a yearly subscription was £1.6s and a single issue cost 6d; by 1895 per annum subscription was £1.8s. A full page advertisement in 1869 cost £12; a half page, £6 and 'six line and under', 3s. As *Vanity Fair*'s reputation grew, advertising became an important source of revenue.

Pen and ink advertisements appeared occasionally in the early editions, but by the 1880s advertising had become an integral part of the magazine. With the advent of photography, improved transfer processes, high speed printing presses and advertising agencies, *Vanity Fair* soon resembled other publications which catered to the middle and upper classes. As the twentieth century began, photographs of smartly attired men and women using the latest products of British industry were splashed across the magazine's pages.

The advertised items revealed the tastes and consumer habits of *Vanity Fair*'s readers: wines, cheeses, cooking sauces, cigars, imported oriental curios, men's boots, ladies' dresses and gloves, furniture, pain remedies, vases and fountains for gardens and conservatories, resort hotels and excursions hinted at a way of life. By the mid-1890s a pronounced shift had occurred in the types of products being sold in *Vanity Fair* – prepared foods, sweets and chocolates, champagnes, holidays in Nice at the Riviera Palace and travel on the Orient Express all appeared to tempt the reader. Ten years later, in 1905, the magazine included the Trades Register: a listing of services and goods provided by London's leading businesses for young brides and homemakers. These 'reliable Firms', some of which still exist, offered everything from 'Alpine requisites' and antique furniture to uniforms and wigs.

Features

The advertisements and format of *Vanity Fair* may have contributed to the magazine's image and certainly to its income, but its weekly features and urbane prose style ultimately accounted for the publication's individual character and phenomenal popularity. The magazine's two distinct categories were the news columns and the regular features. In its earlier issues, the columns on the first pages summarized the political, economic and social news – Continental wars, colonial skirmishes, European governmental crises, Parliamentary debates and political developments in Britain. Detailed accounts and interpretations of these events often ran into hundreds of words. As the magazine evolved, the emphasis changed: political reports were abridged and Society news and gossip came to dominate the opening pages. Even when political events were noted, they were usually identified with the personalities involved – diplomats, Cabinet ministers and members of Royal households – rather than being discussed as issues.

While the contents and emphasis of the front pages varied over the years, the second major category of *Vanity Fair*, its regular features, seldom changed. These weekly features – word games, book and play reviews, travel reports, financial advice columns, serialized novels, fictionalized exchanges of letters, special reports on the Season and on Society's habitats, and the chromolithographic caricatures – all captured the interest and imagination of the *Vanity Fair* subscriber.

The word games and special contests, which called for the reader's answers each week, included 'Double Acrostics', 'Doublets', and 'Hard Cases'. 'Double Acrostics', which today are still challenging addicts in other publications, was the first word game to appear in *Vanity Fair*. Each week the reader was confronted by a puzzle. He or she had to make one word out of each of the numbered stanzas in the series of verses. The first and last letter of each word, where listed and read down, would reveal the meaning of the opening stanza. For example:

Come let us leave war, politics, and bother,
And seek the sea-breeze at the one in t'other

1. Born within earshot of the magic bells,
   His native town his accent surely tells.

2. To hear the music of the past or present,
   Or even of the future is most pleasant,
   When here surrounded by the genial glow

Of those we love and hate or only know.

3. A postal district that requires no guess,
   Two letters only, and you can't have less.

4. The universal debt he did not pay,
   And so is a defaulter to this day.

5. Tis fish or participle as you may wish
   To take it, or as you occasion find;
   But often participle applied to fish,
   Will cause much horror to your sense refined.

Answer to Double Acrostic

C	ockney	Y
O	per	A
W.		C.
E	noc	H
S	mel	T

'Doublets', which first appeared in January 1880, were devised exclusively for *Vanity Fair* by C. L. Dodgson, the mathematics don who is better remembered as Lewis Carroll, the author of *Alice's Adventures in Wonderland*. The challenge was to make one word into another word by substituting one letter at a time through a succession of words until the desired word was formed. Two early examples of 'Doublets' illustrate the intricacies of Carroll's game.

Change Moses to Aaron	Send Monk to Rome
Moses	Monk
Roses	Mock
Rases	Cock
Bases	Cork
Basis	Core
Basin	Come
Bason	Rome
Baron	
Aaron	

Another weekly pastime to amuse the reader and bring in his or her response was 'Hard Cases'. Most of the 'Hard Cases' focused on delicate social problems, although they also addressed themselves variously to knotty points of legal, military and clerical etiquette. The eternal triangle was the root of many a 'Hard Case', often carrying the reader through interminable issues of *Vanity Fair* before arriving at a resolution. The contestants, whose pseudonyms were as enterprising as their answers, offered wonderfully intricate solutions to these problems. How serious or how whimsical the replies were may be difficult to determine at this distance, but for many years solutions to 'Hard Cases' arrived at the editor's office from Britain and from the far corners of the Empire – Burma, India and Africa.[1]

HARD CASES
Hard Case No.20 – In One Incident

Mr. A. is much in love with Miss B, who, however, is in love with Mr. C. But Mr. C is in love with Miss D, who in her turn is in love with Mr. E. Now E is desirous of marrying Miss F, but knowing that she has long been ready to marry either him or anybody else, delays proposing.

What should A do?

Correct Answer
Make love to Miss F. This brings E to the point of marrying her, throws D back on C, and leaves B open to A – No correct answer received.

Answers adjudged incorrect:
a. Marry Miss F. – 'pour encourager les autres.' 'La Favorita.'
b. Propose to Miss B. – 'Brunette,' 'Burncoose,' 'Floreant ludi,' 'Rusticus.'
c. Persuade E to propose to Miss F, and himself propose to Miss B – 'Bremenien-sis,' F.C.S.
d. Wait. – 'Jumbo,' 'Ozokeritikos.'
e. Get Miss F to refuse him, and let E know it – 'Unconsecrated Trout.'
f. Endeavour to win Miss B, and if he can't, look out for Miss G – 'Paul Ferrol.'

Other regular features, less taxing of the reader's social sensibilities, were designed to entertain and inform. In the early years of *Vanity Fair* contrasting viewpoints on timely issues were published in a column entitled 'Both Sides'. 'Both Sides' was intended to be 'an easy "coach" for those idle people who cannot make out "what it is all about" and as a simple abstract of the avowed arguments used on both sides of current questions'. 'Well-informed persons' were 'warned off'. One week, for example, 'Both Sides' asked whether universal education should be made compulsory or not. The magazine thought that most Radicals, many Liberals and 'one or two' Conservatives would say 'yes' because they felt it was the state's duty 'to insure that every child should have the elements of knowledge' and that education could 'never be made universal without compulsion'. On the other side, most Conservatives and a few Liberals would reply 'no' because they feared compulsory education would 'hamper industry', and they knew that people could never 'be made effectually to submit to compulsion'. Other topics argued in 'Both Sides' included the pros and cons of the purchase of military commissions, whether the supply and quality of English horses was improving or deteriorating, the advantages and disadvantages of impending trade treaties and whether women should be allowed to vote.

'Both Sides' was eventually discontinued and other features filled the pages of *Vanity Fair*. Serialized novels and fictionalized letters became very popular. The novels were usually of little weight – their plots revolved around the successes and failures of young men and women constantly pursuing one another through the balls, dinner parties, At Homes and other entertainments of The Season. *Lady Hetty*, by 'Wanderer', appeared first in *Vanity Fair* and then on the London bookstalls. One reviewer hailed it as 'a story of to-day'; another called it a 'very gay, readable little romance of modern life'.

The exchange of letters complemented these serialized stories. For many weeks letters would pass between father and son, mother and daughter, or aunt and niece in the columns of *Vanity Fair*. From the young and innocent came laments over rebuffs, cruelties and 'the cut'; from the parents and guardians flowed first consolation, and then advice on how best to survive in their newly discovered, exciting but often heartless world.

These weekly features and the word games were supplemented by special seasonal columns on Ascot and Cowes, hunting, Society balls, European hotels and spas, and travels of prominent people around the world. They provided *Vanity Fair* with the opportunity to record the major social events of the year and to expose the foibles of their compatriots, particularly their habits of dressing and eating. *Vanity Fair* lamented British culinary ignorance by recounting a Frenchman's efforts to educate an Englishman on the finer points of ordering and enjoying a meal in a Parisian restaurant. He prefaced his instructions with Gallic philosophy assuredly alien to his guest: 'Ah, my dear sir, when you have exhausted Love, Patriotism and Religion, you will prostrate yourself before the kitchen, believe me.'

Vanity Fair was often whimsical, but could and did present more serious, informed comment when it came to the arts and finance. Its candid reviews of books and plays provided incisive critiques of London theatre and English literature. Many of these assessments have endured; its distaste for the three-decker novel has been sustained by modern critics and readers and its judgement of Hardy's novels and Shaw's plays have stood the test of time.[2]

The magazine's weekly column on business and finance offered advice on investments and business trends. In particular, it pointed out the potential growth of new firms in America, the colonies and Eastern Europe which needed funding and promised high returns. Because many of the readers of *Vanity Fair* were constantly looking for new markets in which to invest their surplus capital, this useful and popular feature continued throughout the life of the magazine. Arthur H. Evans, who succeeded Bowles as owner, was the author of these columns for many years, and his frank appraisals made *Vanity Fair* a power in the financial world.[3]

These weekly news columns and many of the regular features were written from a clearly defined political point of view. *Vanity Fair* was supportive of the Conservatives and Disraeli, the Church of England, Imperialism, the Crown and the class system. Gladstone and the Liberals were the sworn enemies, the Radicals were beyond redemption, the Russians untrustworthy and the Irish Home Rulers and their sympathizers highly suspect. *Vanity Fair* stood ready to attack those who desired to modify the Imperial system or change the established social structure. These attitudes no doubt reflected the political prejudices of Bowles, who was himself a loyal supporter of Disraeli, the Conservative party, the social order and the British Empire. Throughout its history, *Vanity Fair* tended to follow his views. Despite these beliefs and prejudices no person or institution was above criticism. On occasion, *Vanity Fair* could be irreverent and iconoclastic and even Disraeli was not immune.

As the years passed, especially after 1890, *Vanity Fair* became more defensive of its reader's values. Nonetheless, it remained capable of censuring the leaders of those institutions it wished to preserve. For example, in 1910, Balfour and Asquith, the leaders of the major parties, were both lambasted.

As the leading Society magazine, *Vanity Fair* inevitably became the target of its rivals. After being criticized for reporting unfavourably on one particular social event, *Vanity Fair* replied in a devastating column that it could not understand why its 'harmless and amusing gossip' has provoked such indignation. The magazine denied that it was the source of such stories, and declared that it had never proposed to print only the best it heard about men and women. A few years later,

Vanity Fair had to defend itself once more against similar charges of 'ill natured remarks' made in one of its Society columns. Rather than hide scandals in Society, they had to be exposed in order to prevent further corruption, argued the magazine. *Vanity Fair* denied that it wanted to stigmatize people; on the contrary, all it wished to do was 'to better the principles'. Furthermore, it printed only one-tenth of what occurred in Society, and if the full truth were known, the critics owed *Vanity Fair* a debt of gratitude for refraining from saying any more! The magazine considered it had a duty to report 'flagrant scandals' and to place the blame where it belonged. Complaints could not deter *Vanity Fair* from exposing scandals, and rather than complaints, it should, in the future, receive 'gratitude and thanks'.

All of *Vanity Fair*'s features, columns and reviews were written in witty, sophisticated and polished prose. Bowles set the standards with his own writing in the formative years of the magazine, and the many anonymous contributors imitated his style. By 1904, when the magazine was printing signed articles, writers still fashioned their columns in *Vanity Fair*'s by then traditional style. The young P. G. Wodehouse's comparison of the jostling, unruly crowds of New York City with sedate, polite Londoners is a good example of such continuity. In terms of the quality of writing, only a few magazines ever matched *Vanity Fair* at its height. Perhaps the American *Vanity Fair* of the 1920–1930 decade, and today's *New Yorker* or *Punch*, might be considered worthy of comparison.

Founder and Owner: Thomas Gibson Bowles

Vanity Fair, in its first twenty years, was largely the product of one man's efforts and energies. Its influence on other publications, its prose style, opinions, prejudices, features and format developed out of the lively vision and hard work of its founder and first editor, Thomas Gibson Bowles. Bowles was reared as the natural son of Thomas Milner Gibson and Susan Bowles. His mother's origins and fate are unknown; under what circumstances she knew Thomas Milner Gibson remain a mystery. His father, on the other hand, was a successful politician. He was a member of the House of Commons, close friend of the Liberal leaders Cobden and Bright, and served as President of the Board of Trade during his career. His property investments have left their mark in the street signs of Islington. Theberton Street is named for Milner Gibson's county seat in Suffolk, and the family is also remembered by Gibson Square and Milner Square. One of the major achievements of Gibson's life was the repeal of the taxes and duties on newspapers and advertising, an accomplishment that brought him recognition and rewards from the publishing world. Upon retirement from public life, the elder Gibson sailed his yacht around the Channel and the Mediterranean. His love for the sea was inherited by his son who became a skilful sailor and a recognized expert on international maritime laws and regulations. Thomas Milner Gibson's wife, Susanna, accepted the child into her household and reared him as one of her own family. Susanna was a strong and resourceful woman who supported women's rights in an unsympathetic age, and was interested in spiritualism. She entertained the leading literary and political personalities of her day. At her salons spiritualism was practised, politics were debated (she was especially

'Tommy': Thomas Gibson Bowles, by Spy 1889

fond of exiled Italians) and amateur theatrical productions were performed. She was a devoted mother to her two sons and to 'Tommy'.[4]

The young Bowles's home life was unusual; his formal education ordinary. He grew up surrounded by some of the most lively literary figures and Society leaders in the country, the guests at his parents' dinner parties and séances. Charles Dickens and Lynn Linton, the novelist, newspaper correspondent and spiritualist, were among the more famous visitors. Bowles's formal education was acquired at Mr Colby's school at Peckham Rye, followed by a few years abroad in northern France and a short session at King's College in the Strand.[5] He had, however, received enough preparation at home and elsewhere to allow him to move in some of the most select circles of London. His acquaintances proved to be valuable sources of information in later years, most useful to the magazine he was to found.

At nineteen Bowles secured a minor post at Somerset House due, no doubt, to his father's influence as President of the Board of Trade. For the next eight years he played the role of a debonair London socialite. He treated his appointment at Somerset House as a sinecure while he drafted leaders for the *Morning Post*, wrote plays, contributed to several fledgling Society magazines, acted in countless amateur performances and enhanced his reputation as a bright, rising young man. His contributions to the satirical Society magazines – *The Owl*, *The Glow Worm* and *The Tomahawk* – helped him improve his prose style, and educated him to the opportunities and pitfalls of journalism. Bowles's coterie included some of the most promising men of the coming generation, and from his circle of friends emerged many well known journalists, judges, politicians, military officers and actors.[6]

Bowles's literary ambitions were aroused and, capitalizing upon his social connections, wit and writing talents, he resigned his position at the Board of Trade. In late 1868, he launched his first publishing venture, *Vanity Fair*. He started with a modest capital of £200, half of which was borrowed, a few suggestions from friends, a title, a slogan and his own idea of what a Society magazine should be. Colonel Fred Burnaby supplied £100 of the £200 original investment and hit upon the title *Vanity Fair*, probably inspired by Thackeray's novel and certainly by Bunyan's *Pilgrim's Progress*. Burnaby might have suggested the masthead subtitle, also from *Pilgrim's Progress*.[7]

Even though Bowles accepted anonymous articles written by London's leading socialites and journalists, in the early days he wrote most of the columns himself under the pseudonyms, Jehu Junior, Blanc Bec, Auditor, Choker and Pantagruel. Jehu Junior submitted the biographical sketches to accompany the chromolithograph caricatures, and Choker devised the weekly Double Acrostics.[8]

From the first issue when Bowles stated the aims of his new Society magazine his personal imprint was firmly established on *Vanity Fair*. His opening paragraphs struck the note of authority, propriety and urbanity which came to characterize the magazine.

In this Show, it is proposed to display the vanities of the week, without ignoring or disguising the fact that they are vanities, but keeping always in mind that in the buying and selling of them there is to be made a profit of Truth.

There will be no long faces pulled, and no solemn praises sung, over any of the wares, neither will magnifying or diminishing glasses be used to them; but they will be spread out upon their own sole merits, ticketed with plain words.

Frank Harris, by Owl, 1913

Dr Thomas Richard Allinson, by Ray, 1911

It is not desired to assume exclusively for the Show the merit of the good bargains, nor to prop up with impersonal 'we' the bad bargains that may be offered in it. Every Chapman, therefore, will distinguish himself by a signature, in order that customers may gain some general and connected idea of him, and may thereby be the better enabled to judge how far they may trust to his account of the wares he displays.

Those who think that the Truth is to be found in the Show will probably buy it; those who do not, will pass on their way to another, and both will be equally right.[9]

Until 1889 when Bowles sold *Vanity Fair* for £20,000 to Arthur H. Evans, he reigned supreme over his publication. By then Bowles was tiring of *Vanity Fair*. Since 1884, when he had founded a magazine for women, *The Lady* (which still exists), his attention had been divided between the two publications. Aside from these practical reasons Bowles had personal cause to sell *Vanity Fair*. In 1887 his wife had died and her death had made him restless. He wanted to forget the past and start life anew. Finally, 'Tommy' Bowles, as he was known to his friends and the publishing world, had become attracted to politics and wished to stand for the House of Commons.

Bowles never achieved the success as a politician that he enjoyed as an editor and publisher. Elected to the House in 1892 as member for King's Lynn, Norfolk, he was in and out of Parliament for eighteen years, first as a Conservative, then as an Independent and, in his later years, as a Liberal who supported Lloyd George's budget. He was an astute, forceful debater who proved to be an expert in financial matters, tax laws and maritime issues. When the Conservatives returned to power in 1895, Bowles seemed a likely candidate for a ministerial post, but he was not chosen. Disappointed, he became a severe critic of the Government and turned Independent. His parliamentary career continued into the twentieth century. He fought Chamberlain's tariff reform programme, supported the strengthening of the British Navy and won a battle with the Bank of England in 1912 over its income tax deduction policy. In 1914 Bowles returned to publishing and introduced a new journal, the *Candid Quarterly Review*, which soon failed. By then, his career was approaching its end and his last years were spent travelling and writing.[10]

After Bowles's departure from *Vanity Fair* in 1889, his general style and ideas were continued by the new proprietors. However, by the mid 1890s *Vanity Fair* had lost some of Bowles's pungent wit and sophisticated irreverence, although it still published many of the popular features and columns he had originated. The tone of the magazine changed; it became more a gossip sheet, a record of Society's activities, a purveyor of advertisements and less an affectionate and perceptive critic of British life. Reminiscences about a glorious past, which it felt it had helped create, began to appear. The editorships of A. G. Witherby, Oliver Fry, B. Fletcher Robinson, and Frank Harris could not match that of Bowles. Harris's attempt, between 1907 and 1910, to revive the slumping magazine failed. It was sold to Dr T. R. Allinson (*Vanity Fair*, 4 October 1911) late in 1911. In February 1914 the leading Society magazine of its day was absorbed by *Hearth and Home*.[11]

The Caricatures

Vanity Fair's reputation and legacy have not rested exclusively on its political views, weekly columns, special articles and its prose style. Its popularity in the nineteenth century and its influence on British journalism are in no small part to be attributed to the caricatures. Like all other features in *Vanity Fair*, they were conceived by Bowles who, in early 1869, brought to his struggling magazine an unprecedented design and style of colour illustrations.

On 16 January 1869, Bowles announced that since the literary offerings of *Vanity Fair* had received so much favour, it was now proposed 'to add to them some Pictorial Wares of an entirely novel character'. Two weeks later, on 30 January, the now famous caricature of Disraeli appeared, the first of over 2300 caricatures published in *Vanity Fair*. It was drawn by Carlo Pellegrini, using the *nom de crayon* 'Singe', which he shortly thereafter anglicized to 'Ape'. Gladstone came next, followed by numerous dignitaries, including foreign Royalty, Earls, Lords, Bishops, politicians and a few women of social position or notoriety. This list was later extended to include such diverse characters as judges, journalists, criminals, sportsmen, artists, actors and Americans.

At first some people were reluctant to be seen in the pages of *Vanity Fair*. However, as the popularity of the caricatures grew, they became less hesitant. In succeeding years, it became a mark of recognition to be the 'victim' of one of the caricaturists hired by Bowles. While most of the subjects took their turns with good grace, there were, of course, exceptions.[12] Some, like Lewis Carroll, a close personal friend of Leslie Ward's (Spy) family, simply refused to pose. Carroll begged to be excused, saying that 'nothing would be more unpleasant for me than to have my face known to strangers'.[13] Carroll's reaction can be attributed to his eccentricities or modesty. Delane, the editor of *The Times*, did not want to be caricatured, and asked William Howard Russell (*Vanity Fair*, 6 January 1875) to intervene for him with Bowles: 'The coin to bribe him with is a review of his book upon the Seige of Paris (*sic*) which he shall have if he will forgo his wicked will upon my poor face and figure.'[14]

Others, perhaps less eccentric than Carroll, were certainly displeased when they appeared in *Vanity Fair*. An amusing but innocuous sketch of the physician, Dr William Broadbent, in 1902, led to his protest in *The Lancet*, the medical journal, that he had been made to appear 'extremely ridiculous'. *Vanity Fair*, in characteristic manner, apparently failed to understand why Dr Broadbent had interpreted the honour of being placed among so many distinguished subjects as an 'indignity'. Furthermore, *Vanity Fair* contended, it was of no possible interest whether or not Sir William objected to the caricature.[15] Earlier, Anthony Trollope had been exceedingly disturbed by his appearance in *Vanity Fair*. Spy and Trollope were invited to the house of a mutual friend, and after returning home, Ward sketched the novelist. The caricature, one of Ward's earliest works, appeared on 5 April 1873. Trollope, according to Ward, was incensed and especially angry over Spy's emphasis of Trollope's right thumb. John Pope Hennessy judged the caricature 'most unflattering' and said that it made Trollope look like 'an affronted Santa Claus'. Yet Pope Hennessy admitted, as did a majority of Trollope's contemporaries, that to have one's caricature in *Vanity Fair* was 'public honour no eminent man could well refuse'. [16] During *Vanity Fair*'s heyday, few eminent people refused this 'public honour', for to be caricatured in *Vanity Fair* was to receive the recognition, if not always the approbation, of England's leading Society magazine.

THEIR ORIGINS

The art of caricaturing dates from the seventeenth-century Italian schools, specifically from the studios of the Carracci brothers, Agostino and Annibale. Agostino's caricatures are extant; if Annibale sketched any, they have never been located. However, Annibale is credited with using the phrase *ritrattini carichi* (exaggerated portrait) which is the basis for the modern English word, caricature. The original meaning of the Italian verb *caricari* is to load or to exaggerate; this verb was eventually transformed into the noun *caricatura*. In the eighteenth century, *caricatura* passed into the dictionaries to describe an exaggerated or somewhat distorted and usually humorous drawing of a person. The French word *chargé*, similar to the Italian *caricari*, is a load or burden. In painting, *chargé* refers to a caricature from which the French coined the phrase *portrait chargé* (a distorted portrait).

Caricaturing began as a private joke and harmless pastime in the studio where the artist, for his own enjoyment and for the pleasure of his friends, drew exaggerated sketches of his patrons or subjects. During the seventeenth century the practice spread to the public, from master to pupil, from one studio to another, from one school of painting to the next, from the Carracci brothers to Domenichino and Bernini, then to the Tiepolos and to Pier Leone Ghezzi. Probably caricaturing as an art form was first brought to England in the early eighteenth century by the Italian opera singers who imported the practice of *caricari* in their presentations. Thus, the concept of *caricature* was established. However, it was not until 1744, when Arthur Pond, the English engraver, published a sheaf of about two dozen caricatures by Ghezzi and other Italian artists, that caricaturing as an art form in painting began in England. Ghezzi's popularity grew, and what had been in the Carracci brothers' studio a personal humorous diversion became an international language. [17]

During the eighteenth century the Italian classical form of caricaturing, which was identified with slight distortions of the subject's physiognomy, spread throughout England. At the same time William Hogarth's pungent artistic style became very popular. Draftsmen and engravers grew increasingly bold and openly criticized government leaders because they were now protected by the Hogarth Act (1753), which guaranteed them a claim to their works. The printshops, from which came the hundreds of broadsides, tracts and prints circulated in the streets of London, multiplied. [18] For a while, the Italian style gave way to Hogarthian influences. Yet it was not completely eradicated as it manifested itself in the caricatures of George, the First Marquis of Townshend, who is credited with using the classical form for satirical purposes. He ridiculed Lord Bute and his Scottish followers in their attempts to influence George III. [19]

The efforts of the First Marquis of Townshend were directly linked to the works of the late eighteenth-century caricaturists who so vividly dominated the Georgian period: James Gillray, Thomas Rowlandson, the Cruikshanks and Robert Newton.[20] However, by the 1830s, the savage wit and explicit sketches of a Rowlandson or a Gillray had lost their popularity in England and were being exported across the channel to re-appear in the pages of Charles Philipon's two publications: *La Caricature,* and after it was suppressed by Louis Philippe, the very successful *Charivari.*[21]

Charles Philipon's satirical magazines established France as the new centre for caricaturing. Philipon was a clever and resourceful editor who hired the best caricaturists in his day, Gavarni, Grandville and above all, Daumier. Daumier is still considered to be the most accomplished artist in the history of caricaturing. He appeared upon the scene when French art was turning towards the subjects of everyday life and reality and when the French middle class had become influential. Daumier, who was a first-rate artist, understood the essential elements of caricaturing in the classical Italian model in which the artist refined reality and concerned himself with the facial features. Daumier worked in the medium of lithography and perfected the *portrait chargé* which was later to be utilized by other French caricaturists.[22]

While Frenchmen laughed at themselves or squirmed in their seats of power, thanks to Daumier's caricatures, Englishmen rejected the crude humour of the Georgian caricaturists and found amusement in the more cultivated and genteel drawings of William Heath, and later, H. B. or John Doyle. The style and message of English caricaturing were changing and the muted tones and subjects reflected the onrush of respectability—the robust laughter of the Georgians gave way to the refined joviality of the Victorians.[23]

By the time *Vanity Fair* was founded in late 1868, Victorian tastes were well established, and the types of caricatures which ran in the magazine mirrored Victorian values. In the wider historical context, *Vanity Fair*'s caricatures were closer to the seventeenth-century Italian style than to later types, and it was an Italian, Carlo Pellegrini, who brought this classical form to its perfection in *Vanity Fair.* Later, an upper class Victorian, Leslie Ward, would perpetuate the classical style through his more precise and formal caricatures. Yet, neither Pellegrini, Ward nor any of their fellow caricaturists would have been able to succeed without the technological advancements in the fields of lithography and printing which had been achieved by the middle of the nineteenth century. The caricaturists owed a large debt to the inventors, printers and printmakers who preceded them. Caricaturing was especially beholden to lithography.[24]

The inventor of lithography was Aloys Senefelder (1771–1834), a German who, in 1798, introduced what he called Chemical Printing. This was a surface or planographic printing process that was based on the fact that water runs off a greasy surface and will not take ink. A design would first be drawn on stone with a greasy chalk and the stone then wetted. Greasy ink was rolled on the stone which would not adhere to the wet part but would stick to the greasy section. From these simple steps came modern day lithography. Senefelder is also credited with inventing chromolithography or the printing of lithographs in colour from several different plates. But more important for the careers of Pellegrini and Ward was Senefelder's invention of transfer paper. Transfer paper allowed the artist to work in his studio without being obliged to make the drawing in reverse for application to the stone. As the drawing was transferred to the stone, the artist would usually continue to work on the drawing. When properly used, the transfer method had no adverse effect on the quality, authenticity or value of a lithograph. Since Ward, Pellegrini and most of the caricaturists (except J. J. Tissot, the French painter) were not lithographers, they were totally dependent on the lithographers to reproduce their watercolour sketches from the transfer paper to the stone. Transfer paper was greatly improved about 1868, just before *Vanity Fair* was founded, and this development probably enhanced the quality of the lithographs in the magazine. Although experts maintain that the transfer method does not impair the quality of the original work, a close study of the original watercolours by the *Vanity Fair* caricaturists does reveal qualitative differences between the watercolour sketches and the printed lithographs. The vitality and nuances of the watercolours are much more vivid than the lithographs which appeared in *Vanity Fair*.[25]

Senefelder's invention came to London as early as 1801. Philip André, a friend and co-worker of Senefelder, established a shop on Fitzroy Square where he made every effort to develop lithography as a graphic art. Senefelder himself was in London in 1801, but neither his labours nor those of André proved effective. It was not until after 1818 that lithography, under the direction of Rudolph Ackerman and Charles Hullmandel, began to thrive. By this time the process was becoming well known in France, and, just as with caricaturing, the French took the lead in lithography during the decade 1830–1840. Daumier was one of the most sensitive artists in the medium of lithography; and his employer, Philipon, who was something of a lithographer himself, adopted the process for his publications.[26]

The history of chromolithography also began with Senefelder. However, his system of colour lithography was less than satisfactory, and in 1837 another German, Gottfried Engelmann of Mulhouse, obtained a patent for a colour reproduction process that used the three basic colours in combination to create other tones. A way to reproduce both oil paintings and watercolours was now available. At the time that Engelmann was perfecting his technique, Charles Hullmandel in London offered a new method whereby each colour stood on its own, separated and balanced. The printing houses accepted this more efficient process, and chromolithography expanded as a commercial success, especially in the firm of Day and Son, lithographers to the Queen. In 1867 the Vincent Brooks publishing company took over the lithographic business of Day and Son to form Vincent Brooks, Day and Son Lithographers. George Baxter, the younger, the son of a pioneering colour lithographer, George Baxter, took his father's expertise and plates with him when he went to work for Vincent Brooks, Day and Son. This new firm was later to print the excellent quality chromolithographic caricatures for *Vanity Fair*.[27]

These new developments in caricaturing, lithographing and printing provided Thomas Gibson Bowles with the opportunity to produce a magazine of *Vanity Fair*'s calibre. Working with the staff and owners of *The Owl* and *The Tomahawk* had convinced Bowles that a Society magazine could be profitable if it were efficiently managed and closely

Vincent Brooks, by WH, 1912

controlled by one person. He had also observed at first hand the influence of the illustrations, political prints and caricatures by Matt Morgan in *The Tomahawk*. This seemed to influence Bowles's decision about caricature for his own publication. T. H. S. Escott, the editor of *Fortnightly Review* and a victim of *Vanity Fair* (2 May 1885) believed that Bowles's adventures and genius made *Vanity Fair*, 'the real parent of all subsequent growths in that department of journalism (Society magazines) at a date when it seemed as fashionable to run a weekly sheet for one's friends as to endow a theatre for one's mistress'.[28]

The popularity of *Punch* probably forced Bowles to avoid competing with that established institution; furthermore, his experiences had led him to a vague notion of what he wanted – a publication similar to but distinct from earlier Society magazines in format and style, and also financially solvent. The concept of *Vanity Fair* slowly emerged in Bowles's mind and the first issue was circulated in November 1868. Around the same time, through a series of events whose precise details are absent from the historical record, Bowles met Carlo Pellegrini and signed an agreement with Vincent Brooks, Day and Son which resulted in the first caricature in late January 1869 (see p. 52).[29]

THEIR CONCEPTION

The caricatures, with only a few exceptions, have always been similar in style, and thus instantly recognizable. The setting, the victim's pose and stance, the colours and the size of the sketch have given them a clear identity. Such identity provided *Vanity Fair* with one more distinct feature to separate it from its rivals.

To Thomas Gibson Bowles the caricature was more than a quaint or clever sketch. It was an integral part of the magazine. Furthermore, its concept, by Bowles's own words, was identified with the classical form of caricaturing which he clearly understood and nurtured in his magazine. In replying to an article in *The Daily News* of September 1869, which had asserted that the caricatures in *Vanity Fair* were not really caricatures, Bowles summarized the classical definition and offered his own interpretation of caricaturing. He first observed that *The Daily News* was mistaken in its definition of caricaturing and then noted:

The Daily News says that the 'original' and 'genuine purpose' of caricature is that of 'giving amusement' by a droll presentation of persons and things, and laments the absence of the 'comic' element and the tendency to 'phantasmagoric extravagance' (whatever that may be) 'grimness,' and 'grotesqueness,' which it says characterise modern caricatures.

I might very well altogether deny that these marks apply to the cartoons of *Vanity Fair*, and say that there is not in any one of those caricatures which have been published with it either an essential feature of grimness, of grotesqueness, or an essential absence of comicality. There are grim faces made more grim, grotesque figures made more grotesque, and dull people made duller by the genius of our talented collaborator 'Ape'; but there is nothing that has been treated with a set purpose to make it something that it was not already originally in a lesser degree.

Bowles went on to say that the 'original and genuine purpose' of caricature was not to invent a line or colour but 'to charge and exaggerate', as the original Italian word stated, the existing lines and tones. Caricaturing was to make the bland more bland, the mild, milder, the persuasive, more persuasive; it was not to turn a person into someone else or invest him with qualities he did not possess. Nor was the function of caricaturing to overemphasize the obvious. The caricaturist, unlike the rest of us, was able to tell us about our vague impressions of others. He was, argued Bowles, able to seize the 'essential point' of his victim and exaggerate it. Such a contribution was 'no common service'. Bowles's concluding comments indicate his insight into human nature, and his observation on how we became parodies of ourselves reveals the approach he often took in *Vanity Fair* in analysing his fellow creatures.

> Let it be observed, too, that caricature is not necessarily pictorial. It may and does take any sort of shape. The tee-totaler is a living caricature of temperance. The moralist caricatures both vice and virtue, to induce us to abandon the former and cling to the latter. The politician caricatures his own principles no less than those of his opponents, though with a different object in each case, and consequently without much fidelity in either. The parson caricatures – for what is any sermon but simply the caricature of the text? Finally, even the journalist – that very highest product of civilization – must caricature the questions with which he deals if he would have his readers agree with or even comprehend his argument.[30]

Bowles's assiduous use of the word caricature and not cartoon, which was just then coming into popular use, indicated that he saw a clear difference between the two forms. The purpose of caricature was not to invent something new but to exaggerate what was already in existence. Students of caricaturing have tended to support Bowles's point of view. For example, E. H. Gombrich has argued that while the victim would be transformed into a ridiculous figure, the caricature would still resemble the individual 'in a striking and surprising way'.[31] John Giepel has defined caricature as an 'anti-portrait of recognizable individuals' while a cartoon, in the modern interpretation of the word, has become 'any whimsical or facetious graphic comment intended as a parody or burlesque of some aspect of human behaviour'.[32] The word cartoon, as used today, came into the English language in 1843, when John Leech, the caricaturist for *Punch*, ridiculed the cartoons or designs submitted by England's leading artists in competition for the privilege of painting the frescoes in the new House of Commons.[33]

Bowles, as noted in his response to *The Daily News*, held firm ideas about caricaturing, and he made it his personal duty to see that the caricatures appeared each week. Certain persons – influential politicians, members of the Royal Family, nobility and titled gentlemen, prominent judges and clergymen, celebrated literary and theatrical figures – were prime targets for the caricaturists.

The caricatures created a particular image of a person for the readers of *Vanity Fair;* such an image, being a caricature, was an exaggeration of the individual and was not meant to be a realistic portrait. By publishing caricatures, the magazine was also permitted to conjure up images. These images reflected not only how Bowles and the caricaturists saw their subjects, but also how their contemporaries viewed themselves. Bowles was fully aware of the power of caricaturing to do precisely this. In 1872, in his Preface to the annual *Vanity Fair Album*, he wrote that the purpose of the drawings in *Vanity Fair* was to present influential men of his generation and those who were 'its natural and typical product'. He felt that the victims were to be portrayed 'not as they would be but as they are'. The caricatures,

General Ignatieff, by Spy, 1877

therefore, became a record of Victorians and Edwardians interpreting each other, and how they viewed themselves has, in turn, influenced later assessments of the eras. With the coming of photography, the differences between image and reality became more sharply defined, but while the camera may be a more accurate recorder of reality it may be a less effective indicator of a people's perception of themselves.

Exactly why, how and when the subjects were chosen and what precise role Bowles played in all of this has never been fully documented. Particular people, however, were featured for obvious reasons. For example, General Ignatieff, the Russian general and diplomat, became a victim of *Vanity Fair* when he travelled to London in March 1877 to assess Britain's stance on the crisis in the Balkans, before the outbreak of the Turko-Russian War. Ward stalked Ignatieff at Claridge's and around London. That he had been instructed to caricature the General is self-evident; whether Spy was encouraged by Bowles to depict Ignatieff as he did is uncertain. *Vanity Fair*'s hostility to Russia and sympathy for Turkey were well known, and the caricature leaves little doubt as to what the magazine thought of the Russian diplomat.

Most of the subjects were sketched as Ward drew Ignatieff – in public places such as the lobby of the House of Commons, behind the bench at the Royal Courts of Justice or at Tattersall's. Now and then, however, Bowles would solicit likely candidates through his acquaintances or directly by letter. On 19 January 1872, Bowles wrote to William Hepworth Dixon, former editor of *The Athenaeum*, historian and world traveller, asking if he would be willing to sit for a caricature and if he would agree to meet the artist for a half-hour interview before the sitting 'in order to secure the greater fidelity of the drawing'. The artist for this caricature was to be Adriano Cecioni, the renowned Italian sculptor and painter whose success at the Paris Exhibition of 1870 had brought him to London and into Bowles's circle. Bowles praised Cecioni's talents and his 'extraordinary ability' as demonstrated in the artist's drawing of Thiers which had been featured in a recent edition of *Vanity Fair* (6 January 1872). He then suggested several places where Dixon and Cecioni could meet over the next few weeks for the sitting.[34] Although Dixon's reply is not extant, he must have agreed because on 22 April 1872, his caricature by Cecioni appeared in *Vanity Fair*.

Through the artists' diligent stalking or through Bowles's judicious requests, the caricatures were gathered for the pages of *Vanity Fair*. While they were visually unique, their value was not determined solely by eye appeal. On the contrary, what made them more popular at the time was the accompanying biographical commentary or letterpress. These commentaries were always written by Bowles under the *nom de plume* 'Jehu Junior'. Bowles had gleaned this name from the Old Testament, for the original or 'senior' Jehu was a prophet and warrior who pronounced the downfall of his enemies and then proceeded to destroy them. From 1869 to 1889, Jehu Junior's insights and innuendoes puzzled and amused the curious and knowledgeable members of Society. Bowles's turn of phrase or veiled reference captured in a few words the personality and life of the victim which, in another context, would have required pages. The editor's friends and heroes escaped unscathed for the most part; his enemies received their 'just' rewards.

Yet, neither friend nor foe, those of high station nor of low birth were totally immune to his tart epigrams and penetrating analyses. Bowles felt that the biographical notices were to be written in the same spirit as found in the caricatures themselves. Like the caricature, the entry was to reveal clearly the relative importance of each person in a short, honest, concise manner.

The commentary on Disraeli, who was the subject of the first caricature, set the tone and standards for all succeeding entries. Bowles praised Disraeli highly; his observations on him indicated his respect for the Tory leader as well as his admiration of the British political and social system.

He is not to be matched in our history, and the page on which he stands marks the beginning of a new era; for he has shown us, contrary to all our beliefs and experiences, that it is possible, even in England, for the man whom Nature alone has made great, to win his proper station, although all other things and men are against him. To have done that is to have done the greatest work that has been effected in England these last two hundred years, and the work that will bear the greatest fruit. *Is* that nothing, and are there any who will grudge him the great honour due for it? He educated the Tories, and dished the Whigs to pass Reform; but to have become what he is from what he was is the greatest reform of all.[35]

The following week, when Ape's caricature of Gladstone appeared, Bowles expressed his distrust of the man, his ideas and his followers. Bowles was wary of the possible consequences of the extremes in Gladstone's character; a fearless intellect, an insatiable sense of justice and a genuine enthusiasm for the right were admirable qualities, but when put into the hands of a political party and the foolish, they became defects. Although Bowles could not help but admire Gladstone's political skill and his influence on public opinion, he was highly suspicious of Gladstone's abundant self-confidence (see p. 54).

While Bowles's observations on Gladstone were qualified, they were not severe until later. Other less fortunate victims received the full impact of Bowles's prejudices. His dislike of Russia was revealed when he called General Ignatieff a 'manipulator of phrases' who possessed 'no personal scruples or principles'. For some, Bowles's antipathy was not always so transparent; nevertheless, it often bordered on the libellous. When Spy caricatured the King of Spain in 1876, Bowles described the King's court as 'one of the most stuck-up and tiresome in Europe' and charged that it had brought about a 'continued series of troubles and anxiety. . . .' Occasionally Bowles was even more personal and caustic. In 1874, when Philip Henry, Earl Stanhope, appeared in *Vanity Fair,* Bowles observed:

Lord Stanhope is the archetype of that respectable mediocrity which is so justly revered by the higher orders in England. He is precisely the sort of nobleman whom an elderly spinster of quality would naturally select as her adviser in perplexity.[36]

The style of Bowles's Jehu Junior continued to be maintained in the biographical sketches long after Bowles had departed from the office of *Vanity Fair.* As late as 1905, Fletcher Robinson still exercised the same discernment and piquancy that had characterized the earlier Jehu Junior. When Max Beerbohm, under the sobriquet 'Ruth', drew George Bernard Shaw, Jehu Junior praised Shaw's talents, recognized his influence but was not overly impressed. Shaw was seen as a witty

'Ape': Carlo Pellegrini, by AJM, 1889

'Spy': Leslie Ward, by PAL, 1889

writer, but whatever he criticized could not shake Englishmen's perfect confidence in their own merits. The English were 'neither modest nor clever enough to take Mr Shaw seriously'.

These comments on Shaw, Disraeli and others in *Vanity Fair* have, for the most part, been forgotten; for the articles and columns in *Vanity Fair* have been overshadowed by the caricatures. Indeed, the caricatures have increased in value, and their creators have bequeathed to posterity a rich and varied gallery of Victorians and Edwardians who once dominated British life. The caricaturists who drew for *Vanity Fair* were numerous and some are unknown; but several are remembered for their importance to the magazine and for their contributions to caricaturing. Among them were Carlo Pellegrini (Ape), Leslie Ward (Spy), J. J. Tissot and Max Beerbohm.

The Caricaturists
Carlo Pellegrini (1839–1889) (see p. 27) was *Vanity Fair*'s first caricaturist. The *portrait chargé* which Pellegrini developed became the accepted idiom of *Vanity Fair* and an English institution. It made Pellegrini's reputation and he became the most influential artist on Bowles's staff. Born in Capua, Italy, of aristocratic stock, his father was from an ancient landowning family, and his mother was descended from the Medici. As a young man he was attracted to Neapolitan Society where he was courted and flattered and where, in return, he caricatured its members. His caricatures were modelled on those of Melchiorre Delfico, Daumier and the French school which had been influenced in the 1830s by the Georgian caricaturists. Thus Pellegrini's coming to England and his subsequent triumphs in London closed the circle of European caricaturing.[37]

Because of the turn of political events, an unfortunate love affair, and the death of his sister, Pellegrini decided to leave Italy. In early 1864 he travelled north to Switzerland, France, and then to England in November. The conditions under which he arrived and his impecunious state have never been fully explained, but Pellegrini always declared that he landed destitute and slept on the streets and in doorways during his early days in London. He fostered this story to perpetuate his Bohemian *bon vivant* image, an image that followed him throughout his life. Irrespective of the circumstances of his arrival, Pellegrini was quickly accepted into London Society and soon became a close friend of the Prince of Wales. His eccentric manner, Italian charm, wit and speech and his artistic skills endeared him to upper class circles. As Disraeli's biographer Robert Blake observed: 'The aristocracy has always been tolerant of individual oddities. It has been prepared to put up with entertainers, buffoons, jesters and freaks as long as they gave good value.' Pellegrini did.[38]

Precisely how Bowles came to know Pellegrini is unclear; certainly they moved in the same social circles and perhaps a chance meeting at a dinner party or salon launched their long but erratic partnership. The office at *Vanity Fair* was not always large enough to accommodate both men; on more than one occasion, they went their separate ways. Regardless of their quarrels, Carlo Pellegrini's caricatures ran in *Vanity Fair* for over twenty years, from January 1869 to April 1889. When he was not drawing caricatures for Vanity Fair, he was engaged in portrait painting. Pellegrini was never very successful as a serious painter even though some of his works were exhibited in the London galleries. His forte lay in caricaturing, which he understood so well. He is reported to have defined a caricature as 'a comic portrait yet with as much of a man's disposition as you can get into it'.[39]

Pellegrini was recognized in his own day for his contributions to caricaturing. At the time of his death *Vanity Fair* claimed that his works would picture history as it had seldom been told. His caricatures had been honest, humorous, consistent and always popular with the readers. The man was both a caricaturist and an artist who had taught others to laugh at themselves. Several years later, Max Beerbohm looked to Ape as his model. In Beerbohm's essay 'The Spirit of Caricaturing', he referred to Pellegrini as the one person who tried to force caricaturing upon the English and who, for a while, did succeed. But, Beerbohm lamented, the pressures of the English 'gradually overbore that temerarious alien'.[40] David Low, a successor to Ape and to Beerbohm, also acknowledged Pellegrini's importance to English caricaturing. To Low, Pellegrini was a 'genius' whose caricatures were maximum likenesses in that they represented not only what Ape saw but what he knew. Low felt that Pellegrini's caricatures, in retrospect, were 'probably more like the person they depict than were the persons themselves'.[41] They were considered by some, noted Low, to be 'the most remarkable instances of personal caricature in England, singularly penetrating and masterfully economical in execution. . . .'[42]

While Pellegrini was the most influential caricaturist on the staff of *Vanity Fair,* he was only one of several hired by Bowles. The other artist most closely identified with the magazine was Leslie Ward or Spy. Hardly could two people have been more different in temperament and personality. Pellegrini was witty, volatile and gregarious; Ward was droll, reserved and something of a snob. Pellegrini played the role of the Bohemian; Ward saw himself as a member of the Establishment. Neither had a very high opinion of the other. Pellegrini claimed he had taught Ward all he knew; a charge that Ward predictably denied.[43] Ward, like many of his English friends, thought Pellegrini to be a 'character'. Yet they never could quite accept Pellegrini as one of their own. Indeed, Ward seemed rather to have patronized Pellegrini.[44]

Their work habits were also in opposition. Pellegrini would depend on his memory or quickly sketch his subject and then return to his studio for a final watercolour draft on transfer paper. Although Ward also worked from memory, he was more methodical. He would study his victim for hours and make numerous preliminary drawings. His technique may account for the large number of judges Spy caricatured, for he was able to observe a judge on the Bench for an extended period of time. Ward often drew many individuals at a sitting in his studio; this was the usual procedure when his subjects were members of Royalty.[45]

In comparing the works of both men, the majority of critics and students of caricaturing have favoured Pellegrini's drawings. Pellegrini has always been recognized as the more perceptive of the two, and he has been more closely identified with the classical definition of the art. Yet Ward in his early years at *Vanity Fair* was a very observant caricaturist; he was especially effective in his treatment of judges, preachers and literary figures. However, he was over sympathetic, if not flattering, to women, the nobility and Royalty. Critics have accused Ward of being less of a caricaturist and more of a portraitist. This charge was levelled against Spy in his later years at *Vanity Fair*, and acknowledged by him in his memoirs. Nonetheless, Spy could sometimes be very telling in his latter years. For example, his caricature of Lord Roberts in 1900 was penetrating and clever and his sketch of F. E. Smith in 1907 was a devastating indictment of an ambitious, unpleasant person. Ward was uneven in his efforts and, in the final analysis, Eileen Harris's observation that 'Spy spent forty years being a tamed Ape' is probably accurate (see p. 28).[46]

The reasons why the two caricaturists' personalities and artistic styles were so different can be more readily understood by examining Ward (p. 28). Leslie Ward (1851–1922) was born into a family of artists whose ancestors on the maternal side included a distinguished line of painters and engravers, among them the celebrated animal painter, James Ward RA. Mrs Henrietta Ward, Leslie's mother, established a name for herself as a portrait painter, art teacher and hostess. She was commissioned to do several portraits of the Royal Family, and her studio attracted fashionable English ladies wishing to explore their potential artistic talents. The Ward house was constantly full of prominent artists, writers, actors and Society leaders; and young Leslie, like Thomas Gibson Bowles, profited in the future years from this introduction to London's *haut monde*. Leslie's formal education consisted of a short time in a preparatory school followed by Eton. During his youth he showed flashes of an artistic nature in his numerous sketches and caricatures. However, his father, E. M. Ward, the renowned painter of historical episodes, did not want his son to be subjected to the vagaries of an artist's life, and consequently actively discouraged Leslie from becoming a painter. The senior Ward never gave his son an art lesson, and, in an effort to channel Leslie's talents in other directions, placed him in the studio of the architect, Sydney Smirke. Leslie's reluctance to continue studying architecture led to a confrontation with his father in 1871 which was resolved through the intervention of W. P. Frith and Frith's subsequent offer to apprentice the young Ward. Two years later another artist and friend of the family, John Millais, submitted some of Ward's sketches to Thomas Gibson Bowles who, in early 1873, was searching for a caricaturist to replace Pellegrini after one of Pellegrini's many departures. Bowles was favourably impressed with Ward's work and hired him. On 1 March 1873, Leslie Ward's first caricature, 'Old Bones', Dr Richard Owen, zoologist and superintendent of the natural history department of the British Museum, appeared in *Vanity Fair*. Ward would be identified with the magazine for nearly forty years under the *nom de crayon* Spy, a name he and Bowles picked from the dictionary. Ward quickly became a fixture on the staff. Because of his family connections, education and personal acquaintances he, too, moved in the 'proper' circles. Living a comfortable and pleasant life among London's upper class, he supplemented his income and fulfilled his artistic yearnings by painting portraits, many of which were displayed in the local galleries. In 1918 he was knighted. Four years later he died and was buried at Kensal Green, near the same cemetery where Ape had been buried, thirty-three years before.[47]

While Ape and Spy set the style and format of the caricatures and dominated the pages of *Vanity Fair* during their years of productivity, they were joined occasionally by other artists and caricaturists. Many of these caricaturists, including two well known artists, J. J. Tissot and Max Beerbohm, contributed some excellent caricatures. Tissot worked for Bowles in the early years of *Vanity Fair* while Beerbohm was on the staff during the last years of the magazine.

James Jacques Joseph Tissot (1836–1902) was born in France and began his career as a painter in Paris. He settled in London after the Franco-Prussian War and contributed to *Vanity Fair* while making a reputation with his charming illustrations of social events and his graceful portraits of ladies and gentlemen, catching the garden party side of Victorian life. Tissot's first caricatures in *Vanity Fair*, a series of European 'Sovereigns', appeared in 1869. They had probably been drawn by him at an earlier date and then sold to Bowles. The French painter's use of bright and vivid colours was in sharp contrast to Ape's monochromatic linear caricatures. Tissot was perhaps the most talented artist who ever worked for *Vanity Fair*. He displayed a genuine sense of feeling, and he was well versed in all the techniques of painting. Unlike Pellegrini and Ward, Tissot was trained in lithography, and he worked directly on the stone rather than the transfer paper. His caricatures, therefore, exhibited the mark of a well prepared draftsman who had mastered drawing and who understood the importance and use of colour. His caricatures and his portraits share these characteristics, especially the portrait of Colonel Burnaby, the dashing military officer, world traveller and personal friend of Bowles.[48] Tissot's life was full of professional success and personal tragedy. He and Bowles were together in Paris during the Franco-Prussian War, Bowles as a correspondent for the *Morning Post* and Tissot as a rifleman.[49] After the siege of Paris, Tissot went to London where his fame began to spread. He met Mrs Newton, a woman of some standing, and fell in love with her. They lived together for only a short time before her sudden death. Tissot, in great despair, left London and, after three years of work and exhibitions in Paris, travelled to the Middle East. There he drew his series on the Life of Christ which brought him renewed recognition. He subsequently returned to Palestine and worked on his Old Testament drawings. Tissot's final years were spent between Paris and his home near Besançon where he died.[50]

After Tissot left *Vanity Fair* in 1877, several French painters became associated with the magazine, but they were neither as prolific nor as influential as Tissot. One of the most famous Théobald Chartran (T). This well known artist contributed about fifty caricatures from 1878 to 1884. He left London in 1884 and became a popular and successful portrait painter in New York and Paris. Another French caricaturist, Jean Baptiste Guth, appeared in *Vanity Fair* on a regular basis from 1897 to 1908. The Italian tradition of caricaturing was expressed not only by Pellegrini but also by Adriano Cecioni and Melchiorre Delfico. Cecioni, a sculptor and painter, was an active leader of the Italian anti-academic movement. His caricatures ran in *Vanity Fair* shortly after its founding in the early 1870s. Delfico, who also appeared about the same time in *Vanity Fair*, was the Neapolitan caricaturist who influenced Ape. Towards the end of the nineteenth century, Liberio Prosperi (Lib) painted members of the racing set.[51]

George Alexander, by Max, 1909

In addition to the French and Italian caricaturists, the American, Thomas Nast drew for *Vanity Fair*. Nast caricatured several prominent Americans, including President U. S. Grant, Charles Francis Adams and Horace Greeley. The Greeley caricature is one of the most devastating in the entire *Vanity Fair* collection. In 1872, when Nast's caricatures were printed, he was at the height of his career and engaged in his struggle against Boss Tweed on the pages of *Harper's Weekly*. The evidence indicates that the work of another American, James Montgomery Flagg, appeared in *Vanity Fair* around the turn of the century. In 1898 he was in England studying drawing. He did some illustrations for several magazines, and probably during his year abroad, he agreed to submit caricatures to *Vanity Fair*.[52]

There were, of course, numerous English caricaturists for the magazine who included, among others, Alfred Thompson, Harry Furniss and Sir Francis Carruthers Gould. Thompson worked for *Vanity Fair* in its early days. He was an old friend of Bowles from *The Tomahawk*. Their interest in the theatre had brought both men together. Thompson was a highly successful playwright and costume designer whose talents for drawing proved an asset to Bowles. Harry Furniss, who illustrated several of Lewis Carroll's books and was on the staff of the *London Illustrated News* and *Punch*, submitted only one cartoon, 'Force No Remedy'. Gould contributed seven cartoons between 1879 and 1899.

The high standard of caricaturing established by Pellegrini, Thompson, Tissot and Ward during *Vanity Fair*'s first twenty years began to fluctuate in the 1890s. Although perceptive caricatures often appeared in the magazine after this time, the trend was more towards portraiture. Ward's work was still full of insight but his best years were behind him. One contributor who did possess a penetrating edge in his drawings was A. G. Witherby or W.A.G., the successor to Bowles as editor of *Vanity Fair*. His clever caricatures alone, however, could not revive *Vanity Fair*'s reputation. By the end of the century the *Vanity Fair* colour lithographs were often merely portraits.[53]

One exception to the general decline of the caricatures were those submitted by Max Beerbohm. In 1896 and again from 1905 to 1909, Beerbohm drew several splendid caricatures. Beerbohm's caricatures in Pellegrini's old magazine were a fitting tribute from the student to the teacher, for Beerbohm, in his essays, admired Pellegrini and recognized the Italian's influence on him. He considered Pellegrini to be the only significant caricaturist during the Victorian era.[54] Among Beerbohm's victims were George Alexander, the actor-manager, Arthur Wing Pinero (with an angular George Bernard Shaw in the background), Maurice Maeterlinck and John Singer Sargent. Each is a witty, economical caricature, and their appearances helped refute the charge, as admitted by *Vanity Fair* when it printed Beerbohm's caricature of Alexander (January, 1909), that the magazine had ceased to print caricatures and was only offering careful, if not flattering, portraits. But the efforts of Beerbohm were not enough to stem the tide; and even though other caricaturists like Wallace Hester, Alick P. F. Ritchie and Strickland did, on occasion, draw well executed caricatures, they, too, could not restore the unique bite of Ape's *Vanity Fair*. These developments reflected what was happening to the magazine itself as it became more a purely Society publication.

'Max': Max Beerbohm, by Sic, 1897

A. W. Pinero & George Bernard Shaw, by Bulbo, 1906   John Singer Sargent, by Max, 1909

Maurice Maeterlinck, by Max, 1908   W. J. Galloway, M.P., by Ruth, 1906

The last caricature to appear in *Vanity Fair* on 14 January 1914 was of Joseph Chamberlain. An ill and broken man, 'The Great Imperialist' sits staring from behind a monocle. When compared with the first caricature in *Vanity Fair*, Pellegrini's Disraeli, the rise and fall of *Vanity Fair*, as well as an era, is apparent. Within another month, when *Vanity Fair* was absorbed by *Hearth and Home*, the last remnants of Britain's leading Society magazine faded into history; and before the year had run its course, the way of life *Vanity Fair* had chronicled and caricatured would begin its agonizing death in the trenches of France.

'The Great Imperialist': Joseph Chamberlain, by Astz, 1914

1 B. Fletcher Robinson, 'Chronicles in Cartoon: A Record of Our Own Times.' *The Windsor Magazine*, 1905, p. 42.

2 *Vanity Fair*, 4 June 1892 (Hardy), 28 December 1905 and 16 August 1911 (Shaw).

3 *Vanity Fair*, 16 May 1891.

4 Leonard E. Naylor, *The Irrepressible Victorian*, London: MacDonald and Company, 1965, p. 11.

5 Naylor, *The Irrepressible Victorian*, pp. 11–12. Frank R. Miles, editor, *King's College School: A Register of Pupils in the School Under The First Headmaster* Mr Miles also supplied us with copies of the school curriculum, Bowles's entrance papers and his school record.

6 Eileen Harris, Introduction to *Vanity Fair: an Exhibition of Original Cartoons*, London: National Portrait Gallery, 1976, pp. 5–6. Naylor, *The Irrepressible Victorian*, pp. 13–18; References to Bowles's early years are found in Arthur William a' Beckett, *The a'Becketts of Punch: Memories of Father and Son*, London: Archibald Constable and Co Ltd, 1903; Sir F. C. Burnand, 'Mr Punch: Some Precursors and Competitors' *Pall Mall* XXIX, 1903; T. H. S. Escott, *Masters of English Journalism*, London: T. Fisher Unwin, 1911; Reginald Lucas, *Lord Glenesk and the Morning Post*, New York: John Lane Co, 1910; Erroll Sherson, *London's Lost Theatres of the Nineteenth Century*, London: John Lane, The Bodley Head Ltd, 1925; Anon. [William MacKay] *Bohemian Days in Fleet Street*, London: John Lang Ltd, 1913.

7 Michael Alexander, *The True Blue: The Life and Adventures of Colonel Fred Burnaby*, New York: St Martin's Press, 1958, p. 35. Eileen Harris, 'Introduction to *Vanity Fair*', p. 5.

8 Double acrostics were not original to Bowles. He may have been inspired by John Stuart Wortley, his friend who supplied them for *The Owl*. Lucas, *Lord Glenesk*, p. 205.

9 *Vanity Fair*, 7 November 1868.

10 Naylor. *The Irrepressible Victorian*, p. 126 ff. Bowles had four children. The oldest daughter Sydney married Lord Redesdale and was mother of the Mitford clan. Jessica Mitford described 'Muv' vividly in *Daughters and Rebels*, Boston: Houghton Mifflin Co, 1960. Pryce-Jones refers to Thomas Gibson Bowles in his book *Unity Mitford: An Enquiry into her Life and the Frivolity of Evil*, London: Weidenfeld and Nicolson. 1976, pp. 13–14. Lady Diana Moseley mentions her grandfather in *A Life of Contrasts*, London: Hamish Hamilton, 1977, pp. 3–4.

11 Witherby was also a caricaturist who contributed to *Vanity Fair* under the *nom de crayon* of W. A. G. Harris's efforts were not ignored. Harris claimed he did get *Vanity Fair* out of debt, but his word was not always reliable. His ambitions

eventually overshadowed his interest in *Vanity Fair*'s restoration. Leslie Ward, *Forty Years of Spy*, London: Chatto and Windus, 1915, p. 330; Harris, *Introduction to Vanity Fair*, p. 13. Philippa Pullar, *Frank Harris*, London: Hamish Hamilton, 1975, p. 234 and *passim*. A. I. Tobin and Elmer Gerty, *Frank Harris: A Study in Black and White*, Chicago: Madelaine Mendelsohn, 1931, pp. 145–146, 285. We could find no corroboration for the assertion in *Bohemian Days in Fleet Street* that *Vanity Fair* was owned by the Harmsworths.

12 Robinson, 'Chronicles in Cartoon' pp. 35–51.

13 Roger L. Green, editor, *The Diaries of Lewis Carroll*, New York: Oxford University Press, 1954, II, 230.

14 Delane to Russell, 8 July 1871, *Archive of the Times*.

15 Harry Furniss, *Harry Furniss at Home*, London: T. Fisher Unwin, 1904, pp. 7–8.

16 John Pope Hennessey, *Anthony Trollope*, London: Jonathan Cape, 1971, p. 325; John H. Wildman, *Anthony Trollope's England*, Providence: Brown University Press, 1940, p. 17; Ward, *Forty Years* pp. 104–105. See also *The Observer*, 3 October 1915, an interview with Ward in which he commented on Trollope's objection to the caricature and how angry Trollope became.

17 Werner Hofmann, *Caricature from Leonardo to Picasso*, London: John Calder, 1957, pp. 13–21. See also Hofmann's article 'Comic Art and Modern Caricature in the Western World,' *Encyclopedia of World Art*, III, New York: McGraw-Hill, cols. 755–775.

18 Randall Davies, 'Caricatures of To-Day,' *The Studio* (special edition 1928).

19 Herbert Atherton, *Political Prints in the Age of Hogarth: A Study of Ideographic Representation of Politics*, Oxford: Clarendon Press, 1974, pp. 25ff. Atherton makes a distinction between what he calls the iconographic print and caricature. The iconographic print 'satirizes a particular individual or concept by associating him (or it) with appropriate symbols and stereotypes; the latter concentrating on the individual himself and is of a more subjective personal nature.' p. 37.

20 Biographies and studies of caricaturists of the Georgian era are extensive. Among the general surveys are: Dorothy M. George, *English Political Caricatures*, 2 vols, Oxford: Oxford University Press, 1959; Dorothy M. George, *Hogarth to Cruikshank: Social Change in Graphic Satire*, London: Penguin Books Ltd, 1967; Michael Wynn Jones, *The Cartoon History of Britain*, New York: The Macmillan Company, 1971; Bevis Hillier, *Cartoons and Caricatures*, London: Studio Vista Ltd, 1970; David Low, *British Cartoonists, Caricaturists and Comic Artists*, London: William Collins, 1942.

21 E. H. Gombrich and Ernst Kris, *Caricatures*, London: Penguin Books, 1940, p. 18 ff.

22 Davies, 'Caricature of To-Day,' Gombrich, *Caricatures*, p. 18 ff. Gombrich and Ernst Kris supply historical and psychological dimensions on caricaturing in: Kris and Gombrich, 'The Principles of Caricature,' *British Journal of Medical Psychology*, XVII, 1939, 319–342, Kris, 'The Psychology of Caricature', *The International Journal of Psycho-Analysis*, XVII, 1936, 285–303.

23 George, *English Political Caricatures*, II, 257–258; Davies, 'Caricature of To-Day,' *The Studio*.

24 Hofmann, *Caricature*, pp. 41–46.

25 Stanley Jones, *Lithography for Artists*, London: Oxford University Press, 1967 *passim*; Felix Man, *Artists' Lithographs: A World History from Senefelder to the Present Day*, London: Studio Vista, 1970. pp. 12 ff.

26 Man, *Artists' Lithographs*, pp. 16–19, 37–43.

27 Man, *Artists' Lithographs*, pp. 53–55; E. R. Pennell and Joseph Pennell, *Lithography and Lithographs*, New York: The Macmillan Company, 1915, p. 137; Robert M. Burch, *Colour Printing and Colour Printers*, New York: The Baker and Taylor Co, 1910, pp. 136, 209. Harris, *Introduction to Vanity Fair*, p. 7. On the Baxters' father and son see Charles T. C. Lewis, *George Baxter: His Life and Work*, London: Sampson Low, Marson and Company Ltd, 1908, p. 28.

28 Escott, *Masters of English Journalism*, p. 263. Thomas M. Kemnitz, 'Matt Morgan of Tomahawk and English Cartooning, 1867–1870, *Victorian Studies*, XIX, September 1975, pp. 5–34; Two journals, *Society* and *Mayfair* were modelled on *Vanity Fair* but never rivalled it.

29 Eileen Harris, 'Carlo Pellegrini: Man and Ape,' *Apollo*, Vol. 103, No. 167, January 1976, pp. 54–55.

30 *Vanity Fair*, 11 September 1869.

31 Gombrich, *Caricatures*, p. 12.

32 John Geipel, *The Cartoon: A Short History of Graphic Comedy and Satire*, Newton Abbot: David and Charles, 1972, pp. 13–14.

33 Geipel, *The Cartoon*, p. 14. There is a touch of irony in this incident, in that one of the successful artists in the competition, and who eventually painted some of the frescos in the House of Commons was E. M. Ward, the father of Leslie. See also David Low, *British Cartoonists*, p. 18.

34 Bowles to William Hepworth Dixon, 19 January 1872, Beinecke Rare Book and Manuscript Library, Yale University.

35 *Vanity Fair*, 30 January 1869.

36 *Vanity Fair*, 23 May 1874.

37 Harris, 'Carlo Pellegrini: Man and Ape,' pp. 53–56; *Dictionary of National Biography*, 44, 265; *The Times*, London, 23 January 1889.

38 Robert Blake, *Disraeli*, New York: Doubleday and Company, 1968, p. 486; References to Pellegrini's personality and habits are scattered through the memoirs and biographies of numerous individuals. See Squire Bancroft, *The Bancrofts: Recollection of Sixty Years* New York: E. P. Dutton and Co, 1909; and *Empty Chairs*, London: John Murray, 1925; Sir Francis Burnard, *Records and Reminiscences, Personal and General*, London: Methuen and Company, 1904; Leslie Ward, *Forty Years of Spy*; Sir Henry Lucy, *The Diary of a Journalist*, New York: E. P. Dutton and Co, 1920, Frank Harris, *My Life and Loves*, New York: Grove Press Inc, 1963. Harris claims Pellegrini confessed to him that he was a homosexual, and was the first to prove to Harris that 'a perverted taste in sex might go along with a sweet and generous nature'. Harris took delight in shocking people and his memoirs are not reliable.

39 Robinson, 'Chronicles in Cartoon,' pp. 38–39.

40 Max Beerbohm, *A Variety of Things*, New York: Alfred Knopf, 1928, p. 119. See also John Felstiner, *The Lies of Art*, New York: Alfred Knopf, 1972, pp. 106–107; Harris, 'Carlo Pellegrini: Man and Ape,' p. 57.

41 Low, *British Cartoonists*, p. 33.

42 Low, *Ye Madde Designer*, London: The Studio Ltd, 1935. p. 123. John R. Robinson called Pellegrini 'one of the greatest of caricaturists,' and noted that he drew his cartoons on a card in the palm of his hand and then thought out the final draft afterwards. Frederick M. Thomas, editor, *Fifty Years of Fleet Street: the Life and Recollections of John R. Robinson*, London: Macmillan and Company, pp. 293–294.

43 Ward, *Forty Yeers of Spy*, pp. 95–96.

44 Ward, *Forty Years of Spy*, pp. 96–101. Ward's attitude toward Pellegrini might have been influenced by having to caricature persons Pellegrini had refused to do. p. 112.

45 Bancroft, *The Bancrofts* p. 103; Ward, *Forty Years of Spy*, pp. 112, 115–116, 194–195.

46 Harris, 'Carlo Pellegrini: Man and Ape,' p. 56; Ward, *Forty Years of Spy*, p. 123; Bancroft, *Empty Chairs*, pp. 93–94; Low *Ye Madde Designer*, p. 123; Bohun Lynch, *A History of Caricature*, Boston: Little Brown and Co, 1927, p. 74.

47 Ward, *Forty Years of Spy*, p. 67, *passim*. *The Times* (London) 16 May 1922, Roy T. Matthews, 'Spy', *British History Illustrated*, III, June/July, 1976, 50–57.

48 Harris, 'Introduction to *Vanity Fair*' p. 17. Tissot's oil portrait of Burnaby is in The National Portrait Gallery.

49 Thomas Gibson Bowles, *The Defense of Paris: Narrated as it was Seen*, London: Sampson Son and Marston, 1871. Bowles also sent articles from Paris to *Vanity Fair* in September and October, 1870. *The Defense of Paris* was illustrated with Tissot's sketches of soldiers and civilians.

50 James Laver, *Vulgar Society: The Romantic Career of James Tissot*, London: Constable and Co Ltd, 1936. pp. 16–33, *passim;* Naylor, *The Irrepressible Victorian*, p. 28. Tissot's paintings are now being re-evaluated, and his reputation is increasing. See Jane Abdy's introduction to the catalogue for *J. J. Tissot: etchings, drypoints and messotints* London: Lumley Cazalet Ltd, 1978.

51 Harris, 'Introduction to *Vanity Fair*' pp. 11–12.

52 Susan Meyer, *Flagg*, New York: Watson-Guptill Publications, 1974; Meyer provides no specific information on Flagg's year in England, nor does Flagg in his James Montgomery Flagg, *Roses and Buckshot*, New York: G. P. Putnam's Sons, 1946.

53 Ward, in *Forty Years of Spy* admits that *Vanity Fair* about 1907 began to allow sitters to pay for their caricature to appear in it. p. 123. Edgar Jepson, an editor of *Vanity Fair* in the short Frank Harris regime, asserts the same. Jepson also alleged that the sitters sometimes wrote their own biography. Jepson's account of how *Vanity Fair* was mismanaged in its last several years, about 1907 on, helps to explain why it declined so rapidly. Edgar A. Jepson, *Memories of an Edwardian*, London: Martin Secker, 1939. pp. 106–112; the biography of another journalist who worked at *Vanity Fair* with Harris, W. Sorley Brown, *The Life and Genius of T. H. W. Crosland*, London: Cecil Palmer, 1938, *passim*. A. I. Tobin and Elmer Gerty, *Frank Harris*, p. 145.

54 See note 40; Beerbohm dedicated his first collection of drawings, *Caricatures of Twenty-five Gentlemen*, to Pellegrini in 1896. See also David Cecil, *Max*, London: Constable, 1964, pp. 136–37.

ROYALTY

Vanity Fair's respect for royalty as an institution is understandable. It represented the quintessence of the world which the magazine sought to chronicle, criticize and entertain. The magazine's descriptions of monarchs were usually deferential and often sycophantic, particularly so when its subjects were members of the British royal family. Treatment of non-British royalty was, however, somewhat less restrained. In fact, the further away from the 'scepter'd isle' the subject was, the franker and funnier the description. It could be humorously censorious when it dealt with the activities of potentates in the Far East, Near East, and Africa, and mildly critical of European rulers. Many of the crowned heads of Europe appeared in *Vanity Fair*, including Alexander III of Russia (*Vanity Fair*, 11 October 1884), Victor Emmanuel I of Italy (*Vanity Fair*, 29 January 1870), Leopold II of Belgium (*Vanity Fair*, 9 October 1869) and Alphonso VIII of Spain (*Vanity Fair*, 21 January 1893). The accompanying commentaries were often sympathetic and understanding of the problems facing the kings and emperors. On the whole though, the colour plates of royalty were flattering. In the case of queens and empresses, whether British or not, the images were usually idealized portraits, and the magazine was almost always deferential in both caricature and letterpress. Chartran (T) contributed a series of noble ladies in the 1880s which established this pattern. Earlier, Tissot had drawn a set of satirical drawings of European sovereigns which were a contribution to caricature and some of which, for example Leopold II and Napoleon III, were devastating, but this pattern was not repeated.

This idealization of royalty and aristocracy, especially after Bowles sold the magazine in 1889, meant that the Royals were not of the same quality artistically or historically as were other groups of *Vanity Fair* caricatures. They give one a sense of what the magazine thought the sovereigns and their families ought to be; not what they were. *Vanity Fair*'s more usual veneration of rulers is not reflected in the following selection, for they provide more insight into royalty than was usual in the magazine.

A CIMIEZ.
Promenade matinale.
Her Majesty the Queen-Empress
Diamond Jubilee Number, No. 1494
17 June 1897
Guth

QUEEN VICTORIA (1819–1901) appeared just once in *Vanity Fair*. She was then seventy-eight years old, and the occasion was her Diamond Jubilee, her sixtieth year on the throne. Queen since 1837, she had outlived many of her critics, and become a semi-mystical symbol of the moral virtues of that age – integrity, family loyalty and Christian morality. Her Diamond Jubilee was used by the late nineteenth-century British élite to celebrate the glory and extent of the Empire. Jehu Junior was sycophantic in his commentary when he fervently asserted:

Queen Victoria has constantly proved herself a greater Sovereign than Elizabeth: wiser, gentler, nobler, under harder conditions . . . For her hard work Her Majesty relinquished the more ornamental part of her duties; and with an industry of which her people are little aware, she has ever since devoted herself to the government of a mighty Empire with a success that has altogether left nothing to be desired. Mistakes may have been made during the long reign of Queen Victoria: but they have been the mistakes of the Queen's Ministers. Herself indeed made the world recognize the Divine Right of Kings.

Guth's portrait is far more perceptive than this silly Victorian effusion. He has portrayed an old lady, tired, in decline, but still of considerable character, increasingly arbitrary, subject to curious whims but not entirely lacking in wisdom. The tones are muted and soft, and a feeling of aging sadness is conveyed in the expression on her face, the grey of her garb and of the carriage and its umbrella. Ironically this portrait, commissioned to capture the glories of her reign, anticipates the end of the era with its sad air of resignation and decline. The Diamond Jubilee was perhaps the last burst of Victorian imperial glory and certainty. The controversial Boer War which followed in 1899 heralded a century in which those imperial glories would tarnish rapidly and vanish.

The Queen died in January 1901, tactful in her death by waiting until the nineteenth century was absolutely and indisputably over. To mourn her, *Vanity Fair* reprinted Guth's portrait in simple black and white. Sir Almeric Fitzroy, clerk of the Privy Council, captured the feelings of many when he said:

The heart that beat so true to England and to duty for eighty years is still forever. It is not only the passing of a great personality, the disappearance of a potent influence, the sudden and irreparable rupture of a relation that has bound things to a common centre for so long. It is a change from era to era; it is as if the standards of comparison, the criteria of taste, the very categories of thought which have regulated the judgements and moulded the desires of two generations were abruptly swept into the limbo of the past.

EDWARD VII appeared several times in *Vanity Fair*, unlike his mother. With one exception, the images were what the magazine staff thought the public ought to see. The first is different, possibly because it appeared in a period when his mother's deliberate withdrawal from public life and the Prince's own peccadilloes had contributed to serious criticism of the monarchy. Though hardly exaggerated enough to be called a caricature, Tissot has painted a surprisingly frank, uncomplimentary glimpse of 'Bertie' – as he was known to his family. It closely resembles a photograph taken earlier in 1870. The Prince's heavy-lidded, chubby face tops a short, somewhat rotund body. He looks jauntily dissipated, standing by the seaside, probably at Cowes, one of his favourite haunts. He could

be a 'swell' or a 'blood'—even something of a rake. The personage so portrayed has little or no relationship to the one discussed in the commentary.

Jehu Junior commended the Prince, then thirty-two, for not seeking to 'anticipate the duties which must one day devolve upon him' and for not providing a focus for opposition to his mother, and observed that 'For the last twelve years there have not been wanting opportunities to form a "Prince's Party".' The Queen's self-imposed seclusion at Windsor since the death of Prince Albert had been unpopular. *Vanity Fair* congratulated the Prince for filling the special role of Private Gentleman with 'noticeable credit'.

The commentary then noted his attention to ceremonial duties: 'there are few men in the Kingdom who have worked so hard or travelled so much as he to attend social gatherings, to lay stones, to open public works, and to preside at Charity dinners'. It complimented him on his extreme good nature – a quality not evident in the caricature. Jehu Junior does allude to his delight in the good life and in practical jokes. 'His intimates are naturally good companions from among the young men of rank of his own age; there is not indeed a Fox or a Burke or a Sheridan among them, yet he willingly admits to intimacy even a grey-beard or a bald-head who may be equal to making themselves sources or subjects of amusement.' His tact, excellent memory and social graces are lauded.

The Prince
HRH The Prince of Wales
Season Number
14 December 1878
Spy

sketches of the Prince for *Vanity Fair: The Prince* (*Vanity Fair*, 14 December 1878) reproduced here; *At Cowes* (*Vanity Fair*, 6 December 1894). Both were complimentary images, showing little or no insight into the man's character. According to Ward, the Prince was pleased with the 1878 sketch. When the King sat again for Spy, he told the artist, 'now let me down gently.' 'Oh', said Ward, 'but you've a very fine chest, sir'. Ward's 'diplomacy', as he called it, is reflected in the accompanying commentary on his 1902 portrait. The King is again lauded. Jehu Junior concluded, 'His whole personality is stimulating, and his people are as proud of their sovereign as His Majesty is of his people. He is a great King, and perhaps even a greater man.' J. B. Priestley was more accurate when he said that the King was 'a typical Englishman with the lid off'.

'The uncrowned King', EDWARD VIII, later the Duke of Windsor (1894–1972), was portrayed in *Vanity Fair*, as were his mother, Queen Mary (*Vanity Fair*, 6 July 1893), and his father, King George v (*Vanity Fair*, 24 May 1890; 21 June 1911). Nibs has sketched a slight, small epicene figure who looks younger than his seventeen years. There is a wistful uncertainty in the soft eyes, the stance and the way his figure floats in the frame.

The occasion was Edward's formal investiture as Prince of Wales. *Vanity Fair*, unctuous as usual when describing British royalty, noted, 'There is every possibility that as time goes on he will fill his position with credit to his parents and to the advantage of the Empire which, in the ordinary course of nature, at some distant day he will be called upon to rule.'

To stage the investiture in Wales was an innovation largely inspired by Lloyd George (see p. 61), who wished to turn the ceremony into a Welsh pageant. In the past, princes had been invested in Westminster and in other English towns. Edward, shy and unsure, having just finished a period of training at the Naval colleges at Osborne and Dartmouth, rebelled when he was shown his costume of white satin breeches and a mantle and surcoat of purple velvet edged with ermine. It was 'fantastic', said he. This 'preposterous rig' would make him a laughing stock to his Navy friends. However, his mother finally persuaded him to adopt the 'preposterous rig'!

The young prince then went unwillingly to Oxford and into the Grenadier Guards. Overprotected and prevented from active serivce during the 1914–1918 War, the Prince never reconciled the various demands of his position. The caricaturist captured the doleful ambiguity which plagued his life.

This Tissot (Coide) of NAPOLEON III (1808–1873) appeared in *Vanity Fair* in September 1869. Within a year, the Emperor would be a prisoner of the Prussian army, his outdated, ambitious dreams shattered by the army of a nation which represented the wave of the future. Tissot's prophetic caricature foreshadows Napoleon's fate. Napoleon's bent body and worn countenance personify his own senility and his country's weakness.

He leans heavily on the strong arm of Marianne, the female symbol of the French Republic. She gestures to him to be silent and to proceed cautiously. Her tender assurance evokes the concern of a dutiful daughter supporting her father in his dotage. Behind the two figures loom Paris's most famous religious and political landmarks, Notre Dame, L'Hotel des Invalides and La Madeleine. The muted greys in the distance are contrasted with Napoleon's bright uniform trimmed in green and red which are then repeated in Marianne's dress. The black

His attraction to women is perceived as a natural consequence of his personal qualities and rank. 'He is simply to his wife and children, one of the very best husbands and fathers in England. Indeed, the Prince and Princess of Wales [*Vanity Fair*, 5 December 1882; 7 June 1911] are now after nearly eleven years of married life rather like lovers than husband and wife'.

Vanity Fair asserted that 'nature has endowed the Prince with intellectual qualities distinctly above the average'. This aspect of his personality is also not evident in the portrait. In the last sentence of Jehu Junior's description there is an allusion to the recent criticism of the Prince – the result of his involvement in a sordid divorce trial in 1871: 'When that [his ascent to the throne] shall arrive those who have been unjust to him as a Prince will be constrained to recognize his merits . . .' Aside from this veiled reference, this description of the Prince is almost as fulsome as the one of his mother in *Vanity Fair* in 1897. Perhaps there is irony in the comment by Jehu Junior: 'This day he completes his thirty-second year, and it is to be hoped that he will see many more before he comes to his inheritance.'

Almost three decades later, Spy portrayed the King on the eve of his coronation. Dressed this time in uniform as an Admiral, the King is treated in a respectful, though not servile manner (*Vanity Fair*, 19 June 1902). Ward's portraits were usually flattering to British royalty. He had produced two earlier

boots, shoes, hat, tie and ribbon set off the shadings of grey and stitch together the picture. Unlike many of his fellow caricaturists, Tissot was able to include two individuals in a caricature, utilizing both subjects to convey his message and yet not overcrowding the frame. The figures, background and colour distinguish this caricature as one of the most astutely conceived and best planned in *Vanity Fair*'s collection.

That Tissot shows Napoleon relying on Marianne for support tells us that, by 1869, the Emperor was turning to the republicans for aid. Whether they or the French people would rally to his support was not yet clear; a year later their verdict would be against him. Since 1852 he had been Emperor of the Second Empire. For years he had dreamed and conspired to restore the Napoleonic Legend. Driven by his own personal ego and by a glorious past, Napoleon had attempted to come to power several times through schemes that bordered on the comic rather than the tragic. By a turn of events in the Revolutions of 1848 he was elected President of the Second Republic. He appealed to the French as a symbol of order, security and past greatness. Four years later, in 1852, he engineered a nearly bloodless *coup d'état* that ushered in the Second Empire. During the 1850s he flourished; France prospered; honour returned to the land. In the 1860s, however, a series of disastrous adventures in Mexico and Europe reversed his fortunes and by the end of the decade France and Napoleon were as frail as Tissot has depicted them.

Jehu Junior observed that although one could not forget how Napoleon had come to office, when one examined the origins of other dynasties, his reign compared 'favourably'. The French had tired of revolutions by 1848, and they had need of a strong leader when Napoleon took power. Furthermore, he had brought 'security, prosperity and dignity' to France. These achievements were sufficient to quiet all of Napoleon's critics except those who still believed that 'we live in an ideal world where condonation of misdeeds is impossible'.

Turning to Anglo-French relations, Bowles noted that Napoleon had always been a 'fast friend' to England because Great Britain had been one of the first countries to recognize his government, and because he had learned from England his own belief in self-government. On the second point, Jehu Junior argued that Napoleon had been trying to establish self-government but was surrounded by a reactionary court which hampered him. Now, however, he was attempting to lift the weight of the government from his weary shoulders by calling upon the French people to assist him. Jehu Junior was heartened by Napoleon's move to create *le régime parlementaire;* the French should respond and cooperate to repay him for the 'incalculable and undeniable benefits' he had bestowed upon them, asserted Bowles.

Jehu Junior was more optimistic about France's future than Tissot, who sensed the impending holocaust which he and Bowles would soon personally witness. His caricature is much more critical of Napoleon than Bowles's commentary. Historians have tended to agree with Tissot who, like Victor Hugo, pictured his victim as Napoleon the Little.

OTTO VON BISMARCK'S (1815–1898) caricature in *Vanity Fair* in October 1870 is in startling contrast to that of his adversary, Napoleon III, who had been featured a year earlier. Napoleon was weary and bent; Bismarck is energetic and erect. Napoleon had lost his self-confidence, looked bewildered and was uncertain of his future; Bismarck exudes boldness and appears to have destiny, and the old enemy, France under his fist. Red and gold highlight his splendid white uniform, adorned with

sash, medals and epaulet, the massive black boots and plumed helmet. But the pose of the countenance reveals to us a resolute, determined, worldly man. Bismarck's penetrating eyes and set jaw indicate his self-assurance and sense of power. Tissot, who drew both Napoleon and Bismarck, caught his victims' personalities during crucial periods of their careers. The artist's ability to depict Bismarck so vividly, when Tissot himself was fighting the Prussians during the Siege of Paris, is a mark of his professionalism and sensitivity.

The triumphant Junker had, by 1870, risen to power in Prussia and now dominated European foreign affairs. The son of a noble Prussian family, Bismarck had attended Göttingen University to prepare for a post in the Prussian government. After his appointment to the civil service he lost interest in the position and returned to Prussia to manage his family's estates. He travelled occasionally, read widely and appeared to be settling down to the life of a landed Prussian Junker. A turning point occurred in his life in his late 20s, when he experienced a Christian 'conversion' which he came to associate with nationalism and militarism, a trait repugnant to many Europeans, including Queen Victoria.

In 1847 he began his political career in the United Diet of Prussia. He witnessed the uprisings of 1848 and their subsequent failure. This led him, in 1862, to state that Germany's problems could not be solved by resolutions and decrees but by 'blood and iron'. Meanwhile, he challenged Austria's influence in the Diet at Frankfurt and later served as ambassador to Russia in 1859 and to France in 1862. That year Bismarck was recalled to Prussia to become both Prime Minister and Minister of Foreign Affairs. From 1862 to 1870 he won victories at home and abroad through his astute political and diplomatic manoeuvering and by military threat and force. He broke the back of his opposition in the Prussian Diet, drove Austria out of the German Bund and organized the North German Confederation – a union of small German states under Prussia's leadership. He defeated Denmark in 1864, for which he was created a count in 1865; and, in 1866, he inflicted a humiliating defeat, but conciliatory treaty, on Austria. By late 1870 he was in the process of bringing Napoleon III's Second Empire to its knees.

When Bismarck appeared in *Vanity Fair*, Thomas Gibson Bowles was in Paris witnessing the results of Bismarck's policy and strategy. As a reporter for the *Morning Post* and his own publication, he was sending out weekly dispatches detailing life among the soldiers and civilians. Bowles's historical sense of these events is apparent in these reports and in his letterpress written on Thomas Carlyle for *Vanity Fair* (22 October 1870) which appeared one week after his commentary on Bismarck.

Bowles was fully aware of the momentous importance of the Franco-Prussian War and the recent developments inside Prussia. Jehu Junior noted that it had been only a few years since Prussia had been regarded a 'free and constitutional country' and as the centre for 'liberal thought' in Germany. Unfortunately, Prussia, a country which had not been able to solve its financial and constitutional difficulties, had turned to Count Bismarck who had 'cut the knot' in an unconstitutional but effective manner. Bowles then summarized Bismarck's manipulation of the Prussian Diet and Prussia's conquest of Denmark and Austria. In conclusion, he assessed Bismarck's policy and personality:

He moves the King, the Princes, and the people about like pawns upon a chessboard; he has flagrantly, and in open day, broken every treaty that stood in his way; he has conspired against the liberties

Le Régime Parlementaire
Napoleon III
Sovereigns No. 1
4 September 1869
Coïdé

The Ablest Statesman in Europe
Count Von Bismarck-Schonausen
Men of the Day No. 12
15 October 1870
Tissot (unsigned)

Austria   47
The Emperor-King of Austro-Hungary
Francis Joseph I
Sovereigns No. 13
29 December 1877
Sue

*and the peace of Europe; with Austria, with France and last of all
with Russia, with whom he hopes to make Prussia walk side by side
in a gigantic scheme of aggression, which the war with France is
waged to forward. He is equally familiar with the use of force and of
intrigue; he fears not God, neither regards man; and he hitherto so
succeeded in his schemes that he is well entitled to be considered the
ablest statesman in Europe.*

Bowles's grudging praise of Bismarck would return to haunt
him in the coming years as he called for a stronger British Navy
to combat the rising threat from Germany. The young journalist sensed the implications of Prussia's new-found position
and the methods Bismarck had employed. *Vanity Fair* and
Bowles would live on to witness the growth of a German Empire, the successes and failures of the Iron Chancellor's domestic policies and a combination of international events that would
generate crises until the dénouement in 1914. Thomas Gibson Bowles in 1870 and later, in the 1890s, in the House of
Commons clearly understood the forces of German nationalism,
Prussian militarism and Hohenzollern authoritarianism which
Bismarck utilized and combined to establish a new type of nation state.

Following true to form, *Vanity Fair* sympathized with the
plight of FRANCIS JOSEPH of Austria while, at the same time,
recognizing the Emperor's weaknesses. When his wife the EM-
PRESS ELIZABETH, or 'Sisi', was featured, the magazine gave her
unqualified praises. Her caricature is really a character portrait.
In her case, however, it is difficult to imagine how Constantine
de Grimm, the artist, could have done otherwise. She was one
of the most remarkable women of the nineteenth century.

The unknown caricaturist, Sue, drew Francis Joseph
(1830–1916) in 1877, after the forty-seven-year-old Austrian
Emperor had been in power for twenty-nine years. He was at
the height of his productive years and bore the rigours of the
office with dignity. Sue has captured his sense of self-confidence
and self-importance. Francis Joseph exhibits an imperious
manner offset by a bewhiskered, very human face. A contemporary photograph of Francis Joseph wearing a Hungarian military uniform has left us with a similar impresson of the man.

During his rule, his empire pacified Italy and Hungary in
1849, suffered defeat ten years later in Italy at the hands of
France and Piedmont, won, with Prussia's aid, a war against
Denmark in 1864, lost a war to Prussia in 1866, was expelled
from the German Diet, struck a compromise government with
Hungary in 1867 and in 1872 joined the Three Emperors'
League with Russia and the German Empire. *Vanity Fair* recognized that 'events . . . have always had the mastery in Austria
. . .' Francis Joseph had been a victim of these events when, as
a young man of eighteen, he had been raised 'to the most splendid, difficult and pathetic position in the world' and was made
the 'last hope and refuge of moribund aristocracy . . . in
Europe'. His lack of resolution had cost him support in Europe
when he did not become involved in the Crimean War and
when he stood alone against France and Piedmont in 1859.
Since 1867, to his credit, he had initiated reforms at home,
made an agreement with Hungary to grant it independence and
initiated a 'Constitutional Government according to modern
nations'.

Francis Joseph's foreign policy would continue to be inept
and his domestic reforms were too little and too late. In 1879 he
signed the Dual Alliance with Germany and the Triple Alliance
with Germany and Italy in 1883, two agreements which tied

Austria to the fortunes of these more vigorous and ambitious
powers. By the opening of the twentieth century, the Austro-
Hungarian Empire was enmeshed in Balkan politics and wars
from which it could not, and perhaps did not, intend to extract
itself. Austria's annexation of Bosnia and Herzegovina in 1908,
followed by the Balkan Wars of 1912 and 1913 and the assassi-
nation of the heir to the Austrian Empire, Francis Ferdinand in
July, 1914 were events of monumental consequence. Once the
1914–1918 war began, Francis Joseph withdrew more and
more into the background while his empire's future was decided by others. He died in November, 1916 and his empire
collapsed two years later.

Francis Joseph's private life seemed no more promising or
rewarding than his public career. *Vanity Fair* thought him to be
a brave and diligent man who was ready at all times 'to sacrifice
himself, his ease, his life and even his convictions to the good of
his country'. He was described as a 'fine soldier and a most
gallant gentleman'. Yet, he had been forced to deal with dangers and difficult situations for which he was poorly prepared.
Fortune, observed *Vanity Fair,* had been cruel to the Emperor
for he had been blamed for things he had and had not done and,
as a consequence, the final results were never 'a happy event'.
To his credit, however, he had married 'one of the most beautiful women in Europe'.

His marriage in 1854 to Elizabeth Amalie Eugenie (1837–

pression. In 1898, aged sixty-one, her life was cut short by an assassin.

In 1884 when Grimm drew Elizabeth for *Vanity Fair* she was dressed in a riding habit, sitting on a rail fence. This unusual pose, in an outdoor setting, identified her with her favourite sport. Her obsession with her looks, her constant attention to diet, bathing and body care obviously had helped her maintain her beauty. *Vanity Fair* called her 'perhaps the finest horsewoman in Europe' and a 'most Imperial Empress'. While in England, she had ridden before some of the most critical judges in the world and, according to Jehu Junior, had received their 'universal admiration . . . for her dress, her equipment, her seat, her carriage and her discretion'. Such gentle irony was not lost upon those who marvelled at her irresistible beauty and knew of her numerous admirers.

Her private life could never be entirely separated from her public responsibilities. Like her husband, she shared the fate and misfortunes of the Austrian nation. Like her husband, she was forced to live in two different worlds. Neither world, for neither one, was very happy. Both were victims of their positions in society and of their times in history.

ABDUL AZIZ (1830–1876), Sultan of the Ottoman Empire from 1861 until his deposition in 1876, glares out at us from Coide's (Tissot's) vigorous, colourful, politically charged lithograph. The Sultan was a violent, obstinate, irascible ruler, constantly subjected to internal pressures for change and reform, and external coercion from European Powers seeking to establish their influence in the Ottoman domains. The caption aptly summarized Abdul Aziz's situation. 'Ote-toi de là que je m'y mette', or 'Get up, so I can take your place.' Jehu Junior amplified this theme:

The western nations, in their conceit of civilization, have taken up the song and have clamoured forth instruction and advice until the bewildered Turk, stunned by the discordant chorus, has given himself up to be divided amongst them as they might please.

1898), daughter of the Duke of Bavaria and Princess of Wittelsbach, had held great promise. But even here he was fated to disappointment and defeat. She was only sixteen years old when she was married to Francis Joseph in April 1854. Two daughters were born by 1856; Rudolf, their ill-starred son, was born in 1858. By 1860 the first strains on their marriage had appeared. Elizabeth began to travel, to be alone and to devote herself to her animals. In 1865 she and Francis Joseph separated; a reconciliation followed but she continued to live by herself most of the time, a tragic and lonely figure.

The Empress's travels brought her to England for the first time in 1874. She was received by the Queen, and enchanted the crowds along Rotten Row with her effortless, graceful riding. Over the next decade she returned to England and Ireland numerous times to ride and be toasted by her admirers. Several Englishmen became infatuated with her and she appears to have returned their feelings in one or two cases. She paid her last visit to England in 1896.

During the 1870s, 1880s and on into the 1890s 'Sisi' continued to travel, either on state visits with her husband or alone. Fascinated by Greece, she began reading the classics and visiting archaeological excavations. Meanwhile the Emperor met the actress Katherina Schratt, who became his mistress and confidante. Elizabeth now lived in her world of travel, horses and study. By the mid-1890s she had begun to suffer from de-

By 1869, the Russians, French, Austrians and British were actively interfering in the internal affairs of the Ottoman Empire. Ironically, their wavering encouragement of internal administrative reform contributed to the acquisition by the Sultans of an apparatus of surveillance and repression which gave the dynasty more scope and impact than it had ever had in its days of greatness.

Vanity Fair noted this development:

There is power in Turkey that is little suspected in Europe . . . Abdul Aziz is the creature of the situation, and can in his time do little to improve it – yet he shows signs of knowing how to face it. To have rebuked the Greek, and humbled the Khedive of his own proper motion, indicates the commencement of a new system, and it will be well, not only for Turkey, but for Europe, if it is developed until the Sultan becomes master in his own house.

Sadly, Abdul Aziz never managed to become master of his house. When he toured Paris, London, Vienna and Budapest in 1867, he was the first Ottoman Sultan to visit Europe for reasons other than war. His extravagance, reckless borrowing and his increasing autocracy led finally to his deposition and death in 1876. Among the plotters against him was the great Ottoman reformer Midhat Pasha (*Vanity Fair*, 30 June 1877).

Tissot has captured something of the Sultan's dilemma.

Ote-toi de la que je m'y mette
Abdul Aziz, Sultan of Turkey
Sovereigns No. 5
30 October 1869
Coidé

Abdul Aziz sits glowering, dressed in western uniform and a fez, with a water pipe in one hand. Greece and Egypt are firmly held in his arms as one of the powers is about to encapsulate him. This is a political cartoon, rather than a caricature. The drawing is one of a series of foreign rulers contributed by Tissot during the first year of *Vanity Fair*. The critic Eileen Harris observed that they make a striking contrast to Ape's early 'strictly personal satires of single figures' in blacks and browns.

Vanity Fair's character portraits of foreign potentates, especially those outside Europe, are among the more entertaining series. Their accuracy and artistic quality is uneven, depending on whether the artist had actually seen his subject and on his inspiration and ability. CETEWAYO or Csethwayo (1826–1884), the last King of the Zulus, was brought to London in 1882 by the British Colonial Office, and Ward had the chance to see him several times. The exiled King had gone somewhat to seed by this time. The Queen's artist, Carl Sohn, at her instigation painted an idealized portrait, copies of which were a popular item in stationers' windows during Cetewayo's visit.

Cetewayo's grandfather, Shaka (d. 1828), had forged the Zulu kingdom on a formidable military system that gave the British and the Boers decades of trouble. When Cetewayo appeared to be reviving Shaka's legions, the British intervened in Zululand, and were slaughtered at Isandhwanda in 1879. Shortly after, Zulus killed Napoleon III's heir, the Prince Imperial (*Vanity Fair*, 14 July 1877). Disraeli coolly observed: 'A remarkable people, the Zulus: They defeat our generals, they convert our Bishops; they have settled the fate of a great European dynasty.' Most of the principal actors in this drama that ended with the defeat and subjugation of the Zulus were portrayed in *Vanity Fair*: Sir Bartle Frere, the aggressive colonial administrator (*Vanity Fair*, 20 September 1873); one of the converted Bishops, Colenso (*Vanity Fair*, 28 November 1874); Lord Chelmsford, the foolish general (*Vanity Fair*, 3 September 1881); and Lady Florence Dixie, who championed Cetewayo and the Zulus (*Vanity Fair*, 5 January 1884).

Cetewayo came to the Zulu throne in 1873, when he succeeded his indolent father, Mpande, the only Zulu king to die peacefully. Pressure from the Boers and the British in fear of a rejuvenated Zulu nation under Cetewayo led to war in 1879. Cetewayo's army fought well but the impact of European firepower and organization defeated him. In August 1879, the proud king was brought as a prisoner to General Sir Garnet Wolseley (*Vanity Fair*, 18 April 1874). At the time of his capture he was a splendid man – tall, huge-limbed and very impressive, with a pleasing and intelligent face. When he walked into Wolseley's camp, he evoked spontaneous expressions of admiration. 'By Jove', said one officer, 'he is a fine looking nigger.'

The deposed King was exiled to Capetown, and Zululand was partitioned to preclude further trouble. Cetewayo had his English partisans, among them the influential, elegant aristocrat, Lady Florence Dixie. She led a campaign in Britain for his reinstatement. When the natives remained troublesome, the British officials decided Cetewayo was of further use, and brought him to London on show in 1882. He was presented to the Queen at Osborne and became a great favourite of the London crowds. In 1883, with British backing, he was restored to his kingdom. Under these conditions, he was not acceptable to the resisters and, in 1884 he died, possibly a victim of poison.

Jehu Junior was surprisingly sympathetic to Cetewayo and the Zulu cause. He recounted that their fear of a revived Zulu nation had led the British into provoking a war, and that Cetewayo's forces had initially won a stunning victory. Ironically, said *Vanity Fair*, it was Cetewayo's 'ignorance of civilized ways' and his unwillingness to exploit his victory by invading Natal that allowed the British to revive and defeat him.

Vanity Fair thought Cetewayo was 'a simple man, with a strong will and shrewd perceptions', a man of little refinement, but great dignity. Spy's portrait is inoffensive if not flattering. Spy recalled that he attended a reception for the deposed King at his residence in London and that Cetewayo struck him as 'quite jolly and robust'. In *Vanity Fair*, Spy represented him as he had seen him, 'nearly bursting through his light grey tweed suit with a kingly headgear of black velvet enriched with gold braid and a golden tassel attached.' Cetewayo looks docile, even kindly, and his features hardly resemble those of a furious warrior whose followers had inflicted such heavy losses on the British Army.

POLITICIANS

Bowles launched *Vanity Fair* shortly after the 1867 Reform Act, which
was a significant extension of the male right to vote. This 'leap in the
Dark', the words of Lord Derby, was a firm if reluctant commitment
by the British political élite to democracy, though even then the electorate was still less than one-tenth of the population, and voting was
not by secret ballot until 1872. During an era when the electoral system and the parties were transformed, and the foundations of the
modern welfare state were laid down, many of the major public figures
appeared in *Vanity Fair*. A third of the nearly 2400 colour lithographs
were of politicians. All the prime ministers between 1853 and
1922 were caricatured, except Lord Palmerston and Lord Aberdeen.
Along with a variety of Ministers of the Crown came the Irish Home
Rulers and Ulstermen; the 'new men' from business, industry, (such
as Joseph Chamberlain) and the working classes, (such as James Keir
Hardie). Selected politically active aristocrats, including the Chur-
chills – Lord Randolph, Winston, and 'Jennie' – were portrayed. In
the magazine's last decade the prominent suffragist Christabel Pankhurst appeared, recognizing the vigorous campaign for women's
rights. The politicians in *Vanity Fair*, their poses, their clothes and the
accompanying commentaries form a kaleidoscope of an era which
brought significant changes in British political life.

The Right Honourable Benjamin Disraeli
Statesmen No. 1
30 January 1869
Singe/Ape

The Junior Ambassador
The Earl of Beaconsfield
Season Number, 2 July 1878
Ape

Power and Place
The Earl of Beaconsfield and Mr Montagu Corry
Season Number
16 December 1879
Spy

53

BENJAMIN DISRAELI had, in his own words, 'climbed to the top of the greasy pole' not long before he was chosen by Bowles as the subject for the first caricature in *Vanity Fair*. This extraordinary man had succeeded Lord Derby as Prime Minister in February 1868. A more unlikely character to become the leader of the Conservative Party, the 'gentlemen of England', could hardly have existed.

Born a Sephardic Jew in London, baptized at twelve, he was an exotic, a dandy and a novelist. Moreover, he entered Parliament in his thirties, older than many embarking on political careers in his time. An adventurer at first, he suffered many political setbacks, but after 1846 he began to lead the Tories out of the political backwoods into an accommodation with the new business and commercial interests then emerging in Victorian Britain. Though he established his claim to the party leadership by his brilliant parliamentary manoeuvering for the Reform Act of 1867, his real opportunity came after the waning of his rival Gladstone's volcanic first ministry in the 1870s. In January 1869, when Pellegrini sketched him, the Tories had been soundly defeated, and 'Dizzy' was leader of the Opposition. Jehu Junior was an admirer of Disraeli. In the letterpress which accompanied the caricature, he wrote:

Of all our political leaders, and although I by no means agree with the political opinions he sees fit to assume, I have the greatest admi-

ration and respect by far for Mr Disraeli, for he represents the coming principle of the world – that of Personal Merit. With that for his only patrimony, he has broken through and risen above every one of the barriers that had hitherto stood as the outwork of prescriptive power, so grand and imposing that no man had so much as dared to look over them. With a foot inside one of them, the others might, as was known, be turned; but Disraeli started outside all. The barriers of birth, of race, of religion, of wealth, all frowned upon him, and even now it is astonishing to think that in a country like ours he should have so lightly passed them all, and that he should now stand confessed the first statesman of the day.

Pellegrini's first caricature was a triumph for *Vanity Fair* and for himself. Circulation rocketed, and within four months a third edition of back numbers with caricatures was reproduced at double the original sixpenny price. Ape was now transformed from an amateur entertainer of high society into a professional caricaturist. The full page studies of prominent or notorious individuals, their faces and other features cleverly exaggerated or distorted, set the idiom of the *Vanity Fair* caricatures. They became an institution.

Ape caricatured Disraeli again in 1878, seated in the House of Lords. Captioned 'The Junior Ambassador', it captured the characteristic languid pose he assumed in the House. The drooping lower lip, the air of insouciance, eyes half closed,

Were he a worse man, he would be a better statesman
The Right Honourable William E. Gladstone
Statesmen No. 2
6 February 1869
Singe/Ape

monocle in eye, he would gaze at the clock and lapse 'into simu-
lated sleep'. His attention, however, never lapsed. Robert
Blake, his twentieth-century biographer, has written: 'In an age
of amateurs he was, along with Gladstone, Palmerston, perhaps
Graham and a few others, a professional politican, always in his
place, always alert, a master of the rules of procedure and
debate.'

Spy drew Disraeli for *Vanity Fair* in the late 1870s. Ward had
arranged with Montague Corry, Disraeli's private secretary, to
observe the great man as they strolled arm in arm from Down-
ing Street to the House of Lords. Ward observed: 'Disraeli
walked, or appeared to walk, on his heels as though he were
avoiding hot ashes. In strongest contrast was the walk of
Gladstone, who planted his feet with deliberate but vigorous
firmness as though with every step he would iron his strong
opinion into the mind of the nation.' Jehu Junior observed

Slowly, yet perseveringly they go, now to the Parliament for some
new and unexpected feat of manipulation . . . A surprising and
well-fitted pair are they, each the complement of the other; the
Knight [Disraeli] sprung from a despised race and a repute once
covered with distrust and ridicule, having by sheer force of intellect
won his spurs, and now the master of the proudest nation in the
world; the Secretary [Corry] ready and nimble, with an eye to
smaller methods, social and others, by which mere intellect may be
seconded and fenced about in a feeble and foolish generation.
Neither of them could be what he is without the other. Nor is either
one of them yet truly known for what he is.

Vanity Fair's second caricature subject was WILLIAM EWART
GLADSTONE, who had just become Prime Minister for the first
time. A tall, upright man with an athletic figure, he had a prominent nose, large ears, a piercing gaze, wore enormous collars,
and a posture of stern rectitude. A political contemporary,
Henry Labouchère, complained that he had no objection to
Gladstone's habit of concealing the ace of trumps up his sleeve;
but 'Laby' did object strongly to Gladstone's reiterated claim
that it had been put there by Almighty God!

Gladstone was born in Liverpool, the fifth of six children of a
prosperous merchant family of Scottish descent. Their money
came from sugar plantations, dependent on slave labour, and
from other commercial ventures. He was a prime example of
that unique blend of altruism and self-righteousness peculiar to
so many Victorian leaders, as well as being a clever, practical
politician. Shortly after becoming Prime Minister in 1868, he
wrote in his diary: 'This birthday opens my sixtieth year . . . I
ascend a steepening path, with a burden ever gathering weight.
The Almighty seems to sustain and spare me some purpose of
His own, deeply unworthy as I know myself to be. Glory be to
his name!' Professor Peter Stansky observed: 'They [the Victorian leaders] wanted to do good for others, and were seldom
plagued by self-doubt about what doing good entailed.'

To many contemporaries, the Grand Old Man radiated what
Mark Twain characterized as 'the calm confidence of a Christian with four aces'. Pellegrini in his caricature conveyed this
feeling. Bowles, though politically unsympathetic to Gladstone
and his party, was reluctantly admiring in his commentary:

It happens with Mr Gladstone that the weak cannot comprehend
him, the foolish follow him, the commonplace appreciate him, or the
unfeeling accept him. These are not defects, but as the world goes;
yet in a statesman, who has to lead the world in the way wherein he
finds it, they may be grave defects. Where Mr Gladstone has failed,

he has failed through them; where he has succeeded, he has suc-
ceeded in spite of them; and when his history is written, it will be
seen that they have placed him far below himself; for were he less
admirable, he would be more admired; were he a worse man, he
would be a better statesman.

Gladstone was impossible to ignore. His glowering, sometimes contemplative face appeared nine times in *Vanity Fair* in a
variety of poses and settings.

In 1880, Chartran (T) caricatured the Liberal front bench in
the House of Commons. Gladstone was 'Babble', Lord Har-
tington was 'Birth' and Joseph Chamberlain was 'Brum-
magem'. The last named word was slang for both Birmingham
and showy and trashy.

A year earlier, in 1881, an unknown artist produced 'the
Gladstone Memorial'. The form and style are different from the
usual *Vanity Fair* caricature. Gladstone, informally clad, sits on
the British lion, pondering the future of Britain. The lion's
head is Charles Bradlaugh (*Vanity Fair*, 12 June 1880), the
atheist and birth control advocate whose elections to the House
so infuriated the members that they refused to seat him for
years.

Spy presented two memorable views of Gladstone. The earlier one, in 1879, showed 'The People's William' posed Napo-
leonically, his right hand tucked into his waistcoat. He looks

ministers to Elizabeth I and James I. He feigned a disdain for many of the tasks of high office. Bishops, said he, died only to vex him. He despised democracy. Yet, like his nephew and successor, Arthur Balfour, he enjoyed power.

Spy caricatured Salisbury in 1900, when he was close to retirement. 'The Markiss', was portrayed as a Santa Claus in top hat, bent yet assured. In his later days, he often rode a tricycle for exercise in St James Park when in London, and at his family home in Hertfordshire, Hatfield House. The sight must have been bizarre. Labelled the Hamlet of English politics, he was melancholy, intensely intellectual, and subject to sleepwalking and fits of depression. He was devoted to religion and interested in science, especially chemistry. In 1900 *Vanity Fair* judged him one of the great prime ministers. 'His virtues, indeed, are very many; and his chief fault (in these democratic days) is his capacity for ignoring the views of that person who has come to be known as the Man in the Street.' The disdained masses, however, apparently liked his aristocratic style of aloofness and assurance.

Tamed Ape though he may have been, Spy did capture many personalities of the era quite perceptively. Few photographs tell us as much about the virtues and defects of ARCHIBALD PHILLIP PRIMROSE, the fifth Earl of Rosebery (1847–1929), as do Leslie Ward's two caricatures. Rosebery inherited position and great

irritated, perhaps by his opponents or by Bowles's assessment: 'Such a man, if he wields any power at all, can but use it in such a manner as to get his own and his country's affairs into a muddle. This indeed he has done; yet, in spite of this, Mr Gladstone is still the most popular man in England.'

Seven years later, in 1887, a baleful-looking caricature appeared, entitled, 'The Grand Old Man'. *Vanity Fair*'s commentary is even more scathing this time: 'There is indeed not a cause ever taken up by Mr Gladstone that he has not ruined, not a principle ever advocated by him that he has not deserted . . . Mr Gladstone is indeed the most successful of political hypocrites, for he succeeds in deceiving even himself.'

Disraeli's successor as the leader of the Tory Party was an acid-tongued aristocratic eccentric: the third Marquess of Salisbury, ROBERT ARTHUR TALBOT GASCOYNE-CECIL (1830–1903). Two caricatures of Salisbury appeared in *Vanity Fair*, more than thirty years apart. In both one glimpses a full-bearded, large-headed, short-sighted, stooped figure of an impressive bearing. Ape captured the youthful Tory rebel, who never bothered to trim his opinions to suit the masses or the classes. Jehu Junior observed in 1869: 'He is too honest a Tory for his party and his time.'

Salisbury revived a family tradition of involvement in high politics going back to the time when his ancestors were chief

The Prime Minister
Third Marquis of Salisbury KG
Robert Arthur Talbot Gascoyne-Cecil
Statesmen No. 730
20 December 1900
Spy

Horse
The Earl of Rosebery
Statesmen No. 225
3 June 1876
Spy

Little Bo-Peep
The Earl of Rosebery
Statesmen No. 733
14 March 1901
Spy

wealth, and then married into another fortune, one of the Rothschilds. He had a fine mind which was trained at Eton and Christ Church, Oxford, yet as Prime Minister he proved to be one of the disappointments of the century.

Jehu Junior's assessment of the young Rosebery, in 1876, is uncannily accurate: Bowles wrote: 'He is very fresh and pretty, very popular, well dressed and known in the clubs, and under thirty. He may, if he will, become a statesman and a personage.' Spy painted him in profile, with smooth, intensely pink complexion, big blue eyes, and a rather fatuous if intelligent expression. Rosebery seemed immature for his age.

Then in 1901, Spy sketched Rosebery in his fifties. His large eyes, pink complexion and elegant dress have survived along with an impression that the man lacked firmness and determination. What weight he added does not convey any maturity. This devastating cartoon entitled 'Little Bo-Peep' tells how he has lost his sheep, the Liberal Party.

He fills all sorts of offices, from the Leadership of an absent Party to a Trusteeship of the Imperial Institute, and he sometimes manages to make quite a sensation. He has filled even bigger offices, such as that of the Sovereign's Prime Minister and the Lord Rectorship of Glasgow University; yet he has never redeemed his early promise. For just as he is at the moment a Leader of no Party, so has he been a Statesman full of possibilities but without that balance which is

needed for really great success . . . He is a clever fellow who is often called able; but with all his cleverness, his brilliance, and his wit he reminds one of a man with ten talents who does nothing with them. He has won two Derbys running, . . . yet in the great affairs of the empire he seems to let his chances – and they have been many – slip. He is supposed to know all about Foreign Affairs; . . . but, like a brilliant meteor, he has left no mark upon the shifting sands of time. He still has a future before him, for he is but three-and-fifty. Will he ever overtake it?

He never did.

The languid figure of ARTHUR JAMES BALFOUR (1848–1930), Prime Minister from 1902 to 1905 and leader of the Tories until 1911, graced the pages of *Vanity Fair* several times. His seemingly effeminate, distant manner was responsible for his first public nicknames, 'Pretty Fanny,' and 'Clara'. Both he and his uncle, Lord Salisbury, professed to abhor politics, but were highly effective politicians.

Balfour inherited a fortune and a keen mind, given to philosophy. After Cambridge University, he seemed to gravitate to politics out of family obligation. Then, to the delight of Tories and the distress of the Irish, he proved himself a formidable, ruthless political manipulator after Salisbury appointed him Irish Secretary in 1887. His new nickname became 'Bloody

The Irish Secretary
The Right Honourable Arthur James Balfour PC LLD MP
Statesmen no. 529
24 September 1887
Spy

Balfour'. He soon established his claim to the succession of the leadership of the Tories. No longer was he the self-described 'Great Man's Great Man'.

Spy's Balfour of 1887 is an attenuated figure. His body, clothes, fingers, spats are all stretched out, as Balfour listened with his usual detachment to the jibes of the Opposition.

Jehu Junior observed: 'Mr Balfour is well-instructed, highly cultivated . . . but he does not carry big guns . . . and is somewhat indolent both by temperament and by habit.'

Balfour and his uncle, Lord Salisbury, shared a taste for cutting, often brutal language, and a decisiveness and unscrupulousness that was of great advantage in their respective careers. Balfour loved power, but in most cases remained detached from it, apparently above the battle. His own party deprived him of the leadership in 1911, yet he remained a central figure in the corridors of power. He returned to high office during the 1914–1918 War and became embroiled in the problems of the Middle East. He was proud of the Balfour Declaration and, as a cynic, he might have been amused by the unexpected outcome, the establishment of the state of Israel.

In 1910 an undistinguished portrait of Balfour appeared in *Vanity Fair*. The commentary is one of the magazine's most scathing: 'With enough steam behind him he might just now have rocked all England; he has instead, tickled it with a philosophic doubt . . . with the aid of poverty he might have achieved greatness; he is, instead, merely brilliant.'

SIR HENRY CAMPBELL-BANNERMAN (1836–1908) replaced Balfour as prime minister in 1905. Most of his politically aware contemporaries thought 'C-B' to be an amiable, somewhat ineffectual timeserver; a plodder, content to toil for his party, the Liberals, and the nation, who would retire soon into well-earned obscurity. Balfour and 'C-B' were Scots, wealthy men, both educated at Trinity, Cambridge. But the similarities stop there. Their differences are significant. Balfour was brilliant, unscrupulous and ambitious, and contributed to the downfall of his party in 1906 by his acid tongue and absence of principle. He never married. 'C-B' was practical, a man of habit and of principle, both public and private. He was an old-fashioned Liberal who comprehended the new forces in the country, and he held his party together despite the fissures engendered by the Home Rule controversy, the Boer War and differing views over social reform. He was a devoted husband. Balfour disdained the masses. 'C-B' understood them. He welcomed innovation for he remained close to the British Radical tradition.

His leadership of the Liberals which led to the great landslide of 1906 and his short term as Prime Minister (1905–1908) proved to be a great surprise. He forged one of the strongest Cabinets in recent history. He was unexpectedly decisive and authoritative and his government was strong. The death of his beloved wife weakened his resolve and he died in office in 1908. His eminent good sense might have mitigated some of the political excesses of the next few years.

Spy portrayed 'C-B' as 'the Opposition' in 1899; a well-fed figure, seated alone on the front bench of the House, listening quietly. *Vanity Fair* labelled him 'an arrant Liberal, a gentleman . . . that freak of nature, a Scotsman who likes a joke . . . Altogether he is rather a weak man with amiable intentions.' Rarely sympathetic to the Liberals in general, this time *Vanity Fair* had misjudged their man badly. Measured against the record of the other prime ministers of the era, 'C-B' had a short but notable record of accomplishment. He was a true Liberal, one of the last.

Vanity Fair's appraisal of HERBERT HENRY ASQUITH (1852–1928), 'C-B's successor as Liberal leader and prime minister from 1908 to 1916, was notably accurate. Three lithographs appeared and the accompanying commentaries pinpointed the character of the man who was called by some 'the last of the Romans'. *Vanity Fair*, however, was not an admirer of him, nor of the Liberals he led. Of the rising young barrister-politician in 1891 it said he was a better lawyer than a statesmen. Jehu Junior commented: 'he is a clever fellow who can hold his own; but he does not understand the art of dressing.' In 1904, after tracing his rise to power in the Liberal Party, including a useful second marriage to the fashionable, ambitious Margot Tennant, Jehu Junior observed: 'there were Radicals who thought he had grown to love society too dearly to be the same politician as of yore . . . though he will never arouse enthusiasm and devotion in his followers, he will be the leader of his party . . . he prefers to follow, rather than precede events.' In 1910, the commentary which accompanied a dull portrait by XIT was equally critical. Asquith 'seemed to be physiologically deficient, devoid of all traces of human sympathy . . . politically his chief fault is that he is a lawyer and treats all causes like cases'.

In Spy's 1904 caricature, he stands in rumpled clothes, waiting perhaps to reply to a Tory sally in the House of Commons. He was a skilled debater. Spy exaggerated his head to give emphasis to his 'brains'; the caption of the caricature. Blessed with formidable powers, Asquith too often preferred to wait upon events, and events caught up and passed him.

Brains
The Right Honourable Herbert Henry Asquith MP
Statesmen No. 769
14 July 1904
Spy

A nonconformist genius
The Right Honourable David Lloyd George MP
Men of the Day No. 1092
13 November 1907
Spy

61

DAVID LLOYD GEORGE (1863–1945), 'the wizard of Wales', ranks with Winston Churchill as one of the two best known prime ministers of this century. Both had long political careers, marked with extraordinary ups and downs. Their dynamic leadership, Lloyd George's in the First World War and Churchill's in the Second, was crucial to the survival of the United Kingdom.

Lloyd George was caricatured by Spy in late 1907. His appearance is testimony to the impact this outsider, born poor and from the Celtic fringe, had already had on high politics. By then he had become a force which Englishmen had begun to respect but did not understand. He began his parliamentary career in 1890, in George Dangerfield's words, 'less a Liberal than a Welshman on the loose'. His witty, courageous opposition to the Boer War brought him national notoriety, and subsequent respect. His star rose as Joseph Chamberlain's declined. 'The war made Mr Lloyd George; but even at the end of the war . . . no one dreamed of his constructive ability and fairmindedness.' So wrote *Vanity Fair* in 1907.

By the end of 1907, his record in the Liberal Cabinet, in Labour negotiations and in the House of Commons had established his claim to higher office. 'We think', wrote Jehu Junior, 'it may well be that Mr Lloyd George will reach the highest office in the state; in our opinion there have been few Prime Ministers better qualified to do great work for the country.' When the time came, during the 1914–1918 War, this proved true. A. J. P. Taylor judged him 'the most inspired and creative statesman of the twentieth century'. To this day, though most agree on his genius, historians cannot adequately define or categorize his peculiar qualities. He was a genie who had popped out of a bottle, never to be reconfined. Spy's caricature captured the animation and the elfin charm of the man, the irrepressible humour in the gestures, in the wrinkles about his eyes, in the enlarged head, and in the aggressive posture. Lloyd George was so delighted with Spy's caricature that he bought the original and used it in a subsequent biography.

Strickland's caricature of BONAR LAW (1853–1923) captured the dull, gloomy, stolid quality of the man whom his biographer, Robert Blake, labelled 'the Unknown Prime Minister'. Law's delicate hands are a surprise for so brutal a personality. George Dangerfield summed him up as 'a man without unction'. Law was 'a true son of Empire' born in Canada of Scottish parents with Ulster connections. Dangerfield described Law in these days: 'his face was sad, his forehead crumpled; he had the unfortunate habit of saying the wrong thing in debate . . . He

was absolutely honest, and he was excessively Tory in the matter of having no imagination whatsoever.' He was rude and that prompted *Vanity Fair* to observe: 'he believes in giving it to them hot.' The 'them' was the Liberal Party.

Law was the compromise choice to replace Balfour as the Tory leader in 1911, and as the caricature shows, seemed for a time to exist in his shadow. Men of his background – business – were relatively new to the political inner circle, and Law often chose to violate the unwritten rules of political conduct, though he showed unflinching party loyalty. Tenacious in opposition, stolid when in office, he is remembered chiefly for his vitriolic support of the Orange Cause in Ulster just before the Great War, and for saving his party from Lloyd George just after it.

The expansion of the electorate after 1867 brought a few members of the working classes into roles in high politics.
The first such members elected to the House of Commons just after 1867 were muted or subdued by the traditional politics of deference, compromise and accommodation. Neither the management nor the readership of *Vanity Fair* was sympathetic to this change, but they could not entirely ignore these men.

When a remarkable Scottish miner, JAMES KEIR HARDIE (1856–1915), came to the House in the election of 1892, he openly challenged the traditional class-bound mores of political life. Society was at first amused when Hardie made his initial

appearance in Parliament. Heralded by a trumpeter and riding in a wagon pulled by his triumphant followers, he wore tweeds and a cloth cap. Soon their scorn and laughter turned to shock and outrage when Hardie, snubbed by the acerbic Liberal Leader of the House, Sir William Harcourt, spoke against a motion to congratulate the Queen on the birth of her grandson, the future Duke of Windsor. Earlier, Hardie had sought through Harcourt an expression of condolence from the House for a recent serious mine disaster. Hardie began to make it explicit that the sacred parliamentary proprieties were merely matters of class, for which he had little respect.

The British Establishment sought to kill by ridicule – as *Vanity Fair* spoke of Hardie in 1906, 'with the amused indifference accorded to all members of the society of cranks'. *Punch* turned his dress into a standing joke. But neither quite succeeded in reducing the threat of Hardie. He cut too close to the insensitivity of the Establishment, and exposed its hypocrisy. He was one of the founding fathers of the socialist movement in Britain and of the Labour Party.

Born into poverty, Hardie went to work in the Scottish mines at eight years of age. Self-educated, he used the evangelical church and the temperance platforms as vehicles into politics. He joined the miners union and came under influence of the ideas of Henry George. By the late 1880s he had begun to attempt to free the trades union movement from its class-bound subservience to Liberal ideas and the Party itself. Hardie became a journalist and was one of the organizers of the Scottish Labour Party. In 1892 he was elected to the House from the working-class London constituency of West Ham South. He was passionate, powerful, proletarian in loyalty and evangelical in style. His consistent example made a powerful impression on the emerging political consciousness of many working class men and women.

Spy, somewhat surprisingly, painted an affectionate glimpse of Hardie in tweeds, cap and pipe, papers on unemployment lying at his feet. He conveyed an air of solid good sense; a man who knew who he was. One example of his good sense is enough. In 1909 the Suffragettes embarked on their violent campaign to obtain the vote for women. The leadership of both parties connived to frustrate them, and the Suffragettes increased their violence. What was the answer, asked the political establishment? Jail? Deportation? Forced feedings? Only Hardie suggested logically: 'Give them the vote'. Jehu Junior commented: 'He writes with some ability; this eloquence sounds better in the open air than in confined spaces. Those who do not call him "don't-care-Hardie", with *Punch* speak of him as "Queer Hardie"; but being very much in earnest, he is a man worthy of attention.'

JOHN BURNS (1858–1943) was elected in 1892, along with Keir Hardie, as an Independent to the House of Commons. In 1906 he became the first manual labourer to sit in the British Cabinet. However, Burns, as Home Secretary, was overwhelmed by the temptations of power, his own insecurity and vanity, and became the prisoner of his civil servants and a barrier to needed social reform during the last Liberal Government. In August 1914 he resigned his office, in protest over the decision to go to war.

Spy sketched Burns in 1892, in his typical straw hat, shortly after his election to Parliament from Battersea, a London constituency with a radical tradition. Spy sketched a rough-hewn, simple-seeming young man, red-faced and confident. Jehu Junior judged Burns a 'stubborn, rather self-sufficient man,

Winnie
Right Honourable Winston L. S. Churchill MP
Men of the Day No. 2210
8 March 1911
Nibs

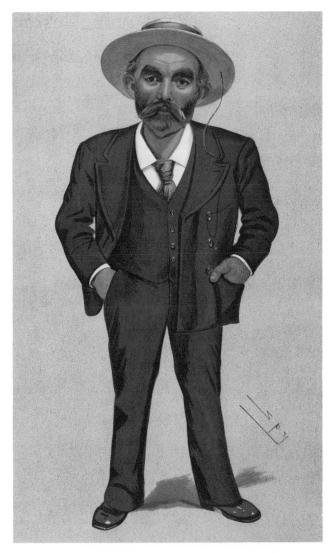

who is inclined to bully where he cannot persuade'. Burns had played a significant role in the trades union movement, especially in the 1889 dockers strike, and in the London County Council. Yet as he embarked on his parliamentary career, *Vanity Fair* sensed his Achilles' heel: 'He has done a great deal of loud talking, for he has a broad chest and a big voice. He is a Socialist who thinks that he believes in the municipalization of land and of the means of production; yet he is less violent than he once was, clothing himself with the dignity of his position.'

The majority of Spy's cartoons during his last two decades at *Vanity Fair* were sycophantic portraits. Only occasionally, as in his cartoon of two 'Labour men', BEN TILLETT (1860–1943) and JOHN WARD (1866–1934), his subjects provoked his imagination, and a livelier caricature resulted.

Tillett and Ward represent, in *Vanity Fair*'s opinion, the two extremes of that necessary evil of democracy – the Labour Party. The giant phlegmatic Ward peers down at the tiny dynamic Tillett, as the latter lectures him on the evils of the day. Tillett, in what Jehu Junior condescendingly describes as a 'memorable if somewhat uncongenial career', had played a major role in the organization of the dockers and in the formation of the Labour Party. *Vanity Fair* said that Tillett was a 'revolutionary Socialist', who believed 'capitalism must die of

its own excesses, assisted by the quickened intelligence of the toilers.' He was 'altogether an interesting personality', but an irresponsible character, in *Vanity Fair*'s view. Ward, said the magazine, was a more balanced representative of the Labour Party. An organizer of the navvies – the railway labourers – he had served with merit in the British Army. He was elected to Parliament as representative of Labour but refused to sign the constitution of the Labour Representation Committee and lost their subsidy of two hundred pounds a year. Jehu Junior approved: 'Mr John Ward has a good deal of quiet character.'
Both men preached a new image or ideal for Britain, said *Vanity Fair*, 'not the warrior-aristocrat, but the workman'. 'Arms and the Man' should be replaced by 'Tools and the Man'.

Chartran's sad, brooding profile of CHARLES STEWART PARNELL (1846–1891) seems, in its gloomy mood, to prefigure the events which wrecked his political career and his cause. Irish Home Rule. Only Gladstone had a greater impact on British politics in the latter half of the nineteenth century. Parnell was half-American, for his mother married an Anglo-Irish landowner. After an upper class English education, he followed a family tradition into anti-unionist politics. By the time of his first appearance in *Vanity Fair*, he had forged a tenuous alliance among the various Irish factions. From 1880 to 1890 he led a group of about eight Irish MPs who sometimes held the bal-

ance of power in a House of Commons split almost evenly between Liberals and Conservatives. By the end of the 1880s Parnell seemed on the verge of seeing his cause prevail. His political leadership and the machinations of his enemies had contrived to make a settlement of the Irish question seem possible. At such a vital stage in negotiations, he was sued as co-respondent in a divorce case. The public outrage ended his career, and shortened his life.

Peter Stansky observed that Parnell's career had 'some suggestion of late nineteenth-century Wagnerian gloom about it'. The 1880 portrait by 'T' conveys this mood with its dull greens, greys and blacks. Parnell looks resigned to a tragic end even then.

Jehu Junior, almost certainly Bowles, was consistently hostile to the Irish cause. *Vanity Fair* acknowledged Parnell's importance as the leader of the Home Rulers in Parliament. 'A union of Saxon, Milesian, and American blood has made him the greatest agitator of the day, and the people of the oppressed Island hold him as a second liberator.' (The word Milesian has a double meaning. It means Irish, but it also refers to a series of witty, sensuous classical Greek fables.) Was Bowles making a veiled allusion to Parnell's liaison with Mrs O'Shea, which began that year?

Parnell appeared once more in *Vanity Fair* when he was in Kilmainham Jail alongside his fellow Home Ruler, John Dil-

lon. ('Force No Remedy', 7 December 1881 by Harry Furniss.) In 1880, Jehu Junior wrote of Parnell: 'He is at this moment an acknowledged power which Ministers treat with deference, if not with kindness; and he has it in his hands to do much for his country, either for good or for evil.' In the end, it was his affair with Kitty O'Shea which destroyed him and his cause. Neither the British nor the Irish were willing then to tolerate open disregard for conventional morality.

SIR EDWARD CARSON (1854–1935), another Irish MP, was as vehemently opposed to Home Rule as Parnell was for it. Throughout his career he championed the Orange cause. His heart and mind, when they were not with Ulster and the Union, were in politics and the law. He once told a friend: 'I died the day I left the House of Commons and the bar.' He had a distinguished career as an advocate in Ireland and in England. After establishing himself at the Irish bar, he was elected to the House of Commons from Dublin University in 1892, and came to England to try his talents further. His relentless cross-examination of Oscar Wilde (*Vanity Fair*, 24 May 1884) in 1895, in the libel case against the Marquess of Queensberry, was his first notable English legal success. George Dangerfield observed: 'He reduced Mr Wilde from a debonair philosopher to a rather fat and greasy gentleman with a peculiar taste for pot boys.' In 1893 *Vanity Fair* described Carson as a 'hardworking,

A Younger Son
Lord Randolph Henry Spencer Churchill MP
Statesmen No. 331
10 July 1880
Spy

Winston
Mr Winston Leonard Spencer Churchill
Men of the Day No. 792
27 September 1900
Spy

painstakingly, lynx-eyed practitioner who can speak strongly'. Throughout his life, his intense moral fervour was devoted almost entirely to one cause, the maintenance of the Union of Ireland with England.

The artist Lib has captured these qualities in Carson by emphasizing his jagged features and prophetic stance and gesture. A second portrait of Carson by Wallace Hester appeared in 1911 in *Vanity Fair*. It is dull and unimaginative and gives little sense of the single-minded dynamism of the man. Carson went on to champion the cause of the Union to the point of supporting armed resistance to the British Government in 1913–1914. Dangerfield has summed up this fervent, hard-jawed Irishman neatly: 'When his moral fervour was aroused he would fight against any odds . . . when it came to fighting against Home Rule, he would take on the English Parliament and the English Army and, if ever he caught one or the other in a careless gesture or hesitant or even sympathetic posture, there was every chance he would win.'

Both LORD RANDOLPH (1849–1895) and WINSTON CHURCHILL (1874–1965) were gamblers in politics. The father failed and the son succeeded. The support and drive of Jennie Jerome Churchill, Randolph's American wife and Winston's mother, was essential for each's public career. They were both young troublemakers in politics, always more interesting than the plodder. Both floundered badly after brilliant starts in politics. Lord Randolph never recovered.

Spy caricatured father and son when they were young men on the rise. Lord Randolph was thirty-one in 1880 and his son twenty-seven in 1900. The artist portrayed them in almost exactly the same pose, elegantly dressed, with arms akimbo grasped at their waists. He captured their engaging arrogance in the liveliness of their expressions. Randolph lacks the solidity of his son, as he seems to float an inch or two off the ground.

Jehu Junior marked Randolph as a coming man in the Tory Party who earlier, in a family matter, had had the courage to oppose so august a personage as the Prince of Wales. 'By making bold and independent speeches in the House of Commons, he has won for himself the interest as well as the attention of that middle-aged assembly. He is so brilliant and witty a speaker, that he is justly looked upon as one of the hopes of his party.' These hopes were dashed barely six years later when Lord Randolph wrecked his political career by 'forgetting Goschen' (his replacement) and resigning from the government he had helped to put in office. He never held office again, wasting away from syphilis and dying in 1895. It was a particular loss for his party, for he was a man of imagination in a party sadly lacking that quality.

Winston, his more famous son, was just on the brink of a meteoric political career when Spy, in 1900, duplicated the pose of his father. Winston idolized his small, slightly popeyed father, and sought both to emulate and to succeed where the erratic Randolph had failed. *Vanity Fair* wrote of Winston in 1900: 'He can write and fight. For himself he has hankered after politics since he was a small boy, and it is probable that his every effort, military or literary, has been made with political bent; He is something of a sportsman who prides himself on being practical rather than dandy; he is ambitious . . . and he loves his country. But he can hardly be the slave of any party . . . and his ways are constant reminders of his father'.

Winston Churchill was again featured in *Vanity Fair* in 1911. Both artists, Spy and Nibs captured the force of his personality by exaggerating his combative posture. The 1911 caricature shows a familiar yet unfamiliar Winston, aged 37, trim of figure, capped with flaming red hair. Both characteristics had long disappeared by the time of the Second World War, but his aggressiveness had not (see p. 64).

Born at Blenheim Palace in 1874, Churchill was the eldest son of a beautiful, spirited New Yorker, Jennie Jerome, who had married the brilliant, erratic Lord Randolph, a son of the Duke of Marlborough. By 1911, when Nibs captured him in profile, 'Winnie' was a young man well 'on the make'.

Before reaching thirty he had made a major name for himself as a young cavalry officer, polo player, war correspondent, and author. Capitalizing on his self-generated fame, his family's political and social connections, and his mother's influence, in 1900 he entered the House of Commons as a Tory. In 1911, Jehu Junior wrote:

In those days he would go anywhere and do anything; and, moreover, he was never too particular what he said or wrote . . . Since his comparatively irresponsible fighting days events have moved rapidly indeed with Mr Winston Churchill. He has written a novel, four books of brilliant battling adventure, and a life of his father which has been authoritatively described as one of the best biographies in the language. He has lectured with distinction, and forced himself to the political front by fearless and fervent utterance on two Party sides before reaching Cabinet rank.

In 1911, Churchill, Home Secretary at 37, was the youngest member of the Liberal Cabinet. Jehu Junior observed:

[He is] one of the most picturesque personalities in his Majesty's Ministry today . . . He qualified . . . for the post of rule of all the King's gaols by experiencing a taste of prison life in Pretoria [in South Africa] and when he visits the unfortunately incarcerated he can do so in the true spirit of fellow-feeling which makes men wonderous kind.

In 1945 Churchill's friends and enemies might have agreed with Jehu Junior's judgements in 1911: 'Assertive and ubiquitous, he is ever to the fore in anything with which he concerns himself . . . Mr Winston Churchill is surely a force to be reckoned with, and seems to enjoy the receiving of "hard knocks" almost as much as he does giving them.'

Vanity Fair portrayed MRS GEORGE CORNWALLIS-WEST (1854–1921), one of the most notable and beautiful women in Society, late in her career, when she and the magazine were growing old. The artist has captured a remarkable personality, still graceful and with a melancholy beauty.

Born Jennie Jerome in Brooklyn, the daughter of a fabulous speculator, Leonard Jerome, and named after one of her father's friends, the 'Swedish Nightingale' Jenny Lind, she married into the English aristocracy. She was one of the most notable of what *Punch* labelled the 'American Invasion'. These were heiresses who brought American dollars to prop up the declining fortunes of British nobility.

Jennie brought more than a fortune and her stunning looks to her marriage to Lord Randolph Churchill. She had courage, stamina, energy and intelligence in abundance, and in a tumultuous life put these all to use. One of her biographers, Ralph Martin, wrote: 'Out of her strength, she helped transform a social dilettante husband [Lord Randolph] into one of the most important men in the British Empire; out of her love and ambition she helped shape her son Winston into one of the great men of this century.'

During her life she edited and published an international literary magazine, *The Anglo-Saxon Review*; set up a hospital ship for the Boer War and travelled with it to South Africa; was a pianist of professional ability; tried her hand as author, playwright and reporter; and organized political campaigns in an age when most women were not permitted to attend the theatre alone.

A snob, like her mother, and a sensualist, like her father, Jennie married three times, and had a number of prominent admirers, including the Prince of Wales, later Edward VII. Her first marriage was flawed by her husband's wayward personality and fatal illness. Her second, to a man twenty years her junior, she characterized as romantic but not successful; her third, as successful but not romantic. At the time of the portrait in *Vanity Fair*, the second marriage, to George Cornwallis-West, had collapsed. They were negotiating about divorce, to which she soon agreed. The artist has captured her mood of sad determination. The letterpress, signed 'Marmaduke,' commented:

A beautiful daughter of a beautiful mother, gifted with exceptional intelligence, singular strength of character, and tireless energy, it has not only been the privilege of Mrs West to know the most prominent men and women of the time, but to render material assistance to several of them in their efforts to add to the security and prosperity of the country of her adoption.

During the decade before the 1914–1918 War, there was a significant increase in violence in parliamentary infighting. Self-imposed restraints between the classes and the sexes appeared to be weakening. At the top of the social pyramid, influential men in the Tory Party and the House of Lords spoke, acted and connived against the erosion of their power and position. The Tory Revolt, as it was called, plumbed alarming depths of irrationality. Professor Robert Webb observed later: 'The movement lacked only the pen of a Rowlandson to make its grotesquerie as permanent a part of our awareness as the vices of the late eighteenth-century rakes he drew so savagely.'

One of the noisiest voices of this Tory Revolt was that of a dynamic, ambitious, young barrister turned politician, F. E. SMITH, later Lord Birkenhead (1874–1930). After his striking debut in the House of Commons (he was known for a time as 'Single Speech Smith'), the usually benign Spy was so struck that he produced a caricature that might have ruined the career of a lesser man. Smith was portrayed as an elegant, oily, tophatted character, the epitome of unprincipled ambition. Jehu Junior labelled him 'naturally a Tory of the crusted sort; but if not shaken by opposition or struggle is reasonably clear of prejudice'. A less sympathetic commentator, George Dangerfield, observed: 'Many people loved him, most dis-

A Successful First Speech. 'Moab is my washpot'
Mr F. E. Smith MP
Men of the Day No. 1049
16 January 1907
Spy

trusted him, and he despised almost everybody.' Smith went on to a distinguished career at the Bar and in politics, but never achieved all he sought.

In 1911, Smith was caricatured by Nibs in *Vanity Fair* in profile. He looks less evil, but still immature.

Women were rarely caricatured in *Vanity Fair*, apart from a few members of the royal family, a foreign queen and several insipid portraits of noble ladies. However, the exceptions were notable: Sarah Bernhardt twice (see. p. 100), the troubled nun Mrs Star (p. 126), Lady Florence Dixie (*Vanity Fair*, 5 January 1884), Mrs Cornwallis-West (p. 69), Mrs Georgina Weldon (p. 119), and in 1910 the militant suffragist CHRISTABEL PANKHURST (1880–1958).

Her zeal, charm, organizing ability and political genius enabled her to move 'straight to the top of the feminist class' in the first decades of this century. Her militant strategy and tactics, in concert with her mother Emmeline and her sister Sylvia, and other notable women and men, kept her constantly in the public eye, and in and out of jail. After taking a law degree in 1906 with first class honours at Manchester, in a profession women could not then practise, she became organizing Secretary for the Woman's Social and Political Union, known by its initials, the WSPU. In 1908 she was responsible for a giant rally in Hyde Park, in support of the vote for women. Estimates of the crowd ranged from a quarter to half a million people! Arrested that same year for appealing to the public to help the 'suffragettes' to 'rush' the House of Commons, Christabel in Bow Street Court cross-examined the Home Secretary, Herbert Gladstone, and the Chancellor of the Exchequer, David Lloyd George, with devastating effect.

When she sat for Ward in 1910, Christabel was world famous. Both Ward then, and Max Beerbohm earlier, were charmed by her graceful eloquence. Ward captured her brilliant colouring, and sought to convey a sense of her 'windmill-like gestures'. Beerbohm, after her court appearance in 1908, observed: 'Her whole body is alive with her every meaning. As she stood there with a rustling sheaf of notes in one hand, the other hand did the work of twenty average hands. . . .'

The anonymous commentator for *Vanity Fair* was surprisingly sympathetic:

She has courage and charm, and would make more enemies if she was less gracious. She has numerous delightful failings: has put the dignities of life into their proper place; proposes to do the same with the male population; and in spite of all, has been accused of having a sense of humour. Nevertheless, she still resents being refused the right to practise as a barrister on account of her sex, though her friends are duly grateful.

She has learned the value of tireless importunity, and has awakened a lively and anxious sense of responsibility in politicians who don't object to making fools of themselves, but resent a bevy of pretty women doing it for them.

She will get it!

Few politicians during the years of *Vanity Fair*'s existence began their careers in Parliament with as much promise or finished them in so much futility as did 'our Joe' – JOSEPH CHAMBERLAIN (1836–1914). As 'The Great Imperialist' Chamberlain's caricature was the last to appear in *Vanity Fair*, before it was absorbed into *Hearth and Home* toward the end of January 1914. Chamberlain and *Vanity Fair* died that year, unwitting symbols of the end of an era. His dreams of imperial unity were subsequently destroyed by the impact of the First World War.

Only Gladstone was caricatured more often than Chamberlain in *Vanity Fair*. Both were a cartoonist's delight, for they were public men who cultivated well-defined images. Chamberlain's 'props' were his long nose and elegant attire, which were accented by the ever-present monocle and fresh orchid boutonnière. In 1877, the jaunty Radical, now up to the House from Birmingham, was sketched by Spy. He stands alertly listening, arms akimbo, hands clasping his waist, sure of himself and his future. Only the boutonnière is missing from his lapel. Jehu Junior observed: 'A very new and noteworthy kind of man is Mr Chamberlain. One of the best of shrewd tradesmen turned politician . . . he has almost the first discovered methods of advocating political heresy with social orthodoxy. For he is a devout Radical Philistine . . . therefore undoubtedly destined to play a leading part whenever the Liberals shall next appear upon the stage in power.'

By the 1880s Chamberlain had fashioned a local political machine in Birmingham which was to perpetuate the Chamberlain family in politics for decades. For himself, he had acquired a national stature such that he seemed likely to follow Gladstone as leader of the Liberals. However, Gladstone's concern over Home Rule for Ireland delayed his retirement, and Chamberlain and others left the Liberals and split the party over the issue. He later joined the Tories, and though they never trusted

Our Joe
Mr Joseph Chamberlain MP
Statesmen No. 241
27 January 1877
Spy

The Colonies
Mr Joseph Chamberlain
Statesmen No. 732
7 March 1901
Spy

him, almost immediately became a power in that party. He subordinated his radical social reform platform for the cause of Imperial unity, and became the most active head of Colonial Office of the century. (He had aged dramatically by 1901 when Spy sketched him as 'The Colonies' for the second time.) The muddle of the Boer War, in which he had actively connived, dimmed his political lustre. Soon after he publically advocated protection and divided his party. He was, by 1908, 'War Worn', the caption of WHO's sketch; the victim of a stroke in 1906 (*Vanity Fair*, 29 January 1908). His sons, Austen (*Vanity Fair*, 3 August 1899) and Neville, made their marks in politics, but none of the Chamberlains managed to accomplish as much as they aspired to. All were gifted with energy, ideals and ability, but none seemed to unite this with good fortune. As a family they seemed to share, somewhere, a failure of vision.

THE ARTS

Vanity Fair's era was one of the most productive periods in the creative arts in British history. The theatre, literature, painting, the graphic arts, and music reached an ever widening audience. *Vanity Fair* was both influenced by and contributed to a popularization of the arts which was taking place in the later decades of the nineteenth century. The advances in education and the urge to self-improvement meant that the demand for some involvement in the cultural and artistic life of the nation, at whatever level, was increasing.

Vanity Fair had, in its first issue, promised to display the merit of the good and bad bargains of the Fair in their show. Taking on the responsibility of informing its readers of developments in the arts, it sought to act as an arbiter of good taste. The founder of *Vanity Fair* was influenced by its predecessors, *The Owl* and *The Tomahawk*, which had often written on the arts, especially the theatre. Thomas Gibson Bowles, since his youth, had regularly moved amongst literary lions of his day. He maintained a lifelong fascination with the theatre, acting in amateur roles and writing plays.

Many other members of the staff who contributed anonymously to the magazine were also involved in the arts; among them was Willie Wilde, Oscar's brother, a drama critic in the early 1880s. Pellegrini and Ward also knew countless painters, authors, artists and actors. The eccentric Pellegrini claimed friends among many of the outstanding creative personalities of his generation. He was a great admirer of Whistler and was, for a short time, his neighbour in Chelsea. Pellegrini's respect for Whistler was returned. Whistler remarked that Ape's caricatures in *Vanity Fair* were very influential because they 'taught all the others what none of them had been able to learn'. Leslie Ward, born to a fashionable artistic family, was an eminently 'clubbable' man: he belonged to the Arts, the Orleans, the Pelican, the Beefsteak, the Fielding, the Lyric and the Punch Bowl. There he encountered many of the leading figures in the world of the arts.

As a result the weekly caricatures included most of the major and minor Victorian and Edwardian literary, theatrical and musical celebrities. Over forty-five artists, eighty writers (novelists, poets, critics, playwrights), fifty musicians, and theatrical figures were sketched. The majority were British, but many influential Europeans and Americans appeared.

Artists

Vanity Fair's admiration for the art world was largely a reflection of its caricaturists and staff whose friends were often fashionable painters. Bowles, Spy and Ape held very strong opinions about certain artists and their works; their prejudices came out in the commentaries and caricatures. Forty painters or sculptors were featured in *Vanity Fair*. Many have been forgotten; four who have not are painters, Sir John Millais, William Holman Hunt, James A. M'Neill Whistler and the sculptor Auguste Rodin.

Millais and Hunt, the two artists most closely associated with the Pre-Raphaelite movement, were caricatured during the 1870s. The impact of the Pre-Raphaelite Brethren on British art has been debated for some years; its influence was intangible but pervasive because it was 'congenial' to the English temper. Charles Marriott called the movement 'a genuinely English thing', and *Vanity Fair* recognized that it was unique to the English experience.

When SIR JOHN MILLAIS (1829–1896) appeared in *Vanity Fair* he had been established as a very successful painter for several years; indeed he had been recognized as the outstanding figure among the Pre-Raphaelites and had, by 1871, gone beyond the movement. According to *Vanity Fair*, Millais was convinced that there was 'more affectation than reality in the new school'. He was now a 'thoroughly converted Pre-Raphaelite'. Not only had Millais passed through the movement, he had outlived it; and, unlike many of his brethren, he had made money from his paintings. His popularity was at its height when he was featured in *Vanity Fair*. Yet he was not without his critics. Among them, according to Spy, was Pellegrini who detested Millais's works and who, at one time in his career, decided to concentrate on portrait paintings in an effort to 'outshine' Millais. Ape is not very kind to Millais, yet he might have been more severe considering his opinion of his fellow artist. The head is too large; the profile is not complimentary and Millais's ear is out of proportion. However, the total effect of the sketch is pleasant and well within the bounds of reality.

Jehu Junior asserted that Millais was the first modern English painter because of his treatment of drawing and colour; many critics would agree with Bowles's opinion. Jehu Junior predicted that Millais would be famous for all time; Bowles's prophesy proved to be an overstatement.

Millais's friend and the guiding spirit of the Brotherhood, WILLIAM HOLMAN HUNT (1827–1910), was caricatured by Spy eight years after Sir John appeared in *Vanity Fair*. Hunt emerged as one of Spy's most honest, effective caricatures; his small frame, large beard, squinting eyes and jaunty smile reveal a secure, self-assured, successful man. The tilt of the hat and the tuck of the handkerchief add a further note of self-confidence. Through his parents, Ward knew Hunt; and his personal knowledge of Hunt's character comes through in the caricature which portrays a candid, confident, moral man.

Vanity Fair identified Hunt as 'The Pre-Raphaelite of the World'; an accolade honestly come by for he was more closely associated with the school than any other artist. Although he was to call the movement a 'tragic failure' later in his life, Hunt's influence on the Brotherhood is undeniable. Hunt, according to Jehu Junior, was the last remaining Pre-Raphaelite who painted some 'fine pictures' for which he was well paid. As a person, said Bowles, he was good, simple, devoted and honest.

The dandy JAMES A. M'NEILL WHISTLER (1834–1903) is the antithesis of Hunt – in character and in art. His personality and life style made him a prime target for *Vanity Fair*; both would have been the poorer if their paths had not crossed. Spy, who caricatured Whistler in 1878, claimed the American expatriate as a friend. Whistler, according to Ward, was an 'excellent subject', but Jimmy's 'unlimited peculiarities' could not be captured in a caricature since they were more associated with his gestures and speech than with his physical appearance. Spy was in Whistler's company often, and was thus able to contribute to the endless Whistler stories. Among them was Spy's account of breakfast at Whistler's: a sardine and cup of coffee. Ward sketched Whistler in a self-conscious pose of disdain peering out at his 'enemies'. Whistler's military bearing – carried over from his three years at the United States Military Academy – provided Ward with a solid form for his study. His left hand on his hip and the twist of his head heighten Whistler's arrogance – his piercing eyes, partly hidden by his monocle, add a final touch. Ward did not caricature Whistler in his famous wide brimmed hat because Ward accidently sat upon it when he came to Whistler's studio to draw the sketch! The small bolero occasionally worn by Whistler heightens his features and frames his famous lock of white hair.

Jehu Junior outlined Whistler's early life in America and recent successes in Paris where his 'power of drawing, sense of

The Pre-Raphaelite of the World
William Holman Hunt
Men of the Day No. 200
19 July 1879
Spy

A Symphony
James Abbot M'Neill Whistler
Men of the Day No. 170
12 January 1878
Spy

He thinks in marble
Auguste Rodin
Men of the Day No. 944
24 December 1904
Imp

77

colour and simple devotion to Nature' had made him famous. Now Whistler resided in London where, according to *Vanity Fair,* he was painting his best canvases and doing 'admirable etchings' which could be compared to the finest plates of Rembrandt. *Vanity Fair* discussed Whistler's efforts to resolve the problem of colour and line in his works, and refuted the charge against Whistler that he did not 'finish' his paintings. Whistler, declared Jehu Junior, put truth in his pictures; and while he did not care for traditions, he did not trifle with the facts. *Vanity Fair* described 'Jimmy' as charming, simple and witty; this evaluation was not shared by Whistler's contemporaries or his biographers.

Later that year Whistler's etching of St James Street appeared in *Vanity Fair* (2 July 1878). In January 1879, *Vanity Fair* questioned Whistler's contention in his *Art and Art Critics* that only artists were qualified to pass judgement upon the merits of art. *Vanity Fair* also corrected the painter's reference to Balaam's ass as the first critic; the ass, indeed, had viewed the angel of the Lord while the prophet had seen nothing. Whistler, in his reply, admitted that he was wrong about the Bible but still refused to recognize the role of the art critic. The tone of their correspondence revealed that both parties were enjoying the exchange and held each other in mutual respect.

In 1903 AUGUSTE RODIN (1840–1917) succeeded Whistler as

President of the International Society of Sculptors, Painters and Gravers. The next year Rodin was featured in *Vanity Fair.* By 1904 Rodin's reputation was well established; for after long struggling against poverty, discouragement and rejection, Rodin, according to Jehu Junior, had finally achieved recognition. His fame was international, and the enthusiastic welcome which he had received in 1902 by Englishmen marked the 'commencement of a feeling which had found expression in *L'Entente Cordiale*'. Jehu Junior denied that Rodin had exercised a 'bad influence' on modern art; quite the opposite, his works marked a new epoch in the history of sculpture comparable to that of Michelangelo or Donatello.

Jehu Junior found Rodin to be a person of simple habits, retiring and shy, whose charm of manner was peculiar but endearing. He was an unassuming man whose anonymity allowed him to go unrecognized in his own home town. Imp's sketch reinforces Jehu Junior's assessment. Rodin's beard, craggy features and heavy eyes are caught by the caricaturist. From under his smock jut his short legs. He looks up wistfully at his masterpiece, 'The Thinker', which he had carved in 1879. This small man was a giant among sculptors, and *Vanity Fair*'s affectionate and perceptive caricature illustrates this opinion.

Poets

Vanity Fair paid homage in its early years to several influential poets. Three of the more prominent, Tennyson, Browning and Swinburne, appeared between 1871 and 1875. Jehu Junior was not, however, their admirer. Bowles's practical experience in the field of journalism had made him less sensitive to the poetic experience. He seemed to think if these poets, in particular Swinburne, had concentrated on more immediate themes (and stayed out of politics) they would have better served mankind. They should have sung the praises of the ordinary in poetic images clear to all. Bowles thought that poets were an English tradition, like plum pudding, to be honoured but not over indulged.

ALFRED TENNYSON (1809–1892) had, in 1871, been Poet Laureate for nearly twenty years. By that date all of his most lasting poetic works were completed: *Morte d'Arthur* (1842), *In Memoriam* (1850), *The Charge of the Light Brigade* (1854), plus parts of the Arthurian legend, *The Idylls of the Kings* (begun in 1859). Since Tennyson had not yet composed his historical novels, the magazine viewed him chiefly as a poet. Jehu Junior denied that Tennyson's genius had waned after becoming Poet Laureate; on the contrary, he was the 'greatest living master, for certain purposes, of the English language', and his poems harmonized with 'the spirit of a sentimental and peaceful generation'. But, Jehu Junior stated, Tennyson lacked the passion and the faith of 'the very greatest' poets for he refused 'to cut loose the bonds that thus bind him to earth . . .' While *Vanity Fair* was critical of Tennyson's inability to touch 'the great problems', the magazine admitted that the poet was at his best when he was not attempting to be mystical but was displaying for his reader 'a full and many-toned sympathy with this fair earth and the creatures that herein inhabit'.

ROBERT BROWNING (1812–1889), who appeared in *Vanity Fair* in 1875, was praised for his poems because they were not 'loose or shadowy'. Neither was there any 'swooning or melting away in emotion . . .' His poems, said Jehu Junior, were a steady building up of thought and feeling through facts and incidents of 'common life'. He was an 'unflinching realist' in his work.

The Poet Laureate
Alfred Tennyson
Men of the Day No. 28
22 July 1871
Ape

Modern Poetry
Robert Browning
Men of the Day No. 116
20 November 1875
Ape

Browning's feelings emerged in his poems; he was capable of hating as well as loving. Jehu Junior did not care for Browning personally; he thought him contemptuous, aloof and conceited. Yet, despite these traits, he possessed 'an unquenchable vitality' which was manifested in his latest work, *Inn Album. Inn Album* was to be one of his last important efforts; by the early 1880s his 'vitality' was ebbing. His marriage to Elizabeth Barrett in 1846, their years in Italy and her death (1861) were memories of the past. Between 1864 and 1869 he had written *The Ring and the Book,* and now, here in 1875, he was experiencing one final burst of poetic greatness which *Vanity Fair* recognized and honoured.

Jehu Junior appreciated most of the poems of Tennyson and Browning; he was less certain about Swinburne's works. Tennyson's poems were practical yet elegant; Browning's poems were realistic but sensitive. As people, Bowles liked Tennyson but not Browning. When he tried to characterize Swinburne, he concluded that he was, simply, 'quite unlike all other men'. Swinburne, seen in his totality, was, however, 'interesting, wonderful and admirable'. Jehu Junior described him as 'nervous, excitable, explosive, rebellious, graphic and ready to revolt against all revealed religions and moralities . . .'

ALGERNON CHARLES SWINBURNE (1837–1909) was thirty-seven years old when Ape caricatured him in 1874. His personal life and exploits, his reputation as a poet, and his avid support of Mazzini had made him a notorious public figure. Wherever he went he consciously shocked others. He also impressed them with his prodigious memory and knowledge. His close friendships with the celebrities of his day added to accumulating legends surrounding him even before his own controversial *Poems and Ballads* was published. It raised an intellectual firestorm and was quickly though temporarily withdrawn from the market. *Vanity Fair* observed that this work daringly glorified sexual passions which had been suppressed by 'Religion, Civilization and Parliamentary Government'. *Vanity Fair* did not think much of Swinburne's other work, *Songs Before Sunrise,* because of its praise of republicanism; *Bothwell,* it felt, was no better. Turning to Swinburne's political views, Jehu Junior asserted that the poet's 'notions of public policy' were those of an 'enthusiastic schoolboy'. Swinburne's political attitudes, formed at Oxford, apparently never changed throughout his life. As a poet, Jehu Junior admitted, Swinburne had no equal in the use of the imagination and the forming of images. As the only modern poet of the flesh, he had reminded his contemporaries that there were still men and women in the world as well as churchgoers and taxpayers, and Jehu Junior felt that was an important contribution.

All three caricatures are by Carlo Pellegrini and they effectively demonstrate his rich talents. Some unique quality of each man is captured in each caricature. Jehu Junior had observed that Tennyson failed to cut loose from the worldly bonds; Ape gives him an earth-bound character. Tennyson could easily be mistaken for a Victorian businessman. While his eyes gaze into the distance, the total impact is one of a rather mundane person. Ape caricatured the aloofness in Browning which so disturbed Jehu Junior. The turn of the head, hands in pockets and set feet express Browning's arrogance. Ape's trick of enlarging the head dramatized the victim's personality. Technically it is a classical caricature which allows us a glimpse into the subject's personality.

Swinburne's physical appearance easily lent itself to caricature. He did have a large head, narrow sloping shoulders, a

slight body and slim arms and legs. His personality was full of paradoxes. Violent and even vindictive, yet often affectionate, courteous and loyal to his friends, Ape has balanced Swinburne's mercurial habits and moods in the caricature. The proportions of the body and head are accurate. The slender form, the tilt of the head and the longing gaze capture the essence of Swinburne. Edmund Gosse, Swinburne's biographer and close friend, owned the original, full length watercolour caricature from which the lithograph was produced. Gosse wrote: 'Although avowedly a caricature, this is in many ways the best surviving record of Swinburne's general aspect and attitude.'

Writers

When this cartoon appeared in *Vanity Fair,* ANTHONY TROLLOPE (1815–1882), 'chronicler of small beer', was furious. One of Spy's earliest cartoons for *Vanity Fair,* it is also, along with one of the preparatory sketches, one of the most affectionately pungent. Ward has given us, and his era, a lovable acerbic portrait of an extraordinary Victorian.

Trollope, like many of the leading figures of his generation, was blessed with phenomenal energy. Arising each morning at 5.30, he worked for three hours on his novels before breakfast, writing at the steady rate of 250 words every quarter of an hour. After breakfast he went to work at the post office. He also found

time to hunt three times a week, and play whist at the Garrick Club in the afternoons. He was a frequent spectator in the gallery of the House of Commons, and he became a sharp observer of the political world. He retired from the post office in 1867, to devote himself full time to writing. He produced sixty-three books. Jehu Junior observed perceptively:

A novelist who would be generally read in this country and in these days should write books with the ordinary young lady always in his mind, books sufficiently faithful to the external aspects of English life to interest those who see nothing but its external aspects, and yet sufficiently removed from all the depths of humanity to conciliate all respected parents. Mr Anthony Trollope has had by far the greatest success in doing this. He is a student and delineator of costume rather than of humanity. He does not, as George Eliot does, pry into the great problems of life or attempt to show the mournful irony of fate. He is not a deep thinker, but he is an acute observer, and with the knack of divining what most impresses the commonplace people who most delight in novels. He is a correct painter of the small things of our small modern English life so far as it presents itself to the eye – deeper than this he does not go – and he is never guilty of a solecism in point of social forms. His gentlemen and ladies are like gentlemen and ladies, and their existence is the existence of people of decent manners. His language is not strong or nervous, but it ripples smoothly along in a well-bred monotone. For Anthony Trollope has lived a quiet life, and writes like a quiet man. He is fifty-eight years of age, and for the greater part of that time has occupied one of those snug berths under Government which are more favourable to good digestion and a placid interest in the struggles mental, moral, and physical of unprovided-for men and women than calculated to develop a great power of grasping the inner meaning of those struggles. He began to write just as he was leaving his first youth behind him; he has produced since a large number of novels of an invariably unobjectionable and a variably interesting kind; and he shows no sign of ceasing to produce them. He has visited various foreign countries for official purposes; he is, if with an undoubted consciousness of his own merits, good-natured and genial as becomes a successful man; and he is very fond of hunting. His manners are a little rough, as is his voice, but he is nevertheless extremely popular among his personal friends, while by his readers he is looked upon with the gratitude due to one who has for so many years amused without ever shocking them. Whether his reputation would not last longer if he had shocked them occasionally is a question which the booksellers of future generations will be able to answer.

THOMAS CARLYLE (1795–1881) appeared in *Vanity Fair* in October 1870, when the Franco-Prussian War was at its height. Napoleon III's fate had been sealed; Paris was under siege, and France's future hung in the balance. Thomas Gibson Bowles, who was in Paris during those days as a correspondent for the *Morning Post*, was viewing first hand what Carlyle had written in his *French Revolution* and *History of Frederick the Great*. Bowles wrote that Carlyle's treatment of the 'weltering chaos' of the French Revolution and his 'apotheosis of kingly power' of Frederick was now transformed into flesh and blood, forcing both sides into a 'death struggle for supremacy'. Bowles's dispatches to the *Morning Post* and to *Vanity Fair* gave a vivid impression of the 'death struggle' which he was witnessing. Later, when Bowles's *The Defense of Paris*, a compilation of his reports, was published he wrote in the Introduction that the Parisians' acts of heroism and cowardice, of intelligence and blundering were found throughout their history; a history, no doubt, fashioned in his mind by Thomas Carlyle.

Jehu Junior considered Carlyle's *French Revolution* unparalleled in its dramatic effects; it was to literature what Dante was to poetry and Doré to art. The Franco-Prussian War was not needed to tell England about Prussia; Carlyle had epitomized and reduced it to a 'few square inches' in his *History of Frederick the Great*. *Vanity Fair* expressed its disappointment that the historian had not spoken out about the war; later Carlyle did support the Germans, writing a letter to *The Times* on the subject (18 November 1870) in which he called Germany 'noble, patient, deep, pious and solid'.

The 'Sage of Chelsea' was also praised by Jehu Junior for his 'grim earnestness and relentless criticism' of society. Carlyle's attack on industrialism, democracy and social changes coupled with his gospel of work, his emphasis on action and his deep religious faith caused him to see disorder as a constant threat. This new world without order had been foreshadowed in the *French Revolution*; Bowles now saw it firsthand during the Siege of Paris. Carlyle's essays and histories had made him one of the more perceptive critics of his age whose opinion, Jehu Junior pleaded, was needed now more than ever. He had established himself as 'the Diogenes of the Modern Corinthians without his tub'; he was 'The Danton of the Revolution in the Republic of Letters' and a 'stout hearted Pagan, tempered by Christianity'. Carlyle was looking for honest men and calling for dedication and obedience in what he considered to be dishonest, turbulent times. However, what Carlyle saw as deceit and chaos became the norm, his writing style fell into disfavour and his appeal to authority was replaced with a belief in rugged individualism.

Ape's caricature captured the irascibility of Carlyle in his small, leaden eyes. His victim's thin body and slumped shoulders supporting his protruding head make Carlyle look like a gargoyle. His wide brimmed straw hat is pressed down on his head, which angles off from his body. One need not have read Jane Carlyle's diary, *Carlyle's Reminiscenes*, published by J. A. Froude (*Vanity Fair*, 27 January 1872), or Froude's biography, to know that Carlyle was a curmudgeon! It is a devastatingly honest caricature.

Trollope was only one of the prominent English novelists who flourished during *Vanity Fair*'s era, 1868–1914. Before the age of radio and television the novel provided escape and entertainment for an increasingly literate public. This growing market supported many new writers. Some are still important; others are seldom now read. The magazine featured both romantic and historical novelists: Anthony Hope Hawkins (*Vanity Fair*, 26 December 1895); Samuel Ruterford Crockett (*Vanity Fair*, 5 August 1897); and George Whyte-Melville (*Vanity Fair*, 23 September 1871); Thomas Henry Hall Caine (*Vanity Fair*, 2 July 1896) and Mayne Reid (*Vanity Fair*, 8 March 1873); all are now largely unread. Among the many influential late Victorian novelists who appeared in *Vanity Fair* were Thomas Hardy, George Meredith and Arnold Bennett.

THOMAS HARDY (1840–1928) was portrayed in *Vanity Fair* in 1892. He had by then written most of his novels, including *Under the Greenwood Tree, A Pair of Blue Eyes, Far from the Madding Crowd, The Return of the Native, The Trumpet-Major, The Mayor of Casterbridge, The Woodlanders* and, recently, *Tess of the d'Urbervilles* which *Vanity Fair* considered to be his best effort. The tragic, sensitive *Jude the Obscure* and his poetical works lay in the future.

Vanity Fair outlined Hardy's early career as an architect and

The Diogenes of the Modern Corinthians without his tub
Thomas Carlyle
Men of the Day No. 12
22 October 1870
Ape

his transition to literature through his essays on architecture. Jehu Junior considered Hardy to be a true artist, a man who wrote about what he knew and who was convinced that 'fiction should embody developments of life in which people silently believe, rather than those in which people pretend to believe . . .' Hardy never forgot his origins, and continued to do most of his writings in 'Wessex', the scene of many of his novels, living in what *Vanity Fair* called 'a queer little house'. Jehu Junior asserted that Hardy knew well the ways of his 'West countymen' and that he was a far greater man than he looked. Spy's rather bland and uninteresting caricature supports Jehu Junior's observation. Ward's caricature also reflects his personal opinion of the novelist whom he described as 'pleasant'. When Hardy sat for Spy, Ward recorded that Hardy did not impress him as being 'the typical literary man'. His clothes, according to Spy, exhibited a 'sporting touch' which was acceptable in rural England but hardly appropriate, by Ward's standards, for London.

Max Beerbohm's sensitive and accomplished caricature of GEORGE MEREDITH (1828–1909) contrasts sharply with Ward's mild character portrait of Hardy. Meredith was caricatured in *Vanity Fair* in 1896, late in his career when he was forced to walk with a cane. Beerbohm's use of the elongated 'S-curve' starts with Meredith's oversized hat, goes down his thin neck,

drooping shoulders, through the torso and to the legs and feet which anchor the figure. Meredith's tilted head permits his large eyes, with only a suggestion of a pupil, to peer out from under the broad brimmed hat. The two hands are cleverly used. The left hand repeats the curved lines in the body; the thin fingers of the right hand point upward and follow the lines of the neck and hat. Meredith seems to be explaining one of the more obscure passages from his novels. Beerbohm has brilliantly captured the subject's physique and personality.

Vanity Fair considered Meredith to be England's 'First Novelist' and described him as the 'best, if the least intelligible of living novelists'. By 1896, Meredith had written all of his major novels and poems. Many of his works were criticized for their obscurity and affectation; however, his penetrating observations on politics and ethics endeared him to many readers. In spite of his obscurity of style and of his vagueness, *Vanity Fair* noted he had been recognized as a 'great artist' and a 'great man'. *Vanity Fair*'s qualified opinion has been endorsed by later generations of readers.

(ENOCH) ARNOLD BENNETT (1867–1931) became a very successful author in his own lifetime and remains respected. His versatile talent produced lively, racy stories such as *The Card*, comedies, essays and plays. His realistic novels of life among the provincial working classes are finely crafted, detailed ac-

The Business Man of Letters
Arnold Bennett
Men of the Day No. 2317
2 April 1913
Owl

G. K. C.
Gilbert Keith Chesterton
Men of the Day No. 1319
21 February 1912
Strickland

85

counts of the life of the industrial poor in the 'Five Towns' of the Potteries. Bennett had learned to write as an editor; he abandoned journalism in 1900 and made his reputation with *The Old Wives' Tale*, published in 1908. By 1913, when his caricature appeared in *Vanity Fair*, he had written two books of his 'Five Towns' trilogy, *Clayhanger* and *Hilda Lessways*. *These Twain* was to follow in 1916.

Vanity Fair called Bennett 'The Business Man of Letters' and predicted that it was highly possible that he would be the first man 'to make a million out of literature'. Bennett did make a very comfortable living; and in his *The Truth about an Author*, he admitted that writing fiction was a lucrative profession. Even the most avaricious could live quite well if they kept to their craft, he advised. Bennett held strong opinions about how to write and who were good novelists. He felt that Meredith's books lacked a sense of direction and shape while Hardy's works were masterpieces of plot and symbolism. Bennett's approach to writing made him, according to *Vanity Fair*, a versatile, cosmopolitan and modern man. (His decision not to use his first name, Enoch, was seen as proof of his modernity.) Owl has not told us very much about the man; the caricature reveals little of Bennett's personality. Although not particularly flattering, it is neither incisive nor clever. When compared with caricatures of other literary figures such as that of Meredith, the sketch is simplistic and superficial.

Poet, essayist and critic, G. K. CHESTERTON (1874–1936) was featured in *Vanity Fair* in 1912. By the first decade of the twentieth century Chesterton had established himself as a promising novelist. His early career as a journalist, as an art critic and book reviewer for such publications as *The Bookman* and *The Speaker* honed his writing style and exposed him to life in London. The early novel which launched his career, *The Napoleon of Notting Hill* (1904), had been inspired by a flight of imagination while walking down the streets of North Kensington. *The Man who was Thursday* appeared in 1908, followed by a work on his close friend, George Bernard Shaw, and, in 1911, the first in the 'Father Brown' detective series. Father Brown was to have an exciting life, prolonged in subsequent novels.

Chesterton wrote in his autobiography that he never took his books seriously, but he was very serious about his opinions. He was concerned about socialism, imperialism, war and religion. His religious convictions led him into the Roman Catholic Church in 1922, and to write prolifically in its defence. Chesterton continued to produce novels, biographies and literary criticism throughout the remainder of his life.

By 1912 Chesterton had removed himself from his London haunts to a rural retreat near Beaconsfield. *Vanity Fair* was saddened that he was no longer a familiar figure on Fleet Street, and it reported that he was sorely missed by his friends. This large ambling hulk of a man, who reminded *Vanity Fair* of Dr

Johnson, was just as genial and pugnacious as his writings. His 'enormous vitality' was found in his work and his personality. Jehu Junior liked Chesterton; so did Strickland, the artist.

The caricature reveals a rather dishevelled man. His pockets bulge with books and papers, the waistcoat strains, the trousers are baggy; but Chesterton is hardly concerned about sartorial splendour. The rumpled hair and stubby hand steadying a smouldering cigar go well with his slippers and socks. The twinkle in his eye hints at his humour and his attitude to life. His caricature is a testament to his dislike of formality and his contempt of pretentiousness. He was once heard to remark that the English were not interested in the equality of men but in the inequality of horses. Those who did put horses before men were Chesterton's sworn enemies.

Vanity Fair honoured not only British writers but also European and American, including Emile Zola (*Vanity Fair*, 24 January 1880), Maurice Maeterlinck (see p. 35), Alexandre Dumas Fils (*Vanity Fair*, 27 December 1879), Henrick Ibsen (*Vanity Fair*, 12 December 1901), Bret Harte (*Vanity Fair*, 4 January 1879) and Count Tolstoi (*Vanity Fair*, 24 October 1901).

COUNT LYOF NIKOLAIVITCH TOLSTOI (1828–1911) was caricatured by Snapp, one of *Vanity Fair*'s several unidentified caricaturists who also contributed Ibsen. Although we do not know Snapp's identity, we can appreciate his talent. He has sketched a finely delineated caricature of Tolstoi as an old man – the face is honest, his bulbous nose dominates; the eyes are set back under a massive brow that curves into a large nose. Tolstoi's white whiskers and hair flow from under his nose and the hair line on his cheek accentuates the face, separating it from the rest of the body. The cane serves as a prop and as a reminder that the Count is no longer a young man. In his left hand he holds rolled up papers, perhaps a manuscript or another open letter to the Czar. The massive coat and fur cap hide the body – only two hands, a head and the lower legs are seen. The distinct colours in the chromolithograph demonstrate how far printing technology had developed since the muted tone caricatures were published earlier in *Vanity Fair*.

Snapp was honest but polite to his victim. Jehu Junior's biographical entry was short and snide; he seemed unconvinced of Tolstoi's goals or influence. *Vanity Fair* admitted that Tolstoi could describe the horrors of war and impress morbid minds, especially with works like his *Kreutzer Sonata*, a tale of sex and murder. In fairness to Tolstoi, this book was a defence of chastity and fidelity in marriage, but many, including Jehu Junior, read it another way. *Vanity Fair* observed that Tolstoi not only wrote novels but was 'guilty of many religiously sensational writings'. Turning to the Count's politics, the magazine observed that he did 'not always hit it off with the Little Father' (Nicholas II). It called him 'a fine old crusted Social Reformer' who had in him a bit of Canon Kingsley, the English Christian Socialist and author (*Vanity Fair*, 30 March 1872), and Ruskin (see p. 92). Obviously, Jehu Junior is referring to Tolstoi's works on socialist Christianity and art.

When Count Tolstoi appeared in *Vanity Fair* he was seventy-three years old, and his most productive and controversial years were behind him. His tremendous literary success of the 1860s, *War and Peace*, and *Anna Karenina* in 1878, had been followed by a spiritual crisis in the late 1870s. Tolstoi's plea for nonviolence, his arguments for establishing a society based on Christ's teachings and his call for a code of morality

became his guiding lights for the remainder of his life. Men and women in and out of Russia took up his crusade and attempted to live by his writings. Tolstoi's creed and personal life stood in sharp contrast to the political turmoil, revolutionary movements, autocratic repressions, industrial expansion and intellectual conflicts occurring in Russia during the last twenty years of the nineteenth century. He denounced the Czar's dictatorial methods, yet he could not identify himself with the militant critics or active revolutionists. He deplored the dehumanization brought on by industrialism, but he could not accept the Marxists' views or their tactics. What he predicted – the breakdown of Russian society – did come true. He and the world caught a glimpse of it in 1904–1905. However, to *Vanity Fair* in 1901 he was a well meaning but somewhat misdirected old man – he believed 'too much' and tried too hard to demonstrate his 'earnest convictions'. *Vanity Fair* was simply not that impressed with true believers.

He is three-and-seventy years of age; he married in 1861, and he has many children. He was born at Yasnaia Poliana, in Russia; he began his education at Kazan University; he continued it as a soldier in the Crimean War, and he believes that he has not yet finished it. Nevertheless, he teaches much and professes to teach more; for he is an Apostle of Philosophic Socialism, who believes too much and digs with his own hands in order to show his earnest convictions. He is an author who can well describe the horrors of war. He first wrote of Sebastopol, then of 'War and Peace', and many other things, until his 'Kreutzer Sonata' made a real impression on morbid minds. Besides these he has been guilty of many religiously sensational writings, from 'Christ's Christianity' downwards; yet he plays chess and swims and reads. He does not always hit it off with the Little Father, yet is he a fine old crusted Social Reformer who, while he may lack the east-winded manliness of Kingsley, yet has in him a dash of Ruskin.

Vanity Fair supported the aims and ideals of that 'Anglo-Saxon' imperialism which was at its zenith in the late nineteenth century, and which were proclaimed in the writings of Henry Rider Haggard and Rudyard Kipling. Their short stories and novels captured an audience that was regularly informed by the daily press of the heroic exploits of the British in faraway India and Africa. Blessed with the craftsman's skill, they spun adventure tales, based on their experience, which brought both men fame and fortune. They were never accepted in their time as outstanding men of letters, but neither the critics nor public protests against wars and imperialism have destroyed their popularity, then or later. Kipling has gone through several revivals over the years and today is seriously studied by scholars.

Kipling's and Rider Haggard's popularity can be attributed in part, to the timing of the appearance of their novels. Their writings were published in the late 1880s and early 1890s, following the generation which included the three-decker novel and authors like Thackeray, Dickens and Trollope, and before the next group of writers: Wells, Conrad, Bennett and Galsworthy. Set in the colonies and constructed around timely political, social and economic issues their shorter novels appeared at the most opportune time. They hit upon a successful formula, and they maintained it for the rest of their careers.

HENRY RIDER HAGGARD (1856–1925) appeared in *Vanity Fair* in 1887. His youth, according to *Vanity Fair*, had not been promising; indeed it was not. Rider Haggard's father consid-

In its commentary accompanying Spy's caricature, the magazine observed that Rider Haggard could tell interesting stories 'in a stirring, powerful, manly, interesting fashion'. He was 'new', 'fresh' and very successful. For the next few years he continued to write, but his all-consuming interest in England and his desire to improve society led him into other careers – agricultural reformer, public servant and defender of the Empire.

Spy's caricature of Rider Haggard gives him a military bearing. Tall and erect, with his hands behind him, the author gazes out to the left. Except for the somewhat large nose and half opened mouth, the sketch is hardly a caricature. His moustache and pince-nez are the only distinguishable features. This pose, by 1887, was quite common in *Vanity Fair*.

When Spy caricatured RUDYARD KIPLING (1865–1936), seven years later, in 1894, he sketched the young author in a pensive mood. Kipling was a small man, and the sketch caught his diminutive stature. In 1894 Kipling was still living in the United States, but he had returned home for a brief time to receive the acclaim of his admiring public. Within four years he had risen from an unknown author to national fame, especially with his work *Soldiers Three*. Ward was kind to Kipling; yet he was also honest. Kipling was a rather quiet and shy man, and Spy's caricature reveals that side of his subject.

ered him equipped only for a mediocre education followed by a position in the lower echelons of the Foreign Office. He was put on Sir Henry Bulwer's staff in South Africa through his father's friendship with the general and went off to help secure the Transvaal. Here he gained a firsthand knowledge of life in the mines and veldt. By the age of twenty-one he was Master of the High Court where he earned a reputation for honesty and proficiency. After a brief visit to England to marry, he returned to Africa only to come home again and begin a new career at the Bar. Bored by law, he turned to writing - *Cetawayo and his White Neighbours* attacked England's policy in South Africa. The book was valuable for its information but failed to sell. Two novels quickly followed; neither was very successful. In 1885 he read Robert L. Stevenson's *Treasure Island* which inspired him to write *King Solomon's Mines*, the first adventure story in English set in Africa. This very popular novel was succeeded by *She* and *Allan Quatermain*. *Vanity Fair*, in its reviews of Rider Haggard's early books, was qualified in praise and reacted to *She* in verse on 22 January 1887

This is the Song of Ayesha
Weird, clever, exciting, full of strange
thoughts and true philosophy.
Written by a dead Princess on a Cracked Pot.
Price, six shillings for the lot . . .

Kipling, like Haggard, received a rather second rate education. He did learn Latin, French and English and the benefits of muscular Christianity at the United Service College in Westward Ho, Devon, but he was denied entry to Oxford and Cambridge. He returned to India to join his family and took a job on the staff of a newspaper in Lahore, the *Civil and Military Gazette*. He turned his keen eye on everything around him, building up a storehouse of anecdotes and situations. Practising writing skills as a young newspaperman, Kipling composed lengthy stories in the *Gazette* about life in India that eventually became *Departmental Ditties* and *Plain Tales from the Hills*. His reputation spread to England. In 1889 he left India for England by way of Japan and the United States. His impressions of these two countries eventually found their way into his work. In 1892 he returned to America to live there for four years. However, his views of the world, his beliefs, his politics had been formed in India; and his attitude toward imperialism, race and Britain's role as a paternalist force in the world never changed. Among the reading public his works withstood the impact of the Boer War and the disillusionment after 1918. No darling of the critics, he nevertheless continued to be widely read. Kingsley Amis has described him as a colonial living in the London of English Decadence who arrived as a hero on the eve of the 1890s symbolized by Wilde's *The Picture of Dorian Gray*. Max Beerbohm sneered at him in caricature; Spy honoured him. The critics were divided then in their opinions, and Kipling remains, in Kingsley Amis's words, 'a haunting, unsettling presence, with whom we still have to come to terms'.

RICHARD BURTON (1821–1890) wrote to Monckton Milnes that he was driven by the devil; his wife observed that he belonged in the twentieth century. *Vanity Fair* called him a wonderful man and pulled a veil of Victorian respectability over him. The obvious omissions in Jehu Junior's commentary of certain phases of his career could only have infuriated Burton who detested English hypocrisy and what he called 'immodest modesty'.

Vanity Fair acknowledged that Burton's education had been 'fitful'. It failed to record that his education had been disrupted by numerous family moves and that he had been sent down from Oxford. At twenty-one Burton went as an Ensign to India where he came under the influence of Sir Charles Napier, the outspoken but highly successful British general, administrator and conqueror of Sind. Unlike the other subalterns, Burton associated with the natives. Gifted with facility for languages and insatiable curiosity, he quickly became knowledgeable about Indian culture. His earliest writings on India, four books on travel and Indian culture, brought him some fame. Back in England in 1849 he was commissioned by the Royal Geographical Society to travel to Mecca in disguise and to report on his findings. He successfully penetrated the Holy City, returned home and wrote *Pilgrimage to El Medinah and Mecca* (1855), an account which enhanced his reputation as a bold adventurer and spellbinding story teller. His next but brief excursion into Somaliland brought him into contact for the first time with the explorer-adventurer John Speke. Burton then travelled to the Crimea where, for a short time in 1855, he covered the war. However, this was a minor detour, as the lure of Africa was strong. With Speke he explored the East African Lake region, discovering Lake Tanganyika, and searched in vain for the source of the Nile. Their joint adventure led to differences that became a *cause célèbre; Vanity Fair* politely ignored the furore.

Burton returned to London from Africa but could not settle down. In 1860 he abruptly left England for America where he visited the Mormon colony, interviewed its leaders and wrote a book on his journey and life among the Mormons, *The City of the Saints*. By the mid 1860s, Burton's zest for explorations seemed to be waning while his marriage to the eccentric Roman Catholic, Isabel Arundell, brought new responsibilities.

Burton's career took another turn in 1864 when Lord Russell appointed him a Consul in Brazil. This move proved to be a mixed blessing. It allowed him to travel throughout certain parts of South America but it also served as an exile from London. In 1869 he was transferred to Damascus and later to Trieste in 1872 where he served until his death in 1890.

During the 1870s Burton published eight books and numerous magazine articles on tribal customs and family patterns. His proficiency in languages and his interest in the sexual habits of various cultures resulted in several books on comparative sexual mores. Often these works were banned or partly censored in England. Today they are seen as important contributions to an understanding of the social and cultural patterns of many non-Europeans. *Vanity Fair* passed over these publications and spoke more of his widely known travel books, but did pronounce his translation of the *Arabian Nights* to be 'complete, laborious, uncompromising and perfect'.

The magazine characterized Burton as a 'bold, astute travel-

I say, the critic must keep out of the region of immediate practice
Matthew Arnold
Men of the Day No. 36
11 November 1871
Coide

ler' and as a 'master of Oriental languages, manners and customs'. *Vanity Fair* thought Burton, at sixty-four, 'still very young, very vigorous, very full of anecdote and playful humour'. The contemporary photographs and paintings support *Vanity Fair*'s observation. All his life Burton was a very active, robust, sensual man. Jehu Junior did comment on his ability to tell a yarn, noting that he liked to watch the reactions to his shocking tales, but Burton's volatile personality and driving spirit are not mentioned; the daemonic force within him is simply omitted.

However, if one looks closely at Ape's caricature of Burton the fierce eyes and determination in his face are apparent. Pellegrini caught the 'devil drive' in Burton's countenance thrusting out from under his arched eyebrows. His fixed, stern eyes glare into a world that only he can see. This same penetrating vision is caught in the photographs and paintings; in every one of his portraits he seems obsessed by some powerful force. Burton felt possessed, and he even prided himself in looking like Satan. Ape's caricature should have pleased his victim, for he captured Burton's eerie glint, and the caricature is much more honest than the biographical entry. But one must look beyond the caricature to gain a true measure of the man – a linguist, explorer, archaeologist, anthropologist, amateur physician, botanist, soldier, swordsman, poet and raconteur. Fawn Brodie asserts that Burton was trapped by the Victorian age. Ape has him looking past his times to another world; his restlessness drove him to search for a future, an exit from the hypocrisy he detested and an identity he never attained.

Critics

Matthew Arnold, John Ruskin and John Stuart Mill had established their reputations by denouncing Victorian materialism long before they appeared in *Vanity Fair*. Jehu Junior tolerated them as useful gadflys but warned that they should not be taken too seriously. All were impractical, Mill being the most sensible, understandable and popular of the three. Jehu Junior respected Arnold's and Ruskin's criticisms of literature and art; both men had made important contributions in these fields. However, he considered that they misjudged Victorian society and offered unrealistic solutions to imagined ills. Their doubts about Britain's future were not shared by *Vanity Fair*, which approved the industrialization of the country.

MATTHEW ARNOLD (1822–1888) appeared in *Vanity Fair* in late 1871 at the age of forty-nine. In his youth he had been subjected to his mother's sense of elegance and his father's decisiveness. His father's concern over the destruction of the English character, which the senior Arnold tried to rescue at Rugby School, influenced Matthew all his life. The young Arnold's misgivings found expression in his poetry and his essays. In 1849 his first volume of poems, which was not well received, was published. They were too serious; they ran against the grain of Victorian optimism. Yet, eight years later in 1857, he was awarded the Poetry Chair at Oxford. During those intervening years Arnold worked in the Education Department as an inspector of schools, and published more poetry. His direct experience in popular education exposed him to the problems of modern life and tended to reinforce his reservations about the future which he presented through his essays and poetry. *Vanity Fair* acknowledged that Arnold was 'eminently fitted' to be a critic because of his extensive writings and experiences. The magazine recognized that Arnold had not been appreciated or understood for his efforts to 'propagate the best that is known

and thought'. Indeed, his hope – to encourage the middle class to transmit the best in culture to others – was in vain. *Vanity Fair* agreed with Arnold that the masses would never see things as they are because, reasoned Jehu Junior, in England men were so 'busied in using things as they seem, that nobody as a rule gives a thought to the necessity of seeing them as they are'. The English 'practical genius' prevailed over the ideal; a 'self-satisfied stability' had settled in, observed *Vanity Fair*. Arnold's attack delighted his supporters, but its impact had been minimal. The magazine admitted that, as a critic, he was 'unsurpassed'; however, *Vanity Fair* disapproved of his proposal to increase the power of the State to solve England's problems.

Tissot's caricature captures Arnold's sense of elegance which he inherited from his mother. Charlotte Brontë, upon meeting Arnold, wrote 'Striking and prepossessing in appearance, his manner displeases from its seeming foppery'. Arnold's serious side, which Brontë appreciated, could not hide his dandyism. He was particularly vain about his hair which he anointed with French lotions. Tissot emphasizes Arnold's hair and his mutton chop whiskers. His foppery is tempered by his clerical attire, but Tissot has caught the essence of his victim.

Jehu Junior appreciated Arnold's struggle against the 'Philistines'. He was much less sympathetic to JOHN RUSKIN (1819–1900) who was, he felt, further out of touch with reality than Arnold. Ruskin was a man 'irredeemably at variance with the spirit of the country and the times . . . [an] incurable poet and artist in a materialistic and money-grubbing generation'.

John Ruskin's childhood, education and early years had protected him from England's 'money-grubbing generation'. The only child of a prosperous wine merchant of Scottish extraction, Ruskin was reared by a mother who read him the Bible and a father who quoted poetry. In his youth he also travelled with his father in England and abroad. His possessive mother followed him to Oxford where she dominated his life. Ruskin's interest in art, and particularly in Turner, had begun in his youth. Given a large allowance by his father, Ruskin lived in London and Venice, travelled to important architectural sites and collected Turner's paintings. A productive writer all his life, Ruskin had transmitted his ideas and criticisms into *Modern Painters* and *The Stones of Venice* by 1860. He also wrote numerous essays and pamphlets, delivered lectures and bombarded *The Times* with letters on current social and political issues. By the time he was featured in *Vanity Fair* in February 1872, Ruskin had been appointed Slade Professor of Fine Art at Oxford (1869) and had established St George's Guild, his utopian agricultural colony formed to protect artisans from the evils of industrialization.

Jehu Junior recognized Ruskin's genius, his sense of social consciousness and his desire to preach to the less well informed. Ruskin labelled his urge to preach to others as his 'hymenopterous instinct'. His sense of mission, his failure in marriage and the history of insanity in his family resulted in states of depression and obsession throughout his life that ultimately led to periodic madness after 1878. In 1872, when he was caricatured in *Vanity Fair*, Ruskin was in a state of euphoria. His productivity and reputation continued to grow after this until 1887 when his mental condition forced him to retire.

Thomas Carlyle called Ruskin 'a bottle of beautiful soda-water' but remarked also that he was a weak man. Bottle of soda-water or not, Ruskin dressed well; he was a dandy whose attire annoyed Matthew Arnold. He is smartly turned out for Cecioni, the Italian sculptor and painter who caricatured him

The Realization of the Ideal
John Ruskin
Men of the Day No. 40
17 February 1872
Cecioni

for *Vanity Fair*. His suit and cravat, perhaps from Stulz the fashionable tailor, cannot, however, hide his large head, protruding nose, thick neck and shoulders. The sweep of the hair line and whiskers is repeated in the curves of the cravat and coat which are contrasted by the straight lines created in the arm and the vertical stripes in the trousers. Ruskin was not a person who mixed easily with the masses whose cause he championed, and Cecioni kept him aloof.

When Spy's caricature of JOHN STUART MILL (1806–1873) appeared in *Vanity Fair*, the famous political economist, essayist and critic had less than a year to live. Spy sketched Mill delivering a lecture on 'Woman's Rights' at Euston Hall and completed the caricature in his studio. Spy reworked the original sketch to highlight Mill's bumpy forehead, beaked nose and elongated head. Ward also made Mill look older by thinning out his body and bending it forward, and by sloping the shoulders and placing Mill's hands behind his back. Ward recorded that Mill's nose 'resembled a parrot's' and while he looked 'ascetic' his 'manner and personality breathed charm and intellect'.

Intellect was indeed what John Stuart Mill possessed; *Vanity Fair* was greatly impressed by Mill's mind. Jehu Junior considered Mill, like Arnold and Ruskin, to be out of step with his times – his lofty ideas fell on the deaf ears of 'practical people'. But, unlike Ruskin and Arnold, Mill had a greater impact in his own day and would have a greater influence on the future. He

was able to put the thoughts of others into a popular and simple form. *Vanity Fair* described him as a 'feminine philosopher', a reference to his personal life and his unquestioned devotion to his wife, to his support of women's rights and to his somewhat idealistic and therefore, to his time, womanly ways of thinking.

Mill's education in Philosophical Radicalism, his later rejection of it, his support of limited governmental control, his career in Parliament and his essays and tracts on society and the individual, on personal and civic rights and economics had made him one of the major voices of the Victorian period. *Vanity Fair* paid homage to Mill and summarized his views on birth control (he was for it), on the ballot (he objected to it), on minority rights (he supported them), on industrialism (he argued that it had enriched the few at the expense of the many) and on the Tory Party (he called it 'stupid'). The magazine predicted that he would be judged 'as one of the few men who have given themselves to thought in an unthinking generation'. Jehu Junior's astute remark has been proven true; Mill has continued to be read and quoted because his observations are still relevant.

Musicians

Vanity Fair was acutely aware of the excellence and abundance of European music produced in the nineteenth century. It paid homage to most of the leading composers and performers of the day, including Mascagni (*Vanity Fair*, 24 August 1873), Gounod (*Vanity Fair*, 1 February 1879), Sarasate (*Vanity Fair*, 25 May 1889) and Jan Kubelik (*Vanity Fair*, 7 May 1903). The magazine was not always pleased with some musical trends but it admitted that music, like life, was subject to change and innovation. Four of the most influential musicians featured in *Vanity Fair* were Giuseppe Verdi, Franz Liszt, Richard Wagner and Jan Paderewski.

GIUSEPPE VERDI (1813–1901) was at the height of his career in 1879 when Chartran caricatured him, rather sympathetically, for *Vanity Fair*. Verdi was to retire in 1882, only to return to the public stage in 1886 to write *Otello* and, in 1893, *Falstaff*. Eight years later, in 1901, he died.

In his youth he trained as an organist, composed overtures and cantatas, studied in Milan and by the age of twenty-six had produced his first opera. Verdi's initial attempts were unsuccessful; *Nabucco,* however, brought him fame in 1842. His international reputation was established in 1851 with *Rigoletto* which, according to *Vanity Fair*, Verdi regarded as his 'greatest work'. Within the next few years came *Il Trovatore, La Traviata* and *Un Ballo in Maschera.* In the early 1870s *Aïda* was produced – first in Cairo and then Italy.

Vanity Fair described Verdi's music as 'essentially the music of the present, shallow and pleasing, sympathetic and tuneful'. Jehu Junior observed that many felt Verdi had encouraged 'a vicious taste' in music. Verdi had taken the popular tunes and folk music of Italy, which he had heard in his youth on the street barrel organs, and then transformed them into operatic works. Moreover, he had remodelled the comic Italian opera into a more serious form and thereby raised the entire level of opera in Europe. Because he had worked under the restrictions of the *opera buffa*, it took him several years to develop a mature style and to free himself from the Italian influence. By 1879 he had not only become a famous composer but was also a hero among Italian patriots. His tunes were turned into rallying cries of patriotism. As a result, he sat in the Parmesan assembly, the Chamber of Deputies, and was made a senator by Victor Emmanuel II in 1875. Although never actively involved in politics

for any length of time, Verdi became a symbol of Italian nationalism. *Vanity Fair* felt Verdi should stay out of politics because he had neither knowledge nor understanding of it. *Vanity Fair* did not understand that, in Italy, music and politics could not be separated, and that opera played an important role in the local community and Italian history. That Verdi's music could influence Italian nationalism, that Verdi would allow himself to be associated with political movements, especially democratic movements, was something *Vanity Fair* could neither comprehend nor condone.

FRANZ LISZT (1811–1886) appeared in *Vanity Fair* in May 1886, when at the end of an illustrious, productive life he had come to England to be honoured by Queen Victoria.
Two months later, in July, Liszt died.

Spy honoured Liszt as a famous musician, showing him as a kindly, bent old man. Liszt's flowing white hair, craggy features, bushy eyebrows, hawked nose and toothless smile seemed to mock his former handsome face and commanding physique which had once had such an effect on women. Dressed in a soutane, Liszt leans forward slightly and smiles faintly.

Behind that faint smile and rugged face was a man who dominated much of the musical world of the nineteenth century. His life was clearly divided into two phases: up to 1848 an accomplished pianist, after then a prolific composer. As a young

man he had been brought by his father from Budapest to Paris where he studied, played the piano and made his name in Society. By the late 1820s he was touring the French provinces and England. *Vanity Fair* observed of his first British tour: 'He came to England and won the praise of George IV, which was nothing; but he also won the praises of the whole musical world, which was something.' During the next decade he became the close friend of Chopin, George Sand and Berlioz, began his relationship with the Comtess Marie d'Agoult and continued to dazzle European audiences on his extended tours. After his affair with the Comtess he met and lived with Princess Sayn-Wittgenstein. Liszt, according to *Vanity Fair*, had 'thrilled Princesses with his smile, and had made some Countesses happy and others envious'. This veiled allusion was understood by all who read it; *Vanity Fair* did not have to state the obvious or indulge in less discreet remarks.

At the height of his career as a virtuoso, Liszt retired from public performances, became the musical director at Weimar and started his second career as a composer in 1848. Ten years later he moved to Rome and spent a part of each year living in Rome, Weimar and Budapest. He continued to write music and gave freely of his time to aspiring pianists. His personal life was well regimented, quiet and productive. On occasion, as in his final trip to England, he accepted the praise of his public. He had, in his old age, according to *Vanity Fair* developed a fond-

The Music of the Future
Richard Wagner
Men of the Day No. 149
19 May 1877
Spy

95

ness for whist, smoked bad cigars and liked weak sherry and water.

RICHARD WAGNER (1813–1883) was, like Liszt and Verdi, approaching the end of his career when he was sketched by Spy, though he still had great works in him. In 1882, only a year before his death, he finished the score for *Parsifal*. Wagner was acknowledged by *Vanity Fair* to be one of the outstanding composers of his day; but the magazine also had its reservations.

That Wagner is one of the greatest of living composers is sufficiently proved by the fact that his very name is a war-cry among all musical people. That he is original beyond the verge of eccentricity and grand beyond the comprehension of ordinary mortals is also certain. The Music of the Future has the undeniable quality of certainly exciting enthusiasm either of delight or disgust. Which it best deserves the Future must decide.

The future would decide in favour of Wagner, but during his lifetime the final decision was often in doubt. Jehu Junior recorded the ups and downs of Wagner's career. The writer understood Wagner's goal of taking Beethoven's music, pictures and actions and welding them into 'one Wagnerian whole'. Wagner possessed this 'idea' as a guide and 'poverty' as his friend for many years. His earliest works were failures, since the Parisian audiences did not understand his innovative operas. After success came with *The Flying Dutchman*, he was employed at Dresden where, in 1848, he participated in the uprising. He next turned to writing essays and books, conducted concerts throughout Europe and in London. His earlier tour in London, according to *Vanity Fair*, had earned him the reputation 'of a tremendous lunatic'.

Wagner's notoriety was enhanced, in part, by how audiences reacted to his operas. His production of *Tannhäuser*, in 1861, created a scandal in Paris when the audience hissed and blew whistles during the performance. Although his next work, *Der Meistersinger* brought him some financial rewards, he was still in debt and was forced to tour Europe and Russia as a conductor. In 1864 he was rescued by the loony King of Bavaria, Ludwig II; but Wagner's stormy relationship with Ludwig was a high price to pay for any semblance of economic security. Eventually he left Bavaria to settle in Switzerland although he still received funds from Ludwig. Wagner married in 1870 the daughter of Liszt, Cosima, who left her husband for Wagner. In 1876 the first Bayreuth Festival was held. It was less than a financial success and for that reason, noted *Vanity Fair*, Wagner had once again returned to England to raise money for his project in his fond hope to write 'music, scenery and acting'.

Spy's caricature of Wagner is one of his best. He caught his subject's personality and physical characteristics. The small glasses resting on a large nose; the hair swept back from the head and the whiskers sticking out from the jutting chin accentuate the physical features. The body rests uneasily on the edge of the chair, ready to spring from the cushion. With arms and legs struggling to control the orchestra, Wagner concentrates on his conducting. Wagner's left thumb is slightly raised and his fingers bent; his right arm holds the baton that points to the members of the orchestra. His right foot beats out the time while his left foot steadies him. During the rehearsal, while Ward was observing Wagner, the composer became 'more and more excited', waved his baton, danced on and off his stool until he was 'very angry', and had to stop conducting out of fear of bringing on one of his 'nervous attacks'.

Spy used the same format in caricaturing IGNACE JAN PADEREWSKI (1860–1941). Still a relatively young man, at thirty-nine, when he appeared in *Vanity Fair*, Paderewski was sketched by Spy playing the piano with his right arm suspended and his left hand descending on the keyboard. Although Spy put Wagner and Paderewski in similar poses, he was kinder to Paderewski. The neck and hair have been emphasized to gain the sense of caricature but otherwise the portrayal is generally flattering, giving the impression of a rather sensitive and soulful young man.

By 1899 Paderewski had conquered the music halls of Europe and America, and had been composing for twenty years. His reputation was firmly established when he appeared in *Vanity Fair*. However, his earlier tours in England, especially in 1890 when he was thirty, had received mixed reviews. His popularity grew among English audiences over the next few years, and by 1899 he could, according to *Vanity Fair*, command 'a thousand guineas for a piece or two'. Jehu Junior called him 'the first of living pianists and a really fine composer . . .' He was charming, and women adored him both for his music and because he was the fashion. Jehu Junior recognized Paderewski's determination to be a great virtuoso through his 'earnest study and incessant practice'. He was an 'indefatigable worker and a poet' who could be compared to Chopin. Mindful of the debate over Paderewski's style and technique, *Vanity Fair* warned its

readers that he must be heard before he could be judged.

This brilliant pianist won fame and fortune over the next years. Like so many Europeans, his life dramatically changed during the First World War, when his patriotic fervour for his beloved Poland forced him into an active political role. Paderewski worked endlessly, first to aid the victims of the war and, later, to establish an independent Poland in postwar Europe. After the war he served for a short time in a coalition ministry, holding the offices of Prime Minister and Minister of Foreign Affairs. He became a symbol of Poland's hope through his performances and selfless dedication to his country's future. His decision to launch a second musical career during the 1920s re-established his reputation as a flawless and sensitive pianist while he continued to defend Poland in the arena of international diplomacy. In his declining years he was to witness the rise of Nazism and the humiliating defeat of Poland. By 1939 the music of Wagner and the music of Paderewski echoed over the plains of western Poland through the screams of Stuka dive bombers; their spirits confronted one another in a deadly war far from the concert stages of nineteenth-century Europe or the pages of *Vanity Fair*.

Gilbert, Sullivan and D'Oyly Carte

The formation of the most famous partnership in the history of the Victorian theatre – Gilbert, Sullivan and D'Oyly Carte – was documented in the pages of *Vanity Fair*. Each had won a name for himself prior to their union, and *Vanity Fair* judged them, particularly Sullivan, on their own merits as well as on their collective efforts. They appeared in the magazine over a twenty-year period, but they were never caricatured together.

ARTHUR SULLIVAN (1842–1900) was sketched by Ape in early 1874, a year before *Trial by Jury* would link together the names of Gilbert, Sullivan and D'Oyly Carte. Pellegrini has the measure of his subject – a shy, polite, well mannered Victorian. Sullivan gazes down as if he is thinking about his recent successes and asking himself whether they have brought him the satisfaction for which he yearned. Ape has made Sullivan's neck and head slightly out of proportion to the body; the round shoulders, engaged arms and short legs purposely diminish the body and force attention on the head. The wavy hair, bushy mutton chops and moustache dominate Sullivan's circular face. His sloped shoulders and round head are separated by a thick neck. We are distracted at first by the physical features which Ape emphasized, but a closer look reveals a respectful and incisive caricature.

Sullivan, aged thirty-two when Ape drew him, had already made a name for himself in English music. He came from a musical family. His father played in the orchestra at the Surrey Theatre and later taught music at Kneller Hall, the military school for musicians. Young Arthur's talents brought him to the Royal Chapel as a chorister, where he launched his career and began to meet prominent people who came to hear the choir. Throughout his life Sullivan followed this pattern, moving in the best social circles and succeeding in the world of music. After studying in Leipzig he returned to London to score *The Tempest* which was performed at Easter, 1862, in the Crystal Palace. The work immediately established his reputation. His serious and religious music was now interspersed with lighter efforts, including *Cox and Box* which was a moderately successful play.

Vanity Fair judged his works as 'first-rate' and asserted that his songs were filling 'every drawing room in London'. The

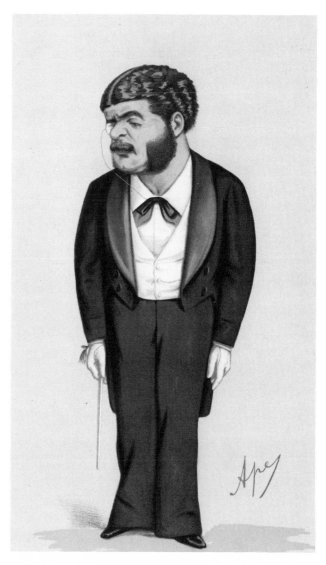

magazine noted Sullivan's close acquaintance with the Duke of Edinburgh (*Vanity Fair*, 10 January 1874) which had exposed the young musician to the 'charms of the court'. Fortunately, observed Jehu Junior, Sullivan had not forgotten the 'claims of art' while under the influences of Royalty. He was still aware that labour was 'the foundation of all things'. Indeed, he always recognized the importance of work for he was an untiring composer who drove himself, in spite of ill health most of his life, to meet his deadlines and contractual arrangements.

The most famous of his contractual arrangements was, of course, with William S. Gilbert. In 1871 they had collaborated on *Thespis* – an unsuccessful venture. From then until 1874, about the time Sullivan appeared in *Vanity Fair*, both men were very productive independently, Sullivan composing music and Gilbert writing plays. On 25 March 1875, after a fervid bout of creativity, revision and cooperation, *Trial by Jury* was presented to the London public. It was an instant success; the press raved. The genius of Gilbert and Sullivan had been brought together under the deft hand of Richard D'Oyly Carte, already a highly successful concert agent and theatre manager. For the next fifteen years this trio generated joy and pleasure for audiences in England, America and Europe.

By the time WILLIAM SCHWENCK GILBERT (1836–1911) appeared in *Vanity Fair* in May 1881, the team of Gilbert and

Patience
William Schwenck Gilbert
Men of the Day No. 244
21 May 1881
Spy

Royal English Opera
Richard D'Oyly Carte
Men of the Day No. 498
14 February 1891
Spy

law suits must have felt that *Vanity Fair* was glossing over this aspect of Gilbert's personality.

Spy, who knew Gilbert, and performed in several amateur plays with him, has sketched an inoffensive caricature. The pose is typical of many shown in *Vanity Fair:* the victim is in profile, hands thrust into pockets, coat open, legs and feet set apart. Spy has kept the legs, arms and body in proportion. His treatment of Gilbert, here in a pensive mood, does not reveal the wit, cleverness, irritability or uncertainty of a man who felt that he had never truly fulfilled his life's ambitions.

Neither Gilbert nor Sullivan had set out in life to find fame in the way they did. Sullivan considered himself to be a serious musician; Gilbert wanted to be a serious playwright. Both men, then, were, in their own eyes, less than successful. Their self images created a number of problems that affected their working arrangements, and only a man of D'Oyly Carte's genius, diplomacy and determination could have made the Gilbert and Sullivan team work as well for as long.

RICHARD D'OYLY CARTE (1844–1901) was caricatured by Spy in 1891, ten years after Ward had drawn Gilbert. By that time Gilbert and Sullivan were nearing the end of their collaborative efforts. Since 1881 they had written, among other operas, *Iolanthe, The Mikado, Ruddigore, The Yeomen of the Guard* and

Sullivan had produced *The Sorcerer, HMS Pinafore* and the *Pirates of Penzance*. Their most recent hit, *Patience*, had just opened in late April. In six years, from 1875 to 1881, they had satirized the Victorian Establishment and its virtues of responsibility and discipline; *Patience* now took on the Aesthetes and their stylized preciousness. *Vanity Fair* declared that through their operas, Gilbert and Sullivan had confirmed 'the triumph of a new school' that had begun with their *Trial by Jury*.

Gilbert's early career as a soldier, then as a civil servant and next at the Bar was noted by Jehu Junior. These adventures, unlike those of Sullivan, were frustrating and did not open the doors of Society to him. While practising law he drew sketches and wrote short articles for *Fun* and *Cornhill* and collected bits of witty dialogue and nonsense stories which he wove into *The Bab Ballads*, published in 1873 to considerable acclaim. He promptly gave up his law career and turned to writing plays. After a somewhat precarious beginning, Gilbert's plays met with increasing approval. By the early 1870s he was well known for his witty scripts, clever parodies and quick-paced burlesques. *Vanity Fair*'s patriotism shows through in expressing its pleasure that Gilbert's plays were 'purely native and yet quite original'; only three had come from the French. Jehu Junior described Gilbert as 'amiable and genial' while admitting that he was capable of showing his temper. Those who suffered the barbs of Gilbert's tongue, his heated letters and threats of

The Gondoliers. In 1890, they engaged in the famous 'carpet quarrel' over refurbishing the Savoy Theatre which nearly destroyed their partnership.

Vanity Fair, in honouring D'Oyly Carte and the construction of his new theatre, the Royal English Opera, which opened on 31 January 1891, made special mention of that 'beneficent triumvirate' of Gilbert, Sullivan and D'Oyly Carte. D'Oyly Carte's success was attributed to his 'hereditary taste' and training in music, his 'natural taste' for the theatre and 'the marvellous business skill' of his wife. Jehu Junior listed D'Oyly Carte's theatrical triumphs, his building accomplishments (including the Savoy Theatre and Savoy Hotel) and his many financial successes. The impresario's large number of companies coupled with his ability to involve himself in the tiniest details explained why he was 'doing good business'. D'Oyly Carte's business acumen was matched by his tact; and, with the help of his wife, Helen, he held together the Gilbert and Sullivan team for over a decade.

D'Oyly Carte's perseverance, breadth of vision and sense of self-importance was caught very clearly by Spy. His expensive fur coat, spats, cigar, cane and gloves are the marks of his success. His stance signals a self-assured man with feet firmly set, eyes clearly fixed on the next goal. His new dream, in its first form as architectural plans, are tucked under his arm. The Savoy and the Royal English Opera were turned from dreams to reality just as the partnership of Gilbert and Sullivan was transformed into words and music – and profits.

The fruits of the labour of these three men have been performed for over one hundred years. The D'Oyly Carte Company and other professional groups along with countless amateur organizations have brought the tuneful melodies, bright patter songs and memorable characters into theatres around the world. Their three caricatures have, in turn, become extremely popular with Gilbert and Sullivan fans, and they have been reproduced in numerous biographies and in programmes and publications by local operetta companies. Enjoying a Gilbert and Sullivan comic opera is a pleasure which also gives us an insight into the Victorian mind. *Vanity Fair*'s assessment of these men and their contributions reveals what the Victorians were, in turn, thinking of themselves. They left us a legacy that sings out now as then.

What though the night may come too soon
We've years and years of afternoon!
  Then let the throng
    Our joy advance,
With laughing song
    And merry dance,
With joyous shout and ringing cheer
Inaugurate our new career!   *The Mikado*

The Theatre

This very complimentary sketch of the actress SARAH BERNHARDT (1844-1923) by Théobald Chartran ☥, the French portraitist, is among the most popular lithographs ever to be published in *Vanity Fair.* It was one of two which had the signature of the sitter as a caption, and 'the divine Sarah' was the only person to be categorized as a Woman of Genius. Her motto, *quand même* was apt: she went on in spite of everything – the consummate professional – and never let a tumultuous personal life get in the way of her art. Her extraordinary career lasted sixty-one years. She was more famous than kings and certainly more notorious. The critic Jules Lemaître wrote admiringly of her: 'She could enter a convent, discover the North Pole, kill an emperor or marry a Negro king and it would not surprise me. She is not an individual but a complex of individuals.'

In 1879, when she first appeared in the magazine, 'the divine Sarah' had just taken London by storm. Her appearance with the *Comédie Française* as Phèdre at the Gaiety Theatre, according to one of the audience, 'set every nerve and fibre in their bodies throbbing and held them spellbound'. She conquered nearly everyone wherever she went – whether the continent, the British Isles or America by her spectacular talent and her exquisite voice – even when few could understand French.

Vanity Fair's 1879 commentary is among its most felicitous:

The Bernhardts were a Dutch family of Jewish race who had adopted France as their home, when that daughter was born who was to render their name famous. This was so few years ago that this daughter is still quite a young woman, and yet there is scarcely a journal published in Europe but her name is found in it. As a child her most ardent desire was to be a painter, but her mother, holding that this was a poverty-stricken career, determined to make of her an actress, and placed her at the Conservatoire *in Paris. Here she soon made herself known by her talent, and after passing through the Odéon she, six years ago, joined the* Comédie Française. *At that time she was known to the public mainly for her extreme strangeness and spareness of figure; but she saw and observed Aimeé Desclée, and resolving thenceforth to let her own individuality have greater scope in her acting, she has within the last four years gradually risen in the estimation of the public, until now she is acknowledged to be the finest of all living actresses. Her voice is of a fine and delicate quality, capable of infinite modulations; her enunciation of the language of Racine and Molière is as near perfection as may be; and she is endowed with a beauty which is all the more fascinating from being so strange and unclassed. In her acting, she has striking resemblances to Rachel, to whom she is held by most to be equal, and by very many to be superior. In her costumes, her port, and gestures, she displays the most correct and severe taste, and by the aid of this she has invested with a new interest those tiresome tragedies which can only be endured when they are a triumph of taste.*

Sarah Bernhardt is herself, when herself, one of the most surprising of women of genius. Her intelligence, her quickness, her vivacity are incredible, and all the more astonishing on account of her being what, if she were any other woman, would be an invalid. She suffers much from a distressing malady, but with her the spirit has so conquered the body that she leads a life of the most arduous and unremitting toil, while she is ever gay, alert, and ready with new and startling theories and conclusions on every conceivable subject. She has given herself to sculpture and to painting with a certain success; she has had her coffin made, and keeps it full of the many love-letters which have been addressed to her; she furnishes her living rooms with skulls; and she has now resigned her place in that Comédie Française which she has revived by her wonderful talent and enriched by her unparalleled success.

Bernhardt appeared again in *Vanity Fair,* late in her apparently endless career. In 1912, the English gave her a National Tribute to celebrate her fifty years on the stage. She was portrayed then by K in profile, wearing the robes of the Queen of Spain from *Ruy Blas,* one of her most famous roles. 'Marmaduke', the commentator, wrote:

Born in Paris in 1844, Madame Sarah Bernhardt entered the Conservatoire *in 1859, made her first appearance on the stage at the Théatre Française in 1862, secured her first success in 1869, and,*

Mademoiselle Sarah Bernhardt
Women of Genius No. 1
5 July 1879
(Theobald Chartran)

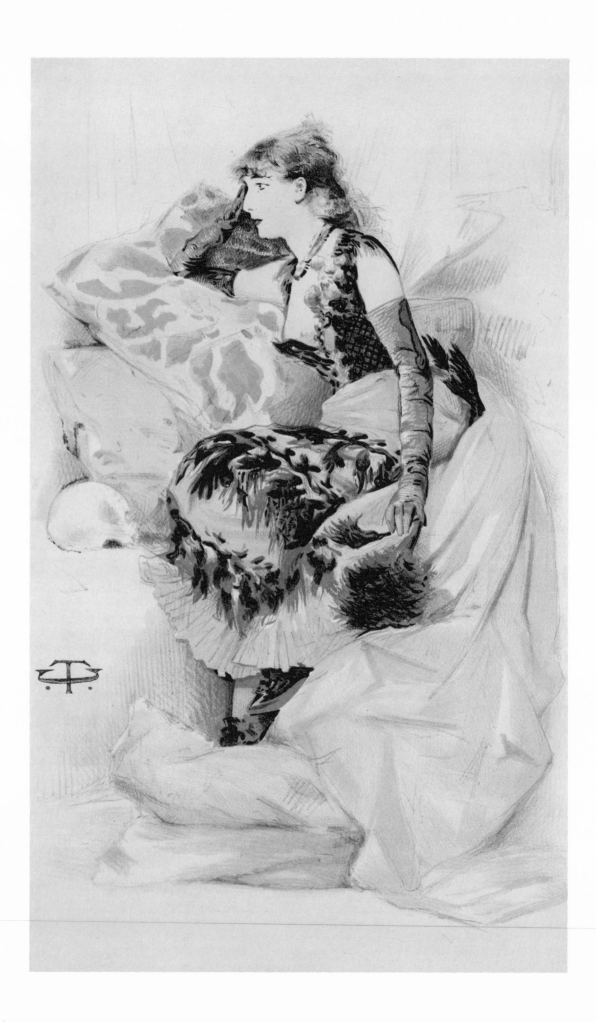

The Bells
Henry Irving
An Actor
19 December 1874
Ape

101

in the character of the Queen of Spain in 'Ruy Blas', attained celebrity at the Odéon in 1872. In 1879, Madame Bernhardt, with the other members of the Comédie Française, *first visited London; it is to the credit of British audiences that her talent and brilliant performances obtained for her the warmest approval here from the outset.*

Great in struggle, great in triumph, in spite of persistent abuse, opposition, and ridicule, Madame Sarah Bernhardt has forced her way to the very front of theatrical celebrity, and in an age of advanced mediocrity stands out as a genius possibly beyond compare.

Not all her contemporaries were quite so ecstatic about her. George Bernard Shaw wrote later: 'I could never, as a dramatic critic, be fair to Sarah Bernhardt, because she was like my Aunt Georgina; but I could not say this at the time, because my Aunt Georgina was alive.'

Unlike many individuals featured in *Vanity Fair*, HENRY IRVING (1838–1905) appeared in the magazine at the beginning of his career rather than the end. Irving had just opened in *Hamlet* in October when Ape sketched this clever, sensitive caricature for *Vanity Fair*'s 19 December 1874 issue. Slouched and shuffling along, he is dressed in the costume for the role of Mathias in *The Bells*, the melodrama that had made Irving the new sensation in the London theatre.

The Bells, which foreshadowed the psychological drama, provided Irving the opportunity to illustrate his acting talents. Mathias, played by Irving, was a man haunted by a murder committed fifteen years before, who finally breaks under the terrible strain and dies clutching his throat, strangled by an imaginary hangman's rope. *Vanity Fair* described the play as a 'harrowing drama' in which Irving 'left a nightmare-like memory on each one of the audience'.

Irving's acceptance into the theatrical world as a serious actor had been preceded by his very popular role in a London comedy, *Two Roses*, and by years in the provinces before less sophisticated audiences. As a young man he spent a short time in an office before turning to the theatre. Having decided to pursue a theatrical career, he left London for Edinburgh in late 1856. Here he played a few roles, returned to London briefly, and then went to Manchester and other cities where he worked in the 1860s. Tom Taylor and Dion Boucicault (*Vanity Fair*, 16 December 1882) formed a partnership in the 1860s, and soon Irving was associated with them. By the early 1870s he had established his reputation as a comedian in *Two Roses*. But his big break came in *The Bells*.

Vanity Fair's drama criticism was particularly well informed, since Bowles, Ward and other staff members all had personal interests in the theatre. It reviewed most of the major plays which opened in the West End. Bowles commented that Irving was 'too confirmed a mannerist to be a thorough artist . . .' Yet, Jehu Junior declared, Irving's artistic talents were far superior 'to the common run of mechanical actors playing solely within the limits of tradition'. *Vanity Fair* praised the company he kept; he exhibited 'a certain careless taste of some pretensions while his manners are considered to be quite equal to those of any unemployed gentleman'. In other words, Irving moved in the right circles; he even belonged to some of the same clubs as did Spy, the Fielding Club and the Lyric Club. The magazine implied that Irving was a greater actor than he had yet shown, and it correctly predicted that he would have an illustrious career.

After his performance in *Hamlet*, which *Vanity Fair* judged was played 'with much intelligence', Irving did a series of

Shakespearean plays and historical roles. When cast in weak plays, such as *Vanderdecken*, an adaptation of the Flying Dutchman legend, he still performed well. *Vanity Fair*, on 29 June 1878, reviewed the play and concluded that Irving's performance, done with all his 'subtle power of characterisation', was the most worthwhile part of the evening. In late 1878 Irving took over the management of the Lyceum theatre and for the next twenty years he was associated with this playhouse. He went on tours to America and Canada from the early 1880s to 1904. Meanwhile, he lectured at numerous universities and to the public; his addresses were later published and widely circulated.

Irving was a thoroughly professional actor. He worked out movements with great precision. The dramatic critic Henry Austin Clapp attributed Ivring's success to his 'intensity, artistic sense and intellectuality'. Irving gave his last performance in *Becket*, on 13 October 1905. He died that night after the play, and is buried in Westminster Abbey.

Vanity Fair suffered a love-hate affair with GEORGE BERNARD SHAW (1856–1950). The magazine admired his wit, insight and independence, but it disapproved of his criticisms of the Establishment and the cherished values of Society. Shaw's plays, articles and lectures could not compensate *Vanity Fair* for his Irish heritage, socialist opinions and political radicalism. Shaw

Magnetic, he has the power to infect almost everyone
with the delight that he takes in himself
George Bernard Shaw
Men of the Day No. 995
28 December 1905
Ruth

G.B.S.
George Bernard Shaw
Men of the Day No. 1292
16 August 1911
Alick P. F. Ritchie

103

was featured in *Vanity Fair* twice, 1905 and 1911. By the time of his second appearance, the magazine had become an uncritical defender of the British way of life; consequently, it found Shaw less amusing the second time around.

In 1905 Jehu Junior depicted Shaw as the personification of British eccentricity tolerated, even admired, by the public. By 1911 he had offended too many people, taken up too many causes. The magazine considered him to be full of contradictions: his original profundity had been exposed as superficial; and he was exploiting his successes for personal gain.

The caricatures reinforced the tenor of the biographical entries. The first caricature, by Max Beerbohm, takes great delight in its victim. This is attributable, in part, to Beerbohm's talents in contrast to Alick Ritchie's more limited skills. Beerbohm has sketched Shaw in the same manner in which *Vanity Fair* described him. With left arm akimbo and legs crossed, eyebrows arched, teeth showing and finger twiddling his beard, Shaw ponders the clever retort. The playwright's impish quality is apparent. Beerbohm has lengthened Shaw's head and legs, pushed out his tummy and put him in slippers and suit – a deft touch of contrast. Ritchie has left us an amusing but less perceptive sketch. Shaw's wink helps, and the outsized hat adds a bit of individuality, but the caricature is not comparable to Max's treatment of Shaw.

In 1905 Jehu Junior observed that in an age of 'personalities',

Shaw cut a 'more salient, and more sharply defined . . . figure in contemporary letters' than anyone else. While Shaw had changed and shifted, he had always been a 'perfect expression of himself'. Jehu Junior argued that the reason why the English tolerated Shaw was because they had confidence in their own merits and contempt for intellectuals. Englishmen, he asserted, 'are neither modest nor clever enough to take Mr Shaw seriously.'

Shaw, by 1905, was taken seriously. Since his schooling in Dublin, his early years struggling to make a living, his first encounters with socialism and his career as musical and literary critic, Shaw had established himself as a promising playwright and social commentator. In 1894 *Arms and the Man* had been produced, followed by *The Man of Destiny* and *The Devil's Disciple* in 1897. He was becoming rich from his plays while writing on socialism and promulgating the Fabian Society's programmes. The year he was in *Vanity Fair*, 1905, *Man and Superman* and *Major Barbara* were staged. Shaw's plays led *Vanity Fair* to admit that no dramatist could compare to him 'in wit, in force of brain and in sense of actuality'. His latest play, *Major Barbara*, disproved the charge that Shaw was 'inhuman'. Personally, confided Jehu Junior, Shaw was a very private individual who shunned Society but was, nonetheless, charming and blessed with a power 'to infect almost everyone with the delight that he takes in himself'. *Vanity Fair*, despite its reservations about Shaw's politics, could not help but admire him:

His opinions are many, and none of them does he hold more sincerely than the one of himself. In the Middle Ages he would have had to choose between these opinions and the stake; and to the stake he would have gone, bless him!

Six years later in 1911, when Shaw again appeared in *Vanity Fair*, the magazine was less enamoured of him. Since 1905 he had written *The Doctor's Dilemma* and *Misalliance*, argued with Wells in the Fabian Society, fought the censors, and published his essays. His reputation had grown, he was now financially secure, and *Vanity Fair* took advantage of the opportunity to point out the inconsistency between Shaw's standard of living, driving about in a 'motor car', and his professions of socialism. Inconsistency, maintained *Vanity Fair*, was the chief characteristic of Shaw; it also recognized this as one of the secrets of Shaw's success. Jehu Junior felt that most of Shaw's plays had to be labelled 'doubtful'. *Vanity Fair* in 1911 emphasized what it had only hinted at in 1905: 'He is clever, no doubt of it; but perhaps not as clever as the world thinks he is; and certainly not so clever as he thinks he is.'

Regardless of *Vanity Fair*'s opinion, the world did think him clever, clever enough to award him the Nobel Prize for Literature in 1925, to attend his plays and to listen to his criticisms of the political and social order. He would live on to see a Labour government come to power. *Vanity Fair* may have sensed in Shaw a voice of the future; regardless of its admiration for the man's wit and thought, the magazine could only dislike that voice.

'The World is a stage, but the play is badly cast.'
Oscar Wilde, from *Lord Arthur Savile's Crime*

'I'll be a poet, a writer, a dramatist. Somehow or other I'll be famous, and if not famous I'll be notorious'.
Oscar Wilde, while at Oxford

By 1884, *Vanity Fair* could hardly ignore OSCAR FINGALL O'FLAHERTIE WILLS WILDE (1854–1900), even had it wanted to. Born in Dublin, Wilde conquered Trinity College and Oxford both socially and intellectually. Then, covered with academic glory, armed with a fine mind, an extraordinary wit, a gift for conversation, prodigious self-assurance, and an unparalleled capacity for self-promotion, he rapidly established himself as one of the ornaments of artistic, literary and social London. In 1881, Gilbert and Sullivan (*Vanity Fair*, 21 May 1881, 14 March 1874) in *Patience* satirized the excesses and manners of the aesthetic movement with which Wilde was identified. The two aesthetic poets of the opera, Bunthorne and Grosvenor, were thought to be partly inspired by Wilde's affectations. He never did 'walk down Piccadilly with a poppy or a lily in your medieval hand'. 'Anyone could have done that,' he observed, 'the most difficult thing was to get people to think I had done it.' Oscar was delighted with *Patience*, and consented to lecture in America where he was a surprising success.

Jehu Junior sympathetically summarized Wilde's career:

Oscar, the younger son of the late Sir William Wilde, archaeologist, traveller, and Queen's Surgeon in Ireland, won the Berkeley Medal for Greek in Trinity College, Dublin, and a Scholarship. Migrating to Magdalen College, Oxford, he took two 'Firsts' and 'the Newdigate.' Then he went wandering in Greece; and, full of a Neo-Hellenic spirit, came back to invade social London. He invented the aesthetic movement. He preached the doctrine of possible culture in external things. He got brilliantly laughed at, and good-naturedly accepted. In 1881 he published a somewhat startling volume of poems, and at once went to America to preach his gospel of culture. Then, as an itinerant art-apostle, he wandered from New York to San Francisco, lectured to all sorts and conditions of men, produced a play, and came back to London. Suddenly he gave up dado-worship for dandyism, cut his long locks, and accepted life. He is a sayer of smart things, and has a rare flow of thoroughly Irish wit and an excellent notion of the advantage that may accrue to any man from drawing attention to himself anyhow.

He has lived through much laughter, in which he has always joined. He has many disciples, and is of opinion that 'imitation is the sincerest form of insult.' He is twenty-eight years old, comes of a literary family, and is essentially modern. He is to be married next week.

Wilde's initial enthusiasm for his marriage soon waned, and he began to seek other diversions. Philippe Jullian observed: 'In Wilde's life the sinister was often not far removed from the amorous'. Wilde himself became one of the symbols of the *fin de siècle:* that creative mix of decadence, disdain for Victorian conventions, artistic, social and sexual experimentation that generated the *Yellow Book*, Art Nouveau and similar expressions in Britain and Europe. His writing, particularly the novel *The Picture of Dorian Gray* and the play *Salomé*, with illustrations by Aubrey Beardsley, shocked and challenged the Establishment. His personal life seemed to endanger his career, particularly after he began his affair with Lord Alfred Douglas, the exquisite third son of the eccentric, vindictive, eighth

Marquess of Queensberry (*Vanity Fair*, 10 November 1877).

At the peak of his career, in 1895, with two plays – *An Ideal Husband* and *The Importance of Being Earnest* – running in London, Wilde foolishly sued the Marquess, his lover's father, for criminal libel. In the trial, the relentless cross-examination of his contemporary at Trinity, Sir Edward Carson (*Vanity Fair* 9 November 1893, 8 February 1911) humiliated Wilde and destroyed his case and his career. Wilde was subsequently prosecuted twice and convicted of seven counts of 'gross indecency', and sent to prison for two years. Several individuals involved in his prosecution or defence appeared in *Vanity Fair*, besides Carson. They included his lawyer Sir Edward Clarke (*Vanity Fair*, 11 June 1903) the Solicitor-General Sir Frank Lockwood; the barristers Charles Gill (pp. 108–109) and Horace Avory (p. 116) who prosecuted him in the second trial; and the judges Sir Richard Henn Collins (pp. 108–109), Mr Justice Charles (pp. 108–109) and Sir Alfred Wills (*Vanity Fair*, 25 June 1896). While in gaol, Wilde wrote to a friend: 'The two great turning points in my life were when my father sent me to Oxford and when society sent me to prison. I will not say that prison is the best thing that could happen to me, for that phrase would savour of too great bitterness towards myself. I would sooner say, or hear it said of me, that I was so typical a child of my age, that in my perversity, and for that perversity's sake, I turned the good things of my life to evil, and the evil things of my life to good'.

George Bernard Shaw (*Vanity Fair*, 28 December 1905, 16 August 1911), a fellow Hibernian, would not tolerate the notion that Wilde's life had been a tragedy. In the preface to Frank Harris's (*Vanity Fair*, 12 November 1913) controversial biography of Wilde, Shaw asserted sympathetically: 'Oscar was no tragedian. He was the superb comedian of his century, one to whom misfortune, disgrace, imprisonment were external and traumatic. His gaiety of soul was invulnerable . . . Even on his deathbed he found in himself no pity for himself, playing for the laugh with his last breath, and getting it with as sure a stroke as in his palmiest prime.'

Ape's brush strokes were equally sure. Pellegrini's own sexual orientation was allegedly similar to Wilde's, and the encounter of the older Bohemian with the artistic dandy produced one of *Vanity Fair*'s most apt caricatures. Ape captured Wilde's willowy, slightly corpulent, dandified, sensual worldliness. Oscar was portrayed in elegant evening dress, his left arm framing his white boutonnière, a lavish pink silk handkerchief stuffed into his velvet waistcoat and a magnificent red stone ring on his finger. His full, sensual lips, arched eyebrows and expression of mild boredom were also captured in contemporary photographs. One wonders if he told Pellegrini that 'caricature is the tribute which mediocrity pays to genius'.

Few have ever talked so well as Wilde. As he wrote in *The Portrait of Dorian Gray*, 'There is only one thing in the world worse than being talked about, and that is not being talked about'. He once told André Gide: 'Would you like to know the great drama of my life? It is that I have put my genius into my life – I have only put my talent into my works.'

Oscar
Mr Oscar Wilde
Men of the Day No. 305
24 May 1884
Ape

105

Sir Horace Davey. Q.C.   Mr Finlay. Q.C.   Mr Coward.
Mr Cozens-Hardy Q.C.   Mr Jelf. Q.C.   Baron Pollock.   Mr Bosanquet.Q.C.
                  Mr Justice Smith.   Mr Graham.   Mr Justice Day.   Sir Hen

The Attorney General.   The Solicitor General.   Mr Justice Williams.
   Mr Gill.   Lord Coleridge.   Sir Charles Russell. Q.C.
                                            Mr R.T.Reid.Q.C.

"BEN

.Esher. Lord Justice Bowen. Mʳ Justice Charles. Mʳ Dugdale. Q.C.

Lord Justice Fry. Mʳ Waddy. Q.C. Mʳ Charles Mathews.

Mʳ Poland. Q.C. Mʳ Justice Hawkins.

STUFF

.hancellor. Lord Justice Lindley. Mʳ Justice Collins. Mʳ Inderwick. Q.C.

Mʳ Murphy. Q.C. Mʳ Justice Jeune. Mʳ Lockwood. Q.C.

BAR."

The Lord Chief Justice
Lord Coleridge
Judges No. 17
5 March 1887
Ape

PAGES 106–7
Bench and Bar
Winter Number, 5 December 1891
Stuff

The Lord Chief Justice
Lord Coleridge

Lord Coleridge was the major, permanent judge of the 1880s. He was a well-known Liberal and political lawyer before his elevation to the Bench and was involved in the notorious Tichborne Heir case. *Vanity Fair* was not impressed: 'Lord Coleridge is far too egoistic for a Judge. . . . If nature had intended anyone for anything, it intended the great nephew of Samuel Taylor Coleridge for an actor. . . . He is a wit, and plays to the gallery. He has been known to dine well on a sleep inducing lunch of steak and porter, and nap during cases. . . . He is not so much a profound thinker as a palpable sophist'.

THE BENCH
AND BAR

Caricatures of solicitors, barristers and judges from *Vanity Fair* have become collectors' items among members of the legal profession. Lawyers and judges are reminded of the procedures, traditions, ceremonies and personalities associated with the English common law by these amusing sketches. There were approximately two hundred of them. Some of the most influential jurists and many of the celebrated advocates of the nineteenth century recorded by *Vanity Fair* grace the chambers of attorneys and judges and the walls of their clubs, restaurants and law schools. Their admiration for the English judicial system was shared by Jehu Junior who considered the law to be one of the finest institutions of western society.

Although *Vanity Fair* praised the ideals and principles of English justice, the magazine was quick to point out that the legal system had its deficiencies. Human frailties often marred the more noble aspirations of fairness and objectivity. Nor was *Vanity Fair* overawed by the solemnity of courtroom procedures. On the contrary, for Spy and the other caricaturists, the Bench and Bar were rich sources to mine for the most human traits and foibles. The advocates and judges were prime targets for the caricaturist's sketch pad. Often the subject appeared in *Vanity Fair*, unaware that he had become another 'Man of the Day'.

The seriousness of the courtroom drama was often counterbalanced by the personalities before the Bench or by the judges themselves. The wigs and robes worn by members of the Bench and Bar became props for the caricaturists to accentuate the individual's personality or to enliven the occasion; as, for example, Spy's treatment of Sir Robert Lush during the Tichborne case.

The visual impact of the individual caricature was complemented by Jehu Junior's commentary. If a judge or advocate was hesitant or bumbling, Jehu Junior said so; the inarticulate and slow witted were not spared the sting of *Vanity Fair*'s barbs. When a barrister misbehaved, defended a cause which *Vanity Fair* did not support or was of questionable character, the magazine expressed its disapproval. But a counsel who performed brilliantly was duly praised. Masters of their profession, like Charles Russell, personified the noblest ideals of English law. Since the practice of law was a lucrative profession, *Vanity Fair* harboured no illusions about the amount of money a resourceful advocate could make. References to opulent styles of life let the reader know that fortunes could be amassed before the Bench. Was it not *Vanity Fair*'s task to display all the merchandise?

While *Vanity Fair* was willing to find fault with individual lawyers and judges, it upheld the judicial institution. The magazine considered the judicial process to be a mainstay of life because it helped support the entire structure of civilization. Although it might have its weaker links (personified in less competent counsels and barristers), the law was strong in its total structure and its purpose. *Vanity Fair*'s confidence in the system was reinforced by its assertion that the judges, though differing in ability, were absolutely incorruptible. Therefore, according to *Vanity Fair*, the judicial system, despite its shortcomings, was ultimately one of the saving graces of mankind.

Group caricatures of prominent members of the legal profession were published twice in *Vanity Fair*, in 1891 and 1902. The first, entitled 'Bench and Bar', was the more representative of the judicial world for it included notable judges as well as barristers. In comparison to the other group caricatures featured in *Vanity Fair*, the figures are crowded together, but its density is offset by the colour, by the positioning of the two groups in the foreground anchored by the central figure, the Lord Chancellor, and by the horizontal line of heads in the background.

'Of all the wares and merchandise that are sold in this *Vanity Fair*, there is none more rightly held in high esteem than Justice,' declared Jehu Junior in his opening observations. Though it was expensive, *Vanity Fair* asserted that English justice was unique and famous throughout the world. The system was renowned for its equality and sagacity. Its dispensers and professors could unravel 'intricate matters only less readily than they observe(d) simple issues'. The judges, because they were learned, incorruptible and above temptation, were the 'envy of every other Fair in the world'.

Having praised the institution and its personnel, Jehu Junior set the scene for 'Bench and Bar' and then briefly described each individual in the caricature. The judges and advocates were milling about the Palace of Justice – the Law Courts on the Strand – on the first day of the Michaelmas Term. Most of those gathered in the Central Hall were, according to Jehu Junior, 'ill-favoured, and all of them curiously clad and with uncouth head-gear'. No matter how silly they looked, their accomplishments could not be hidden by wigs and robes.

In the centre, surrounded by the prominent judges and distinguished advocates, stood the Lord Chancellor, 'the Lord High Jobber', whose responsibility it was to 'keep the Queen's conscience'. To the right of the Lord Chancellor was the Lord Chief Justice, Lord Coleridge, flanked by the Attorney-General and the Solicitor-General. The three gazed upon a reconciliation taking place between Sir Charles Russell, 'the greatest, most intolerant and not least conceited of advocates in our times', and Charles Gill. Russell's offering of a pinch of snuff to Gill symbolized their accord. Poor Gill, noted *Vanity Fair*, was subject to Russell's cross-examining eye, like the cat viewing the timorous mouse.

To the Lord Chancellor's left were Lord Esher, Lord Justice Fry, Lord Justice Bowen and Sir Nathaniel Lindlay, each with a high opinion of his own talents and importance. Lord Esher thought that the other judges' remarks, when not in accord with his own, were uncalled for because he viewed himself as a better judge than any who preceded him on the Bench. Lord Justice Fry, a Quaker. was an habitual dissenter in the Court of Appeals and not to be bullied by Lord Esher. Lord Justice Bowen, standing between Esher and Fry, was a popular and learned judge who did not think much of the Master of the Rolls, Lord Esher.

Jehu Junior then described the other judges. Some were comely, others elicited laughter if not ridicule sitting on the Bench. Many were good fellows, well liked by the courts. A few needed more experience but were quickly learning and earning the respect of their peers.

Stuff, the caricaturist, scattered the members of the Bar among the judges and grouped the rest in the background. In the lower right-hand corner he placed Frank Lockwood, amateur caricaturist and Queen's Counsel, admiring his own sketches. Jehu Junior was less deferential to the Bar than to the Bench because these were the yet-to-be-chosen judges. They lacked the aura that went with judges which so impressed *Vanity Fair*. True, some of the advocates were effective speakers in the court; for example Samuel Danks Waddy and Charles Mathews. Others were experts in their fields and most of them had proved their worth before the Bench. Yet, they were not without their faults. Robert Finlay was 'hard-headed' and 'heavy-footed'; Sir Horace Davey the 'worst of political speakers'; and Frederic Inderwick was 'better known by his grin than by his learned works'. All of the Queen's Counsels, observed Jehu Junior, made handsome salaries and kept themselves distant from their clients except when it was time to collect their high fees. Advocates, like judges, had their weaknesses; no one at the Bench and Bar was immune from *Vanity Fair*'s taunts.

The vast majority of the nearly 200 caricatures of advocates and judges which appeared in *Vanity Fair* were drawn by Spy. They constitute some of his most perceptive and humorous work for the magazine, and closely link his name to the extensive collection of legal subjects.

Ward admitted in his autobiography that the Law Courts were ideal 'hunting grounds'. There he did not have to stalk his subjects for he could observe, unnoticed, 'a host of peculiarities and idiosyncrasies'. Spy began caricaturing lawyers and judges immediately upon joining *Vanity Fair* in the spring of 1873 and continued sketching them until late in his career. Through the years Spy was able to maintain a genuine sense of caricature when drawing a judge or advocate, capturing the most subtle characteristics.

Vanity Fair's sceptical admiration for the judicial world and Ward's respectful, but often irreverent sensitivity made for a happy union. The result was a memorable gallery of the most famous Victorian and Edwardian judges and barristers which are highly prized.

Two of Spy's earliest and best caricatures of judges were printed in succession in late May, 1873. They are Sir John Mellor and Sir Robert Lush. Mellor and Lush presided over the celebrated Tichborne claimant case which attracted the attention of the Victorian public for months. Six of the major principals in the trial, including the alleged Sir Roger Tichborne (Arthur Orton?), appeared in *Vanity Fair* (10 June 1871). During the height of the trial, Ward slipped into the courtroom and sketched Mellor and Lush in typical poses which revealed, with a deft touch of humour, their personalities.

SIR JOHN MELLOR (1808–1887), the son of a solicitor, was a student at the Inner Temple and read law in the chambers of the renowned Thomas Chitty before joining the Midland circuit. By 1873, when he sat to 'judge the claimant' in the Tichborne case, he had been knighted. Spy pictured Mellor on the Bench sucking his little finger while watching the proceedings from 'under his heavy-lidded eyes; over which his eyebrows slanted with sudden fine lines to his big nose, while his humorous mouth seemed ready for a wry smile.'

Jehu Junior further described Sir John as 'extremely well-bred, polite and not condescending to his clients'. Mellor was a very private person but highly professional. His patience and thoroughness in the court were emphasized by Jehu Junior's observation that if he were a victim of an unjust accusation 'likely to need an interminable investigation, he would wish for Mellor; but were he a criminal hoping for an escape from the fatigue of the Bench, he could fear no worse.'

Judges the Claimant
The Honourable Sir John Mellor
Judges No. 7
24 May 1873
Spy

111

advocates by his close friend, the prominent barrister and man about town, Montague Williams. Williams, according to Spy, possessed an acute insight into human nature, and he warned Ward not to be misled by a man's physical appearances. The urbane and debonair Williams himself was sketched by Spy (*Vanity Fair*, 1 November 1879).

Following his established habits and taking Williams's advice, Spy caricatured numerous judges and advocates. In addition to Mellor and Lush, three of his most representative caricatures of Sir Robert Walter Carden, Sir Joseph William Chitty and Henry Barton Buckley appeared in *Vanity Fair* over a period of ten years, 1880–1890.

SIR ROBERT WALTER CARDEN (1801–1888) was sketched by Spy for *Vanity Fair* in December 1880. Spy caught the keeper of 'City justice' in a forbidding pose. Carden's keen eyes are fixed on the accused. They are searching out the truth from behind his snow white bushy eyebrows. His full beard and unruly white hair frame a ruddy face dominated by an oversized nose. Carden is visualized as a stern judge who would not tolerate nonsense or histrionics in his courtroom. Justice was to be dispatched quickly and soberly.

According to Jehu Junior, Carden had served in the army, then became a stockbroker and a member of a City Company. Elected Lord Mayor, he was knighted by the Queen for his services. He was a Tory who had gone to considerable length and costs to attain a seat in the House of Commons. Jehu Junior thought him to be 'a very well-meaning old gentleman', but Spy's caricature makes him appear a much sterner character than such a benign summing up would suggest.

SIR JOSEPH WILLIAM CHITTY (1828–1899) appeared in *Vanity Fair* in 1885. Spy, using one of his favorite artistic devices, placed Chitty behind the bench to enhance his importance and power. Chitty is given a dour expression as he peers over his glasses. His thick, downturned lips indicate a sombre man. However, he possessed a droll wit which led him to observe, on one occasion, that 'truth will sometimes leak out even through an affidavit'.

The Judge came from a long line of distinguished lawyers. His father, Thomas Chitty, had many barristers and judges to read in his chambers and to study his tracts on law. The younger Chitty was an excellent student and versatile athlete at Balliol. His interest in racing continued throughout his life, and for nearly a quarter a century he served as umpire at the annual Oxford-Cambridge boat race. Thus, 'the Umpire' decided the fate of races and alleged criminals.

In his court, business progressed rather slowly, reported Jehu Junior. Chitty's tendency to talk with counsel had earned him the title 'Mr Justice Chatty'. After 1885 he continued to serve with distinction in the courts and was elevated to the Court of Appeals in 1897 where he sat for two years before his death in 1899.

Spy's caricature of SIR ROBERT LUSH (1807–1881) appeared the following week. 'A Little Lush,' the caption on this amusing sketch, was derived from a specific incident in which Sir Robert, on being told that the toast 'Women and Wine' was being changed to 'Lush and Shea,' replied: 'A spell of sobriety will do the Bar no harm, and a little Lush may do the Bench some good.' Jehu Junior said Sir Robert was a just, conscientious judge and a good-natured, good-humoured man, always ready for his or anyone else's jokes. As for a jury, Lush left them nothing to say but 'Amen' or to proclaim themselves fools, observed *Vanity Fair*.

Spy thought Justice Lush wore a very odd round wig 'with the suspicion of a dent on the top.' Lush reminded Ward of a 'champagne bottle, with his queerly shaped wig like a cork on his head, and his shoulders sloping down like a bottle.' Spy's treatment of the learned Judge captured this image. He does look like a champagne bottle, about to bubble! It is a humane sketch of a famous Victorian jurist whose career was totally dedicated to law. Lord Westbury wrote of Lush that he is 'a very learned and distinguished man, who so far as I know, has no politics at all.'

Spy's long hours of sitting in the courtroom, absorbing the features, personality and mannerisms of his victim and returning to his studio to complete the caricature, became a set pattern of work. He was also advised on how to evaluate judges and

Alderman Sir Robert Walter Carden KNT, MP
Statesmen No. 348
11 December 1880
Spy

The Umpire
The Honourable Sir Joseph William Chitty
Judges No. 15
28 March 1885
Spy

Company Law
Mr Justice Buckley
Judges No. 55
5 April 1900
Spy

He resisted the temptation to cross-examine a Prince of the Blood   115
Serjeant Ballantine
Men of the Day No. 4
5 March 1870
Atn

Spy, in 1890, made a penetrating sketch of MR JUSTICE
BUCKLEY (1845–1935), 'Company Law'. Henry Barton
Buckley had attended Christ's, Cambridge, and was called to
the Bar in 1869. His early reputation rested on a classic tome on
company law which he had written when a young man. *The
Law and Practice under the Companies Act* was to reach eleven
editions by 1935. He took silk in 1886 and became a bencher in
1891, a year after his appearance in *Vanity Fair*. He went on to a
distinguished career in law, and was raised to the peerage as
Baron Wrenbury in 1915.

According to *Vanity Fair*, Buckley was 'a cold, able,
hardworking Judge whose head is quite clear.' His manner was
'somewhet repellent'; yet, Jehu Junior mused, Buckley had a
soft spot somewhere because, after forty years, he had recently
'wooed and won a charming lady . . .'

Spy pictured Buckley as *Vanity Fair* described him, 'very
solemn'. Again, Spy used the judicial bench and chair to emphasize his victim's severe, forbidding countenance. As
Buckley writes in the ledger, a sense of gravity exudes from the
caricature. His angular face, long nose and sunken cheeks, topped by the white periwig resting on a high forehead, complement Jehu Junior's assessment of Buckley's style and appearance. Perhaps because of his undoubtedly distinguished air,
this caricature today is highly prized among members of the
legal profession.

When WILLIAM BALLANTINE (1812–1887), Serjeant-at-law,
was caricatured by Atn – Alfred Thompson – in March 1870,
he was at the height of his legal career. The son of a magistrate,
he was called to the Bar in 1834. He joined the criminal court
and travelled the home circuit which included the counties of
Hertfordshire, Essex, Sussex, Kent and Surrey. When a young
man, he haunted London's literary taverns and met many writers, including Dickens, Thackeray and Trollope (see p. 81).
In the late 1840s, Ballantine became involved in several
famous cases in which he displayed his effectiveness as a
cross-examiner. In 1856, he received the coif or white cap of a
serjeant-at-law. Ballantine was one of the last serjeants in the
courts, since this title and function was abolished in the judicial
reforms of the 1870s. During the 1860s, he continued to win
(and to lose) many well-publicized cases, and at the end of the
decade, he served as counsel for Lord Mordaunt in the notorious divorce suit against Lady Mordaunt.

Lord Mordaunt had filed for divorce after his attractive
young wife, Harriet, had informed him that he was not the
father of her child. Indeed, she confessed that she had committed adultery with several men, including the Prince of Wales,
'often, and in open day'.

Lady Mordaunt's sensational disclosures made it likely that
the Prince of Wales would be summoned to the trial. Although
he could be subpoenaed as a witness, he could not be compelled

to testify. The Queen advised him not to appear in court. However, he did appear and agreed to be questioned. The delicate probing by the Queen's counsel left the Prince's honour publicly unimpugned. The Prince denied that 'any improper familiarity or criminal act' had occurred between Lady Mordaunt and himself.

When Serjeant Ballantine, as counsel for the plaintiff, Lord Mordaunt, was allowed to cross-examine the witness, he declared that he had no questions for his Royal Highness. Deference to the Crown was maintained, although everyone familiar with the trial knew that the Prince had perjured himself. The case dragged on. Eventually Ballantine lost because he failed to convince the court that Lady Mordaunt was guilty.

Ballantine earned Jehu Junior's plaudits for his 'tact' in refusing to question the Prince. Jehu Junior, while recognizing Ballantine's reputation as a thorough and often merciless cross-examiner, explained that the 'peculiar circumstances of the case' had resulted in Ballantine's 'want of success'. Although he had not won, Ballantine's reputation remained high, for he was still a 'terror to witnesses'. This bit of praise for the Serjeant was a rationale to cover up a hypocritial act. Bowles's admiration for the man who respected the Crown and who upheld its position despite the glaring publicity of a sensational trial was not, after all, supportive of an equitable judicial system. Bowles and Ballantine, unwittingly or not, had conspired to protect the Prince.

After the Mordaunt case, Ballantine participated in other famous trials. In 1875 he successfully defended the Geakwar of Baroda against an accusation of attempting to poison the British Resident. His cross-examination of one of the key witnesses is still considered a masterpiece.

In the early 1880s, Ballantine retired as an advocate, to write and travel until his death in 1887. His interest in the theatre and journalism made him a well-known figure. He probably was well acquainted with Thomas Gibson Bowles and Alfred Thompson, the costume designer and playwright who caricatured him for *Vanity Fair*. The subject's craggy features are emphasized and the wig adds its usual comical effect, but otherwise the sketch is hardly a caricature.

Although he was recognized as a very skilful cross-examiner who could penetrate the motives of criminals, he was not considered a model legal mind. According to the *Law Times* Ballantine 'left behind him scarcely any lesson, even in his own poor biography, which the rising generation could profitably learn.'

Spy sketched barristers as well as judges. Their gestures, personalities and attire made them likely candidates for Ward and throughout the pages of *Vanity Fair* appeared some of the most well known barristers of the day. Two of these were 'Jumbo', Samuel Pope, in 1885, and 'Slim', Horace Avory, in 1904.

HORACE AVORY, 'Slim' (1857–1935), was sketched by Spy for *Vanity Fair* in early June 1904. Avory's thin body is swallowed up under his gown; his diminutive, delicate facial features and elongated neck are protected by a wig which rests uneasily on his small head. Bracing himself against the desk with his hands, Avory leans forward listening intently to the elders from the Bench.

From his birth, argued Jehu Junior, Avory had been destined to be a criminal lawyer. His family had been associated with the Old Bailey for years. Legend had it that his nurse foresaw his legal future in the 'infantile gravity of his demeanour, a gravity that was eminently judicial'. After rowing at Cambridge, he

plunged into his profession with 'hereditary zeal'. He was now a great authority on crime whose courtroom style made him thorough but dull. Although he was neither an orator nor a maker of epigrams, he did possess flashes of wit. His career was boosted by several famous cases, where he served as counsel for the prosecution: the Jameson Raid trial and the Liberator frauds. The Liberator frauds case, in 1893, grew out of a financial scandal brought on by the failure of a group of companies that caused widespread panic in the financial world. *Vanity Fair* remarked that Avory's wiry frame made him look under forty, even though he was over fifty. The magazine's prediction that this clever, shrewd advocate was destined someday to be a judge came true in 1910. He was made a senior judge of the King's Bench division in 1923 and served until his death in 1935.

The stout advocate, SAMUEL POPE (1826–1901) was a prime target for Spy. Ward caught Pope arguing a point of law, his pudgy hand and fingers reaching out to emphasize the legal complexities of his position. The rotund body is accentuated by the full, flowing robe. Pope's face, with its heavy jowls and double chin bulging from a stiff collar, is made more ludicrous by his small periwig with its dangling tail.

Jehu Junior identified Pope as an Irishman by race, brogue and humour who had been born so long ago that the event had 'by common consent' been forgotten. Actually Pope was born

Jumbo
Mr Samuel Pope QC
Men of the Day No. 346
12 December 1885
Spy

A Splendid Advocate
Mr Charles Russell QC, MP
Statesmen No. 421
5 May 1883
Ver

117

in Manchester in 1826 and studied in London where, in 1858, he was called to the Bar. Always interested in politics, Pope contested unsuccessfully for the House of Commons in 1859, 1865 and 1868. He practised in Manchester until 1865 when he moved to London where he devoted himself to parliamentary practice and, at the time of his death, was leader of the parliamentary bar. His ability to present complicated facts, as Spy caught in his caricature, made Pope a very prosperous advocate. He was kept busy in the United Kingdom Alliance and the temperance movement. However, Jehu Junior pointed out, Pope was not a teetotaller. A rich, vulgar, effective humour made him good tempered and persuasive. Spy left us a caricature which supports *Vanity Fair*'s opinion that Pope was a 'good fellow of the Irish variety'.

CHARLES RUSSELL (1832–1900), the Irish barrister who rose to become Lord Chief Justice of England, had such a long, illustrious and lucrative career that he was featured twice in *Vanity Fair*, in 1883 and 1890. Francois Verheyden, the Belgian sculptor, sketched the first; 'Quiz' or John Page Mellor, the lawyer, submitted the second caricature. Both men produced character portraits rather than caricatures; however, Verheyden tells us a little more about Russell than does Mellor. Verheyden has portrayed a determined, confident counsel pressing his argument – but nothing is revealed of Russell's human side.

Verheyden's benign if not flattering sketch reflected the respect given to Russell by the public and by *Vanity Fair*. Despite *Vanity Fair*'s hostility towards Irish Home Rule which Russell supported, the magazine recognized this extraordinary man's talents in the courtroom. He was the most effective advocate of his generation. Russell possessed the ability to convey his deepest emotions and to ferret out the truth from a witness while holding the court spellbound. Moreover, he was as thorough in his preparation and research as he was skilful in his presentation. After a highly successful and profitable law practice in Ireland and England, he became a Liberal MP, represented his Government on several important commissions, and ended his career as one of the most distinguished and respected members of the legal profession in the nineteenth century.

Russell was reared by a mother whose devotion to Catholicism and education instilled in him a respect for both. He was trained in law in Ireland where he won several important, highly publicized cases early in his career; but his heart was set on becoming a barrister in London. In 1856 he arrived in London and soon became a pupil of Henry Bagshawe who described the young Irishman as 'grave, reserved and hard-working'. Taking advantage of the increased number of teachers appointed to the Inns of Court, Russell read under these men and prepared himself for the Bar, specializing in the fields of equity and constitutional law. Meanwhile, he contributed articles to newspapers and magazines and wrote a weekly column for the Dublin *Nation*. Called to the Bar in 1859, he quickly established his reputation as a forceful and well prepared barrister. In 1872 he took silk. In 1880 Russell was elected to Parliament as a Liberal. By 1884 he had become a supporter of Home Rule for Ireland.

When Russell appeared in *Vanity Fair* in 1883 he stood on the threshold of his political career. Jehu Junior recognized him as 'indisputably the foremost advocate of the English Bar'. Given Thomas Gibson Bowles's dislike of the Irish, Russell was generously described as a man of 'extraordinary abilities' who possessed 'all the brilliant qualities and discloses none of the countervailing defects that we are accustomed to recognize in the very best kind of Irishman.' Russell was a 'marvel' in court with his clear resonant voice, his grand presence and commanding powers. He was a 'giant among pigmies' rather than a competitor among equals, declared Jehu Junior. While Russell was a terrible adversary, he was congenial in company, gregarious and 'a most rare and brilliant companion'. Similar accolades followed Russell throughout his life – in the House of Commons, in the courtroom, as Attorney General, as an international arbitrator, and finally, as Lord Chief Justice – until his death in 1900.

GEORGINA WELDON (1837-1914) repudiates our often stereotyped view of Victorian ladies. She and others like her are causing us to reassess our opinions about the role and impact of women in the nineteenth century. Her life demonstrates that respectability and decorum, mixed with determination and skill, can change attitudes and customs. In her struggle to bring about these transformations she foreshadows her more liberated sisters of the modern world. *Vanity Fair* observed with sublime patronage that Mrs Weldon was not like other women because she possessed an 'indomitable courage, a marvellous energy and an incredible activity and industry . . .'

This remarkable woman was born into an upper-middle-class Victorian family. Her father was a barrister, but, being independently wealthy, devoted his time to politics and farming. She spent much of her youth in Europe, living in Florence and Brussels and being pursued by her many admirers. Her beauty inspired G. F. Watts (*Vanity Fair*, 26 December 1891) to paint her in 1857, at about the same time she was presented to Queen Victoria. A year later, in 1858, she met Harry Weldon, an unambitious and dissolute young man whom she decided to marry. She got her way in 1860 and although they were happy during the first few years of their marriage, their relationship was doomed to fail because of their conflicting personalities and values. Weldon had inherited her father's Puritanical streak which blended with her own courage, curiosity, amibition, affection for animals and humans to form a romantic and ingenuous spirit.

A pretty face, soft blue eyes, fair complexion and pleasing manner won Weldon many friends. Her good looks, which Spy portrayed so well, were matched by a melodic voice that became her entrée into the circles of proper Victorian homes. She enjoyed being part of the London Season and during the mid-1860s was the toast of Victorian Society. However, by the end of the decade her life had begun to change: her father died, she suffered a miscarriage and marital problems surfaced.

In early 1871 Georgina Weldon met Gounod (*Vanity Fair*, 1 February 1879), and for the next several years her life evolved around the career of one of France's most celebrated composers. Before their paths crossed, she had already established a music school at her London residence, Tavistock House. In Gounod she beheld the person who would bring prestige to her enterprise. Likewise, Gounod needed someone to manage his life and affairs. They seemed destined for each other, and for over two years he lived at her home. Tavistock House became a training school for young vocalists, a haven for orphans, a beacon for musicians and a source for scandal. In June 1874 Gounod left the Weldons and England under a cloud of ill feeling. Meanwhile, Georgina's marriage continued to disintegrate, and she and her husband agreed to a separation. By Victorian standards, she stood alone and as a helpless and disgraced woman.

She was now forced to try other means to make a living. The orphanage for the homeless but talented children was kept open. In order to raise money, she decided to carry her wards on a world tour but they got no farther than France. On returning home she discovered that all of her belongings were being removed from Tavistock House. A more immediate personal danger threatened when her husband tried to have her committed to an asylum. She escaped her captors by running away from her house and sought refuge among friends.

This episode marked another turning point in her life that would eventually bring her fame in the law courts. Meanwhile she managed to continue a musical career which was marred by uneven performances and mixed reviews. In the early 1880s, as a result of a difference of opinion with her impresario she was sued for libel and sentenced to four months in Newgate, where, according to *Vanity Fair*, she spent her time 'mending the linen of the establishment'.

Weldon's imprisonment convinced her that she, as a woman, was a victim of unjust laws and she came to see herself as 'a martyr of the Lunacy Laws, the Libel Laws and the Marriage Laws'. By 1882 Weldon was determined to test the laws and attitudes of Victorian England regarding private asylums and marriage contracts. The passage of the Married Women's Property Act of 1882 provided her with the legal grounds she needed to file a civil action without her husband's consent. She proceeded to sue the owner of the private asylum, Dr Forbes Winslow, and her husband as a co-conspirator of the 'Mad Doctors' who had attempted to incarcerate her. The case began in March 1882 and Weldon served as her own lawyer. She did not win, but her reputation was established as a shrewd and clever examiner who refused to be intimidated by judges and solicitors. Overnight, she became the darling of the press and public.

When Mrs Weldon appeared in *Vanity Fair* on 3 May 1884, she was entering into her next famous law suit. The caricature shows her holding the papers of her earlier trial, Weldon v Winslow. Now, in 1884, she sued Dr Semple, the doctor Winslow had hired to certify her insanity. She won this case and was awarded £1000 plus £20 for trespass. Grierson, her biographer, asserted that the Semple case 'confirmed Georgina's position as the most admired badgerer of lawyers since the death of Dickens . . .' She went on to win several other cases and to earn rightfully the title *Vanity Fair* bestowed upon her, 'the new Portia'. While performing in the courts, she continued to publish music, write books and pamphlets, operate a newspaper and perform in music halls. Weldon became more deeply involved in spiritualism during these years and also found time to take up the causes of the Salvation Army and Charles Bradlaugh (*Vanity Fair*, 12 June 1880).

In 1885 Weldon lost her second case against her impresario and was sentenced to six months in prison. This term in prison

Mrs Weldon
Mrs Georgina Weldon
Ladies No. 10
3 May 1884
Spy

119

brought her more public attention. Life in confinement she found not at all inhibiting, for she busied herself in various activities and made many new friends. While in Holloway Gaol her case against her old friend, Gounod, was won by her advocates. When she was released she was given a public reception organized by none other than Drs Winslow and Semple.

As a result of her sometimes sensational and sometimes even comic efforts in the law courts, Lunacy reform was started, the Court of Criminal Appeal was established and women's rights were re-examined. Although her days in court were over after 1885, she remained in the public eye through her acting career, and as the model for the Pear's Soap advertisement. By the mid 1890s she withdrew from public life and moved to France. In 1905 she returned to England to spend the remainder of her days among old friends and admirers, until her death in early 1914.

CLERGY
AND DONS

As part of the Establishment, clergymen and dons were ready victims for *Vanity Fair*. They occupied important and influential positions in society, and many clergymen were prominent in public life. Spy implies in his autobiography that they, like judges, were prime candidates in their academic garb or vestments. Because some of them, especially the Dons and Fellows, were rather eccentric in their manners or dress, their distinctive personalities easily lent themselves to some amusing caricatures.

Dons and teachers proved especially popular in *Vanity Fair*, since the readers of the magazine often remembered them from their days at Eton, Harrow or Winchester, and Oxford or Cambridge. Among those included in *Vanity Fair* were Robinson Ellis (*Vanity Fair*, 24 May 1894) the classical scholar; Edward Laird (*Vanity Fair*, 4 April 1895), former student of Jowett and later his successor at Balliol; Max Müller (*Vanity Fair*. 6 February 1875), renowned philologist and student of Oriental mythology; and the Reverend Lionel Ford (*Vanity Fair*, 1 May 1912), of Harrow.

Clergymen were more in the public eye than Headmasters and Dons; many of them, especially the Archbishops, Bishops and popular preachers, were featured regularly in *Vanity Fair*. Describing the clergy gave Jehu Junior the opportunity to express the magazine's views on current religious issues, such as the Oxford Movement, rights of Dissenters, policy in the Church of England and the debates raging in the Roman Catholic Church. Generally speaking, *Vanity Fair* was opposed to change in the Church of England, but quickly pointed out the Established Church's weaknesses and called for reform where the magazine thought it was needed.

Over one hundred leaders of various denominations and faiths appeared in the pages of *Vanity Fair*. Among the Roman Catholics, Popes headed the list. They included Pius IX (*Vanity Fair*, 1 January 1870), Leo XIII (*Vanity Fair*, 18 May 1878) and Pius X (*Vanity Fair*, 10 December 1903). Among the Dissenters featured were the Reverend Thomas Binney (*Vanity Fair*, 12 October 1872) and the Quaker, Joseph Sturge (*Vanity Fair*, 20 November 1886). The largest group, of course, consisted of the Archbishops, Bishops and clergymen of the Church of England. Several Archbishops of Canterbury were victims; one of the best is Spy's caricature of Archbishop Temple (*Vanity Fair*, 11 September 1902). The Bishops of Oxford (*Vanity Fair*, 24 July 1869), Ripon (*Vanity Fair*, 8 March 1906), Winchester (*Vanity Fair*, 19 December 1901), Peterborough (*Vanity Fair*, 3 July 1869) and, twice, York (*Vanity Fair*, 24 June 1871, 5 September 1891) were also included. Perhaps the most startling pose of a Bishop was struck by the Bishop of London, Bishop Ingram (*Vanity Fair*, 22 April 1897), tennis racket in hand, delivering a vigorous forehand!

Tracts for the Times
The Reverend John Henry Newman
Men of the Day No. 145
20 January 1877
Spy

For *Vanity Fair* the Church of England was an integral part of the foundation of civilization. Along with the Queen, the Bench and Bar, the Empire, the Royal Navy and the Army, it stood as a bulwark against the rising tides of barbarism. The magazine, however, recognized that like the other institutions of society, the Church was being buffeted by social, economic, political and intellectual upheavals which caused numerous crises within the organization. Church leaders, confronted by pressures for change, either called for modernization of the Church or looked to the past for guidance. While some members supported programmes of social justice and accepted the implications of scientific discoveries, others felt that the Church should combat scientific secularism and remain aloof from the problems of society. This stance against industrialism and rationalism manifested itself, in varying degrees, first in the Oxford Movement and, second, in the conversion of some Anglican leaders to Roman Catholicism.

By the time the proponents of the Oxford Movement and neo-Catholicism appeared in *Vanity Fair* in the 1870s, the Movement had run its course, the heated debates had cooled and the Church of England had accepted the secessions of Manning and Newman. Indeed, when Newman, Pusey and Manning were featured in the magazine they were old men whose influence was waning. Nonetheless, *Vanity Fair* acknowledged their impact on Anglicanism and Roman Catholicism and the contributions they had made during a turbulent time in the history of the Church of England.

JOHN HENRY NEWMAN (1801–1890) entered Trinity College, Oxford in 1817 and remained there as a tutor at Oriel where he became associated with Edward Pusey, John Keble and R. H. Froude, the future leaders of the Oxford Movement. From 1828 to 1843 Newman was vicar of St Mary's, the university church. The series of sermons he preached while at St. Mary's was possibly as influential a part of the Movement as the Tracts themselves. During this time he read extensively in church doctrine, helped launch the Oxford Movement, published poems and books and wrote some of the more important of the *Tracts for the Times*, the major statement of the Movement.
Newman's Tract 90 (1841), the most famous of them, asserted that the Thirty-Nine Articles of the Anglican Church were Catholic in spirit and intent. It created a storm of protest and set him on his road to Roman Catholicism. *Vanity Fair* asserted that Newman, in his essay, 'blew a blast which shook the whole fabric of the Church to its foundations'. Newman's Tracts, which *Vanity Fair* described as 'profound learning' couched in 'marvellous eloquence', had been attacked by 'puny theologians' and Bishops who eventually drove him out of the Church in 1845. Anglicans and Catholics clearly understood the importance of Newman's conversion; Disraeli remarked that the Church never recovered from this crushing blow. The magazine pointed out that Newman had not found a 'rest' or 'acceptance' in Catholicism because the Roman Catholic Church hierarchy constrained him as much as that of the Church of England. His years as Rector of the new Roman Catholic University of Dublin ended in his resignation; his commentaries on the Douay version of the Bible were denied publication; his establishment of a seminary in Birmingham was denounced by his superiors. *Vanity Fair* felt that because of these differences of opinions and because of Newman's attack on some of the supporters of Papal infallibility (he personally upheld the doctrine), Newman, were he a younger man, might well revert back to the Church of England. The magazine, in conclusion, praised the 'great purity

and moral robustness of his character, the breadth of his intellectual grasp, and the acuteness of his perception . . .' which had made him one of 'the most subtle and delicately shaded' theologians for centuries.

This 'delicately shaded' genius was effectively caricatured by Spy. Newman's physical features are clearly accentuated – the large nose, small mouth, drooping shoulders. The umbrella and hat, clutched in front, are effective props. Ward's treatment of clerics, like that of lawyers, was incisive. He did not overrate them.

Ape caricatured the REVEREND EDWARD PUSEY (1800–1882) three years before Spy drew Newman. By 1875 Pusey was seventy-five years old; the once rebellious professor who had been suspended for three years from preaching at Oxford on charges of heresy was now in his declining years. Ape was kind to Pusey. Pellegrini has given him a doleful countenance; his heavy eyes look back upon a lifetime of struggles, debates and controversies. Always somewhat a recluse, Pusey was not naturally a public figure, and Ape has evoked that side of the man.

Vanity Fair summarized Pusey's education at Oxford and at several German universities where he was exposed to the schools of Higher Criticism and German Rationalism. At twenty-eight he was named Regius Professor of Hebrew and became, according to *Vanity Fair*, the 'most prominent apostle'

High Church
The Reverend Edward Bouverie Pusey, DD
Men of the Day No. 95
2 January 1875
Ape

The Next Pope
Archbishop Manning
Men of the Day No. 20
25 February 1871
Ape

123

of the Oxford Movement and its most powerful exponent because he never 'openly deserted to the enemy'. After Newman and Manning left the Church, Pusey and Keble became the chief spokesmen for the Movement and Pusey's influence at Oxford flourished. Indeed, Pusey struggled to reassure followers of the Movement who had been shattered by these defections. However, he lacked the dynamic qualities of leadership, and *Vanity Fair* observed that he spent most of his time in 'an inaccessible study in company with a crucifix . . . and the heaviest works that theology has produced.' Yet, to his credit, which *Vanity Fair* recognized, Pusey stood up for his beliefs and defended those whom he felt were unjustly accused in public controversies. The magazine was convinced that if Pusey had lived during the Middle Ages he would have been rewarded a 'Doctorate and crowned . . . with a chaplet of latinized superlatives . . .', but could not resist ending its comments tongue-in-cheek, remarking that the 'most astounding fact' about Dr Pusey was 'that he did marry'.

Lytton Strachey in his *Eminent Victorians* observed that the Middle Ages lived again in HENRY MANNING (1808–1892). While *Vanity Fair* did not place Manning in the Middle Ages, as it had Pusey, the magazine, nonetheless, associated Manning with the medieval world. He was, to *Vanity Fair*, a 'spare, spiritual, intellectual, elegant ascetic . . .' To have lost a person

of Manning's talents to Roman Catholicism was 'one of the most discouraging of all the discouraging facts that surround modern Protestantism in England', lamented Jehu Junior. And this at a time when 'any one faith is too commonly regarded as being as good as any other' was offered by Jehu Junior as proof of Manning's earnestness and sincerity.

Henry Manning had been educated at Oxford, and although not directly associated with the Oxford Movement, became identified with the stresses and strains being placed upon the Church of England during the 1830–1850 decades. After serving as Archdeacon of Chichester from 1840 to 1851, he converted to Roman Catholicism. In 1865 he was appointed Archbishop of Westminster, the position he held when he appeared in *Vanity Fair*. The magazine observed that Manning had passed through all the honours that the Roman Catholic Church 'assumes to bestow in England' and he had been duly appreciated and rewarded. He might 'probably be the next Pope – should there be a next', concluded Jehu Junior. Manning, of course, never became Pope; he was appointed Cardinal in 1875 and spent the remainder of his life writing books and pamphlets, crusading against alcohol, serving on commissions to aid the poor and intervening in labour disputes. He was actively involved in the famous dock strike of 1889.

Ape's caricature of Manning is harsh, though respectful. Manning's stern and dour presence is clearly depicted. His refined features, beak nose and sharp chin are well done. His characteristic high forehead has been covered by his hat. The caricature reveals Manning's ascetic style of life. Ape agrees more with Strachey than with Jehu Junior; he has put his victim back in the Middle Ages.

Rabbi Adler and General Booth represent opposite ends of the religious spectrum: the former a cultivated, cultured leader, driven by a social conscience and respect for learning, who worked within the Establishment; the latter, an uneducated, passionate nonconformist, spurred on by his desire to save souls and eradicate poverty through zeal, fervour and a touch of showmanship. They both personify changes within the religious life of nineteenth-century Britain, which included an increasing acceptance of Jews into the social order and a rising sense of social justice. They came to represent the widening of the social system and the deepening of class conflict.

When RABBI ADLER (1839–1911) was sketched by Spy in 1907, he had been Chief Rabbi in London for ten years. Ward, in *Forty Years of Spy*, records that he went to the Rabbi's home to draw his subject. While there Rabbi Adler's daughters came into the room, peeped at the caricature and exclaimed that it looked just like their father, to which he, in mock anger, re-

plied: 'How dare you! I'll cut you both out of my will.' The Rabbi certainly could not have been upset by Spy's interpretation, for the caricature is mild and inoffensive. No physical feature is emphasized at the expense of another – head and body are correctly proportioned; the attire lends dignity, not ridicule, to the subject. We observe a quiet, composed, earnest individual before us. Peering out over his glasses, the Rabbi looks like a pleasant man worthy of his office and the honours bestowed upon him.

Jehu Junior, likewise, is respectful, if mildly condescending, of Adler. The Chief Rabbi of the United Hebrew Congregations of the British Empire was the 'greatest Jew Minister in the world . . .' His education, scholarly publications and social commitment had made him a popular and influential person. He could claim as his friends and admirers Cardinal Manning, Joseph Chamberlain and the Lord Mayor of London. He had gained a reputation outside Jewish circles for his tact, culture and committee work. The Rabbi had been able to bridge the gap between Gentile and Jew, serving as the Vice-President of the Anglo-Jewish Association and being received into the Athenaeum Club in 1900. Later he was awarded the CVO from Edward VII. Jehu Junior admired the Rabbi, praised his contributions to society and education and, by implication, took great delight in seeing an outsider make his mark within the system and be rewarded for his efforts.

Twenty-two years before Spy caricatured Rabbi Adler, he sketched a much more revealing work of 'GENERAL' WILLIAM BOOTH (1829–1912), the founder of the Salvation Army. The angular body, folded arms, bony hands, craggy features, hawk nose, stringy beard and tousled hair reveal a man who cared not a whit for his physical appearance. The crows' feet and dark recesses circling the eyes tell us more about Booth: a childhood of want and and degradation, his early struggle to keep body and soul together working in a pawnbroker's shop, his increasing sensitivity to poverty, his commitment to the downtrodden, his zeal of religious conviction, his imperviousness to ridicule and his dedication to long hours of endless labour. Unlike Adler, Booth was neither born to nor blessed by fortune.

William Booth's formal education was meagre. Growing up in squalor in Nottingham left him with a sense of bitterness and determination to improve the lot of the worker which remained with him all his life. His poverty and disillusionment cut him adrift from the Church of England and diverted him towards the Methodist movement. He supported the Chartists in the 1840s and might well have become a political radical except for his deep religious belief and burden of conscience. After his conversion to Methodism in 1844, he became a street revivalist in Nottingham. In 1849 he went to London and when not working at the pawnbroker's shop, devoted himself to church activities. Eventually, through members of the Church, he met his future wife, Catherine Mumford, an invalid who was the antithesis of Booth – cultured, refined and restrained. They were married in 1855. Six years later, disappointed with Methodism and unable to achieve his goals, Booth broke with the Church and launched his own revival movement. He established a mission in Whitechapel that was to become the genesis and eventual headquarters of the Salvation Army.

By the time he appeared in *Vanity Fair*, in 1882, he had become the subject of both calumny and praise. The magazine reported that the Salvation Army, only four years after its creation, had grown to 740 paid officers. Booth, declared Jehu Junior, had managed to make himself 'an absolute ruler' who

The Salvation Army
'General' (William) Booth
Men of the Day No. 267
25 November 1882
Spy

Fearless but Intemperate
The Reverend R. J. Campbell
Men of the Day 940
24 November 1904
Spy

125

advised his subordinates to 'Excite your audience, and look after the collection.' Such a 'simple and beautiful principle' had had good results so far. If Booth's dream of the future were to come true, if the British workman engaged in manly toil all day and divided his evenings between 'out-door pedestrianism and in-door convalescing', then the nation's manners, predicted Jehu Junior, would be sweetened and the brewers be injured. In conclusion, *Vanity Fair* attested that Booth interpreted the Gospels in an 'airy and gamesome way'. Indeed, he did have a touch of commercialism in his sermons and his organization. But because of his zeal and dedication, he saw nothing evil in employing such techniques to achieve his ends of eradicating poverty and saving souls. Such mild criticisms from Jehu Junior would hardly hinder a man of Booth's perserverance who replied to the charges levelled against him by T. H. Huxley (see p. 151), convinced Cecil Rhodes (p. 143) to pray on his knees in a railway carriage and who, as his biographer Begbie stated, 'unroofed the slum to Victorian respectability'.

The REVEREND REGINALD J. CAMPBELL (1867–1956) was born the son of a Methodist minister, of a long line of Ulster Protestants. He lived in Ireland and England in his youth, receiving a private education before attending Christ Church, Oxford where he graduated with Honours. In 1895 he entered into the Congregational Ministry and became a very popular preacher in

Brighton. From there he moved to London in 1903 as Minister of the City Temple. Here he quickly established a local following and national reputation by embroiling himself in current issues, taking on the London newspapers and delivering direct and persuasive sermons. This 'grey-haired boy with mesmeric eyes, a musical voice, and a mission in his soul', as *Vanity Fair* described him, became so famous that his likeness was sold on postcards along with actresses and other celebrities of the early Edwardian era. Later he was to be ordained in the Church of England, become a prolific writer, and, for years, be associated with Chichester Cathedral. But in 1904 he was the toast of an adoring public.

Vanity Fair could hardly pass up the opportunity to feature the Reverend when he was at his height of popularity. Jehu Junior liked the man. He found him engaging, effective and honest. Reverend Campbell had not been afraid to speak his own mind. He had assailed 'scamped work' and gambling among the British working class, much to the horror of the Radical Nonconformists. But he had held firm and withstood their attacks, noted *Vanity Fair*. The magazine asserted that Campbell was an intelligent preacher, remarked on his many publications and commented on his appearance – a neatly dressed man but one who obviously did not 'bore his barber'.

Spy's caricature of Campbell is the final product of his numerous visits to the City Temple. Ward made several prelimi-

126

I felt very uncomfortable
Mrs Star, Late Mother Superior of the Convent of Our Lady of Mercy at Hull
People of the Day No. 1
20 February 1869
Ape

nary drawings before deciding upon the one he picked for *Vanity Fair*. Spy says that he found it difficult to capture Campbell's personality because of his constant gesturing. However, as Campbell worked himself up in his sermon he tended to project over the pulpit like a gargoyle, Ward noted. It was this pose that Spy caught. Some time after Campbell appeared in *Vanity Fair*, he met Ward at a luncheon where he told Spy that he had 'hit him rather hard'. When they parted, Campbell warned Spy that if he caricatured him again, he expected to be treated more gently. Whether Campbell can be compared to a gargoyle or to a bowsprit, he closely resembles, in mannerism and physical appearance, one of today's popular and forceful evangelists, Billy Graham. Indeed, the thrust of Campbell's jaw and his flowing hair would be an effective 'image' for the television generation.

Why did *Vanity Fair* feature a nun among its famous victims? What had she done to earn the distinction, after Disraeli, Gladstone and Bright, to be the fourth individual caricatured in the magazine? What attracted Bowles and Pellegrini to MRS STAR?

Mrs Star played a central role in Saurin *v* Star, one of the most sensational trials of the Victorian era. Her testimony inflamed anti-Catholicism, stimulated the perverse corners of Victorian minds and has left us with another example of Victorian voyeurism. As *The Times* (4 February 1869) predicted, it turned out to be a 'very remarkable case' that was bound 'to excite an unusual degree of public interest'. The trial possessed all the ingredients a curious populace could desire: an exposé of life inside the walls of a convent; the disclosures of politics and personalities hidden behind the nun's habit and priest's collar; a revelation of the rules, policies and punishments which seemed to destroy a sister's character rather than strengthen her soul. On 6 February 1869, *The Eastern Morning News and Hull Advertiser* echoed the opinion of many of its readers when it observed that a young girl 'would do well to pause' before entering a convent if the testimony given in the court was indicative of how she would be treated.

The case, heard before a special jury of the Queen's Bench, resulted from a suit filed by Miss Saurin, a former member of the Sisters of Mercy, against Mrs Star and other Superiors of Our Lady of Mercy Convent in Hull. Miss Saurin charged that Mrs Star and her staff had conspired to drive her out of the convent and had deliberately falsified evidence before a church commission and the Bishop to have her expelled. She was asking for compensation of £5000 for damages to her reputation and character. Saurin was represented by the Solicitor-General, Sir John Coleridge (*Vanity Fair*, 30 April 1870) and his legal staff. The counsels for the defence were Henry Hawkins (*Vanity Fair*, 21 June 1873), George Mellish (*Vanity Fair*, 30 December 1876) and Charles Russell (*Vanity Fair*, 5 May 1883 and 29 March 1890). The Lord Chief Justice, Sir Alexander Cockburn (*Vanity Fair*, 11 December 1869) presided.

The daily press accounts heightened the drama. Every day the courtroom was packed. Each morning crowds gathered outside Westminster Hall to queue for a seat. Large groups of nuns and priests were conspicuous in the courtroom. Solicitors, attracted to the case, were often spotted among the spectators. The packed court listened to the testimony of both parties, followed the cross-examinations and were stirred by the counsels' closing pleas.

The public was titillated, shocked and entertained by this fascinating trial. Critics of Roman Catholicism had their suspi-

cions confirmed, while the faithful suffered another attack on their beliefs and practices. Guests at fashionable dinner parties, members of the clubs, pub dwellers and back yard gossips fed their conversations with titbits of hearsay and rumour.

Vanity Fair was quick to take advantage of the publicity given to the trial. In its commentary which accompanied the caricature, the magazine printed extracts of Mrs Star's testimony. Bowles did this to protect himself against libel and to conform to the laws. Mrs Star's revealing, salacious comments still evoke a sense of the trial's excitement. Mrs Star, according to *Vanity Fair*, had known Miss Saurin for some length of time; reports concerning Miss Saurin's behaviour had come to her in recent years; these reports, she admitted, had been destroyed since 'action was commenced' against the plaintiff. Mrs Star, during the cross-examination, replied several times that in regard to certain details she could not remember or did not know. Mrs Star, it was revealed in *Vanity Fair*, had spoken to Miss Saurin about the tone of her letters to relatives which were, in Star's opinion, 'too tender and affectionate'. She felt a letter addressed 'My ever dearest uncle' was 'deemed excessive in affection.' As to Miss Saurin's behaviour, Mrs Star had 'perceived a great forwardness in Sister Mary Scholastica's [Miss Saurin's] conduct with regard to one of the priests at Hull . . .'. The Mother Superior denied that she was accusing Miss Saurin of doing anything wrong, but she had a 'feeling' that 'all

The Infallible
Pius IX
Sovereigns No. 6
1 January 1870
Coide

127

was not right on her [Miss Saurin's] side'. The priest, according to Mrs Star, had been 'completely deceived' about Miss Saurin's real character and for him to have spoken of her as a 'saint of the community' made Mrs Star feel 'very uncomfortable'.

Other papers printed Mrs Star's testimony in greater detail. Witnesses against Miss Saurin accused her of exhibiting many worldly interests, in particular her fondness for clothes; of wandering about the convent late at night; of being unwilling to teach the children at the convent's school; of stealing the children's food; of eating strawberries and cream in the pantry. To pay for these, and many other sins, she had to make public confessions; she was forced to undress in front of Mrs Star and her assistants; she was ordered to turn over to the convent some of her clothes and was issued leaky boots to wear; she was given unsavoury, if not spoiled, mutton; she was deprived of her straw mattress; she was ordered to wear a duster on her head after she had not properly cleaned the rooms. Miss Saurin was kept under surveillance. Her cell was secured with a latch string to alert other sisters of her nightly wanderings; and her mail was withheld, read and censored.

Disciplinary action taken from 1861 to 1865 seemed to have had no effect on her, according to the defendants. Consequently, the head of the convent and her advisers had appealed to the Bishop to name a special commission to investigate the situation and to call for her dismissal. After the hearing, the commission decided to expel Miss Saurin. Now, four years later, in February 1869, Mrs Star and her staff were being sued by Miss Saurin.

By the end of February the trial was drawing to a close. On 26 February the Lord Chief Justice instructed the jury to render its verdict. Within an hour they had decided in favour of the plaintiff on the two counts of libel and conspiracy. She was awarded £500. The crowd outside the courtroom, upon hearing the decision, cheered loudly. The trial had, indeed, as *The Times* (27 February 1869) noted, caused 'an excitement quite unprecedented within living memory'.

The defendants appealed the results. In April 1870, both sides agreed to an out-of-court settlement and the 'great convent case' was over. By that time Mrs Star had faded from the public's short-lived memory. More famous trials – the Tichborne claimant and the Mordaunt divorce case – were to capture the Victorians' imagination and later attract the historians' attention.

But *Vanity Fair*'s selected extracts of testimony and Pellegrini's caricature have bequeathed to us a fascinating record that arouses our curiosity. Ape's sketch is one of his best but least known caricatures. He caught Mrs Star at a moment during the trial when obviously she was not sure where she was or what was happening. She not only felt uncomfortable because of Miss Saurin's reaction to the priest but also because she herself was in an alien atmosphere and uncertain of her own testimony. Ape's caricature of Mrs Star, with her furtive glance, downturned mouth, clasped hands and hunched shoulders hints that she was not free of guilt, that there were problems in the convent and that she was 'very uncomfortable' on the witness stand.

Tissot's imposing caricature, or rather character portrait, of POPE PIUS IX (1792–1878) appeared in *Vanity Fair* in the first issue of the new year, 1870. It was to be a momentous year for the Pope and the Church. The Vatican Council, convened by the Pope in 1869, would promulgate the doctrine of papal in-

fallibility, and the Pope would lose his temporal power to King Victor Emmanuel (*Vanity Fair*, 29 January 1870).

Pius IX had been elected Pope in 1846 after a distinguished career as an administrator and diplomat. His personal experience of the Revolution of 1830 and his plea to Pope Gregory XVI for clemency toward the rebels hinted at a desire to be more tolerant of liberal movements in Europe. Because of his apparent liberal sympathies when Bishop of Imola and because the Cardinals recognized the last Pope's unwillingness to accept change, they chose Mastai-Ferretti, the Bishop of Imola, as Pope. The new Pontiff's first act was to declare an amnesty for the political prisoners in the Papal States; he next established a council of laymen to advise on the government of Rome and approved some reforms. The Revolution of 1848, however, brought a halt to any more reforms. Political assassinations followed by the personal humiliation of having to flee Rome before the advancing Italian troops, soured the Pope to any future changes or compromises. From 1860 to 1870 Pio Nono ruled the Church under the protection of French troops. His advisers, coupled with his own inability to understand movements for change in Europe, forced him into a more conservative position during the 1860s. In 1864 he issued an encyclical condemning the principles of Piedmont's secular government and attached to it a Syllabus of Errors, a list of eighty condemned propositions on politics, science and rationalism. Three years later he called for a General Council at which, it was widely believed, the question of papal infallibility would be discussed.

Vanity Fair, in looking back over the Pope's reign, wryly observed that recent events in Italy should not be blamed on the Pope but on those people who believed in 'such things as representative institutions, freedom of religion, moral and scientific research, and other superstitions of civilisation . . .' The Pope himself declared that they were in error 'who regard the reconciliation of the Pope with modern civilisation as possible or desirable.'

Now here in 1870, noted Jehu Junior, the Church was meeting to decide whether or not the Pope's claim to absolute and universal infallibility should become dogma. Jehu Junior was not particularly alarmed over such a prospect; if the Church did decide in the Pope's favour, it would be conceding in name what had already been established in practice for centuries. Faith, of course, was the cornerstone of all religions, but it was only in Roman Catholicism, Jehu Junior asserted, that there could be found 'an avowed abnegation of Reason'. Bowles argued that it should not be too difficult, given the past demands of the Church, to ask for a belief in papal infallibility. After all, concluded Jehu Junior, a famous Jesuit scholar had previously observed that an ignorant Pope may well be infallible because God had, in the past, 'pointed out the right road by the mouth of an ass'.

Whether the road was right or wrong, the Council approved the Doctrine of Papal Infallibility in 1870; later that year, in September, Papal temporal power in Italy ended when the French troops, protecting the Pope, were withdrawn to defend France against Prussia. The Roman Question which had concerned the Church for several years was now settled once and for all; the Pope would be only a spiritual ruler. During the remainder of his life, Pius IX resisted Bismarck's (*Vanity Fair,* 15 October 1870) influence in Germany and expanded the Church's missionary work around the world. Despite his blind spots to modernity, he was an immensely popular Pope among the masses, and under him, a genuine revitalization of piety and devotion to the Pope grew. However, intellectuals and politicians saw him as a reactionary who refused to allow Roman Catholicism to recognize, much less accept, developments in science or the tenets of rationalism. He continued in this paradoxical situation until his death in 1878.

Jehu Junior's condemnation of Pius IX has been supported by many historians but not by Tissot's caricature. Due reverence has been paid to the Pope and, consequently, little is revealed of the man. The drawing is one of Tissot's less perceptive efforts at caricaturing. His deference may be because of his education and training in France, or it may well foreshadow Tissot's later life when he abandoned his upper-class Victorian world and gained solace in the new-found faith so clearly expressed through his religious paintings.

Among the numerous teachers and headmasters who appeared in *Vanity Fair,* two of the best known were Benjamin Jowett and William A. Spooner. Both men left their mark on Oxford through their scholarship, teaching and unique personalities. Of the two, however, Jowett has to be considered the more influential.

BENJAMIN JOWETT (1817–1893), Master of Balliol College and Regius Professor of Greek, attended St Paul's School. The skill in Greek and Latin which he acquired at St Paul's quickly earned him a reputation as an undergraduate at Balliol that

Greek
Reverend Benjamin Jowett
Men of the Day No. 124
26 February 1876
Spy

brought him an election as a Fellow in 1838. In 1842 he was appointed as a tutor. Although embroiled in the Oxford Movement, he found time to work closely with his students and pursue his studies of St Paul. Jowett's interpretation of St Paul caused him many problems. First, he was made suspect in the eyes of some Church authorities; later, he was forced to submit to the Thirty-Nine Articles to clear his name. Some time after this episode, he was brought into the Vice-Chancellor's court over his article 'On the Interpretation of Scripture' in *Essays and Reviews* (1860).

During the 1860s Jowett devoted much of his time to organising and reforming education at Balliol, travelling with his students and translating Plato. His efforts bore fruit, for in late 1870 he was elected Master of Balliol and the next year his translation of Plato appeared. His caricature was printed in *Vanity Fair* in 1876, soon after his second edition of Plato's *Dialogues* was released. His scholarship was equalled by his administrative talents. Management and educational reforms were carried out which made Balliol the most influential college at Oxford. Many bright young men including Curzon (*Vanity Fair,* 18 June 1892), Milner (*Vanity Fair,* 15 April 1897) and Asquith (see p. 61) came under Jowett's influence at Balliol, and his impact on the lives of England's leaders carried on into the twentieth century. According to Faber, Jowett set his

Spooner
Mr W. A. Spooner MA
Men of the Day No. 711
21 April 1898
Spy

129

students an example through his 'gospel of hard, honest, brainwork'.

Spy caricatured Jowett in his academic robe, complete with mortarboard. He caught the distinguished scholar peering over his pince-nez, which hang precariously on the end of his nose. Jowett's cherubic face and faint smile hint at a pleasant demeanour, but this mild mannered pose belies the tremendous energy and dedication to his profession and to his contributions to education.

Jowett taught Spooner; Spy caricatured him. When Spy decided to sketch W. A. SPOONER (1844–1930), he went to his class disguised as a student for what Ward termed a 'complete stalk'. One student nearly gave everything away by asking, in a loud whisper, how Ward was 'getting on'. Spy quickly hushed him for fear of being discovered by Spooner. The student replied 'that's all right if he does. I'll tell him you're my guv'nor!' Spy emphasized Spooner's poor eyesight by having his subject adjust his glasses while leaning over the lectern. Spooner's mortarboard rests upside down on the top of the stand. Spy does not reveal much about his victim in the treatment of his facial features; the sense of caricature is expressed in the totality of Spooner's posture and action.

Spooner was fifty-six years old when Spy caricatured him. He had been at New College, Oxford, nearly all of his life. In his youth he had overcome the handicaps of an albino through sheer determination. First as a scholar, then as a Fellow and later as Warden, he was to make his reputation as a knowledgeable and popular personality at New College. He lectured on ancient history, philosophy and divinity. In 1899, the year after Spy drew him, Spooner was made honorary canon of Christ Church. In 1903 he was unanimously elected Warden of New College and from that date until his retirement in 1924, Spooner was a familiar character around Oxford. He has been remembered, of course, not for his lectures on Aristotle, nor as the Warden of New College, but as the inventor of Spoonerisms. *Vanity Fair* noted that his chief 'flaim to came' lay in his genius for metathesis or the re-ordering of letters in words. He was a learned, gentle, amiable and modest man:

The half-warmed fish has risen in his breast; he knows all about Kinquering Congs; his cat has popped on its drawers; he has unwillingly addressed beery wenches; and he will doubtless be grattered and flatified by his appearance in Vanity Fair.

THE MILITARY

The serving officers of the Army and Navy were an ornament to and a bastion of the Victorian and Edwardian world. Until the end of the century, most wore colourful, elaborate uniforms on all occasions. Over two hundred British and other nation's officers appeared in all their finery in *Vanity Fair*. At the turn of the century, the magazine offered a set of forty-five officers who had served in the Brigade of Guards for £2.12s6d; twenty-eight officers who served in the South African War for one guinea, and twenty-four British admirals for £1.11s6d. Framing was extra. These sets found their way around the world. In the 1930s, John Masters, then serving with the Gurhkas in India, observed: 'There was almost always a club, sometimes a dusty shack, sometimes a portentous mausoleum. However small it contained a men's bar decorated with Spy's cartoons . . .' The student of costume can follow in colour the various embellishments that these dandies wore, from their formal mess dress to examples of their field uniforms.

These cartoons reveal an array of characters who delighted the caricaturist, even when in mufti. Ape contributed a number of memorable military figures, including 'the Beau Brummel of the day'. That was 'Bwab', Lieutenant Colonel John Palmer Brabazon (*Vanity Fair*, 29 May 1886) of the Hussars. He was the epitome of the Victorian swell, elegantly dressed, with a fastidiously curved moustache and a posture to match! Another moustached ornament of the parade ground and drawing room was 'Henry', Lieutenant Colonel Sir Henry Stracey, whom Ape depicted elegantly bent about his epée (*Vanity Fair*, 24 April 1880). Ape also captured the red-faced determination of lean old General Sam Browne, who 'with his one arm and various ingenious arrangements of straps contrived by himself, he is as good a shot, and even as good a salmon-fisher, as most men with two' (*Vanity Fair*, 5 February 1887). Earlier in the decade, Pellegrini's profile of another Colonel, Charles 'Chinese' Gordon, (*Vanity Fair*, 19 February 1881) evoked the atmosphere of slightly bogus piety that surrounded the soon-to-be martyr.

Spy also painted a large number of serving officers, including most of the higher command involved in the Boer War. Late in 1900, he

posed most of the senior British officers in a double print, 'A General
Group' (*Vanity Fair*, 29 November 1900). 'Bobs', Field Marshall Lord
Roberts was among Spy's most popular caricatures. In 1900, Spy also
painted 'Oom Paul' Kruger (*Vanity Fair*, 8 March 1900) the President
of the Transvaal, and General Baden-Powell, who founded the Scout
Movement (*Vanity Fair*, 5 July 1900) though these were taken from
others' descriptions. Normally Ward refused to caricature anyone he
had not personally observed, so he signed these drawings, 'Drawl'.
Earlier Spy had fun exaggerating the height of 'Ossie', Captain Os-
ward Henry Ames of the Life Guards (*Vanity Fair*, 27 February 1896),
who was six feet eight inches tall, and the ample belly of Major General Sir Frances Grenfell, the Sirdar or Commander of the British-
controlled Egyptian Army (*Vanity Fair*, 19 October 1889).

The Senior Service was well-represented in *Vanity Fair*. Spy
painted the jaunty 'Jacky', Admiral Fisher (*Vanity Fair*, 6 November
1902) and a large-nosed Captain Jellicoe (*Vanity Fair*, 26 December
1906). Somewhat over thirty 'sea dogs' and desk admirals appeared in
the magazine.

Foreign military officers also found a place among *Vanity Fair*'s
Men of the Day. Aside from Guth's Dreyfus and Esterhazy, a number
of other French officers appeared over the years, including the
dynamic Trouchu, 'the hope of France' (*Vanity Fair*, 17 September
1870), by Tissot; the foolish Boulanger, 'La Revanche' (*Vanity Fair*,
12 March 1887); and the simple MacMahon, 'J'y suis. J'y reste.' (*Vanity Fair*, 11 October 1879). These were both by Chartran, who also
contributed the Garibaldi included in this volume. Other notable
foreign military officers included the hapless Russian general
Kuropotkin ('I regret to report') after his defeat by the Japanese
tember 1905) and the impish Austrian soldier of fortune, Slatin Pasha,
who became an administrator of the Anglo-Egyptian Sudan (*Vanity
Fair*, 15 June 1899).

The military and naval officers who were caricatured in the
magazine were usually accorded an affectionately critical wave of
brush and pen. As a group they constitute one of the most colourful
and distinctive sets of *Vanity Fair* caricatures.

Revolution
General Giuseppe Garibaldi
Men of the Day No. 181
15 June 1878
T

Revolution
General Giuseppe Garibaldi
Men of the Day No. 181
15 June 1878
T

This mournful, humane image of GENERAL GIUSEPPE GARIBALDI (1807–1882), the architect of Italian unification, and one of the most popular heroes of the nineteenth century, appeared in *Vanity Fair* only four years before his death. The glorious days of the Thousand, and countless other exploits, were long over, and Garibaldi, in failing health, was in retirement on his island Caprera, worrying about Italy, the problems of the South and all the issues which he had hoped might be solved by the creation of a united Italy. Mazzini was gone; in 1878, King Victor Emmanuel (*Vanity Fair*, 29 January 1870), Pio Nono (*Vanity Fair*, 1 January 1870), La Mamora, and Pallavicino had all died. Two years later Garibaldi finally married his beloved companion Francesca Armosino. His marriage certificate described him simply as *Giuseppe Garibaldi, agricoltore*, a description he had long preferred. Christopher Hibbert has written:

He was not, and he admitted with pride that he was not, a clever man. He was more inclined to be ruled by instinct than by reasoning. He saw problems without gradations of emphasis. But this very lack of chiaroscuro *in his vision, this certainty unclouded by doubt, had always been the main source of his power and influence. And he was never in any sense arrogant at home . . . He could never see a joke, and that, after all, was part of his strength.*

The artist, 'T' (Théobald Chartran), recruited by Bowles after Tissot withdrew, had neither the acid wit of Ape, nor the more respectful, humorous exaggeration of Spy. Still, this portrayal of the aging Italian titan captured his essential character. At seventy, his fair reddish hair had turned grey, but he still took great pride in it. Tired, worn down by disappointment and illness, there is still greatness in the old man, clad in his embroidered hat and snow-white poncho, topped by a red neckerchief, his arthritic hand grasping his spectacles. All seems accurate and fair but for his small eyes, painted by T an intense blue. In fact they were brown. T had treated a living legend with sympathy and humour. So did Jehu Junior who wrote:

Personally General Garibaldi is one of the most lovable of men. The son of a poor fisherman of Nice, he owes the unexampled position he has achieved solely to the qualities with which nature had endowed him. For the most part without fixed purpose himself, and always with the haziest notions as to whither his action may lead, he yet can command the most devoted support for any enterprise he may undertake. His voice acts like a charm, and there is no living man who by his sole individual influence has worked so powerfully upon the events of history. He is withal entirely disinterested, and while there is no public man who has had so many opportunities to become rich, there is none who has of choice remained so poor; so that his greatest foes and those who most uncompromisingly condemn the purely lawless acts by which he has made himself known, cannot but admire while they pity this splendid child of Revolution.

HELMUTH VON MOLTKE (1800–1891) was the most famous European soldier of the second half of the nineteenth century. The image of Moltke by the German artist 'Go' (F. Goedecker) is one of the notable examples of the consistency of *Vanity Fair*'s style of caricature created largely by Carlo Pellegrini. The aging general's features and figure are sharply exaggerated, so that in a glance the viewer can comprehend the essence of the individual, yet recognize the man. We see an ascetic, wrinkled face, peering through his binoculars, while holding a map of France behind him. All Moltke's energies focus on his task.

Moltke was the descendent of a line of Prussian officers from Mecklenberg, but he was born in Holstein, then part of Denmark. Thus he was trained as an officer in Copenhagen before transferring to the Prussian infantry. Marked by his seniors as a brilliant prospect, he was given a variety of positions which included a term as an advisor to the Ottoman Sultan's army. Seconded to the Prussian General Staff, he became its chief in 1858. He was the chief planner of the series of wars against Denmark, Austria, and France which had, by 1870, made Prussia the dominant power in central Europe. Jehu Junior observed in 1884: 'He wielded the tremendous instrument that a severe and uncompromising militarism had made of the Prussian Army . . . and in 1870 Europe to its surprise, became aware that in von Moltke, Prussia possessed the greatest master of modern strategy.'

Moltke belonged to the old world of the aristocratic military officer as well as the new of the technocratic servant of the industrial state. Some of his critics in the Prussian Army called him 'Der Grosse Schweiger' – the great silent thinker. A systematic student of the history of warfare, he combined this knowledge with practical experience and scientific calculation to create in the Prussian Army the finest military machine of its era. The military organization he helped make became the model for most others in Europe.

War, to him, was a fact of life, and he wrote in 1880:

The man who won't stop
Sir Garnet J. Wolseley, Bart, KCB
Men of the Day No. 83
18 April 1874
Ape

Khartoum
Lord Kitchener of Khartoum GCB KCMG
Statesmen No. 706
23 February 1899
Spy

135

War is an element in the order of the world ordained by God. In it the noblest virtues of mankind are developed: courage and the abnegation of self; faithfulness to duty and spirit of sacrifice; the soldier gives his life. Without war the world would stagnate and lose itself in materialism.

His was a voice echoing a stern nineteenth-century rightist European tradition. Jehu Junior noted that his 'fame [is] second in the art of war to none, not even of the great Napoleon'. Moltke's motto was: 'First ponder, then dare'.

The comic opera nature of the career of SIR GARNET J. WOLSELEY (1833–1913) inspired Gilbert and Sullivan to use him for 'the very model of a modern major-general', in *Pirates of Penzance* in 1880. George Grossmith (*Vanity Fair*, 21 January 1888), who first played the part, tailored the role to the mannerisms and dress of Wolseley. 'Our only general' as he was then known, was delighted and, in private, would sing the famous patter song for his family.

Sir Garnet became the master of the small war, and seemingly fought in every one of them from the time he entered the Army at the age of eighteen, in 1851. He appeared to believe that the best possible way to get ahead was to try to get killed every time he had the chance. However, he also happened to be one of the few British officers of his generation who approached war as a science. 'All Sir Garnet' became a late Victorian expression for all is in order. Wolseley was healthy, organized, intelligent, well read, ambitious and lucky. In a little more than twenty years he became the youngest general in the British Army. Along the way he wrote a military manual, *The Soldier's Pocketbook for Field Service* – the first to attempt to prepare soldiers for war, rather than the parade grounds. It enlightened the troops and infuriated the Colonel Blimps of the time.

When Ape caricatured 'Our only General' in 1874, Wolseley was at home, basking in public adulation after a whirlwind campaign against the Ashanti on the Gold Coast of Africa. Many British people had felt disgraced when Britain did not intervene on the continent in 1870 in the Franco-Prussian War. As *Vanity Fair* observed: '. . . There was a great opportunity for England and the Penny Papers . . . Here was an opportunity to to regain all the lost position by fighting a mob of Ashantees [sic] armed with seven and six-penny muskets. So the troops were sent and the papers thenceforth were filled with more print than ten Waterloos would have produced. The English prestige has been, as was anticipated, entirely regained by it; and it is now patent to all the world that having burnt Coomasie [Kumasi] we can when we will burn also St Petersburg or Berlin.'

Sir Garnet became the leader of reform within the British Army. The opposition was formidable and included most of the generals, the commander-in-chief, the choleric George, Duke of Cambridge, and his cousin, the Queen herself. The Army itself was at this time more of a social organization than a fighting machine. Meanwhile, Wolseley spent the remainder of his career either fighting colonial wars or the entrenched forces of tradition. He won the former and lost the latter. When he finally became Commander-in-Chief, after the doddering Duke was retired in 1895, he was deteriorating both physically and mentally.

Jehu Junior described him in 1874 as 'a soldier, who has been successful, and who has been rewarded in full proportion to his achievements, is a phenomenon in the British Army . . . Like all successful men, he has gained much from fortune . . .

for indeed he has never slept since he began life. Most men might be or might do something did they but seize one chance in ten of those they have, but this is a man who has never missed a single chance. . . . He has shown himself a great General on a small scale'.

Ape caricatured Wolseley in one of the uniforms he designed for battle. One of his heretical notions was that soldiers should be dressed for fieldwork, not to enrich tailors or to delight nursemaids!

Few men captured the public imagination during the era of *Vanity Fair* as did the soldier, HORATIO HERBERT KITCHENER (1850–1916). When Spy caricatured the tall, bronzed General, Kitchener had just returned from the Sudan to the cheering London crowds and the rewards of the Establishment. At a minimal cost, he had slaughtered the forces of the Khalifa at the battle of Omdurman, and avenged General 'Chinese' Gordon, a fellow hero (*Vanity Fair*, 19 February 1881). After his victory near Khartoum in 1899 a mystic union took place between the masses and Kitchener. 'The initials "K of K" were a magic formula and his broad martial moustache a national sym-

Bobs
Field Marshal Lord Roberts VC KP
Statesmen No. 726
21 June 1900
Spy

bol that was to England what the *pantalon rouge* was to France,' observed the historian, Barbara Tuchman. Kitchener's victory in the Sudan made him, in Jehu Junior's opinion, 'a pet of the Great British Public'.

Vanity Fair summarized his characteristics: 'He is a first rate soldier. He is also a hard, obstinately-decided man who has made himself; for his success in life is in no way due to anything but his own determined merit . . . [and] foresight, to his complete method of organization, and to his own resolute, personal attention to detail, for he is a man who leaves no loophole unguarded. He may not be very popular with his army; but that army does not include a man who does not respect him'.

Unlike most of his military contemporaries, who have faded into a deserved oblivion, Kitchener is still remembered, although less for his accomplishments, than for a World War One recruiting poster. In 1914, Alfred Leete drew the moustachioed Field Marshal, now the Minister of War, pointing his finger and saying, 'Your country needs YOU!' It was one of the most effective works of graphic art of that era. Hundreds of thousands rushed to take the King's shilling. In America, James Montgomery Flagg used the idea and replaced Kitchener with Uncle Sam.

Behind the giant moustache, which Spy also captured, lay a complex man whose reputation, forged on colonial battlefronts, turned out to be more myth than reality. Single-minded, virulently ambitious, a ruthless intriguer, he cared little for others, except those who could be of use. *Vanity Fair* noted that 'He is a very sensible fellow who knows his business. But he does not care for ladies.' A more sympathetic biographer called him 'a natural celibate'. Most people found something strange and disturbing behind his fiery, intense gaze.

His career and military triumphs were fashioned overseas. Despite his notoriety, he was, like many who made their reputations abroad, a stranger to England. Brought back as War Minister at the start of the War in 1914 in order to lend his prestige to the weak Liberal Government, he turned out to be an administrative liability except as the recruiting poster. Spy has left us a memorable image of a single-minded giant of a man, more symbol than substance.

The other military hero of the turn of the century was the tiny 'Bobs' or 'Babs Bahadur', FREDERICK SLEIGH ROBERTS (1832–1914). Like Kitchener, his reputation was forged overseas, largely on the Indian frontier. Unlike Kitchener, he possessed the 'common touch' and was humane, lively, and beloved of his troops. His career spanned the Indian Mutiny of 1857–1858 (when he won the Victoria Cross for heroism at Khaudaganj), the Abyssinian and Lushai Campaigns, the second Afghan Campaign of 1879–1880, and the Boer War. He rose to command the Indian and British Army and led a national campaign for military conscription before the 1914–18 War.

At the time of Spy's caricature, 'Bobs' had been sent by a troubled Cabinet to South Africa to recoup a series of humiliating defeats inflicted on the British Army by the despised Boers. Kitchener went along as his Chief-of-Staff. *Vanity Fair* judged 'Bobs' to be 'the most popular man in the British Isles and the most unpopular – or at least the most feared – in Boerdom.' Spy wrote that his cartoon of the diminutive Roberts was one of the most successful ever sold. It is certainly one of his cleverest, for he sketched the tiny Field Marshal standing on the veldt, clasping his binoculars. Outlined on the rock outcrop behind him is the silhouette of 'Oom Paul' Kruger, the Boer leader (*Vanity Fair*, 8 March 1900). This caricature, perhaps unintentionally, symbolizes the difficulty the British had in finding the Boers!

In less than a year, Roberts and Kitchener appeared to have defeated the Boers, and Roberts left to become Commander-in-Chief of the British Army. However, more than eighteen months of guerrilla warfare ensued before peace between the Boers and Britain was made in 1903.

'Bobs' was a Tom Thumb sized man and blind in his right eye since childhood. He would have been disqualified from the twentieth-century officer corps. Astride his famous grey drab stallion, Vololel, he led the Diamond Jubilee parade to the ecstatic cheers of the London crowds. Kipling immortalized him in song (1893): 'There's a little red-faced man, which is Bobs, Which rides the tallest horse he can – Our Bobs.'

Vanity Fair lauded him: 'his breast is covered with medals . . . He is a strategist as well as a soldier; who in spite of his work has found the time to write books, to hunt, and to cycle . . . In a word, he is a great general, who does his duty, loves his country, and is no respecter of official persons. Consequently, he has a few enemies whose enmity is tribute to his merit.'

In the 1890s, France was convulsed by a spy scandal. Somebody was leaking military secrets to the Germans, and, in 1894, a Jewish captain on the French General Staff, ALFRED DREYFUS (1859–1933), was accused of the crime. Although he protested his innocence and the evidence presented against him was almost worthless, he was swiftly convicted in a secret, closed military court, publicly degraded, and banished into exile on the desolate Caribbean isle, Devil's Island. There he was kept in solitary confinement, often in leg irons, and given the silent treatment by his jailors. Although normally wives were allowed to join their deported husbands, this was not the case for Dreyfus. The announcement of his conviction resulted in a fever of anti-semitism and anti-republicanism in France, so severe that it appalled most foreigners. One of these, Theodore Herzl, despaired of the assimilation of the Jews and began to foster the notion of Zionism – Jewish nationalism – as a solution.

Secrets, however, continued to be conveyed to the Germans. The new head of French military intelligence, Colonel Picquart, discovered that the case against Dreyfus had been fabricated. When he conveyed this information to his superiors, he was threatened, blackmailed and transferred to a foreign post. Meanwhile, Dreyfus's family, especially his brother and wife, sought for new evidence to clear the unfortunate man who was wasting away on Devil's Island.

Gradually, and then in a rush, evidence of the innocence of Dreyfus and the conspiracy against justice perpetrated by the French General Staff began to emerge. The Army conspirators forged more evidence to substantiate the case against Dreyfus. While much of the public raged against Dreyfus and for the Army, a brave minority began to campaign for Dreyfus, justice and the Republic. Clemenceau (*Vanity Fair*, 27 May 1908) and Zola (*Vanity Fair*, 24 January 1880), aware of the threat to republican ideals, published Zola's *J'accuse* in January 1898. In ringing prose, the eminent novelist focused the attention of the world on this drama in which the innocence or guilt of an unknown soldier had become the centre of a battle for the survival of justice and the ideals of the Republic.

Vanity Fair followed the case with a series of colour lithographs by Jean-Baptiste Guth of the principal figures in the case. In asserting Dreyfus's innocence, Zola had pinpointed the

Major Esterhazy
Major Esterhazy
Men of the Day No. 714
26 May 1898
Guth

139

guilty parties, in particular the well-born but disreputable officer, MAJOR CHARLES FERDINAND WALSIN ESTERHAZY (1857–1923). He was caricatured as an aristocratic rascal. Jehu Junior, cautiously moving to a pro-Dreyfus position, wrote: 'Six years ago he was mixed up in the memorable duel between Captain Cremieu Foa and Edouard Drumont' (a notorious anti-semitic journalist) who was in the vanguard of the anti-Dreyfusards, '. . . and he [Esterhazy] recently acquired a quite sudden notoriety by implication in l'Affaire Dreyfus; of which, perhaps more will be heard. He has been heard to say that he does not love Zola.'

That year, another major figure, Henri Brisson, then Premier of France, appeared in a character portrait entitled 'Justice to Dreyfus' (*Vanity Fair*, 6 October 1898). *Vanity Fair* complimented him: 'Being a man of strength, and not to be bullied by the military, he has now shown himself so much a friend of Justice that he has secured a Revision of the Dreyfus trial, has given that unfortunate and degraded soldier a chance, and has earned renown.'

During the second trial held a year later at Rennes, Guth painted two views of the now celebrated victim. The few terrible years on Devil's Island had dramatically aged and emaciated Dreyfus. Guth's first portrait is of a slim, prematurely-aged, dignified man seated on a chair facing his accusers.

Vanity Fair's commentary is clearly sympathetic.

Nine-and-thirty years ago he had the misfortune to be born an Alsatian Jew, at Muhlhausen; and from what has happened during the past few years it would seem that, with very few exceptions, no one has liked him. He went into the French Army, and as a Captain of Artillery he has not, probably, ceased to regret it for years. Convicted of treason five years ago – without evidence, as one may safely say – he has since lived in death; and now he sits at Rennes the most pathetic figure of the end of Century. But he has set France by the ears, and is now opposed, almost single-handed, to the whole Army of France. He has borne up through a long trial and against enormous odds with quite unsemitic courage; and he still hopes.

He is the most miserable man living, but he has a good wife.

The second portrait is 'At Rennes' a 'Winter Double Number' (*Vanity Fair*, 3 November 1899) – a double page cartoon showing the trial setting and most of the important participants. *Vanity Fair* compassionately observed:

A few short weeks ago Captain Alfred Dreyfus was prominent before the civilized world as few men have been in our times. And now, although as a personality he may be retired into obscurity, the pathetic picture of the man as he stood up against his accusers on his return from that Devilish Island is a picture that should take place in the history of the world. There is the wretched prisoner before his Judges; labouring under a measure of injustice that must have appalled any innocent man: whose shame was France's. It is a picture to which the pencil can do better justice than the pen.

Whether Alfred Dreyfus was, or was not, innocent of the crime laid to his charge will never, perhaps, be certainly known. It is possible that the man was a traitor: it is certain that he was most unjustly dealt with. For to condemn a man on a most hideous charge, with practically no evidence, is to do a thing that is altogether shocking to English notions of right; and it can be no answer to such injustice to urge Expediency. But in the end the man who seemed to stand up so bravely, so pathetically, against the French world only to be condemned again, has accepted a pardon; and in all

the French circumstances of this terrible case it is not for us to say that he has done wrong.

In 1906, Dreyfus and Colonel Picquart, the honourable officer who had discovered the conspiracy, were formally rehabilitated. The passions aroused did not settle then or later, even after evidence of Dreyfus's innocence and Esterhazy's guilt was supplied in 1930 by the German officer involved. What began as a case of espionage became a morality play in a struggle for the survival of the ideals of the French Revolution and the Republic. National security became the cloak for prejudice and criminality. It took brave acts to secure justice.

BUILDERS OF THE EMPIRE

Vanity Fair flourished during the height of the far-flung, diverse British Empire. The lithographs are a colourful record of the variety of individuals who explored, ruled, exploited, administered and financed British activities on nearly every continent and ocean of the world. Captain Frederick Lugard, 'an earnest African'; Cecil Rhodes, 'The Cape'; the Earl of Cromer, 'Egypt'; Sir Wilfrid Laurier, 'Canada'; and Richard Seddon of New Zealand, 'King Dick', whose caricatures appear in this section, are only a sampling of the hundreds caricatured in *Vanity Fair* who played a part in establishing and maintaining the Empire. Even Antarctica is represented, through Ernest Shackelton's (*Vanity Fair*, 6 October 1909) and Robert Scott's (*Vanity Fair*, 19 February 1913) attempts on the South Pole. *Vanity Fair* included in its gallery of notable explorers Lieutenant Verney Lovett Cameron, RN, of whom Jehu Junior commented: 'He walked across Africa . . . He has learnt to disbelieve in teetotalism and missionaries' (*Vanity Fair*, 15 July 1876). Others found in this book are Richard Burton, 'The Arabian Nights' (see p. 89), and Henry Morton Stanley, 'He found Livingstone' (see p. 168).

Over the years some of the rulers from territories the British sought to influence, dominate or exploit were also portrayed. The artistic quality and accuracy of these caricatures vary with the skill and imagination of the artist, and the availability of information on each ruler's appearance. The few Chinese mandarins are pleasant images. Guth's 'Li', Li Hung Chang, a war lord and ambassador (*Vanity Fair*, 13 August 1896), and Imp's 'Chinese Customs', Sir Robert Hart (*Vanity Fair*, 27 December 1894), make an interesting pair from the age of European intervention in the Middle Kingdom. Portraits of the emperor of 'Corea', Li Hsi, by Pry (*Vanity Fair*, 19 October 1899) and the white Rajah of Sarawak, Sir Charles Anthony Brooke, by Spy (*Vanity Fair*, 19 January 1899), are mainly of historical interest.

The Indian princes make a splendid set. Two of them are featured in this book: 'Ranji', the Maharaja Kumar Shri Ranjitsinhji Vibhaji of Nawanagar, the great cricketer, and Sir Rajindra Singh, His Highness the Maharaja of Patalia, a noted horseman and polo player. (See pp. 183, 181.) There were nine more, including the Aga Khan, portrayed in 1904 by Spy as a dapper, smiling, shiny-haired Europeanized young man. Of the Viceroys of India, a few such as Lord Curzon (*Vanity Fair*, 18 June 1892) and Lord Northbrook (*Vanity Fair*, 9 December 1876) were caricatured, along with a number of Anglo-Indians. Two Shahs of Persia, Nasser ed-Din (*Vanity Fair*, 5 July 1873) and Muzaffer ed-Din (*Vanity Fair*, 29 January 1903), and two emperors of Abyssinia, Menelik II (*Vanity Fair*, 29 July 1897) and Ras Makunan (*Vanity Fair*, 12 February 1903), one sultan of Morocco, Muley Hassan (*Vanity Fair*, 4 July 1891), and one sultan of the Ottoman Empire, Abdul Aziz and one King of the Zulus, Cetewayo (see p. 50) add to the range of exotic sovereigns found in the *Vanity Fair* caricature gallery.

Britain's concern over passage through the Suez Canal, which led to its military intervention in Egypt in 1882, evoked a kaleidoscope of caricatures. Aside from the Earl of Cromer, the proconsul, and many of his underlings, two Khedives, Ismail (*Vanity Fair*, 7 May 1881) and Tewfik (*Vanity Fair*, 20 January 1883), and the defeated patriot, Arabi (*Vanity Fair*, 6 January 1883), were portrayed. South of the Sahara, Lugard is only one of a galaxy of personalities involved in Africa who were featured in *Vanity Fair*. Prominent Boers included 'Oom Paul' Kruger (*Vanity Fair*, 8 March 1900) and an assortment of British officials, missionaries, soldiers and businessmen appeared over the years. As well as Rhodes, a sampling might include Sir Bartle Frere (*Vanity Fair*, 20 September 1873), Bishop Colenso of Natal (*Vanity Fair*, 28 November 1874), 'Dr Jim' Leander Starr Jameson, of the Raid (*Vanity Fair*, 9 April 1896), the 'High Commissioner', Alfred Milner (*Vanity Fair*, 15 April 1897), 'Barney' Barnato (*Vanity Fair*, 14 February 1895), and 'Rhodes the Second,' Abe Bailey (*Vanity Fair*, 9 September 1908).

The white dominions were more sparsely treated in *Vanity Fair*. Other than Laurier, most of the Canadians portrayed were entrepreneurs such as Lord Strathcona and Mount Royal of the Hudson's Bay Company (*Vanity Fair*, 19 April 1900), Sir Charles Tupper of the Canadian Pacific (*Vanity Fair*, 30 July 1913), and Price Ellison of British Columbia (*Vanity Fair*, 25 January 1911). Prominent Australians were few; included were 'the demon bowler', Fred Spofforth (*Vanity Fair*, 13 July 1878); 'Australian Cricket', G. J. Bonner (*Vanity Fair*, 9 September 1884); 'Kismet', the actor Oscar Asche (*Vanity Fair*, 29 November 1911); and 'Australia', the politician Alfred Deakin (*Vanity Fair*, 2 September 1908).

The caricatures of *Vanity Fair* constitute a unique visual record of the sorts and conditions of individuals in that empire on which, it was alleged, the sun never set. At the Diamond Jubilee in 1897, the Queen's subjects numbered nearly four hundred million over five continents. They were of every race and every colour, of a thousand religions and a thousand languages. James Morris observed: 'Such a variety of peoples as had never before, in the whole history of human affairs, owed their allegiance to a single suzerain.'

An earnest African
Captain Frederick John Dealtry Lugard DSO CB
Men of the Day No. 639
19 December 1895
Spy

During the 'scramble for Africa' by the European powers late in the nineteenth century, *Vanity Fair* portrayed a number of personalities entitled 'notable Africans'. These were British men and women who participated in the exploration, exploitation and administration of that vast, diverse continent. Captain FREDERICK LUGARD (1858–1945), later Lord Lugard of Abinger, was among the most influential in a group noted for its abundance of characters.

Spy produced one of his most amusing, effective caricatures depicting Lugard as a perky, grown up Boy Scout. The intrepid explorer was bemoustached, smoking a cigar, with some reserve smokes peeping out of his pocket. He had a pocket knife clasped to his belt, a spear leaning on his arm, and looked ready, willing and prepared to lead a safari, pacify the natives, map a territory, and campaign among the opinion makers at home for the benevolent expansion of British control in 'Darkest Africa'.

Lugard exemplified the best qualities of the British adventurers who went out to Africa to 'take up the white man's burden'. Born in Madras, the son of a respectable, impecunious missionary, young Lugard was brought by his mother (with his five siblings) back to England in 1863. Ineffectively schooled for the examination for the Indian Civil Service, he then opted for the Army, as had many of his relatives. After eight weeks at Sandhurst in 1878, his entire class was hastily commissioned on the possibility of a war with Russia. He later recalled that an American newspaper wrote: 'England has let loose one hundred war pups from Sandhurst! Let Russia tremble.'

Jehu Junior summarized Lugard's career up to 1895 as follows:

Born too late by three years for the Crimea, he joined the 9th Foot after leaving Rossall, and presently won his first medal with 'the Holy Boys' in the Afghan War of '79–'80. Five years later he was a Captain in the Soudan with the Indian Contingent, and earned a second medal with two clasps. Yet a year later he won a third medal in the Burma War, and got thrice mentioned in dispatches. Then he began work in earnest. He went to Nyasaland in command of an expedition against slave-raiding Arabs, and got very severely wounded by a bullet, which made six holes in him at once. Next he took service with the British East Africa Company in Uganda; where he commanded till he returned to England, made a stir in behalf of the retention of Uganda, and got his way. Last year he tried West Africa and made treaties; beating the French and German expeditions sent out in their behalf by a few days. Since May last he has been in England writing vigorously, lecturing forcibly, and generally devoting himself to African matters; for he is an earnest African without fads, who knows the country.

His big work, 'Our East African Empire', was very well received, and he is now busy with another and greater book on African problems. He has been covered with glory and with wounds; one of the latter inflicted by a poisoned arrow, making him acquainted with many disagreeable, native-grown antidotes. His name is very closely identified with the great questions of the Slave Trade and of the Liquor Traffic with Native races; as to which questions he soundly urges moderation, being a practical man and not a fanatic. His methods are not Mr Stanley's methods, yet Lord Salisbury believes in him, although he has made a bitter enemy of France by serving his own country; which owes him something.

This stalwart 'earnest African' went on to become the most renowned colonial administrator in Africa south of the Sahara. In Nigeria he created a system of shared administration called 'the Dual Mandate'. It was a form of indirect rule, using the existing local élite to administer British rule. His biographer, Dame Margery Perham, judged him to have become 'a, perhaps *the*, chief figure in the sphere of British colonial affairs' during his long career, which lasted more than a quarter century after his formal retirement.

In 1894, during one of his countless expeditions, an attacker shot an arrow through his sun helmet into his head. One of his men pulled at the arrow, but it would not budge till someone braced his foot on Lugard's shoulder and brought the arrow out accompanied by a good hunk of Lugard's skull. Undaunted by the poison from the arrow, Lugard munched some antidotal roots, led a successful counterattack, and marched thirteen miles before ending the day's activities.

Vanity Fair summed him up: 'Despite his hard work, his serious ideas, and his lean presence, he has a very merry wit . . . Yet he does not know fear.'

By 1891 the rumple-suited figure of CECIL RHODES (1853–1902), the South African 'Diamond King' and gold magnate, had become familiar in London. Despite his extraordinary wealth, Rhodes 'was notable for the shabbiness of his suits'. Only thirty-eight years old, Rhodes had established control over the world production and marketing of diamonds, paid his own way through Oxford, made an immensely profitable corner

in the gold business of the Rand, obtained personal control over the territory soon to be known as Rhodesia, and become the Prince Minister of the Cape Colony.

What Rhodes most wanted was power, in order to pursue and promote his dream – the creation of a secret white male élite which would control the world. He embodied the ideals of rugged individualism, having the will to 'expand' into the territory of others. In the process, Rhodes created the image of the typical Victorian imperialist and patriot of empire. As the apostle of British race patriotism, his career has become the focus for critics of imperialism.

Spy's image of Rhodes is down-to-earth and not at all reverential. Pictured in profile, hands on his waist, he resembles an impatient and unimpressive middle-class businessman. Vanity Fair's commentary does not fawn. It tersely summarizes Rhodes' South African accomplishments and wonders about the possibility of conflict between his political and business interests. Jehu Junior observed: 'He is now Premier of the Cape, and the leading spirit of the British South Africa Company; in which dual office he has, so far, managed to avoid clashing with himself – He is a versatile, strong man, an able negotiator, and good financier. When in England he is as popular with Dukes as he is with Irish Nationalists.' This last is a reference to the fact that Rhodes gave Parnell (Vanity Fair, 11 September 1880) and his Irish Home Rule Party £10,000 to assure their acquiescence in a particular South African matter; but he also believed in their cause.

In 1891 Vanity Fair concluded its assessment of Rhodes on a warning note: 'He holds a large portion of South Africa in the hollow of his hand, confidently. He has got himself up on a pedestal so high that he needs a steady hand to maintain his position; but he is a self-made man, who believes in himself, and he knows what he is about.'

Hounded by fears of an early death (his heart was weak), Rhodes rushed on. In 1897 he connived in the Jameson Raid as part of a plot to undermine the Boer Republic in the Transvaal. As a result, he lost his pre-eminent political position in South Africa, tarnished his imperial image, and helped bring about the British-Boer War.

Still pursuing his imperialistic dream, always with the necessary power and money, Rhodes died in 1902, leaving his fortune to fund Rhodes Scholarships to Oxford University. His will actually intended that the Rhodes Scholarships should create that secret élite which would control the world for Anglo-Saxon glory. His trustees, however, reinterpreted his imperialistic desires, with the result that the holders of the scholarships have gone on to become distinguished in their individual vocations and countries. Thus, an adolescent dream of a jesuitical-masonic-imperialist secret society devoted to the control of the world by the Anglo-Saxons produced, instead, scholarships for an élite of merit. Professor J. H. Plumb noted recently: 'By that very irony in which history delights, Rhodes aided humanity by his death.'

EVELYN BARING, Earl of Cromer (1841–1916), was among the most distinguished of those who went abroad to rule 'the natives' for Britain during its imperial heyday. In 1902, Jehu Junior summarized his early career before his Egyptian proconsulship began. Cromer was:

. . . a young man of fifty and much talent . . . for he came from a house of much ability [the Baring Brothers Bank] financial and otherwise. Himself began life as a member of that destructive force,

the Royal Artillery . . . He went into the staff college as a Captain, wrote some military essays, went as ADC to Sir Henry Storks to Corfu, and to Jamaica when the late Governor Eyre had suppressed a negro outbreak, became Private Secretary to his cousin, Lord Northbrook, then Viceroy of India [Vanity Fair, 9 December 1876] and retired from the service as a major.

The financial rapaciousness of the European financiers and the fiscal naïveté of the Khedive Ismail (Vanity Fair, 7 May 1881) precipitated Egypt into near bankruptcy in the 1870s. Cromer was sent as the representative of the English bond holders to look after their money. He and his European colleagues cut the Egyptian budget and services so drastically that their interference set in motion the proto-nationalist rebellion led by Arabi Pasha (Vanity Fair, 6 January 1883) against growing foreign interference in Egyptian affairs. This revolt was used by the British as an excuse for armed intervention in 1882 to save the nation from itself. They set up a 'temporary' occupation which lasted until 1956.

Cromer, after organizing the draconian debt collection which led to the revolt and occupation, returned to England. In 1882 the British Government appointed him the caretaker of Egypt As Her Majesty's Agent and Consul-General and Minister Plenipotentiary until 1907, he salvaged Egypt's finance and 'reformed' its administration and economy. To do so he recruited a cadre of able young gentlemen who forged a semi-modern administration under his calm, stern control. Several of these men were portrayed in Vanity Fair, including J. Rennell Rodd, the diplomat (Vanity Fair, 7 January 1897); Sir Edgar Vincent, later Lord D'Abernon, the financier-diplomat (Vanity Fair, 20 April 1899); Alfred Milner, the apostle of imperialism (Vanity Fair, 15 April 1897); and the soldiers: Sir Reginald Wingate of the Sudan (Vanity Fair, 9 September 1897), Lord Edward Cecil (Vanity Fair, 9 November 1899), Sir Claude MacDonald (Vanity Fair, 10 October 1901), and the eccentric Austrian, Sir Rudolph von Slatin (Vanity Fair, 15 June 1899). The pathetic puppet, Khedive Taufiq (Vanity Fair, 20 January 1883), whose regime the British had intervened to save, also appeared.

Spy captured the stolidity and sureness of this epitome of the Victorian proconsul. His nicknames were well earned. 'The Vice-Viceroy', was acquired during his short tour in India as the power behind his cousin, and 'Overbearing' and 'the Lord', resulted from his twenty-four year dominance over Egyptian public affairs. Sent by a Liberal Government to salvage the wreckage of an 'oriental despotism', the irony is that he created a western one in its place. A self-taught classical scholar of some note, Lord Cromer never in those twenty-four years found it necessary to learn Arabic, the tongue of his subjects. He had most of the virtues of his class, and some of its failings, including a benevolent impenetrability and anti-semitic prejudices. All in all, he probably did deserve Vanity Fair's accolades: 'He has since been called the Maker of Modern Egypt . . . He is a good servant whom his country has not found wanting.'

In 1897, SIR WILFRID LAURIER (1841–1919), the Prime Minister of Canada, was, according to Jehu Junior, 'probably the most remarkable of all the Colonials who came to England for the Diamond Jubilee'. The popular newspaper, the Daily Mail, asserted with its usual chauvinist condescension: 'For the first time on record a politican of the New World has been recognized as the equal of the great men of the Old Country.'

Laurier was the first French-speaking Canadian to become the leader of his nation. Unusually fluent in both French and

Egypt
The Earl of Cromer
Statesmen No. 744
2 January 1902
Spy

145

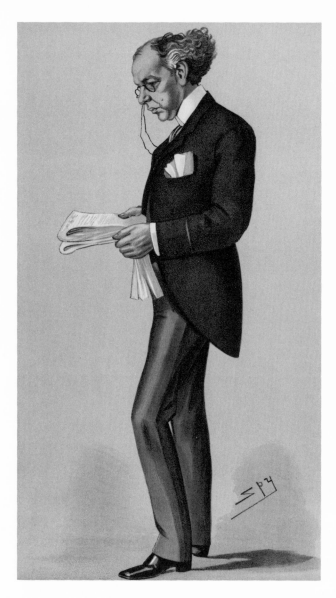

English, he was a dynamic orator, who was also reserved and often remote. He was something of a dandy, which Spy conveys in his sketch. In one of his campaigns he cried: 'Follow my white plume and you will find it always in the forefront of honour.' Canadians both French and English followed the debonair figure of the 'knight of the White Plume' for a lengthy time.

Born in St Lin, a placid, isolated small village in French Canada, Laurier had a happy childhood. His Canadian father, a land surveyor, encouraged him to read and sent his son at the age of eleven to a neighbouring English-speaking village, New Glasgow. There Laurier acquired a facility in English which alternately fascinated, soothed or tormented his hearers. He became a noted lawyer in Montreal, and entered Quebec politics as a Liberal. Though he was a subtle politician, he refused to bow to the dominant priests, and looked for the centre course between anti-clericalism and subservience to the reactionary Catholic church in French Canada. At national level, he tried to bridge the two Canadian national traditions, and to come to an accommodation that would ensure Canada's independence from the giant to the south, the United States, and the 'old country', the United Kingdom.

Laurier's maiden speech stunned the Quebec Legislature with its boldness, dexterity and authority. He went on to become leader of the Liberal Party and, in 1896, Prime Minister, when the Liberals won the national elections. He was to be Prime Minister until 1911. Then, in a sense, his successes were his downfall. The Liberals, in power so long, ossified and fragmented. The tensions in Canadian politics, between the French and English provinces as well as amongst other politicians eager for power, coupled with controversy over an independent navy and economic relations with the American republic to the south, swept him out of office.

When Laurier and his regal wife, Zoe, came to London for the 1897 Diamond Jubilee, they were immediately lionized. *Vanity Fair* observed: 'He is marked out among men by his quick progress, his blameless character, his kindly honesty, his graceful speech, and his winning ways. He can be lucid, sarcastic, and diplomatic; and he can hit hard. He has done much to make friends of French and English; but he has done even more for Canada. He is a very able, sensible, honest, yet discreet fellow; who is gifted with much clear foresight.'

The imperialists, led by the Colonial Secretary, Joseph Chamberlain, found this out when they sought to entice this charming man and his nation into their schemes for imperial federation. In the end, the wily hard-nosed businessman from Birmingham was out-haggled by the courtly lawyer from St. Lin. 'Our Joe' forgot that Laurier was a Gaul who found the pretentions of 'Anglo-Saxonism' foolish. Said Laurier: '. . . England has no more rights over us than are allowed by our own Canadian Parliament. If this is not a nation, what then is a nation?'

Vanity Fair wrote admiringly that Laurier, 'though French and Catholic, in spite of his comparative youth, . . . now shines even in England, as Prime Minister of the Confederated Provinces of Canada.' Laurier, the author of the Canadian Independence, had about him 'a sunniness of soul that brightened his time'.

Another remarkable colonial leader who came to the Diamond Jubilee was RICHARD JOHN SEDDON (1845–1906), the Premier of New Zealand. Under his formidable, dominating leadership, New Zealand, in the 1890s, became the 'world's social labora-

King Dick
The Right Honourable Richard John Seddon PC LLD
Men of the Day No. 838
17 April 1902
How'

147

of imperial unity. Jehu Junior labelled him 'an earnest imperialist', who ought to be encouraged, 'for he has done much, and is capable of doing more for the Empire.' New Zealand sent the first colonial military contingent to support the British in the Boer War, an act much appreciated in Britain.

Seddon's imperialism was certainly appreciated by *Vanity Fair,* even if the magazine found his style rather vulgar. In describing him, it wrote: 'For he is a very remarkable, if a self-made man, who is full of unshaken confidence in himself, strong in his beliefs, and, though he may be a little rough, altogether of sound stuff.' The artist captured the massive bulk of man and his combativeness but did not convey his geniality. With his left hand clasped firmly on his waist, and his right fist raised, he looks as ready to fight as to talk. Seddon was a loud, forceful, verbose speaker and had enormous physical strength. By the standards of the Edwardian élite, he was not a gentleman. He had refused a knighthood in 1897 on democratic principles. *Vanity Fair* was admiring but patronising: 'He is a man of his word, who has kept an inn, has led labour, and has made many enemies. But he has worked hard all his life, and is now known as "King Dick".'

tory'. In the aftermath of a severe slump – the Long Depression – Seddon and his party, the Liberals. supported or initiated a unique series of political, social and economic reforms. Women were given the vote, the criminal code consolidated, the Bank of New Zealand bailed out and brought under state control, graduated land and income taxes initiated, large holdings broken up and absentee landlordism reduced, the first compulsory state system of labour arbitration created, the eight-hour working day made law, old age pensions enacted, and a free place system for secondary schools established.

In the process, Seddon became the most popular figure ever in New Zealand politics. Lancashire born, he emigrated to the antipodes at eighteen, and was a gold miner and storekeeper before he entered politics. A contemporary described him as 'without a doubt, a jolly, good-tempered despot'. One of his parliamentary opponents observed: 'The greatest cause of Richard Seddon's universal success [was] that no human being – no man, woman or child – could ever be too high or too low for him to address with familiarity and apparent interest.' 'Our Dick' was re-elected repeatedly, and died in office in 1906. One of his countrymen observed recently: 'the country was very content to warm itself in the climate of his geniality.' Unlike Lauriėr, the Canadian leader, Seddon was a strident supporter

SCIENTISTS

Vanity Fair recognized some of the contributions made by the men (and one woman) in science whose theories and discoveries radically altered life in the nineteenth and early twentieth centuries. But the magazine did not revere scientists and science to the same degree that it did judges and the law or clergymen and the Church because, in the nineteenth century, science was seldom associated with the Establishment nor was it seen as supporting the social order. Since scientists received neither the adulations nor criticism reserved for the more easily identified institutions of Society, *Vanity Fair* produced a collection of rather bland caricatures and commentaries which lack the sense of historical cohesion or purpose that is found in their treatment of the Bench and Bar or Church of England. Science was a relatively new arrival upon the British scene. *Vanity Fair* could not gain an historical perspective on its causes and effects. Since science was a Johnny-come-lately, it never was viewed by *Vanity Fair,* as it might be today, as a pillar of the social and economic edifice; the magazine did not see the scientist personifying the virtues, and sometimes vices, of British life. Consequently, each scientist was interpreted in isolation, on his or her own merits; nor was each person's work placed into a larger framework of scientific developments.

For example, while *Vanity Fair* understood quite clearly the arguments and implications of Charles Darwin's writings, it did not directly associate Huxley with the movement. Huxley was judged on his own as teacher, biologist, materialist and proponent of mass education, not as 'Darwin's bulldog'. Nor did *Vanity Fair* place the critics of Darwin, such as Dr Richard Owen, into the opposite camp. On the contrary, Owen was rightly praised for his contributions in comparative anatomy and as a capable administrator of the natural history section of the British Museum.

Although *Vanity Fair* failed to acknowledge the interrelationships of scientific developments, it did realize that science was making tremendous strides in important areas. It recognized two men active in the study and control of diseases, Louis Pasteur and Rudolf Virchow (*Vanity Fair*, 15 May 1893). Sir William Ramsay (*Vanity Fair*, 2 December 1908) and Professor John Hall Gladstone (*Vanity Fair*, 11 November 1891) were featured for their work in chemistry; Ramsay for his discoveries of inert gases and Gladstone for associating refractivity and chemical problems. In astronomy, *Vanity Fair* honoured Sir William Huggins' (*Vanity Fair*, 9 April 1903) contributions in astrophysics, Sir George Airy (*Vanity Fair*, 13 November 1875) for his work at the Royal Greenwich Observatory and Richard Anthony Proctor (*Vanity Fair*, 3 March 1883) who charted over 1600 stars and studied Mars and Venus. Some of the famous physicians included in the magazine were Sir Morrell Mackenzie (*Vanity Fair*, 15 October 1887); Sir Francis Henry Laking (*Vanity Fair*, 19 February 1903), physician to the King; Sir Felix Semon (*Vanity Fair*, 1 May 1902), the noted laryngologist; Sir James Paget (*Vanity Fair*, 12 February 1876), the surgeon and pathologist; and Sir Alfred Pierce Gould (*Vanity Fair*, 27 September 1911), surgeon and lecturer in academic surgery.

Nearly eighty scientists and doctors were caricatured; some, such as the Curies, *Vanity Fair* immediately realized had made astounding discoveries which could change the course of history; others featured in *Vanity Fair* made little lasting impact and have been forgotten. In 1875, *Vanity Fair* proclaimed that it was acquainting the world 'with the remarkable men of our times in a manner which renders a true estimate of them . . .' By their times perhaps it was rendering a true estimate, but the magazine did not always understand the importance of their victims from the world of science.

Natural Selection
Charles R. Darwin
Men of the Day No. 33
30 September 1871
Coide

A Great Med'cine-Man Among the Inqui-ring Redskins   151
Professor Thomas H. Huxley
Men of the Day No. 19
28 January 1871
Ape

When CHARLES DARWIN (1809–1882) was one of *Vanity Fair*'s 'Men of the Day' in September 1871, the magazine competently summarized one of the burning issues of the moment, the debate over the theory of evolution. Jehu Junior clearly understood Darwin's central thesis of natural selection, the naturalist's key role in the formulation of the theory and its implications and his tremendous impact on Western thought.

Darwin's earlier years, however, hardly promised his later fame. His education had been quite conventional and his stay at Edinburgh and Cambridge anything but outstanding. At Cambridge, however, Darwin awakened to the mysteries of natural history and upon graduation was asked to serve as an unpaid naturalist on the voyage of the survey vessel, HMS *Beagle*. For five years, from 1831 to 1836, he circumnavigated the globe, observed flora and fauna, collected specimens and wrote up his notebooks. Darwin returned to England with a vague notion of evolution which, through his writings, began to take shape. All fell into place in 1838 when he read the Reverend Thomas Malthus' *Essay on the Principle of Populations*. Meanwhile, his association with leading naturalists, including Charles Lyell and Joseph Hooker, and his research in geology and zoology, helped further crystallize his views. By the mid-1840s his basic theory had been outlined and by 1858 he had the bulk of evidence supporting his ideas on evolution on paper. It was at this time that Darwin received from Alfred Wallace a tract on evolution that was strikingly similar to his own analysis.

In 1859, both men read their papers before the Linnean Society; later that year Darwin's abstract of his famous talk was published: *On the Origin of Species by means of Natural Selection*. All 1250 original copies sold out the first day. The debate was now public and during the 1860s arguments over evolution resounded throughout the land. On 30 June 1860, the Reverend Samuel Wilberforce (*Vanity Fair*, 24 July 1869), coached by Dr Richard Owen, President of the British Association, debated with Thomas Huxley at Oxford. Huxley's replies to Wilberforce's questions were so devastating that he won the day and set Darwin's ideas on their road to triumph. The year Darwin appeared in *Vanity Fair*, 1871, saw the publication of his *Descent of Man*. This book did not generate the furor of Darwin's first work because public opinion was becoming more receptive to his theories.

The notoriety that Darwin received was in sharp contrast to the tone of his personal life. Darwin was always something of a recluse. He suffered from a debilitating malady which doctors were unable to diagnose; it was probably Chagas' disease, carried by the Benchuca, a bug which bit Darwin while he was travelling in the Argentine. Whatever the cause of his lassitude and intestinal ailments, Darwin was subject to ill health that forced him to live a sedate life.

Tissot's caricature has caught something of the semi-invalid quality of Darwin's existence as he sits on a thick cushion, his thin hands and legs dangling from his body like the disjointed limbs on a puppet. His habitual stoop causes him to lean forward slightly in the chair. What is most intriguing, however, is the grin on Darwin's face. It is more than that of a genial and pleasant man, because behind the smile lies a brain which had brought the world some unpleasant truths. Does Darwin's grin tell us that he is delighted by all the fuss? Could the 'cushion' be a Pandora's Box?

Jehu Junior was certainly delighted by the debate; he was pleased that Darwin had provided answers which had until then been couched in fables 'of the most childish invention'. While Darwin's theories did not provide all the answers, they were, he

argued, certainly 'more presentable than any of the old fables'. Darwin, asserted Jehu Junior, was an accomplished naturalist whose researches had to be regarded with great respect. His books were written in a style which ordinary persons could understand, and, indeed, it was possible for the average person to comprehend Darwin's arguments. His writings were, in Bowles' judgement, 'a record of earnest and honest devotion to the solution of the most momentous of the problems by which mankind are surrounded.'

Charles Darwin's most vocal disciple, THOMAS HENRY HUXLEY (1825–1895), appeared in *Vanity Fair* on 28 January 1871, nine months before Darwin himself was featured. Ape has sketched his subject standing ready to take on all critics – feet apart, arms crossed, mouth twisted, eyes set. In this characteristic pose, defiant but thoughtful, Huxley could have been before an audience pondering a new insight or at Oxford contemplating his famous response to Bishop Wilberforce.

Jehu Junior praised Huxley for being a 'popular teacher' who had contributed much to the awakening of the minds of Victorians. Indeed, before Huxley became identified with Darwin and Darwinism, he had been engaged in public lecturing. His workingmen's lectures, begun in 1855, had made him a well-known figure in London. Huxley had dedicated himself to this

task because he was convinced that the public should be made aware of new scientific discoveries and their implications. At the beginning of his lectures, he wrote:

I want the working classes to understand that science and her ways are great facts for them – that physical virtue is the base of all other, and that they are to be clean and temperate and all the rest – not because fellows in black with white ties tell them so, but because these are plain and patent laws of nature, which they must obey under penalties.

His was a practical philosophy rooted in the Socratic tradition. Out of education came the will and ability to act. The individual, argued Huxley, should train his faculties and be made aware of the connection between learning and living. He wished to join the basic disciplines of reading, writing and arithmetic with the natural sciences, history and the arts. *Vanity Fair* admitted of Huxley's popularity, his 'matter-of-fact' approach and his 'happy talent' for lecturing before various audiences.

Jehu Junior went on to note Huxley's campaign for educating women and giving them equal rights; his belief in scientific materialism and the power of the human mind. Bowles asserted that there was no one who had contributed more to the awakening of the intellect, no one who was more progressive in 'social science' or more 'comprehensive . . . in physical research'. He had played the role of a 'great Med'cine Man' among the 'Inqui-ring Redskins'; he had brought knowledge to those who wanted to know.

Huxley has too often been remembered as 'Darwin's bulldog', the role he played in the controversy surrounding Darwin's work. This identification is too restrictive of Huxley's life and influence. Before he became a defender of Darwin's theory, Huxley was spreading the value of education and rooting out ignorance among the masses, and it is for these individual contributions that *Vanity Fair* recognized him.

T. H. Huxley had come to his commitment to education and science from a background of medicine. His medical interests changed to natural history as a result of a four-year cruise as surgeon on the HMS *Rattlesnake*. At sea, his study of planktonic life led him to some discoveries that won him the respect of London's scientific community when he was only twenty-seven years old. In 1854 he became Professor of Natural History at the Government School of Mines. Here Huxley was forced, because of his teaching programme, to study fossils. This led him into new areas of scientific interest. His research into fossils and animal classification in turn put him on a collision course with Dr Richard Owen (see p. 152). Their differences of opinion became entangled in the evolution controversy after 1859 and were, consequently, public knowledge. When Darwin decided to publish his *On The Origin of Species*, he sent Huxley a copy. Huxley was greatly impressed by Darwin's arguments and praised the work in an anonymous review in *The Times* in late 1859. As part of the debate over Darwin's theory, Huxley continued to attack Owen's classification system and research on vertebrates until the climactic debate in Oxford where Huxley humiliated Samuel Wilberforce and, indirectly, Owen, who had prepared the Bishop of Oxford for this famous meeting. This dramatic confrontation marked the opening round of the contest over evolution that would go on for at least a decade.

By 1871, when Huxley was featured in *Vanity Fair*, many of the issues had been resolved or were no longer considered immediately important. For ten years Huxley and others had ar-

ticulated the basic arguments over evolution which were, of course, only part of a larger scientific movement in the nineteenth century. As Gertrude Himmelfarb has observed, the debate over *On the Origin of Species* did not revolutionize beliefs so much as give public recognition to a revolution that had already begun; the debate was a belief now made manifest.

Huxley, during the remainder of his career, would be identified with Darwinism through his writings on the topic, *Zoological Evidences as to Man's Place in Nature* (1863) and, late in his life, *Science and Victorian Tradition* (1893). His personal contributions to scientific progress were outstanding. He continued to do important work on paleontology and geology, to deliver his famous public lectures, to defend academic freedom, to serve on numerous public commissions, to encourage scientific societies and to win many awards and medals. For some years he was President of the Royal Society of London, the highest of scientific distinctions in Britain. In his private life he and his wife reared a son, Leonard, the well known teacher and writer, who was the father of Julian, Aldous and Andrew. The brilliance of the Huxley line surely supported Thomas's belief in the survival of the fittest.

It is unfortunate that PROFESSOR RICHARD OWEN (1804–1892) is remembered chiefly as the recipient of T. H. Huxley's stinging attack on Samuel Wilberforce at their famous debate,

because in his lifetime Owen made important contributions to science. Had he recognized and accepted certain anatomical structures and relationships which were self-evident to Darwin, Huxley and others, his name would be associated today with those whose theories have been adopted. Although Owen ended up on the wrong side of the Darwinian debate, he was still a prominent scholar who occupied a very important position in nineteenth-century British science.

Owen's career falls into two periods. In his early days at the Royal College of Surgeons he worked in comparative anatomy. His dissecting and classifying of animals which had died in the Zoological Society of London gardens resulted in a series of important papers on anatomy and the orders of primates. After 1856, when he became superintendent of the natural history department of the British Museum, he switched to paleontology. It was his studies in this field and his system of classifications that led him into conflict with Huxley's findings who, even before 1860, was prepared to question Owen's work.

Owen's distinguished career as scientist, naturalist, anatomist and administrator made him an outstanding and well-known Victorian figure. His scientific accomplishments sprang from an indomitable drive; his research in anatomy and paleontology strained the publishing resources of the scientific societies in London. Such intriguing titles as 'Memoir of the Gorilla' or 'Memoir of the Dodo' were matched by his extensive printed lectures on the anatomy of invertebrate animals. Owen's scientific research was complemented by his interest in museums and his administrative talents which eventually resulted in the construction of the Natural History Museum in South Kensington. He saw his original plans, submitted in 1859, become reality after 1871, and he lived long enough to occupy the new building as superintendent until his retirement in 1884.

Throughout his life Owen received numerous awards and medals, served on royal commissions and belonged to many British and foreign scientific societies. He was knighted in 1883. His outstanding administrative career and prodigious bibliography assured him a well-earned reputation; his personality and appearance marked Owen as a unique character and likely target for *Vanity Fair*. The *Dictionary of National Biography* described him:

Owen was a very remarkable personality, both physically and mentally . . . tall, and ungainly in figure, with massive head, lofty forehead, curiously round, prominent and expressive eyes, high cheekbones, large mouth and projecting chin, long, dank, dark hair . . . with a very florid complexion. Though of the old school in manners, . . . and when in congenial society a delightful companion, owing to his unfailing flow of anecdote, considerable sense of humour . . . and strongly developed . . . imagination, he was not only an extremely adroit controversialist, but no man could say harder things to an adversary or rival.

Professor Owen unwittingly played an important role in the career of caricaturist Leslie Ward. Ward encountered the famous naturalist at a garden party. He arrived clad in his best clothes and a pair of old boots, his distinctive florid features and unkempt locks topped by a tall white hat. Sir Leslie recalled: 'I saw Professor Owen, or "Old Bones" . . . and struck with his antediluvian incongruity amidst the beautiful surroundings of the garden . . . I resolved to caricature him.' Ward's family friend, John Millais (see p. 74), advised him to redraw the caricature, and to show it to Bowles who was then looking for new

talent during one of Ape's frequent departures. Ward did, and Bowles published it, unsigned. It was very popular. While in Bowles's office both men discussed a suitable *nom de crayon* for Ward. Bowles handed Ward Dr Johnson's *Dictionary* which, according to Ward, fell open 'in a most portentous manner at the "S's".' 'How's that?' he asked Bowles. 'The verb to spy, to observe secretly, or to discover at a distance or in concealment.' 'Just the thing,' said Bowles, and forty years of 'Spy' cartoons were launched – thanks, in part, to 'Old Bones'.

LOUIS PASTEUR (1822–1895) was caricatured by his fellow Frenchman, Chartran, in 1887 near the end of his distinguished yet controversial career. Chartran and Jehu Junior were sympathetic to Pasteur and honoured him in word and in picture. Compared to Tissot's Darwin or Spy's Owen, Chartran's Pasteur is more of a character portrait than a caricature. This placid sketch may be in deference to Pasteur or, perhaps more accurately, may be Chartran's attempt to depict an old man, exhausted from innumerable public debates, scarred by academic politics and handicapped by a brain haemorrhage which had left him partially paralysed since 1868. By 1886 he was suffering from cardiac problems and in October of 1887, ten months after he appeared in *Vanity Fair*, a stroke further enfeebled him.

This benign sketch, however, must not be misinterpreted: underneath the outward appearance seethed a tough, determined, opinionated will which served Pasteur well in his scientific pursuits but embroiled him in countless heated debates. Jehu Junior hinted at the quarrels surrounding Pasteur's career when he observed that although Pasteur was a 'very humane and kindly man' (which he was personally), he had been 'greatly denounced by his opponents' (which he certainly was).

Throughout his life Pasteur linked academic science and industry in solving practical problems. He established his reputation in crystallography and structural chemistry which earned him an appointment in chemistry, aged twenty-six, on the faculty at Strasbourg in 1848. Six years later, in 1854, he was named Professor of Chemistry at Lille; and here, in this industrial heartland he applied his expertise to solving problems besetting local manufacturers, while beginning his study of fermentation and micro-organisms. Then, in 1857, Pasteur moved to Paris and the École Normale Supérieure as director of scientific studies. His discoveries in fermentation soon resulted in a new scientific process for manufacturing vinegar and the preservation of wine by heating, a process known as 'pasteurization'. In the early 1860s Pasteur, through his experimentations and discoveries, was emerging as an opponent to the theory of spontaneous generation of disease and a supporter of the airborne germ theory. Meanwhile, during the 1860s decade, he turned his attention to a blight that was rapidly destroying the French silkworms. Through painstaking research he identified the lethal parasite and proposed a method to combat the disease.

For many years Pasteur had believed that fermentation and disease were caused by similar micro-organisms, and this belief led him to suspect that both could be explained in terms of germ theory. During the 1860s and 1870s vast strides were made against the spread of diseases based, in part, on the germ theory. One of these was Joseph Lister's introduction of antiseptic surgery for which he recognized Pasteur's contributions. Another was the final conquest of anthrax. Robert Koch, in 1876, had already identified the anthrax bacillus. Now Pasteur entered the picture and proved by experiment that the dis-

Hydrophobia
Louis Pasteur
Men of the Day No. 372
8 January 1887
T

ease was carried by germs. Pasteur eventually produced a vaccine for anthrax.

Pasteur's work in immunology encouraged him to search for a rabies vaccine for animals. He was using one by 1884. A year later a rabies vaccination was administered to a young boy and by November 1886 nearly 2500 persons had been treated. On the whole, the vaccine was successful, but the tendency to play up the deaths rather than the successfully cured patients brought him some bad publicity.

Pasteur, or course, was not entirely innocent in all of this for he had made many enemies who wished to settle old scores. Nevertheless, he did win recognition in the end. In 1889, the famous Institut Pasteur opened. Three years later, in 1892, a jubilee brought him honour at the Sorbonne. He was a frail man by then, and through the voice of his son he called on the coming generation of young scientists to 'live in the serene peace of laboratories and libraries'. He had not always followed his own advice. Whether he would have made even greater contributions to chemistry and biology had he done so remains as haunting a question as the look in his eyes captured by Chartran.

Vanity Fair witnessed the final phases of the debate over evolution; it participated in the birth of the Atomic Age when in 1904 the magazine featured MARIE and PIERRE CURIE. Jehu

Junior showed that he understood the repercussions of the discovery of radium, as he had recognized the consequences of the theory of evolution. In his opening paragraph, he observed:

When the mouse freed the lion, that self-assured beast was never more astonished than was the scientific world when, from an unimportant villa in a dowdy quarter of Paris, there sprang a discovery that upset half its preconceived ideas . . . The scientific world differs from the lion in that it does not yearn to be freed from the net of tradition by nibbling investigations.

Radium, according to *Vanity Fair,* had been displayed to the public in the Paris Exhibition of 1900, but it was quickly withdrawn from public view because of the 'audacious pranks' it began to play on the older exhibits. This new discovery proved to be 'a veritable *l'enfant terrible'* so it was taken back 'to its nursery'. But once the press explained radium to its readers, civilization had, since then, 'radium on the brain'. Having described the potential heating power of radium, *Vanity Fair* remarked that the 'imagination shrinks from the idea' of its immense applications and possibilities.

Vanity Fair then commented upon the Curies who, regardless of the honours bestowed upon them, had remained 'unspirited'. Both were immune to the praises of an adoring public. Monsieur Curie, wrote Jehu Junior, was 'negligent in his attire', being wrapped in theories, shy to strangers and contemptuous of worldly affairs. Madame Curie was also 'impatient of the dressmaker and careless of society'. In conclusion, Jehu Junior wrote: 'They are a notable pair, a marriage matched by fate; and their child is radium.'

Matched by fate they seemed to be. Both had been born to parents trained in science or medicine. Marie Curie's (1861–1934) early life was marked by genteel poverty and noble sacrifice for her education. She grew up with a love of nature and a geniune concern for poor people; perhaps this helps explain why she was never impressed by those with money or in Society. The young Pierre (1859–1906), in contrast, was reared in a permissive atmosphere, taught by his parents and sent off to the university as a matter of course. Marie struggled through on a limited income, read Marx, Dostoevsky, engaged in political movements, served as a governess for several years and made her way to Paris from Warsaw in a fourth class rail coach sitting on a camp stool. By the time Pierre met Marie in 1894, he had already established a name for himself in the study of crystals and in the area of magnetism. Marie, who had trained as a chemist and later in physics and mathematics, was working as an assistant in a laboratory. After their marriage in July 1895, Pierre turned his attention to working with his bride in the newly discovered field of radiation. Their ability to work closely together produced, in 1898, the first samples of radium.

They were a remarkable team, fully complementing one another. Pierre was a true physicist; a theoretician, experimenter, philosopher and builder of equipment. Marie, with her background in chemistry, was driven by a sense of dedication and thoroughness that would not tolerate disappointment or discouragement. For months they toiled in their wretched, poorly equipped workshop, reducing the huge amounts of pitchblende ore to the minute particles of radium. Each step was tested, measured and recorded. After they isolated and identified radium in 1898, it was displayed at the Paris Exposition. Three years later in 1903, the Curies were awarded the Nobel Prize.

From 1903 until Pierre's death in 1906, when he was hit by a

Radium
Monsieur and Madame Curie
People of the Day No. 1
22 December 1904
Imp

155

wagon in the streets of Paris, the Curies worked together. However, they shunned the mounting publicity and were dismayed, if not repulsed, by their sudden fame. Jehu Junior's comments pointed out their reluctance to accept the public's adulation. Imp, the caricaturist, has caught their reserved quality, even Pierre's shyness. A photograph of them with their daughter Irene, taken in 1904, reveals a comparable soberness in their lives. Their faces, like the ones depicted by Imp, are deadly serious. In both poses they sit reserved, lost in the thoughts of their intense hard work.

After Pierre's sudden death in 1906 Madame Curie continued her research alone. In 1908 she became the first woman ever to teach at the Sorbonne; three years later she was awarded her second Nobel Prize, the first person to receive it twice. During the First World War she developed and designed radiological (x-ray) units for the French Medical Corps. She accompanied the ambulances carrying this equipment to the front lines and drove her own vehicle. After the war Radium Institutes were established and foundations formed to receive gifts and support. During the 1920s she supervised the extension of her work, fought for safety regulations among workers exposed to radiation and served on a League of Nations Commission.

Madame Curie's deep reserve and untiring commitment lasted into the final months of her life. According to her daughter, her mother felt that 'life was negligible, without proportion to the work undertaken'. Madame Curie's contributions were squeezed out of a life that knew few pleasures in childhood and untold hours of toil as an adult. The responsibilities of working with the discoveries which she and her husband passed on to the world were recognized by *Vanity Fair* as early as 1904 and understood by Pierre Curie when he accepted his Nobel Prize:

We might still consider that in criminal hands radium might become very dangerous; and here we must ask ourselves if mankind can benefit by knowing the secrets of nature, if man is mature enough to take advantage of them, or if this knowledge will not be harmful to the world.

We are still asking ourselves the same question.

BUSINESSMEN
BANKERS & BUILDERS

Britain's position in the nineteenth century as a world power was due, mainly, to competent business leadership. The first nation to industrialize, during much of the nineteenth century Britain led the world in the technical innovations and quantity of goods produced. *Vanity Fair* realized the important role that these new men were playing in bringing prosperity and growth to the British people, and the magazine featured outstanding members of the business community including bankers, financiers, industrialists, entrepreneurs, retailers, engineers and architects.

Among the financiers and bankers (exclusive of the Rothschild clan which appeared nine times in *Vanity Fair*) were Arthur Fitzgerald Kinnaird (*Vanity Fair*, 15 January 1876), of the banking firm of Ransom and Co, and George Grenfell Glyn (*Vanity Fair*, 24 February 1872), who was a partner in Glyn, Mills, Currie and Co and later served in Gladstone's cabinet. Businessmen and entrepreneurs included Christopher Furness (*Vanity Fair*, 21 October 1908), Douglas Vickers (*Vanity Fair*, 30 December 1909) and Frank Ree (*Vanity Fair*, 5 June 1912), all identified with ships, armaments and railways.

The crest of mid-Victorian prosperity, which began in the 1850s, came just before *Vanity Fair* was founded. Heavy industry was expanding, and the growth and wealth of the middle classes was reflected in the fact that over a million people were engaged in domestic service. Although the British economy went into a slump between 1873 and 1896 as prices and profits fell, this recession did not visibly affect *Vanity Fair*'s financial state, nor its optimism. The Edwardian mini-boom tended to reinforce what the magazine had always contended – that British products and management were the best in the world. Statistics which revealed the relative decline of Britain's world economic strength were discussed in *Vanity Fair*. Its weekly column, 'Other People's Money', continued to advise readers on where to invest their savings, and the biographical descriptions accompanying the caricatures of the business men and entrepreneurs imparted a sense of confidence in the continued economic growth of the United Kingdom.

Members of the business community also personified the Victorian ideal of just reward for honest toil. Many of them were imbued with a moral code that gave them a feeling of achievement and righteousness. These men felt that God was on the side of the custodians of the machine and that He was guiding the impulses of this new industrial age. While their goals were not always achieved, such businessmen were recognized for their honesty, efficiency, hard work and thrift. Moreover, once success came many of them men turned to philanthropy. Their ideals of fair play and self help were thus extended to the less fortunate in society. Socially and politically these successful men were eventually accepted by Society. Their daughters married into the aristocracy, the public schools educated their sons and the political processes and playing fields were slowly opened to men of wealth rather than birth.

Businessmen

Three businessmen who personified the 'getting and spending' of the Victorian-Edwardian eras were Henry Bessemer, Walter Gilbey and Thomas Lipton. All were 'self-made'; and all were accepted into Society. Upon making their fortunes they turned their interest in a variety of directions: to astronomy, to cart horses, to yachting. Spy caricatured all three men at the height of their business careers, after they had amassed their fortunes and were devoting their time to other matters. Each man possessed a keen sense for making a profit, obviously a quality that *Vanity Fair* was coming to admire in its victims.

HENRY BESSEMER (1873–1898) may be best described as a practical man of science. Full of energy, inventive talent and artistic feelings, he capitalized upon the skills and common sense his father had taught him, went on to amass a fortune and to win the respect of his fellow countrymen and, eventually, the world. When caricatured by Spy in 1880, Bessemer was sixty-seven years old and had been knighted and made a member of the Royal Society the previous year.

The Bessemer steel process, his most famous invention, had been in operation since 1856 when he received his first patent. Over the years the process had been modified until, by 1879, it was fully perfected with the application of Sidney Gilchrist-Thomas's discovery of a way to eliminate phosphorus in the Bessemer Converter. Although Bessemer's reputation rests mainly on his steel-making system, his other inventions could have earned him a place in history, and probably a page in *Vanity Fair*.

Sir Henry inherited his father's skill, craftsmanship and shrewd business mind. In 1830 he left the Hertfordshire village of Charlton to make his way in London. He immediately came to public notice through his metal art work and castings which were exhibited in the Royal Academy. He was soon producing large quantities of embossed work in different materials and at a handsome profit. In 1833 he made his first important invention: a set of perforated discs which made it impossible for forgers to reuse stamps on government documents, an illegal process which had cost the British government £100,000 a year in revenues.

In rapid succession Bessemer developed a process to use graphite or plumbago in pencils, designed a type composing machine, discovered a way to make imitation Utrecht velvet and hit upon the secret of making bronze powder and gold paint by a cheap method. Profits from these allowed him to turn to steel making. *Vanity Fair* recognized Bessemer's changing interest: '[he] preferred modelling to painting, and as he modelled he found he preferred mechanics to both.'

The perfection of the Bessemer system led *Vanity Fair* to observe that his new method of making steel so cheaply and speedily had caused 'iron to be all but superseded, has ruined or revolutionized all iron-work and has made [him] a colossal and well-earned fortune.' Huge profits were made; estimates of a 100 per cent return every two months on the original investment have been calculated. Cheaper steel, boosted by large profits, made a fundamental change in the world. Abraham S. Hewitt, the American steel manufacturer, compared the Bessemer process to the invention of printing, the discovery of America and the introduction of the steam engine.

His colossal and well-earned fortunes allowed Bessemer to turn his attention to his home on Denmark Hill where he constructed telescopes, conducted solar heat experiments and laid out lakes and ferneries. *Vanity Fair* claimed that his four foot

lens telescope would be the largest in the world once it was completed.

Spy was unusually kind to his subject. He appears to us as a genial old man; the facial features, body and head are in proportion. While time had taken its toll, Spy did not capitalize upon the by-products of old age. Jehu Junior described Bessemer as one of 'the strongest, ablest, simplest men of his time'.

Spy treated Gilbey and Lipton with less deference. He portrayed these two men in similar poses, facing left, in half profile. Their tight collars accentuate their facial features and effectively separate the body from the head. Gilbey's slight frame, his pince-nez and chain, his whip, high collar and hat are well utilized by Spy to capture the man's personality. Lipton, on the other hand, was treated more respectfully; a sportsman in white duck pants and white shoes. His interest in yachting is further emphasized by the pennant of the *Shamrock* in the upper right corner.

WALTER GILBEY (1831–1914) founded a wine business with his brother after beginning his working life as an estate agent and serving in the Convalescent Hospital during the Crimean War. The firm took in more relatives, prospered and expanded with the tobacco trade. Gilbey's success in business permitted him to pursue his private interests. His cultivated tastes, according to

cart horses
Walter Gilbey
Men of the Day No. 404
30 June 1888
Spy

Shamrock
Sir Thomas Johnstone Lipton, KCVO
Men of the Day No. 824
19 September 1901
Spy

159

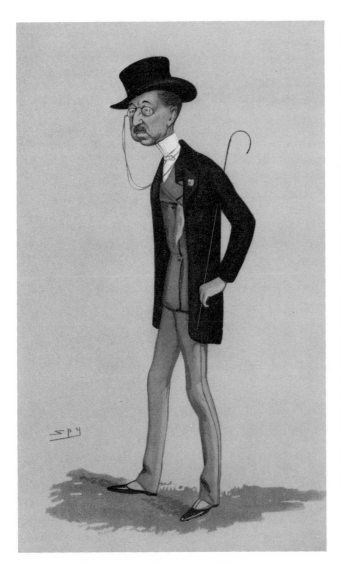

Jehu Junior, embraced 'agriculture, nankeen [buff coloured cotton] trousers, and the fine arts'. His interest in agriculture was nearly as extensive as the quality of his wines, for he sat on numerous important committees dedicated to the improvement of farming and animal husbandry. He also established several societies dedicated to the breeding and care of various types of horses. Gilbey's 'pet hobby' was the British carthorse. 'This animal', noted *Vanity Fair*, 'he may almost be said to have re-created.' Gilbey's interest in horses and farming lasted many years after he appeared in *Vanity Fair*. He wrote on a variety of agricultural topics that included horses, a biography of George Stubbs, styles of carriages, pigs, poultry and cockfighting. In the eyes of the public his name is identified with a very popular gin, but in the hearts of horse lovers he is remembered for help-ing organize the London Cart Horse parade in 1885 which is still held each Easter Monday in Regent's Park and which is carried on by his namesake, Walter A. Gilbey, vice president of the London Harness Horse Parade Society.

THOMAS LIPTON (1880–1931), like Gilbey and Bessemer, made his own fortune and left his name on his products. By Victorian standards, Lipton was perhaps more admired than Gilbey, hav-ing accumulated his money from groceries and tea rather than spirits and tobacco. Lipton's father, an Irishman who left his homeland during the potato famine to live in Glasgow, operated a small grocer's shop and made a modest living. Lipton's mother, Frances, a kind, loyal and shrewd woman, was an in-spiration to him all of his life.

Young Thomas left Scotland in 1865, aged fifteen, for Amer-ica where he worked for five years on plantations in the South and in a big grocer's shop in New York. He became homesick and returned to Glasgow in 1870 – on a Saturday afternoon with a rocking chair and a barrel of flour strapped on top of the cab.

Such a talent for publicity not only impressed his neighbours but served him well throughout his career. A year later, in 1871, he founded his own grocery shop and proceeded to buy directly from suppliers in order to undersell his competition. His reputation for quality food at a low price spread; soon he established other stores. He drew upon his advertising skills to put together attention-rousing campaigns to announce the openings of new shops. For example, he would sponsor a big parade and display a monster cheese that, when sliced open, spilled out gold coins, or he would hire a balloonist to drop leaflets entitling customers to prizes in his store. By 1889 he was expanding and experimenting in the production and distribu-tion of foods. That year he moved his headquarters from Glas-gow to London. He acquired tea plantations in Ceylon and a slaughter house in Chicago. He ran his own printing, paper bag and food processing plants around England.

In the late 1890s Lipton became involved in philanthropy and in yachting. He came to know the Princess of Wales through his gifts of food for her projects to feed the poor, and his interest in yachting opened doors for him to British Society. He entertained the king himself, Edward VII, on board. In 1898 he was knighted for his services to charity and in recognition of his business successes. The next year, in 1899, he issued his first challenge for the America's Cup. His yacht, the *Shamrock I*, was defeated then, and again in 1901, the year he was featured in *Vanity Fair*. He never won the race even though he competed over a thirty-year period at a cost of nearly £1,000,000. This result earned him the unenviable reputation as 'the world's best loser'.

The year after his appearance in *Vanity Fair*, Lipton was created a baronet. During the First World War his famous steam yacht, the *Erin*, delivered medical supplies between Marseilles and Salonica until it was sunk by a submarine. Lipton continued to be active in his various enterprises and charities until 1927 when he retired. He died a few years later.

Vanity Fair ranked Lipton as 'one of the most prominent men in the world'. He was possessed of 'Irish ambition and parents, Scotch abilities and birth, [and] British pluck'. Though he had amassed millions and had corporate and financial interests and charities, *Vanity Fair* observed that his personal habits of simple living, of hard work and keeping excellent health and of 'no vices' made him a 'cheerful, modest, popular fellow and a cheery companion'. Apparently the joys of life that attracted his friend, Edward VII, never tempted Lipton. He abstained from alcohol and tobacco. Thomas Lipton was the ideal model of the successful, enterprising, honest, charitable, sport-loving Victorian business man. He stood for all that was best in the Victorian business world and set an example of Victorian decorum in his private life.

Bankers

The Rothschild dynasty arose in the eighteenth century in the Frankfurt Jewish Quarter where Mayer Amschel (1744–1812) sold old coins to members of the court of Prince William of Hanover. Meyer Amschel then started a money exchange, the first Rothschild bank, made handsome profits and reared five sons. Four of the five sons were sent abroad to establish branches in Naples, Vienna, Paris and London. Nathan Mayer (1777–1836) went to England, where he opened a bank at London's New Court and founded the English line of Rothschilds. He managed the financial arrangements of Wellington's Peninsula Campaign and by a series of complicated manoeuvres poured money into the hands of Britain's European allies. Nathan's most well known financial coup occurred in 1815 when, upon being the first person in England to be informed of Napoleon's defeat at Waterloo, he went to the Stock Exchange and purchased huge amounts of government stock. He emerged from the Napoleonic Wars as one of the most powerful bankers in England. Nathan had four sons; two of them appeared in *Vanity Fair*, Lionel Nathan, or Baron Lionel, and Mayer Amschel. Seven more Rothschilds were later featured in the magazine: the three sons of Baron Lionel, Lord Rothschild (the first Lord) (*Vanity Fair*, 9 June 1888), Alfred (*Vanity Fair*, 31 May 1884), and Leopold (*Vanity Fair*, 13 December 1884); two members of the French branch, the Baron Alphonse (*Vanity Fair*, 20 September 1894) and Arthur (*Vanity Fair*, 2 August 1900); Baron Ferdinand (*Vanity Fair*, 15 June 1889), the Austrian cousin who came to England and built Waddesdon Manor, and Walter Lionel (*Vanity Fair*, 13 September 1900),

the heir of Lord Rothschild who became a famous naturalist for whom a giraffe was named and to whom, because of his role in the Zionist movement, the Balfour Declaration of 1917 was addressed.

The first Rothschild to be caricatured in *Vanity Fair* was MAYER AMSCHEL (1818–1874), namesake to the founding father and fourth son of Nathan Mayer who had established the London bank. Known as Baron Mayer (a title given to the family by the Austrian rulers), he played only a minor role in the banking business· and devoted his life to collecting art and racing horses. His mansion, Mentmore, became a showplace of art treasures and celebrated for its hospitality. In 1871, the year he was featured in *Vanity Fair*, in addition to winning the Derby with Favonius he won so many important races that 1871 was called 'the baron's year'. The Baron was elected to the House of Commons as a Liberal, from 1859 to 1874. Hannah, his only child, married Philip Primrose, the fifth Earl of Rosebery (see p. 58).

Jehu Junior outlined the rise of the Rothschild dynasty in his commentary, reminding his readers of Bismarck's famous remark that the family was the 'sixth great Power in Europe'.

Although the Rothschilds were 'of a more ancient race and nation than any of those which hold a position in Europe', they had come to identify themselves 'with their place of habitation' – they had readily assimilated themselves into their adopted countries. Indeed, Nathan Mayer had supported England 'through the darkest moments' of the Napoleonic war. Now, his son sat in the House of Commons and was the 'sporting member of the great house'. Baron Mayer had begun racing horses with the 'energy of his family'; but, added Jehu Junior, 'not at all with that single eye to gain with which his race is credited'. His triumph at the Derby was symbolic; as the first Rothschild to win this coveted race, he had taken one more step into the inner circles of British Society.

Vanity Fair recognized this step with a degree of approval, but not without a condescension which hinted at anti-Semitism. Ape's caricature of the Baron is not flattering. He has emphasized his subject's large nose, protruding mouth and lips. The stance is hardly becoming as the Baron leans forward, stiff legged and slightly bent, resting on a cane.

When Ape sketched the Baron's older brother LIONEL NATHAN in 1877 he was much kinder to him. The heavy eyelids and large nose dominate the face, but the features are softened. He looks like a pleasant elderly man, wise in the ways of the world. His head is in proportion to the body; his clothes compliment him. Nevertheless, the caricature hints at a nineteenth-century stereotyping of Jews.

When Baron Lionel appeared in *Vanity Fair*, Jehu Junior again summarized, in his commentary, the rise of the House of Rothschild. Like his father, Baron Lionel has been close to the 'great political events' surrounding English history; for example, he informed Lord Russell of the United States Government's decision to hand over to Great Britain the Confederate emissaries who had been captured on board the *Trent*. In 1871 he had been the first person to tell Gladstone of the fall of Paris. The Baron, through long hours of hard work and skilful moderation, had held together the family and extended its fortunes until he was now 'the undisputed Emperor of Legitimate Finance'.

The Baron's success in finance was in sharp contrast to his difficult struggle in the House of Commons to be seated without

The Winner of the Race
Baron Mayer Amschel De Rothschild
Statesmen No. 85
27 May 1871
Ape

Builders

ALBERTO SANTOS DUMONT (1873–1932) appeared in *Vanity Fair* in November 1901 soon after he had won the Deutsch Prize. The Deutsch Prize was offered by the Aero Club of France to anyone who could fly from St Cloud around the Eiffel Tower and return in a period of thirty minutes. This feat was seen as more than a flying stunt; it was a symbol of the beginning of a new century and a new mode of transportation. Santos Dumont accepted the challenge and captured the prize. His victory brought him worldwide fame and, after 1901, he continued to be a pioneer in the conquest of the air.

Santos Dumont was the son of a successful and wealthy Brazilian coffee producer. His father, from French immigrant stock, married the daughter of a prominent Brazilian family. He made a fortune and divided it among his children, telling his youngest son, Alberto, to 'go to Paris' to seek his fame.

From his childhood Alberto had been fasincated with machines and balloons. On his father's coffee plantation he observed the harvesting equipment and learned how to make and fly fire-balloons and kites. Like S. F. Cody (see p. 199), Santos Dumont profited from these children's delights, although he was not, like Cody, taught by an expert in kite flying, a Chinese cook. After his arrival in Paris in 1892, he began to study engineering. By 1897, he had made several balloon ascents and the following year he built his first gasoline-powered balloon. Over the next three years he constructed and tested five airships and, in 1901, he built 'Number Six' to compete for the Deutsch Prize.

To commemorate his triumph and to welcome him to London, *Vanity Fair* had Santos Dumont caricatured upon his arrival. The magazine called him 'the greatest flyer that has yet seen the world from above . . .'. Santos Dumont was 'eminently adapted by nature' to be an 'Aeronaut' because he possessed 'the agility of a cat, the feet of a climber, the hands of an engineer, and the airiness of barely seven stone'. Jehu Junior noted that he was a diminutive man with a tiny voice who was always smartly dressed. Santos Dumont stood only 5 feet 5 inches and weighed 110 pounds. He had an oversized head, with a wide forehead above dark brown eyes, a big nose and protruding ears, a clipped moustache and large white teeth.

The caricaturist captured Santos Dumont's physical features very clearly. Here is the 'smart dresser' in his striped shirt, high collar (which he always wore), tie, waistcoat and boater. Geo-Hum, the caricaturist, capitalized upon his victim's features. Their incongruity helps to make the drawing an effective caricature. Santos Dumont's personality, appearance and passion for balloons have been united in the caricature, making it one of the most amusing found in *Vanity Fair* in its last years.

That *Vanity Fair* should put JOHN CHETWYND-TALBOT, the Earl of Shrewsbury and Talbot (1860–1912), into a motor car was clear evidence to its readers that times were changing. The automobile had first appeared in England in 1895. In 1889, the Comte de Dion was caricatured by Guth, sitting on a motorized tricycle, clad nattily in jacket, plus fours and a straw boater. The caption read 'Automobile' (*Vanity Fair*, 12 October 1899). By the Edwardian era, the upper classes were using the motor car as their adult toy and status symbol. In 1904, a year after the Earl was featured in *Vanity Fair*, the number of cars in England was estimated to be at 24,201, a third of them in London.

The upper classes not only used motor cars as status symbols; some, like the Earl, were actively engaged in the manufac-

taking the Christian oath. *Vanity Fair* discreetly failed to mention the reason why he was not seated. His assault on the House of Commons was one of the most famous battles for Jewish emancipation in England in the nineteenth century. He was elected, as a Liberal, from the City of London to the House in 1847. For eleven years the House of Lords rejected the House of Commons' bill allowing the Baron to take his seat and still adhere to his religious beliefs. Finally, in 1858, after being re-elected five times, he was permitted to occupy his seat when a compromise was reached granting each House the power to determine its own form of oath. The Baron sat in the House for the next ten years and never spoke in debate. He had established the principle; the contest had been won. Several years later his efforts were rewarded when his son was made a peer. Gladstone had recommended that the Baron Lionel himself be raised to the peerage, but Queen Victoria said she could not bring herself to make a Jew a peer. However, his son, Nathaniel Mayer, was named Lord Rothschild in 1885, at Disraeli's insistence. Jehu Junior described the Baron as a great lover of art, a 'splendid entertainer' (although he was rather reserved), and a generous philanthropist who gave liberally 'to the deserving'. According to Jehu Junior, he had been 'completely adopted' into Society and was 'loved and courted to the full as much as the best of Englishmen'. In spite of such comment – or perhaps because it was made – the barrier of prejudice still remained.

the Deutsch Prize
M Alberto Santos Dumont
Men of the Day No. 829
14 November 1901
Geo.Hum

ture of automobiles. The links between aristocracy and industry were strengthening. The Talbots traced their lineage back to the Domesday Book. The Lord Talbot who fought for Henry VI and was made Earl of Shrewsbury, has been immortalized by Shakespeare in *Henry VI, Part 1*. His later successor was the premier Earl of England and Lord High Steward of Ireland. According to *Vanity Fair*, the history of the Earl's 'eminent House' filled more than six pages of *Burke's Peerage*. Regardless of his esteemed position, in 1903, the Earl was one of the 'keenest of motor drivers' and chairman of a 'big motor manufactory . . .' He was also the first person to fit cabs with noiseless tyres in London and Paris. *Vanity Fair* noted that the Earl 'shoots all the autumn, hunts all the winter, plays polo all summer, and motors all the year . . .' and 'his hobby is cabs'.

Spy, especially after 1890 when the aristocracy were less reluctant to sit to him, was very sympathetic. His work on the Earl is a complimentary character portrait. John Chetwynd-Talbot is a handsome man. His manner and dress are impeccable; a well trimmed moustache and a clipped haircut lend dignity to his erect posture. But therein lies the incongruity of the sketch, for no serious motor car owner, having to face the dust and wind on primitive roads, would travel about in such attire. *Vanity Fair*, at the sacrifice of accuracy, associated the Earl with his hobby and business.

Although it was accepted slowly and with some scepticism, if not hostility, the motor car was here to stay. Ordinances controlling its operation literally slowed development. For a time, car drivers had to have a man with a flag running in front to clear the way. As the car became more acceptable, others besides members of the aristocracy became enthusiasts. *Vanity Fair* reported on 2 October 1902, that W. S. Gilbert, in a letter to *The Times*, had narrated his experiences as a 'lately turned motorist', and he had informed *The Times* that the 'twelve-mile limit is quite reasonable, and should not be exceeded'. As a gesture to the famed lyricist and his newly discovered pastime, *Vanity Fair* composed 'The Very Mild Motorist' (after *Patience*):

If you're anxious for to shine
In the motor-racing line,
* Set out with caution rare;*
You must not, on any terms
(So William Schwenk affirms)
* For 'scorching' feats prepare;*
As the country roads you scour
At a dozen miles per hour,
* You must call it break-neck speed;*
And the pace of Piccadilly
For your new bought 'puffing-billy'
* Never venture to exceed.*

CHORUS:
Then everyone will say,
As you dawdle on your way:
'If this young man's enjoying himself,
The fun I fail to see;
Oh, what a most particularly mild young man,
Is William Schwenck, J. P.!'

Vanity Fair also recognized the contributions of entrepreneurs and engineers who made fortunes outside Britain. Among those honoured in *Vanity Fair* were the two French builders, Ferdinand de Lesseps and Alexandre Gustave Eiffel.

FERDINAND DE LESSEPS (1805–1894) had begun his career as a diplomat in the French consular service in Lisbon. Later he served in Rotterdam and was Minister to Spain. As early as 1832 when stationed at Alexandria, he had thought of digging a canal across the isthmus of Suez; but it was not until 1854 he received the permission of Said Pasha, the Viceroy of Egypt, to start construction. In 1869, ten years after the project began, *Vanity Fair* featured de Lesseps.

The magazine noted that the workers on the canal had had only the 'passive resistance of nature' to overcome while de Lesseps had had to contend also with 'the active opposition of man'. His critics, among them many Englishmen, had argued that it should not and could not be done. Yet, due to his 'indomitable perseverance and unflagging energy', the canal had been a success. Exhibiting its usual Francophobia, *Vanity Fair* observed that normally Frenchmen were better known for their ideas than their 'practical qualities', but de Lesseps combined the 'boldness and grasp of the idealist with the working capacity of the practical man'. He had never relaxed in his efforts or been discouraged by his momentary defeats, added *Vanity Fair*. Now he had 'suppressed an isthmus, and brought together two sides of the world.' Later on he was not so successful in Panama, where his herculean efforts to build a canal in Central America failed. He died a broken man, under suspicion from the scandals surrounding his Panama adventure and disap-

He Supressed an Isthmus
Le Vicomte Ferdinand de Lesseps
Men of the Day No. 2
27 November 1869
(unsigned)

Gustave Eiffel   165
Alexandre Gustave Eiffel
Men of the Day No. 424
11 May 1889
Guth

pointed over his inability to conquer the country's rugged terrain and deadly diseases.

Tissot has combined East and West in de Lesseps's attire by putting an Egyptian cloak over his European business suit. With a shovel in his left hand, he presents to the world, with his right hand, his handiwork. The caricature is complimentary; de Lesseps looks pleasant and, indeed, pleased with himself. He was sixty-four when Tissot caricatured him; no longer a young man, de Lesseps showed his age. While the sketch reveals age it tells little of the man's character or past.

Another Frenchman, ALEXANDRE GUSTAVE EIFFEL (1832–1923), had just completed his most famous landmark – the prefabricated iron tower – when Guth caricatured him. Like Tissot, Guth has been kind to his subject; and the caricature, more like a character portrait, does not offer any revealing traits of Eiffel. A sombre, serious man, somewhat stiffly posed, Eiffel exudes self-confidence, but little else is disclosed. Jehu Junior's only vcomment about Eiffel's physical appearance dealt with his clothes. Because Eiffel still patronized his provincial tailor, he wore the 'worst-fitting trousers in Europe'.

Although Eiffel's name will be forever associated with his structure in Paris, he had made his reputation as a construction engineer. The first of his famous works was the bridge over the Garonne at Bordeaux completed when he was only twenty-six

years old; later he built bridges in Portugal and Indo-China, the train station in Pest, the dome of the Nice Observatory and the framework for Bartholdi's Statue of Liberty. Jehu Junior called the Eiffel Tower 'an audacious structure', the 'chief wonder of the day' that beggared the Tower of Babel.

Like de Lesseps, Eiffel did not end his career with his best known structure. He went on to design locks for the Panama Canal and founded the first laboratory for aerodynamics. His contributions to aeronautical engineering helped others pioneer the age of the flying machine.

JOURNALISTS

The repeal of the duties on paper and advertising in 1861 allowed specialized weeklies such as *Vanity Fair* as well as provincial dailies and the cheap mass circulation newspapers in London to flourish. More than fifty of the 'new journalists' – and a few of the old – were portrayed in *Vanity Fair*. Bowles's own father, Thomas Milner Gibson, had brought about the repeal of the last 'taxes on knowledge'. His natural son served his apprenticeship in journalism partly as a political writer on the *Morning Post*. Its proprietor, Algernon Borthwick (*Vanity Fair*, 17 June 1871), probably contributed to the initial expenses of *Vanity Fair*.

The caricatures and the commentaries of this collection of correspondents, editors and proprietors are among the most pungent of the sets of *Vanity Fair* caricatures. Bowles's own contacts and personal sympathies accounted for the attention given to this relatively new professional class who, at mid-century, were barely respectable. Palmerston, in replying in 1855 to a complaint of the Queen about *The Times*, observed: 'There is no Doubt some inconvenience in the admission of Editors and writers of newspapers into general society, but if they happen to be in a Position in Life which would naturally lead to their being invited, it would not be easy to exclude them merely on account of their connection with a newspaper.'

Bowles had little fondness for 'The Thunderer'. In 1881, the proprietor of *The Times*, John Walter III, was dismissed as an old fogy. 'He has never yet added a new idea, a new fact, or even a new phrase to any subject of public import . . . It is felt that it is not he who inspires the *Times*, but the *Times* who coaches him' (*Vanity Fair*, 10 September 1881). Other Timesmen caricatured besides William Howard Russell the great war correspondent (see p. 171), were Thomas Chenery, the editor from 1878–1884 (*Vanity Fair*, 4 October 1879), and 'The prince of journalists,' Henri Stefan Opper de Blowitz of the Paris Bureau. Both Ape (*Vanity Fair*, 29 August 1885) and Guth (*Vanity Fair*, 7 December 1889) tried their brush on this extraordinary little eccentric. Alfred Harmsworth, Lord Northcliffe, founder of the *Daily Mail*, was unimaginatively sketched by Spy (*Vanity Fair*, 16 May 1895).

A sampling of other new journalists includes Frederick Greenwood, 'He created the *Pall Mall Gazette*' (*Vanity Fair*, 19 June 1880); Edward Levy of the *Daily Telegraph* (*Vanity Fair*, 22 March 1873); James Johnstone of *The Standard* (*Vanity Fair*, 14 February 1874); and Harry Marks of the *Financial News* (*Vanity Fair*, 8 June 1889). Correspondents and columnists, or leader writers, included Russell's successor as the top war correspondent, Archibald Forbes of the *Daily News* (*Vanity Fair*, 26 November 1892), George Augustus Sala of the *Daily Telegraph* (*Vanity Fair*, 25 September 1875), and 'Mr Dooley' – the American, Finley Peter Dunne (*Vanity Fair*, 27 July 1905). Other American journalists were an impatient James Gordon Bennett of the *New York Herald* (*Vanity Fair*, 15 November 1884), a dishevelled Horace Greeley (see p. 189) and Whitelaw Reid of the *New York Tribune* (*Vanity Fair*, 25 September 1902).

Newspaper cartoonists were not ignored. *Vanity Fair* affectionately caricatured John Tenniel, 'Punch' (*Vanity Fair*, 26 October 1878); F. Carruthers Gould, 'He believes that he is an artist . . .' (*Vanity Fair*, 22 February 1890); Phil May, 'Phil' (*Vanity Fair*, 21 February 1896); and Max Beerbohm, 'Max' (see p. 33).

Thus, Henry Morton Stanley, William Howard Russell, Baron Reuter and J. L. Garvin are offered as a tantalizing sample of the newspapermen in *Vanity Fair*. As a set they are representative of the era when modern journalism took shape.

HENRY MORTON STANLEY (1841–1904), the finder of the lost explorer-missionary, Dr David Livingstone, in East Africa, was cruelly caricatured in 1872 by Montbard, the *nom de crayon* of Charles Auguste Loye, a French caricaturist-illustrator. He portrayed Stanley as a *poseur*, a small, swarthy man with heavy-lidded eyes and features that might be a mixture of negroid and oriental. The cartoon reflected the initial hostility and distrust of the English élite for this little, aggressive, lowborn reporter on a notorious American newspaper, the *New York Herald*, who had done what only gentlemen were supposed to do in a terri-tory reserved for British imperialists. He led an expedition into 'Darkest Africa' and found Livingstone, one of the heroes of the age, who had vanished more than five years earlier on the last of his efforts to explore and 'civilize' that vast unknown continent. Stanley's greeting to this hero, 'Dr Livingstone, I presume?' became part of his historic scoop, and the pellmell gusto of his book on the subject, *How I Found Livingstone,* brought him world fame. Snobbish carping such as Florence Nightingale's: 'the very worst book on the very best subject' could not seriously lessen his coup.

Jehu Junior observed in a commentary which was friendlier than the accompanying caricature:

Some persons who knew no more of Mr Stanley than he was the correspondent of a newspaper not of unimpeachable veracity hesi-tated at first to accept his unsupported announcement; but when let-ters were received through him from Livingstone himself all doubt was at an end, and Mr Stanley has since been regarded and treated as a more important personage than the original traveller.

Finding Livingstone was an extraordinary achievement, especially for a young, unknown, illegitimate Welshman. At seventeen, Stanley (baptized John Rowlands) left a poorhouse school in Wales for the slums of Liverpool. He then worked his passage to New Orleans where he found a life where fewer cared about his origins and more valued his talents. He was adopted by Henry Stanley, a New Orleans cotton broker. He served on both sides in the American Civil War, then found his first pro-fession – journalism – in the postwar Indian campaigns on the Great Plains. *The New York Herald* hired him and sent him as their 'danger-correspondent', in *Vanity Fair*'s words, to cover wars in Abyssinia and Crete. Then Stanley's employer, James Gordon Bennett Jr (*Vanity Fair*, 15 November 1884), the im-mensely wealthy, temperamental publisher of the *New York Herald,* dispatched him to 'FIND LIVINGSTONE' and forget the cost.

While seeking Livingstone, Stanley found his second profes-sion – as an explorer and developer of central Africa. His ca-pacity for sudden, determined action, his quickness to see an opening, his ruthless competitive drive, his organizational skills, his eagerness to make an impression, his skill at public-ity, while initially offending the British Establishment, sus-tained three further expeditions into Africa. From 1874 to 1877 he journeyed from Zanzibar to the Atlantic and became the first white man to explore the River Congo. Then, from 1879 to 1884, he systematically investigated the Congo region for the avaricious King of the Belgians, Leopold II (*Vanity Fair*, 9 Oc-tober 1869), and became the 'Smasher of Rocks', 'Bula Matari', the founder of the Congo State. Finally, from 1886 to 1889, he made his last cross-country journey, at Britain's request, to rescue the mysterious Emin Pasha.

In 1890, he published the last of his best sellers, the lavishly illustrated *In Darkest Africa,* and, exhausted, settled back in

England to a distinguished but premature old age. His march, during the Emin Pasha expedition, from the Atlantic to the In-dian Ocean was the grandiose finale to an era of African explora-tion. The continent was now open to the colonizers and exploiters.

'As foreign news is now managed it is not too much to say that he who has the command of telegrams, has the command of public opinion on foreign affairs.' So began Jehu Junior in the commentary on BARON PAUL JULIUS DE REUTER (1816–1899). The son of a rabbi of Cassel, he went from banking to the book trade in Berlin. When the political climate became too hot for him there in 1848, he left along with many others for Paris. After working a short time for Havas, the pioneer French news agency, Reuter branched out on his own. He recognized the need for a speedy, accurate and reliable commercial news ser-vice and met it – first with a pigeon post. The spread of the telegraph lines on the continent, and then to England, led him to give up his pigeons and come to London in 1851. By the early 1860s, Reuter's Agency had established a virtual monopoly on the distribution of foreign news. He proceeded to extend the Reuter's Telegraph Company all over the globe. Most news-papers in the Empire came to depend on Reuters for essential facts, and on foreign correspondents, when they could afford them, for the 'colour' and background.

Telegrams
Baron Paul Julius Reuter
Men of the Day No. 55
14 December 1872
Delfico

Reuter's name became a household word in England, where the *St James Gazette* sought to clarify its pronunciation:

I sing of one no Pow'r has trounced
  Whose place in every strife is neuter,
Whose name is sometimes mispronounced,
  As Reuter.
How oft, as through the news we go,
  When breakfast leaves an hour to loiter,
We quite forget thanks we owe
  To Reuter.

His caricature is one of six in *Vanity Fair* by the Neopolitan master of the art, Melchiorre Delfico. It conveys the essence of this natty, vivacious businessman, the Napoleon of telegrams. To emphasize his shortness, Delfico has given him a giant head. The fluffy side whiskers were no exaggeration, nor were the bird-like eyes. The dramatically enlarged nose is another sign of Victorian anti-Semitism, also shown in the comment by Jehu Junior: 'when he arrived in England, Mr Reuter with the shrewdness of his race caused himself to be naturalized as an English subject.'

Vanity Fair fully recognized Reuter's power, derived from his control over swift, accurate information. Jehu Junior wrote:

One of the most remarkable incidents of modern international relations is the fact that all the telegrams of Europe are indeed practically in the control of one man and the correspondents in his pay; and it is pleasing to know that he has never yet been suspected of a conscious purpose to use them for the interests of a particular individual or country.

The *St James Gazette* must be allowed the last lines on this pioneer of news distribution:

His web around the world is spun,
  He is indeed the world's exploiter:
'Neath ocean, e'en, the whispers run
  Of Reuter.

In 1875, Jehu Junior teasingly lauded the accomplishments of one of the pioneer figures of modern journalism, WILLIAM HOWARD RUSSELL (1820–1907):

An Irishman by birth, and by profession an advocate, Mr Russell has been devoted from the first years of his manhood to the task of modernizing the English Press. He rightly judged that the work could best be effected through the [Times] newspaper, which was at the time of his advent to it esteemed the most independent and trustworthy of the London daily journals, and undertook to write for it contemporary epics of a kind hitherto unknown on the heroic incidents of the day. He described the Irish famine with so much success that he was allowed, when the Russian war broke out, to appoint himself as 'Our War Correspondence,' and to invest that post with a portentous importance.

During the Crimean War, Russell virtually created the role of war correspondent. The telegraph was now available to transmit news from the battlefield to the world and he used it to great effect. Despite hostility from the British Army, he covered this war with a series of pungent dispatches and letters to his newspaper, and exposed the mismanagement, inefficiency and general muddle of the campaign. Jehu Junior observed: 'His

labours, his valour, the refusal of his rations, and the control he exercised over the reputation of the commanders of the ridiculous Crimean expedition soon became matters of history.' His coverage of that war marked what the journalist Phillip Knightley has called: 'The beginning of an organized effort to report a war to the civilian population at home using the services of a civilian reporter.' *The Times* cited its coverage of the war as 'a brilliant phase in the history of *The Times*'. It could claim to have made the war; it had saved the remnant of an army; destroyed one Ministry and forced changes in another; and caused removal of a Commander-in-Chief. Jehu Junior added: '. . . and Mr Russell was so thoroughly recognised as a high military authority that on his return he was not only made a Doctor of Laws by the chief university of his native island, but was thenceforth for ever affectionately adopted as "Billy" by all arms of the service.'

'Billy' Russell used his great personal charm, energy and his competitive drive after the Crimean War to carve out a place of unusual distinction in the history of journalism. He covered the coronation of the next Czar with impartiality; his reports on the Indian Mutiny helped to moderate demands in England for revenge; he started a newspaper of his own – the *Army and Indian Gazette;* offended both the North and South by the frankness of his dispatches during the early years of the American Civil War; and covered the Austro-Prussian War and the Franco-Prussian War. *Vanity Fair* congratulated him for his reporting of the latter: 'The accounts he sent home of the fighting and capitulation at Sedan, and the thrilling records of his personal adventures and intimacies at Versailles, stamped the *Times* for ever as possessing not merely the most able but the most important of all the correspondents.'

In the caricature, Ape has sustained the affectionate tongue-in-cheek tone of the commentary by Jehu Junior. 'Billy' Russell is portrayed as a dandy, eyes partly hooded, with his shiny top hat perched raffishly on his head. He looks the part of an energetic, charming though cynical man.

Russell referred to himself as 'the miserable parent of a luckless tribe' – the war correspondent. Jehu Junior thought well of his particular talents and personal qualities:

Dr Russell, in truth, is a man of great cleverness, and of a remarkably agile intelligence, very fitly representing the modern Press. He is full of varied information of every description, a major portion of which is correct; and he is a most admirable teller of good stories. With a very few facts to work upon, he will sit down and build up a full and impressive account of a battle or a negotiation so vivid and life-like that a reader may fancy he has actually seen the battle or been present at the negotiation himself. He first discovered and utilised the discovery that in these days it is neither Ministers nor Generals, nor even Success or Failure, but only Newspaper Correspondents who make and mar reputations; and he has used his own great power in this respect to so much purpose, and yet with so much good-fellowship, that he is courted and petted wherever he goes. The superior ranks of Society admire him, his Editor believes in him, and his varied experience and inexhaustible fund of good temper and stories would justify far more than the modest belief in himself which has been less conceived by himself than forced upon him by others.

J. L. GARVIN (1868–1947), editor of *The Observer* from 1908 to 1942, told a stunned young man the first time he appeared in the office: 'Boy! We are going to make *The Observer* sell like hot cakes!' In the last years of *Vanity Fair*, Garvin's dynamism inspired the artist Alick Ritchie to produce a lively, accurate

Our War Correspondence
Mr William Howard Russell LLD
Men of the Day No. 96
16 January 1875
Ape

171

caricature of the popeyed, energetic, able 'new journalist' who had been brought in by Lord Northcliffe (*Vanity Fair*, 16 May 1895) to make the failing *Observer* a financial success and an influential journal of opinion. Holding his newspaper, Garvin stands surrounded by scattered cigar butts and correspondence. In the wastepaper basket lie some letters initialled A. J. B. by the leader of the Conservative Party, Arthur J. Balfour.

In three years Garvin accomplished his goals: *The Observer* was selling well, and he had become one of the chief advisers to the Tory Party leadership. His success was based on three things: his lengthy, sprightly and carefully laid out leaders or editorials; his access to early, accurate and confidential political information (mainly from Arthur Balfour); and finally, his ability to influence opinion through his relationship as a political adviser to the press baron, Lord Northcliffe. Garvin turned *The Observer* into a new type of Sunday paper. He broadened its appeal and made it 'a companion for the weekend', according to Barrington-Ward of *The Times*.

Tongue-in-cheek, *Vanity Fair* recognized Garvin's initial accomplishments. Jehu Junior wrote:

A very, very few years ago Mr Garvin did not figure in 'Who's Who'. It is all right now; the oversight has been corrected . . . The vehemence, persistence, ability, rhetoric and metaphor with which his advocacy is conducted are unique. So is the columnar quality of his output. It is titanic. People have said that there is an inscription over the mantel of his home. 'Never whisper in three inches what you can say in a yard and a half.' But the fact has been distinctly denied.

Irish and proud of it; with a torrential volubility befitting his nationality. No one can accuse Mr Garvin of having kissed the Blarney Stone. There's too much solid reasoning and sound sense in what he writes . . . an enthusiast with a restless eye, Mr Garvin has a following which trots along behind him blindfold, yet admiring.

He neither bears nor brooks malice; he is a staunch friend, an inspiring personality . . . His adaptability is amazing.

That year, 1911, Garvin had to be adaptable. *Vanity Fair* noted some potential trouble: 'On one occasion, at least, he made some remarks that were not strictly in accordance with Carmelite.' (A reference to the headquarters of Lord Northcliffe, the owner of *The Observer*.) Garvin and Northcliffe fell out suddenly over food taxes and Tariff Reform in Canada, and Garvin had to find a new proprietor or lose his paper. He quickly found William Waldorf Astor to take Northcliffe's place and enable him to continue his influential career.

?-!
James Louis Garvin
Men of the Day No. 1296
13 September 1911
Alick P. F. Ritchie

The Favourite Jockey
Fred Archer
Men of the Day No. 245
28 May 1881
Spy

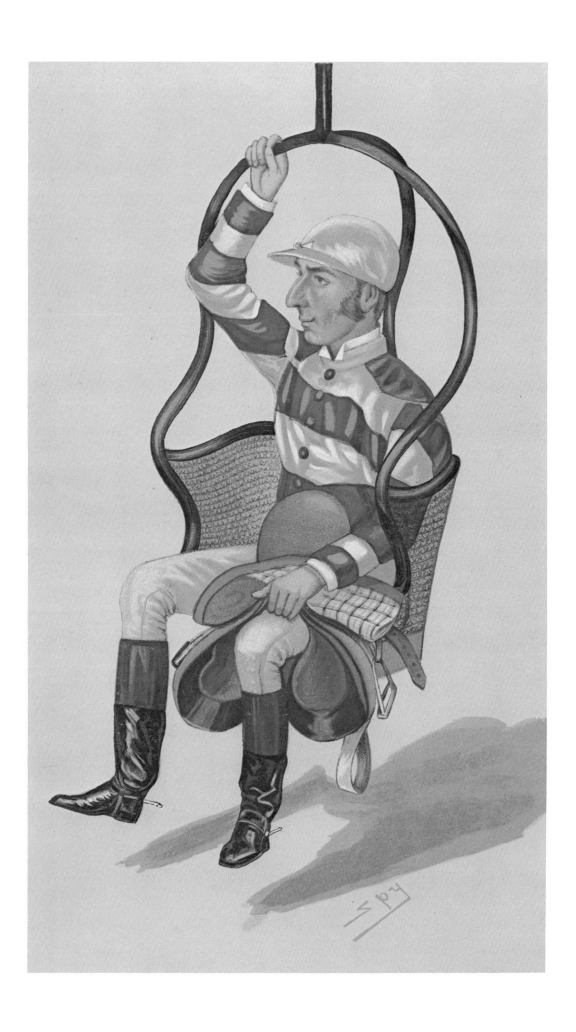

Cricket
Mr William Gilbert Grace
Men of the Day No. 150
9 June 1877
Spy

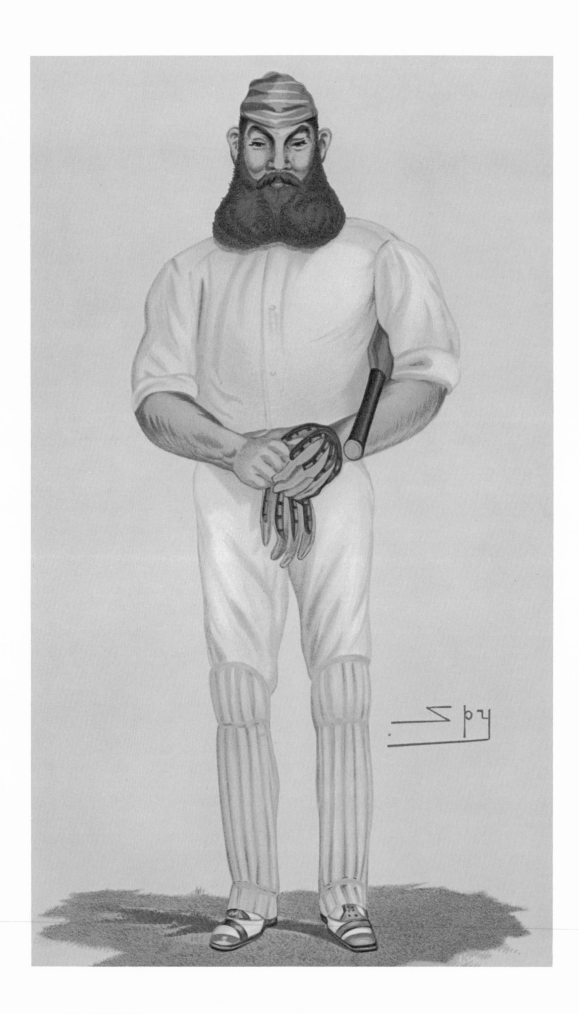

SPORTSMEN

The Victorian and Edwardian eras were a golden age of adult play. Individual and team games flourished as never before. Idols of the turf and the cricket pitch became national figures. The aristocracy, the gentry and many of the newly rich gave much of their life to sport, especially hunting. The British loved to bet, and rich and poor flocked to horse racing. Cricket flourished, particularly in the north of England. The working man took association football to his heart, while the middle classes favoured rugby. The notion of 'muscular Christianity' had considerable popular support. Wellington's apocryphal conclusion that Waterloo had been won on the playing fields of Eton became conventional wisdom.

In the 1860s the Queensberry Rules for boxing were formulated and the Football Association was established – illustrations of the Victorian tendency to discipline, regulate and organize their play as well as their work. The Royal and Ancient Golf Club at St Andrews, 'The R and A', and the Marylebone Cricket Club, 'The MCC', became the ruling bodies of golf and cricket. The All England tennis tournament at Wimbledon was first held in 1877, and the Jockey Club fought for and obtained the right to regulate thoroughbred racing. W. L. Burn has observed that 'the same phenomena of organization, clarification, discipline and regulation had been evident in Englishmen's work before it became much evident in their play.'

The pages of *Vanity Fair* chronicled these sporting phenomena. The British at play, for both pleasure and profit, were among its most popular caricatures. Cricketers and jockeys appeared in abundance, more than seventy-five of them. The wide range of sporting life is evident in the horsemen, oarsmen, yachtsmen, swordsmen, golfers, runners, boxers and managers, polo, tennis and billiard players and even the curler and the roller skater who were sketched in *Vanity Fair*.

Mr. John Ball, Jun.
John Ball, Junior
Men of the Day No. 534
5 March 1892
Lib

An American Jockey
Tod Sloan
Men of the Day No. 750
25 May 1899
G.D.G.

179

The Turf

The elongated profile of FRED ARCHER (1857–1886) was one of Spy's most popular caricatures. Archer, twenty-four years old when Spy drew him in 1881, was the premier rider in Britain. Jehu Junior recorded: 'His score of winning mounts has since 1873 been the highest reached by any jockey, and in five instances has been above 100 over that of his nearest competitor. No wonder that he has become the favourite jockey of his time . . .' (see p. 174).

Archer was the son of a distinguished jockey of the old school, 'Billy' Archer. He virtually grew up in the saddle. Apprenticed at ten to the famous trainer Matt Dawson, Archer won his first victory at eleven in a steeplechase at Bangor. By his mid teens he had become an established winner, and the first jockey for Lord Falmouth's famous stable. After 1874 'his career has been one of unbroken success', wrote Jehu Junior admiringly. In 1885 he won almost all the major stakes races including the Derby, the Oaks and the St Leger in England and the Grand Prix in France.

His iron nerve and exceptional judgement of pace were the principal attributes that made him the most successful jockey of his era, coupled with a determination to win which allowed no one to outdistance him if at all possible. He is reported to have ridden 2748 winners out of 8084 mounts, and made a considerable fortune. He is also known to have put his own brother over the rails in his anxiety to win. At 5 feet 10 inches he was tall for a jockey, and making his racing weight became increasingly difficult in his late twenties. In order to reduce, Archer resorted to a combination of Turkish baths, starvation and 'alkaline medicine'. The caricature captures Archer as almost skin and bones. In October 1886 he starved himself in order to ride in the Cambridgeshire. He won the race, but fell into a feverish depression afterwards and shot himself at home. He had been champion jockey since 1874, and the turf had lost one of its greatest riders. The Prince of Wales (later Edward VII), for whom racing was a mania, sent a wreath to Archer's funeral.

Modern thoroughbred racing style was transformed by an aggressive American from Kokomo, Indiana, JAMES FORMAN 'TOD' SLOAN (1874–1933), who was caricatured in his famous 'monkey crouch', bent over the head of his mount, in *Vanity Fair* in 1899. A tiny infant, he was nicknamed 'Toad' by his father; and his playmates changed the name to Tod. Though afraid of horses, Sloan was drawn to horse racing by an elder brother who was a jockey. He became famous for his ability to master the most rebellious mounts.

Sloan had a quick, observant mind and excellent reflexes. He studied the problems of wind resistance while racing, and adopted a posture of crouching along the neck and shoulders of the horse. This new technique brought him ridicule at first. 'He rides like a monkey on a stick', noted Jehu Junior, 'but he wins races.'

Aside from his 'peculiar seat', Sloan popularized the practice of forcing the pace or 'waiting in front'. He rode in front from pillar to post, instead of waiting to win, as had hitherto been the custom, especially in Britain. 'To do a Tod Sloan' became Cockney rhyming slang for going out on your own. After conquering the racing world in America, in 1897 Sloan took his style and technique to England and France, where his string of victories quashed the ridicule that his riding innovations had attracted. His success was crowned when he was selected to ride the Prince of Wales's horses.

Lutteur III
Famous Racehorses No. V.
13 October 1909
Emil Adam

Sloan's spectacular career was suddenly shattered in 1901, when the Jockey Club banned him from racing for conduct 'prejudicial to the best interests of the sport'. Though he had powerful friends, the Club refused to restore his licence, and he quickly lost a substantial fortune by a combination of high living and bad investments. This pioneer of the modern jockey's technique died penniless in Los Angeles in 1933. *Vanity Fair* had complained at the height of his career: 'He is a great little jockey who is popular; but he is hardly so polite as a good American should be.'

Jehu Junior observed that TOM CANNON (1846–1917) 'enjoys a reputation enviable and rare among jockeys, for no whisper of scandal has ever been breathed upon his name, and he is one of the few professional jockeys who are allowed by the Jockey Club to own as well as ride race horses' (see p. 175).

A contemporary of Fred Archer and 'the demon' George Fordham (*Vanity Fair*, 2 September 1882), his sensitivity to horses and his business talent enabled him to become a trainer, a horse breeder and a landed proprietor. His intelligence and good sense are captured in Spy's attractive, colourful portrait, and in Lib's sketch 'The Winning Post', which featured most of the major jockeys of his day (*Vanity Fair*, 8 December 1888).

Vanity Fair extolled Cannon:

He is gifted with unfailing good nature; he is absolutely free from that bumptiousness which is so often bred of exceptional success; he is as hospitable as he is discreet; he can sing a good tenor song; and his only weakness seems to have been the purchase of church livings which he cannot fill with little Cannons of his own; for his sons are impelled to the scales by their hereditary instincts.

Several celebrated racehorses of the late Victorian and early Edwardian eras were portrayed in *Vanity Fair*, notably the outstanding fillies Sceptre and Pretty Polly, the brilliant colts St Simon and Bayardo, and two of the royal Derby winners of the period, Minoru and Persimmon. Steeplechasing was at this time very much the poor relation of flat racing, but the inclusion of J. Hennessy's 1909 Grand National winner LUTTEUR III is indicative of the hold which that race exerted, then as now, on the public. Bred in France though his pedigree was English (his sire St Damien was a son of St Simon), Lutteur III was not the first French-bred horse to win the National, but he has the particular distinction of being the last five-year-old to win. (Today the race is for six-year-olds and older.)

Lutteur III was bought by Hennessy as a yearling for 610 guineas, but was so slow as a two-year-old that he was used as his trainer George Batchelor's hack, and was put into training only eighteen months before his Grand National victory. Having won five races in France, he came to England with the reputation of being an outstanding young horse, and this was confirmed when he won the Champion Chase at Hurst Park before going to Aintree. He completed his preparation with the trainer Harry Escott at Lewes.

Carrying 10*st* 11*lb* in a field of thirty-two runners (the biggest field since 1850), Lutteur III started the big race (run on 26 March) at 100–9. He moved up from the rear halfway round the second circuit and, in the words of one writer, 'fairly flew past his field' to win easily by two lengths from Judas. His victory was the more full of merit, wrote 'Nimrod' in *Vanity Fair*, 'in that neither the horse nor George Parfrement, who rode him with marvellous skill and nerve, had ever previously faced such fences as those at Aintree.' He contested the Grand National

twice more: in 1911 he fell when 7–2 favourite, and was placed third in 1914 when carrying the considerable burden of 12st 6lb.

A rather washy chestnut, Lutteur III was a beautifully balanced horse, and had a good deal more quality than most Grand National winners of the time – one of whom is reputed to have been pulling a milk-cart before his victory! This quality is well captured by Emil Adam in *Vanity Fair*, though later photographs of Lutteur III show him to have grown considerably sturdier and less leggy.

'Nimrod' noted that 'Mr J. Hennessy may well be proud of such a horse, and had he himelf been present at Aintree he would perhaps have been still more proud of the splendid reception given to his victorious colours'. (Hennessy himself was portrayed by 'HCO' in *Vanity Fair* on 24 February 1910.) The Hennessy family has continued to support the sport. The Hennessy Gold Cup, sponsored by the family cognac firm, is today one of the most important races in the British steeplechasing calendar. It is pleasing to recall that Mme K. Hennessy's Mandarin was sent over from England to win the French Grand National at Auteuil in 1962 despite the horse's bit breaking early in the race, a victory which has been described as 'a feat of courage, skill and horsemanship never excelled'. M. Hennessy, the son of Lutteur III's owner, bred Mont Tremblant, winner of the 1952 Cheltenham Gold Cup.

Polo

By the turn of the century genuine caricatures were the exception in *Vanity Fair*. A most enjoyable exception is the subtly coloured, elongated yet delicate portrayal of the eminent polo player SIR RAJINDER SINGH MAHINDER BAHADUR, the Maharaja of Patiala (1872(?)–1900). The caricature appeared a few months before his death in November, 1900. Jehu Junior summarized his career:

. . . *he is now one of the Ruling Chiefs of India and the premier Prince of the Punjab. He is also the descendant of an ancestor who stood by the English in the Mutiny at a time when his support was worth having; and the head of the Sikhs, a great Chieftan amongst Chiefs, and the leader of a fighting race. As becomes his ancestry, he is himself a keen fighter in the field, and in the polo field; and as a pigsticker he is in the very first flight. A fearless and accomplished horseman, he is also a good cricketer, who keeps a polo team, a cricket team and an enormous stable of racehorses – hacks, hunters and pigstickers – his teams and horses giving good accounts of themselves on every occasion: as his* Cherry *did last week winning the Viceroy's Cup. He is indeed the chief supporter of the Turf in Upper India; and in the late frontier war he went out with his transport and bore himself so well that he was rewarded with the Grand Cross of the Star of India. He is a generous and a good friend, and though he was 'privately educated' he is full of quality. He invented the Patalia riding trousers, which are English, and the elastic strap to his Turban, which is Sikh. He is capable of many inventions.*

In the drawing (see p. 182) he looks as if a strong wind might blow him over. It is one of the most witty among an attractive set of Indian Princes produced by *Vanity Fair* over the years.

Cricket

'In any history of cricket for the last forty years of the nineteenth century, W. G.'s performance with bat and ball must necessarily run like some inevitable fugue', declared the cricket writer Altham of WILLIAM GILBERT GRACE (1848–1915) (see p. 176). This remarkable man began to play first class cricket at an age when most schoolboys were still struggling for a place on their house or school eleven. His sporting career spanned fifty years. He revolutionized the game, and left a set of batting records that may never be equalled.

Jehu Junior observed:

Born at Bristol twenty-nine years ago of a family long given to the national game of Cricket, he found himself with a father and uncles reputed famous in its pursuit, and with brothers known for excellence in its practise. Devoted therefore though he was to the medical profession, he took up the game with enthusiasm, and his natural gifts of eye and hand have made him what he is – the best cricketer that ever played. Not only has he made the highest scores off his bat against the best bowling of the day, but he fields as well as he bats, and he gets as many runs in a season as most cricketers do in the course of their lives. He once achieved as many as four hundred runs without losing his innings.

Yet his proficiency in this particular game is not his only claim to renown; for he has proved himself an admirable runner, rider, and shot; and in addition to all this he has been a student of medicine, to which he henceforth intends to devote himself, reserving his play solely for his County and the Marylebone Club. He has excited some envy but more admiration; so that a national testimonial is about to be given to him, as he deserves who has proved himself so preeminent in the sports that still delight his countrymen.

A history of cricket written in the 1920s said of W. G:

. . . *he did more to popularize cricket than any man who ever lived. His Jovian form, his inexhaustible vitality and stamina and enthusiasm, all combined with his prodigious prowess to make him the focus for an empire's devotion to the game.*

Grace himself was never preoccupied with theory. His plan consisted of putting the bat against the ball. This was the cricket equivalent to baseball's 'I hits 'em where they ain't'.

Alongside the powerful Grace, the willowy figure of 'Ranji' stands as one of the symbols of late nineteenth-century cricket. MAHARAJA KUMAR SHRI RANJITSINHJI VIBHAJI, the Maharaja Jam Seheb of Newanagar (1872–1933), set new standards of batting which were not broken until the 1930s, the era of Don Bradman and Wally Hammond. At Sussex, at the turn of the century, he teamed up with the inimitable all rounder, C. B. Fry (*Vanity Fair*, 10 April 1894), in one of the most formidable batting pairs of all time.

Born to the princely state in western India, Ranji, aged sixteen, was brought to England in 1888 to continue his education. At Trinity College, Cambridge, he found his métier, and became, in *Vanity Fair*'s opinion, 'one of the finest bats in the world'. So successful was he at university and town cricket that he decided to remain in England. He qualified for residence, captained Sussex from 1899 to 1903, and was chosen for England in 1897 for the Test against Australia. In Manchester his batting saved the match. In 1904 he returned to India to assume his public duties.

Jehu Junior described him aptly: 'He is a slim, exceedingly lithe fellow, whose action on the field sometimes reminds you of a panther, and a genial and very casual person . . . he is full of unassuming pluck, and he may be known a mile off by the elasticity of his walk . . . and the people idolize him.' Ward's sketch captured Ranji's sinuous grace and modest air.

Ranji, by his success at cricket and because of his social

Patiala
HH the Maharaja of Patiala GCSI
Princes No. 21
4 January 1900
MR

Ranji
Kumar Shri Ranjitsinhji
Princes No. 19
26 August 1897
Spy

graces, is said to have put India on the map for the ordinary Englishman. One of his biographers extolled his diplomatic talents, and his understanding of people of all races and classes: 'He was not only the perfect host, but the perfect guest.'

Tennis

Lawn tennis became a popular sport among the aristocracy and upper middle classes of Europe during *Vanity Fair*'s era. The willowy, lanky figure of the volatile GRAND DUKE, MICHAEL MICHAILOVITCH (1861–1929) of Russia, the cousin of the Czar, 'who always plays up to the net,' appeared in 1894 in a caricature by one of *Vanity Fair*'s proprietors, A. G. Witherby. The Grand Duke was an ornament of a class soon to disappear. According to Jehu Junior, he 'decided that his chance of the bomb-proof throne of all the Russias was well lost for love, and married the beautiful and delightful Sophie', later the Countess Torby. A keen sportsman, he founded the Golf Club at Cannes. He lived a pleasant life devoted to his family, sports, and some piano playing 'in a military manner'. He was a friend of the Prince of Wales.

In the 1890s the Grand Duke discovered the joys of the life of a wealthy English gentleman, and bought Keele Hall, near Newcastle. He was welcomed into the district and the City of

Newcastle made him its High Steward. *Vanity Fair* observed that he remained a prudent man: 'Fond as he is of the country of his adoption, he is careful not to affront the horrors of its winter later than January when he retires to the sunnier climes of Cannes till May has made England habitable'. In 1908 Spy produced a second and dull portrait of the Grand Duke for *Vanity Fair* (22 January 1908).

Curling

Vanity Fair immortalized one of the most famous travel agents of the era, Dr (later Sir) HENRY SIMPSON LUNN (1859–1939), crouched over a curling stone. Curling is one of the more curious winter sports. A person propels an oval stone with a handle attached over the ice towards a mark. Grown men run, slide or stumble alongside the moving stone, seeking to change its velocity by madly stroking the ice in front of it with brooms. Lunn's interest in curling allowed him to combine business with pleasure for profit – he had recently established a series of travel clubs for sports and games of all sorts. The first was the Public Schools Winter Alps Club.

Lunn went out as a medical missionary to India, where he discovered, in *Vanity Fair*'s words: 'the hopeless system of hypocritical luxury in which much of the Oriental Mission work is conducted'. Ostracized by his peers, and in ill-health, he returned to England in 1888. While pursuing his interest in the union of the churches, he discovered Switzerland, winter sports and the travel and hotel business. In a few years, he had established one of the largest travel businesses in the world. In the early 1900s he organized an ever proliferating set of clubs to attract special groups whose interests could be combined with tours. Among the most notable was the Hellenic Traveller's Club, which fostered serious study and research into the classical world. Lunn's Tours to Greece are still popular with travellers.

Vanity Fair thought Lunn to be 'one of the most remarkable pioneers of travel ever known'. Dubbed 'the King of Clubs' by his friends, Lunn was an organizer par excellence, who unleashed such groups as the Headmasters of the Public Schools upon the classical sites of Europe, and English municipal officials upon their German counterparts. 'In doing this,' wrote *Vanity Fair*, 'he has done as much for the *entente cordiale* between England and the rest of Europe as any man; perhaps more . . .' Lunn, added *Vanity Fair*, 'is the most restless man the British Empire has ever known.' And he turned this trait into a profit (see p. 185).

Shooting

Shooting game was an obsession among many of the Victorian landed gentry, and they organised it systematically. On their great estates thousands of birds and animals were slaughtered each year. Edward VII as Prince of Wales and as King vastly enjoyed this activity. One of his companions was FREDERICK OLIVER ROBINSON (1852–1923), then the Earl de Grey and later the Marquess of Ripon. Once while shooting at Sandringham, the Earl alone shot 28 pheasants in 60 seconds. Jehu Junior approvingly listed some of his other accomplishments in the field: 'In Yorkshire he has killed five hundred grouse in a day; in Hungary he has brought down over that number of partridge; while on another occasion he has killed no fewer than seven hundred and fifty pheasants; all those falling to his own gun.'

This determined, accurate shot was the scion of an intensely political family, the son of the Liberal Marquess of Ripon who

The King of Clubs
Dr H. S. Lunn
Men of the Day No. 1193
6 October 1909
Elf

185

The best game shot in England
The Earl de Grey
Men of the Day No. 460
15 February 1890
Spy

Roller-skating

Pellegrini's skill at caricature caught the essence of this forgotten young Victorian, HERBERT PRAED (1841–1921). Jehu Junior described him as amiable, well connected enough to be 'known to Duchesses and held to be in considerable favour with them'. He was also a sportsman, fond of exercise and a good skater, fencer and racquet player, who did not neglect the family banking business. Then, he quietly became the Secretary of the Charity Organization Society and devoted himself to the well-being of the working classes. Not long after, Praed won a seat in the Commons as a Conservative. Society was sceptical and astonished. Jehu Junior noted the reaction: 'Though some admired that one of the fashionables should devote himself to good works, many predicted that he would come to a poor end. Therefore, it was felt that anything might happen to him, and it was in sorrow rather than in anger that the Duchesses found him forsaking their neighbourhood for that of Bermondsey, and their commerce for that of the working man.'

Ape has captured this apparently aloof young gentleman poised delicately on his roller skates, perhaps capable of going in any of several directions. Jehu Junior is also sceptical of Praed: 'Whether he will make a figure in public life equal to that which he has shown in private remains to be seen.'

among other posts was Viceroy of India, and Lord Privy Seal in the Liberal Government of 1906. He held this last post until his death in 1909. Unlike his political father, Lord de Grey devoted most of his life to the social world. Spy sketched him in hunting garb, tweeds, plus fours, spats and shotgun, directing his beaters on some unnamed moor. His wife Gladys, the former Countess of Lonsdale (*Vanity Fair*, 6 October 1883), was considered by Jehu Junior 'a very handsome lady'. His other interests included Italian opera and fine china. *Vanity Fair* noted that he was 'such a good fellow that none of his excellences have made for him enemies.'

In 1923 he died suddenly while shooting in his Dallowgill Moors. The *Annual Register* observed that 'he was recognized in his day as undoubtedly the finest game shot in the country, perhaps in the world.'

The Philanthropist
Mr Herbert Praed MP
Statesmen No. 179
18 July 1874
Ape

187

AMERICANS

Over the years a variety of Americans appeared in *Vanity Fair*. Four presidents – Grant, McKinley, Theodore Roosevelt and Wilson – were among the nearly fifty individuals who can be identified. Hester's portrait of Wilson in 1913 shows only his head and shoulders – a deviation from the established *Vanity Fair* style during its last year of publication. In 1872, Thomas Nast, the famous political cartoonist, wittily sketched Charles Frances Adams, Hamilton Fish, and Charles Sumner. Spy contributed Joseph Choate (*Vanity Fair*, 28 September 1899) and John Hay (*Vanity Fair*, 24 June 1897). These could form the beginnings of a representative gallery of American statesmen of the era.

Yankee financiers and businessmen were not neglected by *Vanity Fair*. Among those included were the Scottish-born Andrew Carnegie (*Vanity Fair*, 24 October 1903), who made his fortune in steel and spent it on libraries and peace; Chauncey Depew of the New York Central (*Vanity Fair*, 26 October 1889); Alfred Gwynne Vanderbilt (*Vanity Fair*, 31 July 1907); Gordon Selfridge (see p. 198); and the financier, diplomat and publisher, Morgan Shuster (*Vanity Fair*, 28 February 1912). Newspapermen from across the Atlantic were featured as well. Nast cruelly caricatured Horace Greeley in 1872 (see p. 189), and 'Nemo' (Constance de Grimm) sketched an impatient, peripatetic James Gordon Bennett Jr., of the *New York Herald* on 15 November 1884. Notable American writers included Mark Twain (see p. 192), Bret Harte (*Vanity Fair*, 4 January 1879), Dr Oliver Wendell Holmes (see p. 193) and Finley Peter Dunne (*Vanity Fair*, 24 July 1905). The evangelists Dwight Moody and Ira Sankey (see pp. 195, 196) were castigated by Jehu Junior in 1875; Ape's caricatures were kinder. On the whole, Americans were treated with a mixture of amusement and condescension. By the first decade of the century, Jehu Junior's commentaries allude to what *Punch* described as 'the American invasion'.

Many of these 'invaders' made lasting contributions to English and European life. William Gillette, the actor who created the stage image of Sherlock Holmes (see p. 194), Hiram Maxim of Maine, the inventor of the machine gun (see p. 197), and S. F. Cody, the Texan who made the first airplane flight in England (see p. 199), inspired witty drawings and commentaries. Three jockeys – 'Tod' Sloan (see p. 179), and the brothers John (*Vanity Fair*, 23 August 1900) and Lester Reiff (*Vanity Fair*, 30 August 1900) – were recognized for their winning records on the English turf. Last but not the least, that most crucial export to the British aristocracy, the heiress, was not entirely forgotten by *Vanity Fair*. Jennie Jerome, Mrs George Cornwallis-West, was portrayed in graceful middle age in 1912 (see p. 69).

Captain, Tanner, Farmer, General, Imperator

**General Ulysses S. Grant,
President of the United States**
Sovereigns No. 10
1 June 1872
Nast

Anything to beat Grant

**Mr Horace Greeley, Candidate for
the Presidency of the United States**
Statesmen No. 118
20 July 1872
Nast

189

The first President to be portrayed was the stolid GENERAL U. S. GRANT (1822–1885). The 'father of American political cartooning', Thomas Nast (1840–1922), was the artist. He originated or popularized several political symbols, the Democratic donkey, the Republican elephant, the Tammany Tiger, and is thought to be responsible for the existing forms of Uncle Sam, John Bull, Columbia, and Santa Claus. In 1872 Nast also contributed caricatures of Horace Greeley, Grant's opponent, the Senator, Charles Sumner (*Vanity Fair*, 25 May 1872), and the diplomats, Hamilton Fish (*Vanity Fair*, 18 May 1872) and Charles Francis Adams (*Vanity Fair*, 5 October 1872).

The caricature of Grant is for Nast unusually benign. The President sits in a rocking chair topped with a carved American eagle, cigar in hand, embodying the modest man he was. He had been dubbed 'old useless' by his mother, reported Jehu Junior, and sent to West Point 'to prepare him for an honourable extinction in the Army'. Despite a nondescript career, Grant had risen to the challenge of the American Civil War and after the conflict was elected President by a grateful people.

Vanity Fair asserted that Grant meant business, 'meaning more business perhaps than some of his countrymen would like, stern, resolute, unbending, yet simple and plain.' Bowles marvelled at Grant's ability to overcome his weaknesses, and wondered whether he would triumph over his shortcomings as President. Grant's administration proved to be scandal-ridden, though he was not involved personally.

After Grant, until the end of the century, *Vanity Fair* chose to ignore the American Presidents. Then a character-portrait of William McKinley (*Vanity Fair*, 2 February 1899) signed 'Flagg' appeared. This was probably the work of the American artist, James Montgomery Flagg (1877–1960), later famous for his adaptation of the Alfred Leete recruiting poster using Kitchener's moustache and finger to the 'Uncle Sam wants you for the USA' during the First World War. Flagg portrayed McKinley in a Napoleonesque pose, right hand thrust into his frock coat, a man of simple taste, kindly, good and astute '. . . conducting a little war with Spain quite ably'. His major failing, said Jehu Junior, lay in his choice of servants: 'His steward, cook, coachmen, footman and waiters are all coloured. His chief fault, indeed, is his liking for niggers.'

Nast's treatment of Grant for *Vanity Fair* was mild when compared to his sketch of Grant's opponent that year, HORACE GREELEY (1811–1872). So scathing were Nast's cartoons of Greeley during the ill-fated presidential campaign of 1872 that Greeley remarked he was not sure whether he was running for the presidency or the penitentiary.

Greeley's manner of dressing and attitudes were a caricaturist's delight. The historian Allan Nevins has noted:

'Few Americans were more intimately in the public eye than he, and none commanded such a mixture of admiration with affectionate amusement. The oddity of his appearance, with his pink face of babylike mildness fringed by throat-whiskers, his broad-brimmed hat, white overcoat, crooked cravat, shapeless trousers, white socks, his shambling gait and absent-minded manner, was exaggerated by every caricaturist.'

Greeley came from a poor farming family in New Hampshire. After an irregular schooling he was apprenticed to a small town newspaper in Vermont where he learned the printing trade. At twenty he gravitated to New York City with twenty-five dollars and all his personal possessions tied in a handkerchief. Ten years later he had established himself as a journalist with considerable influence in the Whig Party. In 1841 he founded *The New York Tribune*. This newspaper set new standards for American journalism with its energetic news gathering, its good taste, its high moral standards and intellectual appeal. Under Greeley's leadership the *Tribune* was the most influential newspaper in the country.

Greeley's rusticity of manner and eccentricities shocked many, but his homely wisdom appealed to the masses. Though not physically strong, he lectured, travelled and wrote indefatigably. Everyone remembers the phrase he made famous, John Babsone Soule's 'Go West, young man and grow up with the country'.

Greeley's political ambitions contributed to his tragic death. In 1872 he was nominated for president by some dissident Republicans and the dispirited Democrats. The campaign was one of the most abusive of the century, and Nast caricatured him with unusual venom. Greeley suffered badly from these attacks. The death of his wife and the decline of his influence at the *Tribune* combined to break him mentally and physically. He died insane in November 1872.

Nast's drawing was matched in vituperation by *Vanity Fair*'s commentary. Greeley was 'not a statesman, scarcely even a politician, but merely a journalist with all the worst journalistic faults highly developed'. The magazine called him 'illeducated', 'entirely untrained for public life' and without 'those qualities which have sometimes stood in lieu of training.' If the cry was 'Anything to beat Grant' then, said *Vanity Fair*, 'Mr Greeley is the anything that has somehow blundered to the surface.'

Flagg has portrayed an uncharacteristic THEODORE ROOSEVELT (1858–1919). The ebullience and bombast of the man is not adequately conveyed, perhaps because the caricature reflects wishful thinking on the part of the artist and *Vanity Fair*. Professor Ray Ginger observed: 'He [Teddy] shouted and waved his arms, but his feet never moved.' Mark Twain told Andrew Carnegie: 'Mr Roosevelt is the Tom Sawyer of the political world of the twentieth century: always showing off; always hunting for a chance to show off; in his frenzied imagination the Great Republic is a vast Barnum circus, with him for a clown and the whole world for an audience.'

Jehu Junior wrote:

Theodore Roosevelt, twenty-sixth and youngest President that the United States have ever known, was born in 1858; but no Washingtonian boyhood will ever be accorded to him. Such myths will not fit him. He was a blunt, well-read, ambitious young fellow when illhealth and good fortune made him a cowboy. Western plains expanded his chest and his mind, developed a notable biceps, and taught him much that is useful and decorative. With his lariat he

could noose the off foreleg of a running Texan steer – a feat which lifted him to a high place amid cowboy aristocracy. He became one of the finest rifle shots of his country, shot pumas with certainty, and would have been notable after tigers if his country had grown any. Incidentally he learned to sit a broncho or a cayuse with the seat of a Sioux Indian, and picked up much knowledge of men, while they picked up much knowledge of him; for he was a very striking young man who commanded attention which he did not seek. His forceful and engaging personality won the heart of the Farther West, and when subsequent events made him National he became its Idol. At twenty-four he was elected to the New York State Legislature; and on this lively body, which makes laws in response to the demands of some seven millions of people and two or three bosses, had a measured success in suppressing the irrepressible. Then he thought he would like to be Mayor of New York; but the voters did not sympathise with his desire, and so he filled in three years by writing books which his countrymen admired. He was appointed Civil Service Commissioner by President Harrison, and surprised people by developing tact, which, joined to his powerful will, solidly founded the reform, and smashed a maxim – 'To the victors belong the spoils' – that half a century of practice had lifted into natural law. He stepped from Washington to New York, became head of the Police Department, and by two exciting years spent in the attempt to protect the people from their own constables, trained himself for the milder game of war, and organised a regiment of Cavalry Volunteers which rendered picturesque service at Santiago de Cuba. As Colonel of Rough Riders he dashed into the Spanish lines and into the hearts of his people, and so returned from the front to have the Governorship of the State of New York thrust upon him. Then political pressure forced him into the uncongenial serenity of the Vice-Presidency, whence by the assassin's bullet he was raised to the seat of power. The startled public waited in vain for rash or headstrong action from their ebullient President; who has passed a year and a half in a position of immense difficulty – holding his great Office through succession, not by the votes of the People – and has already silenced criticism: to raise it anew in interested quarters by his bold pronouncement in the matter of big trusts. It is not too much to say that his reasonable conservatism, his capacity for honest compromise, his candid, able utterance, and his practical ideals, have won the confidence of his people.

Among the dozen books of which he has been guilty is one called The Strenuous Life. *Such is his own.*

Not all the wit disappeared from the *Vanity Fair* caricatures in its last decade. Spy's sketch of the seventy-two-year-old MARK TWAIN (1835–1910) is instantly recognizable, and enjoyable. A great mop of white hair and moustache, a matching white suit, on which, reported *Vanity Fair*, 'he is believed to have refused enormous offers of money for stencilling space', and a large calabash pipe combined to produce an irrepressible animation. They inspired one of Ward's most popular cartoons.

The commentary captured Twain's mood of good natured cynicism. *Vanity Fair* wrote 'For ourselves we hope that he will live to be at least a hundred; for we have every respect for grey hairs and we wish no man discontinuance. It is further to Mr Clemens' credit that in our English *Who's Who* he describes himself as an "American novelist and lecturer" – not, you will note, as humorist'. *Vanity Fair* complained that Twain was 'the parent of cartloads of American humour', and 'we have suffered accordingly'. Grudgingly, the commentator admitted that Twain was a great favourite of the English:

He is a sportsman and dislikes Mrs Baker Eddy and the King of the

U.S.A.
The President of the United States, Theodore Roosevelt
Men of the Day No. 849
4 September 1902
Flagg

191

Mark Twain
Samuel Langhorne Clemens
Men of the Day No. 1118
13 May 1908
Spy

Barnum
Phineas Taylor Barnum
Men of the Day No. 448
16 November 1889
Spy

The Autocrat of the Breakfast Table
Dr Oliver Wendell Holmes
Men of the Day No. 362
19 June 1886
Spy

193

Belgians. The people in America who do not happen to love him have to put up with him. The people of England love nobody else when he happens to be here.

The dynamic showman and circus impresario P. T. BARNUM (1810–1891) was a living event. One of his biographers has written that Barnum 'was himself the greatest of his shows and knew it'. That year at the apex of his career, he had brought his famous circus, the Barnum and Bailey, to London. The town was enthralled from commoner to royalty. Prince George, later George V, asserted that he was going to stay at one performance until they sang 'God Save Grandmother'.

Barnum's career was devoted to public entertainment. F. L. Paxon wrote: 'He found the American public without an easy means of innocent diversion, and left it changed in habit, taught to play, and served with entertainment of complex variety.' Barnum turned his youthful dislike of manual labour into fruitful channels, drifting inevitably into show business. He opened the American Museum of Curio's in New York in 1842, where he made an engaging dwarf, Tom Thumb (Charles Sherwood Stratton), into an international celebrity. He organized the first concert tour of Jenny Lind, the 'Swedish Nightingale', in 1850, and opened his famous circus, 'The Greatest Show on Earth', in Brooklyn in 1871.

Early in the 1880s Barnum purchased a huge African elephant, 'Jumbo', from London Zoo. The British press, outraged momentarily at this act of 'American vandalism', delighted Barnum for he relished any publicity. He had already written to the editor of the *New York Tribune* 'I don't care much what the papers say about me, provided they will say something'. Jumbo, in life and death, was a great hit with the public in America. According to Barnum, Jumbo died saving a baby elephant from being run down by a locomotive.

'There's a sucker born every minute', is perhaps the most famous of Barnum's sayings. Both Spy and *Vanity Fair* were enormously entertained by this character. Jehu Junior wrote: 'He says that he is not a humbug; but he is a very great friend to the bill-stickers, and one of the best advertisers of his own wares that ever lived . . .'

When Madame Tussaud asked Barnum if he was willing to allow his effigy to appear in wax in her famous London museum, he responded, 'Willing? – Anxious! What's a show without notoriety?' and sent her an entire outfit, including his socks.

Spy was in his prime as a caricaturist in the 1880s, and his sketch of DR OLIVER WENDELL HOLMES (1809–1894), the writer from Boston, was most delightful. Holmes looks like a whimsical elf.

Mark Twain once observed about Americans: 'In Boston

Sherlock Holmes
Mr William Gillette
Men of the Day No. 1055
27 February 1907
Spy

Prayer and Praise
Mr Dwight L. Moody
Men of the Day No. 101
3 April 1875
Ape

195

they ask, How much does he know? In New York they ask, How much is he worth? In Philadelphia, Who were his parents?' The eminent Dr Holmes knew a lot, and wrote prolifically about it to the entertainment of readers on both sides of the Atlantic. Born in Cambridge, Mass., he trained in medicine at Harvard, becoming Professor of Anatomy there. Before turning to literature, he sought to correct his contemporaries' ignorance about childbed fever. His international fame arose from his series of witty essays in the *Atlantic Monthly* entitled 'The Autocrat at the Breakfast Table', some novels, and excursions into poetry such as *The Chambered Nautilus*, and *Old Ironsides*.

Holmes charmed both Ward the artist and Bowles the journalist on a visit to London late in his life. Jehu Junior observed approvingly:

He has written a great many books. His poems are quite harmless and full of common-sense and flippancy . . . and are excellent examples of what poetry ought not to be. His novels . . . are very fantastic, very imaginative, and read like the conversation of a medical student in love. His essays are a sort of Montaigne for families . . . He is the last of the laughing philosophers . . . His style scintillates with wit, and, when it is at its best, has all the charm of an exploding cracker. When he lectures on anatomy, he is a poet. His novels are the note-books of a physician; and his philosophy is the kindly observation of man of the world, the wisdom of one who has dined well.

Personally he is a brisk, dapper little man, very brilliant and very bright-eyed; a Puck without malice, an Ariel with a sense of humour. He is very much loved by all who know him, for he has a wholesome dread of people who impart useful information, and thinks that serious conversation is a form of solemn trifling. Attic wit, Yankee humour, a very large supply of human nature, and an absence of any ambition to be President, have made him the most popular man in America. He has been made much of recently in London Society, and has delighted The Duchesses, for unlike many Society lions, he has the most genial manners and no mane. On the whole he is a great success. Though a Bostonian, he is not a prig; though a brilliant conversationalist, he can listen; and though seventy-seven years of age, he is still a very young man.

One of the most popular fictional creations of the late nineteenth century was Arthur Conan Doyle's intellectual detective, Sherlock Holmes. It is now hard for many people to believe he did not really exist, operating out of 221B Baker Street, with his faithful companion, the slow but steady Dr Watson. Holmes was brought to life on the London stage by an American actor, WILLIAM GILLETTE (1855–1937), in 1901. By 1907, when Spy drew the actor in this role, Gillette had created the archetypal Holmes. Among collectors this caricature has become one of the most popular.

Ward found Gillette an interesting man to draw. He had a typical American face, Ward thought, with strongly marked features which had an open-air quality. 'I suppose', wrote Spy, 'the effect of climate and the method of heating rooms "across the pond" produces that parchment-like complexion.' At the sitting, Gillette asked Ward for his suggestions for a mild pipe tobacco, which would not burn the actor's throat while on stage.

Gillette was born in Hartford, Connecticut, and gave up college to go on the stage. By the age of twenty-two he was a success. He made his London debut in 1897 in his own play, *Secret Service*, a Civil War melodrama. In 1901 the original play, *Sherlock Holmes*, based on three of Conan Doyle's characters,

Holmes, Watson and Moriarty, was brought by Gillette from New York to the Lyceum Theatre, London. His thin, handsome face, topped by a deerstalker cap, set the public's image of Holmes. *Vanity Fair* judged it a fine interpretation, though 'perhaps a trifle more full-blooded than Holmes of the stories'.

Following his success as Sherlock Holmes, Gillette appeared as Crichton in J. M. Barrie's *The Admirable Crichton* and in many other roles. Booth Tarkington told him: 'I would rather see you play Sherlock Holmes than be a child again on Christmas morning'. He came out of retirement in 1924, in his early seventies, to play Holmes. He was seventy-six when he last played Holmes, though he carried on acting until he was eighty-two. During his life he wrote twenty-nine plays. One biographer, William Van Lennep, wrote: 'No actor has ever been more eloquent in silence . . . In his acting and his methods of mounting a play, he is probably the first person in America who can be called natural in the modern sense of the word.'

Two Americans, the leaders in one of the most successful religious revival tours of Britain in the nineteenth century, were caricatured by Ape and vilified by Jehu Junior in the spring of 1875. DWIGHT MOODY (1837–1899). the preacher, and IRA SANKEY (1840–1908), the gospel singer, were the Billy Graham and George Beverly Shea of that era. Moody and Sankey arrived

in the British Isles in 1874. For more than two years they toured, arousing a stunning, dramatic response. The culmination of their mission came in London in 1875 where their 285 meetings spread over four months attracted an estimated 2.5 million people.

Bowles was highly disturbed by their successes. He thought Moody was a vulgar man who had cheapened religion. Jehu Junior commented: 'He [Moody] is a shrewd, commonplace person, absolutely without culture, utterly without literary education, coarse sometimes, familiar always.' He was equally scornful of Sankey, the bulky baritone: 'Mr Sankey's singing is as vulgar as Mr Moody's preaching . . . it is probable that early training as a nigger minstrel before he had become regenerated has taught him something of the art of producing sounds.' In spite of his hostility, Bowles admitted '. . . there is not a Bishop or other dignitary of the church whose presence could command a tenth part of the audiences which Mr Moody brings together daily.' Ape's two caricatures are somewhat kinder, though there is a hint of the anti-semitic imagery in Sankey's features.

Moody believed in the kind of evangelism that leads to social service. The pair's British successes led to greater ones in America. Proceeds from the sale of their hymn books went to support two schools established by Moody, the Northfield Seminary for girls and nearby Mount Hermon for boys. He founded the

Chicago Bible Institute for those without a college education who wished to become missionaries. Moody was an able, sympathetic organizer who often said: 'Better set ten men to work than do the work of ten men.'

It was Britain's gain and America's loss when the inventor HIRAM MAXIM (1840–1916) established his laboratory at 57 Hatton Garden, London, in 1881. Shortly thereafter he developed the first efficient machine gun. *Vanity Fair* observed:

He first thought of the Maxim gun by receiving a jar on the shoulder at the firing . . . The name of the inventor has gathered popularity thereby amongst all peoples, save a few barbarians, such as the Matabele, Soudanese, and Somalis, where there is such an odd prejudice against him. But your true barbarian is ever a foe to the progress of civilisation.

Born in Maine, in an area where bears outnumbered men, Hiram was stimulated by a father with philosophic tastes and a talent for invention, who encouraged him to use his hands and brain. Apprenticed at fourteen to a carriage maker, Hiram rapidly learned several trades, studied scientific books when possible and developed an uncanny skill with tools. He heeded a friendly physician's advice not to waste time as a fighter, either in the boxing ring or in the Civil War. He worked in Quebec and upper New York State as a carriage-painter, cabinet-maker and bar-tender, and became renowned as a bully tamer and practical joker.

His wanderlust satisfied, in 1864 Maxim joined his Uncle Levi Stevens' engineering works and embarked on a career as an inventor and entrepreneur. One of his biographers observed: 'He could use no machine or process without seeking to improve it.'

His first patent for an improved hair curler was followed by a variety of inventions: a better mouse trap, automatic devices for gas generating plants, water sprinklers, steam pumps, engine governors, vacuum pumps and an improved incandescent lamp. He lost by accident and machination the patent to his lamp and thereafter hated lawyers. Rival inventors, especially Thomas A. Edison and Maxim's younger brother, Hudson, excited his jealousy.

Maxim decided to establish his arms business in Europe after a friend, also an electrical engineer, told him: 'Hang your chemistry and electricity. If you want to make a pile of money, invent something that will enable these Europeans to cut each other's throats with greater facility.'

In England in 1884 he formed the Maxim Gun Company, which was amalgamated with Nordenfeldt Company in 1888; then in 1896 it was merged again to create Vickers Sons and Maxim. Once he had perfected the machine gun, he developed a smokeless gun powder and other contributions to gunnery. He was knighted by the Queen in 1901.

At the same time, he decided that 'if a domestic goose can fly, so can a man,' and set about building an aeroplane. The result, a steam driven plane, did just about leave the ground in 1894, but the weight of fuel and water made it impracticable.

This self-made Maine Yankee was six feet tall, strongly built and a fastidious dresser. Spy has caricatured him in front of one of his more whimsical creations – a merry-go-round.

'The "Invasion by the American" is a topic which Londoners have rolled under their tongues for many moons', wrote *Vanity Fair*. One American 'invader', H. GORDON SELFRIDGE (1858–

In the Clouds
Sir Hiram Stevens Maxim
Men of the Day No. 943
15 December 1904
Spy

Self -
H. Gordon Selfridge
Men of the Day No. 1308
6 December 1911
Alick P. F. Ritchie

ALICK.P.F.RITCHIE.

All British
S. F. Cody
Men of the Day No. 1303
1 November 1911
Alick P. F. Ritchie

199

1947), must have relished the marvellous free advertisement when he was caricatured for *Vanity Fair* in 1911. By then few in London could have been unfamiliar with his great store on Oxford Street. His dapper welcoming figure, orchid in buttonhole, proudly pointing over his shoulder to his splendid emporium, is a tribute to his vision and energy.

Born in Wisconsin, Selfridge started from the bottom and rose meteorically to a junior partnership with Chicago's Marshall, Field & Co, by the age of thirty-two. Optimistic, energetic, accessible and agreeable, such diversions as the theatre, raising orchids, bookbinding and travel were not enough to keep him busy when he retired for the first time in 1904.

Then a millionaire, he arrived in London in 1906 to assess its commercial possibilities. Sensing that there was room for a distinctive store with a wide range of goods and services, including groceries as well as clothes and sundries, he secured a site on the north side of Oxford Street. In March 1909 his store was opened. It had 130 departments, a library, a roof garden, rest rooms and a free telephone information bureau, and prided itself on the courteous service it offered to customers. A master of advertising, Selfridge paid any customer who pointed out errors in their copy. To the surprise and chagrin of other West End merchants, the store was a smashing success, setting practices and standards for similar emporiums worldwide.

Selfridge settled in England and became a citizen in 1937. He died in London in 1947. Business to him was an exciting and romantic adventure. Jehu Junior commented:

Mr Selfridge is the most genial of men – and seriously, one of the strongest it has been my lot to know. He is not the man who has lost his star in the mists – or anything . . . I have tried hard to discover his recreations, but unsuccessfully. I imagine he uses his beautiful motor-car occasionally, because if I remember correctly, he was tipped out of it once. But like most of our earnest cousins from over the west-going sea, I think he likes business better than anything.

That must have pleased him.

SAMUEL FRANKLIN CODY (1861–1913), a Texan, was one of the pioneers of aviation in Britain. Born on the frontier, in Birdville, Texas, he was not related to Buffalo Bill (W. F. Cody), except in appearance, flamboyance and career. On the frontier he apprenticed himself to show business and aviation in such trades as buffalo hunter, Indian fighter, Klondike gold digger, horse trader and kite flyer. Horse trading and his own wild west show brought him to Britain in the 1890s, where he married a lively English horsewoman, Lela Blackborne Davis. About the turn of the century he began to experiment seriously with passenger-carrying kites, then dirigibles and finally heavier-than-air craft.

Like his namesake, Cody cultivated a glamorous image. His flowing hair, waxed moustache, broad brimmed hats, thigh boots with enormous silver spurs and white horse delighted the public. However the War Office and the Army, with whom he had to deal, found them distracting.

When George V greeted him as 'Colonel Cody' after he had won a series of flying prizes, Cody remarked: 'If the King of England calls me Colonel, that's good enough for me.' He took British citizenship, and became, according to *Vanity Fair*, 'The British Public's chief and best beloved showman of flight.'

In 1907 Cody constructed an airship, the dirigible *Nulli Secundus*, for the Army, and flew it from Farnborough over London. It was the first 'invasion by air' of the capital. A year later,

he flew the first heavier-than-air craft over England on a sustained and controlled flight on 16 May 1908. Soon after he took his wife up with him on a plough seat; she was the first woman to fly and the first aeroplane passenger in Britain.

In 1912 Cody won the Military Flying Trials against an international field, and that year the Royal Aero Club gave him their gold medal for his pioneer work in aviation. A year later, while preparing a new biplane for the Northcliffe Prize Competition – a flight around Britain – his plane crashed on Laffin's Plain on 7 August 1913. Cody and his passenger, the Oxford University and Hampshire cricket Captain, W. H. B. Evans, were killed when they were thrown out of the plane. This disaster led to the adoption of seat belts for aeroplanes. Cody the cowboy died as he wished, with his flying boots on. He had once told a friend: 'When death comes to me I should like it to be . . . sharp and sudden. Death in one of my own airplanes.' This flashy cowboy, horse trader, showman, skilled engineer and pilot has a memorial – a dead, withered tree at the end of a runway at the Royal Aircraft Establishment at Farnborough. 'Cody's Tree', where he used to tether both planes and horse, has been preserved by the Royal Air Force as an honour to the Texan who did so much to advance aviation in Britain before the Great War.

Collecting 'Vanity Fair' caricatures

What happened to Vanity Fair's unsold stock?

The dispersal of Vanity Fair's stock of unsold caricatures, proofs and original watercolours is a fascinating, confused tale. When the last proprietor, Dr T. R. Allinson (*Vanity Fair*, 4 October 1911), sold the magazine in early 1914, there was apparently an immense stock of prints left over, perhaps some two to three million. These were stored some time later in the Bonnington Hotel on Southampton Row in Bloomsbury. Early in the 1920s David R. Weir, a London antiquarian book and print dealer, bought this immense collection for about £500. A brochure printed by Weir to advertise these caricatures states:

All these cartoons comprise the stock of the late Dr Allinson, Proprietor of 'Vanity Fair' and were acquired by us some time ago, through the death of the late owner.[1]

Dr Allinson died in August 1918. His only surviving son, C. R. Allinson, cannot recall any stock left over after the sale of the name of magazine in 1914.[2] Thus at present, the disposal of the stock between 1914 and the early 1920s remains a mystery.

DAVID WEIR AND THE VANITY FAIR CARTOON COMPANY

Weir moved the *Vanity Fair* stock to his shop at 5 Sandland Street, nearby in Bloomsbury, and devoted the remainder of his life to ordering and selling the prints. He formed the *Vanity Fair* Cartoon Company to market the caricatures and built his life around them.[3] His wife and some of his children helped to sort and label the cartoons and send enquiries to possible customers. Various groups and individuals in Britain and North America were approached with offers to buy the prints, the proofs and the originals. He sought to locate the family of *Vanity Fair*'s victims in *Debrett's*, then wrote a letter informing them of their ancestor or family member who had appeared in *Vanity Fair* and offered them the prints. Family legend has it that one peer had Weir bring him the copies of his caricature, bought them and burned them. Weir also marketed and sold sets such as cricketers, judges in their wigs and robes, and scientists to interested organizations in the English speaking world.[4] Judges, jockeys and some Americans were popular, and he received half-a-crown per cartoon. The rarer proofs were offered for two guinea each and an original watercolour for thirty guineas.

By the early 1930s, the Depression, the availability of large numbers of the caricatures, and Weir's declining health combined to lessen the *Vanity Fair* Cartoon Company's business.[5] Paul Victorious, a young American medical student, had come to London between the wars, and began to accumulate and sell books and prints, especially those associated with scientific subjects. In the course of his searches, he discovered the scientific figures caricatured in *Vanity Fair*. For his own print and book shop at 30 Museum Street, Bloomsbury, Victorius purchased *Vanity Fair* prints from Weir. As Weir's business declined, Victorious began to buy the prints in larger lots. Eventually, when Weir's health failed, Victorious bought perhaps two-thirds of Weir's huge stock for about £500. Weir died in 1936. His family inherited the remaining stock of the *Vanity Fair* Cartoon Company, numbering prints in the thousands, a few original watercolours, preliminary sketches and several hundred proofs.[6]

PAUL VICTORIOUS AND THE 'VANITY FAIR' PRINTS

Weir's stock of prints, when acquired by Victorious, filled a basement in Sandland Street, estimated by Ron Chapple, a book runner who helped Victorious move them, to be about 12,000 cubic feet in size. The bulk of the prints were stored in packets of 250 copies per single individual, and the text was separately wrapped. Some complete albums in their green cloth bindings and some proof in brown moroccan leather bindings were also included.

Victorious sorted through this mass of cartoons, saved the sets and individual prints which he thought marketable and sold the rest for waste paper to a pulping mill on the South Bank. Chapple recalls that it took ten days to haul away, by four horse drays, all the discarded prints. The impending war had forced up the price of paper, and Victorius received £20 per ton. If he sold eighty tons, as commonly reported, then he earned £1600 – a clear profit. The remaining caricatures were carried in hand carts by Chapple and Ada Victorious, Victorious's wife, over a period of weeks, to a low-rent basement warehouse in Streatham Street.[7]

THE PRINTS GO TO THE UNITED STATES

When the Second World War broke out, Victorious moved his business to Charlottesville, Virginia. Before he left he sold perhaps half of his stock of *Vanity Fair* prints to a London book and print dealer, Andrew Block. Block also helped to arrange to ship Victorious's stock to Virginia. He subsequently had the bad luck to lose all the *Vanity Fair* prints he had bought in a flood.[8]

Along with a vast amount of other prints, Victorious kept the *Vanity Fair* caricatures in Charlottesville, largely untouched. For a time the bulk was stored in two old bread delivery vans outside his picture frame factory and the rest in a warehouse.[9] Pleas by prominent print dealers to Victorious later in his life to allow them to sort out and catalogue his vast holdings were never granted. He died without heirs in the early 1970s.

THE ORIGINS OF VANITY FAIR LTD

In 1973, notice of an offer of *Vanity Fair* caricatures from Victorious's estate attracted the attention of a Cincinnati, Ohio, businessman, Morton W. Olman, whose golfing memorabilia shop had led to an interest in the *Vanity Fair* cartoons of golfers. With his son James and an associate, Thomas S. Benjamin, they travelled to Charlottesville to assess what Victorious had left. They found a substantial number, mostly unsorted in boxes, filling about one quarter of a large warehouse. The lot also included a couple hundred *Vanity Fair Albums*. They bought all the *Vanity Fair* prints, which came to about fifteen tons, and shipped them back to Cincinnati, where they spent fifteen months sorting and cataloguing them. They found they had an entire run of prints, as far as they could determine, including all the larger double prints, unfolded. *Vanity Fair* Ltd was formed to market these prints, and their first sale was made in March 1975.[10] Their sale catalogue divides the prints into sixty-nine categories, and was the first systematic catalogue to appear since the 1930s. Their stock of caricatures constitutes the largest available source in the world.[11]

Types of Prints

THE ORIGINAL WATERCOLOURS

During its heyday, three versions of each individual caricature were usually produced. First, there are the original watercolour cartoons. Their average size is about 30.5 x 17.8 cm (12 x 7 inches) corresponding to the size of the published lithograph. The early ones are on white or green-tinted paper, the later on blue transfer paper.[12] The cartoon was transferred at the printers to the lithographic stone. These sketches are often more subtly coloured, and the characterization is keener than the resulting lithograph. In 1912, *Vanity Fair* sold a large number of these originals through Christie's and Sotheby's. Later in 1916, more were auctioned at Puttick and Simpson.[13] The National Portrait Gallery in London has acquired over three hundred of the original watercolour cartoons, and some preliminary sketches by Ape, Spy and the other artists. Once in a while a few of these watercolours come on the market, as do some of the artists' preliminary sketches.

THE PROOFS BEFORE LETTERING

The second versions of the *Vanity Fair* caricatures are the proof prints or proofs before lettering. Produced to verify the colours and lines of the lithograph, no more than twenty copies were printed. These prints have no captions or dates, or other descriptive type, and the magazine bound them in numbered albums, in green leather with gilt tooling. They were offered for sale, and also awarded as prizes in the magazine's acrostic contests. At the front of each volume is a printed note from *Vanity Fair* giving the number of proof volume and the numbered volume in the series. The quality of the colours in the proof prints, their clarity of line and detail and their scarcity make them of considerable interest to the collector.

THE WEEKLY AND ALBUM PRINTS

The weekly lithograph (or colour offset) or album print is the third and most familiar version of the *Vanity Fair* caricatures. Over the years they were reprinted in large numbers. They were published in three forms. First, as they appeared as the centre feature of the weekly magazine, with the accompanying description. Second, each print was again reproduced as part of a yearly or sometimes half-yearly *Vanity Fair Album,* with the description often edited and reset on a separate page. The changes were not often significant. Occasionally, the numbering of the 'Statesmen' or 'Men of the Day' series in the weekly magazine and the albums did not agree. These attractive albums were described by *Vanity Fair:* 'Each volume [was] handsomely bound in green cloth, bevelled boards, gilt and gilt edges.'[14] Thirdly, the caricatures were sold individually or in sets, framed or unframed. Sets of privately bound albums do exist, mostly in the hands of private individuals or organizations.

THE FORMAT OF THE CARICATURES

The format, or the layout, of the *Vanity Fair* cartoons underwent some changes over the years. From 1869, when the printers were Rankin and Cox, to 1873 printers' hatchmarks were left on the proof and final prints and the coloured caricature was framed by thin black lines crossed at the corners. The paper used was a type of newsprint. Starting in 1874, the hatchmarks were eliminated, the weight and grade of paper improved and the quality of the colour printing enhanced. This became the standard *Vanity Fair* caricature format. VANITY FAIR, in capital letters, appeared on the top left-hand corner, and the date – month, day and year – on the right-hand top corner. The portrait would usually be signed with the artist's acronym. Under the cartoon, on the bottom left corner, was stamped after 1873, in small type, the lithographer's name, Vincent Brooks, Day & Son, Lith. Below, centred under the caricature, ran the caption in larger letters. The name of the victim appeared at the top of the accompanying text, with a few exceptions. In 1898, however, after the works of Vincent Brooks, Day & Son were destroyed by fire, a few prints (including that of Dr Spooner) were produced instead by P. W. van de Weyer in Holland by colour offset. On 20 July 1905, this format was altered slightly, as were the paper and the printing process. The prints were no longer dated. The top left-hand corner over the cartoon now read VANITY FAIR Supplement. Under the caption, on the bottom right-hand corner, the sitter's name was placed in parenthesis. The publishers began to use slick, or glossy, magazine style paper, and until 4 October 1911 the prints were reproduced by the newer and cheaper colour offset process, which employs a series of dots unlike the continuous colours of a lithograph.

Between 18 January 1906 and 4 October 1911 Vincent Brooks, Day & Son were replaced by a series of other printers:

Bemrose Dalziel Ltd, Watford and London, 25 January 1906 to 16 October 1907.
Hentschel Colourtype, London, 23 October 1907 to 11 November 1908, and again, 12 May 1909 to 20 September 1911.
John Swain & Son Ltd, London, 18 November 1908 to 5 May 1909.
David Allen & Sons Ltd, Fleet Street, E. C. and Harrow (16 January 1907).
The Grout Engraving Co (27 September 1911).

Early in August 1911, Jehu Junior announced:

The reversion to the lithographic process of reproduction has been made in the conviction that the most satisfactory results are thus obtained. With the issue of the first week in August 1911, the new Proprietor presented *Vanity Fair* in confidence and hope. He promised to re-establish its olden fair name, and with no o'erweening vanity he feels that his efforts have attained justification . . .

The artists have been instructed to approach, as nearly as in them lies, to the traditional line of genial caricature, in distinction from the fashion-plate type of informal portraits which latterly had prevailed.[15]

Vanity Fair returned on 4 October to Vincent Brooks, Day & Son for their colour lithography, and probably used that firm until their demise in January 1914[16] although there is no printer's name on the caricatures after 5 February 1913.

THE SPECIAL NUMBERS
Beginning in 1878, *Vanity Fair* published, at irregular intervals, a different size and style of lithographs, under a variety of labels. These included frontispieces, double prints, Summer and Winter numbers, and special supplementary cartoons. We have called these thirty-four

cartoons collectively Special Numbers. Included in the Special Numbers are twenty-one double print lithographs approximately twice the size of the standard *Vanity Fair* print. If included in the magazine or the album, they were folded.

The Special Numbers began with an etching 'St James Street, June 1878' by James M'Neil Whistler, published in July of that year. Those interested should consult the list we have provided on pp. 254–255. Until 1902 two Special Numbers were usually printed each year on a variety of subjects from politicians to royalty to horse racing, the Bench and Bar, the Dreyfus trial and the Boer War. After 1902 there were only two more: 'A Fox Hunting Constellation' in 1905 and 'Collapse of the Conference', possibly in 1913.

The artistic quality of these Special Numbers is uneven, but as a group they provide a splendid panorama of the late Victorian era, and the collector and social historian will find them amusing and full of insight.

Availability of the Caricatures

Until the last few years, the large number of cartoons published by *Vanity Fair* during its lifetime meant that the collector could find them easily, especially in London. The destruction of so many late in the 1930s or early 1940s had had little immediate impact. Now the cartoons have become scarce and certain figures are very difficult to find. Complete albums are becoming rare as well. Over the years they have been broken up; the most desirable caricatures kept, and the rest discarded. Some complete sets and individual albums are occasionally offered for sale in Britain and North America.

Between 1869 and 1910, *Vanity Fair* offered the yearly albums for two or three guineas. Between 1900 and 1910 they sold individual caricatures for as little as sixpence, many for half a crown, and a very few for a guinea.[17] By the turn of the century *Vanity Fair* was marketing a variety of sets, such as jockeys, university oarsmen, golfers, judges, surgeons and doctors, artists, authors, actors, musicians, Oxford dons, Eton masters, railway men, Masters and huntsmen, British admirals, officers who had served in the Brigade of Guards or in the Boer War, and Americans.[18] In June 1899, the magazine headlined 'a new offer' modelled on Sir John Lubbock's 'The Hundred best Books'.

We offer a set of Vanity Fair cartoons of the HUNDRED BEST MEN
or rather of the BEST WOMAN AND THE NINETY-NINE BEST MEN
OF THE HALF CENTURY.

The complete set cost £10, and any fifty could be purchased for £6. Framing was £10 extra. Their list includes very few individuals who have since been forgotten.[19]

This active promotion of the sale of the coloured caricatures happened after Bowles had sold the magazine in 1889. In the 1890s and the first decade of this century there are indications that the sale of the cartoons was an important, perhaps crucial source of income for the magazine's proprietors. One apparent result was that considerable numbers of lithographs were reprinted. Earlier in 1878, and again in 1879, *Vanity Fair* warned its readers that editions of the prints and the volumes were going out of print and that the lithographic stones had been destroyed.[20] In 1885, four years before Bowles sold out, he announced that they could no longer supply individual prints. Of the seventeen volumes they had only two hundred fifty copies left. The conclusion was obvious: '. . . the exhaustion of the 250 sets now remaining must amount to the exhaustion of the whole work in its complete form. This explanation is here given in answer to repeated appeals for copies of single Portraits, which it has been impossible to satisfy; and in order to explain the exact limits of the power there still remains to supply copies of this Album'.[21] If this was true, the quantity of lithographs which survived from the 1869–1889 era must have been augmented by reprints.

A comparison of the pre-1890 prints with those which can be traced to the stock left over after *Vanity Fair* was sold in 1914 and which were brought to America by Paul Victorious revealed differences in colours, in tones and in some of the shapes of the details in the lithographs. However, it should be noted that lithographs published in the 1890s also show striking differences as well.[22]

Colour lithographs from the 1869 to 1900 period remain the most abundant. Our conclusion, lacking as we do any accurate information on circulation of *Vanity Fair,* is that this was the period when it flourished. After 1900, the fewer available prints, whether lithograph or half-tone, is a sign of the magazine's declining popularity. Victorious's destruction of a large amount may also have reduced the supply.

THE CARTOON SETS

Caricatures of the Bench and Bar, mostly by Spy, have remained highly popular since they were first offered as a set by *Vanity Fair* in the 1890s. 'Red-robed judges', whether known or unknown, sell quickly, when available. They adorn the walls of countless law schools, lawyers' offices, barristers' chambers and the clubs and restaurants they frequent. They have recently cropped up on the covers of primers for the Bar examinations in North America. Sportsmen, especially the more colourful jockeys and others associated with the turf, are likewise highly prized. Cricketers, particularly if they are in playing gear, have a steady market, as do the few golfers. Most varieties of sportsmen are nearly out of circulation.

Musicians, some of the well-known literary figures and the recognized actors are also scarce. Scientists and medical men are collected avidly and not easy to find. The Special Numbers, particularly the double prints, when in good condition – not folded for the albums – are almost unobtainable. In general the colour offset prints of the 1905 to 1911 era are scarcer than the earlier chromolithographs. Too many of these are little more than sycophantic character portraits, though one or two of the later artists succeeded in reviving *Vanity Fair*'s previous stinging humour.[23]

Other sets, such as the many forgotten politicians, foreign personages, most of the peerage and the numerous military and naval officers, are relatively easy to locate. Collectors could still amass a colourful selection of Indian princes, foreign royalty, newspapermen, businessmen, and individuals associated with the scramble for Africa and the assumption of British control in Egypt. A smaller number of personalities identified with the history of South Africa, Rhodesia, Canada, Australia, New Zealand and the United States are also available to the collector of sets.

Individuals interested in Ape, Tissot, Chartran or Spy as artists can find examples of their caricatures for *Vanity Fair* with little difficulty. However, Max Beerbohm's nine graceful, witty caricatures are few and far between.[24] Caricatures of women are also scarce, partly because *Vanity Fair* seldom featured them. Until 1882, only three women had been caricatured, noted Jehu Junior, 'who presented themselves as taking men's parts in life'. Bowles explained further that *Vanity Fair*'s essential principle of truth in its caricatures had 'been sometimes regarded as severe'. Ever the upper class Victorian, who put women on a pedestal, he asserted: 'With ladies no amount of truth could justify any suspicion of severity, still less any suggestion of caricature; wherefore the ladies have been left out of the collection altogether, rather than run the risk of appearing to sin against the canons of taste.' In 1883 Bowles announced that portraits of ladies would begin in his magazine with HRH Alexandra, the Princess of Wales.[25] Theobald Chartran (T) drew a series of titled ladies in 1883–4 that conformed largely to Bowles's desire for 'graceful truth'. Other artists, including Spy, contributed sympathetic portraits of women, but on the whole they are a reflection of Victorian and Edwardian wishful thinking about 'ladies'.

INDIVIDUAL CARICATURES

Many of the individuals in these cartoon sets have become exceedingly scarce. Among the sportsmen, Fred Archer and George Fordham are difficult to locate. The double print, 'Tattersall's 1887', *Vanity Fair*, Winter Number, December 1887) which shows the paddock filled with luminaries of the late Victorian racing world is very rare. Furthermore it is associated with a legend about 'Bertie', the Prince of Wales, whom Lib, the artist, placed standing in the centre of the Paddock near an attractive blond woman. Some thought that the Prince was portrayed in a state of sexual arousal, and it is said that demands were made to withdraw the cartoon from circulation. In any case individual figures associated with the turf are always in demand. Perhaps the most popular sportsman is Spy's W. G. Grace (*Vanity Fair*, 9 June 1877). It was reprinted 14 April 1898 after the fire that destroyed the Vincent Brooks, Day & Son printing works.[26] Ranji (*Vanity Fair*, 26 August 1897) is also difficult to find.

The 'Sherlock Holmes', William Gillette by Spy (*Vanity Fair*, 27 February 1907), though a colour offset print, is exceedingly difficult to locate as are Spy's lithograph of 'Winston' Churchill (*Vanity Fair*, 27 September 1900) and Nibs's colour offset version of the great man 'Winnie' (*Vanity Fair*, 8 March 1911). The drawings by Guth of Captain Dreyfus (*Vanity Fair*, 7 September 1899) and figures associated with his ordeal, the villain Captain Esterhazy (*Vanity Fair*, 26 May 1898), Premier Brisson (*Vanity Fair*, 6 October 1898) and the double print of Dreyfus's second trial 'At Rennes' (*Vanity Fair*, 23 November 1899) are likewise scarce. Guth's Queen Victoria (*Vanity Fair*, 17 June 1897) is also in demand.

Caricatures of two flamboyant personalities, Spy's 'Mark Twain' (*Vanity Fair*, 13 May 1908) though not a lithograph, and the two Sarah

Bernhardt's (*Vanity Fair*, 5 July 1879, 30 October 1912) have virtually disappeared from view. J. Montgomery Flagg's Theodore Roosevelt (*Vanity Fair*, 4 September 1902) is highly valued.[27] Gilbert (*Vanity Fair*, 21 May 1881), Sullivan (*Vanity Fair*, 14 March 1874) and D'Oyly Carte (*Vanity Fair*, 14 February 1891) along with Verdi (*Vanity Fair*, 15 February 1874), Wagner (*Vanity Fair*, 19 May 1877) and some other composers and musicians are highly sought after by their fans, and are not easy to find, with or without the accompanying text. However, the persevering collector may yet discover several of these prized prints if alert. He or she should be looking for the rarer proof prints, without lettering, which are generally sharper in detail, line and colour.

Known copies of Vanity Fair caricatures

The demand for certain sets and individual cartoons has led, naturally, to the production of copies. It should be relatively simple for the collector, armed with knowledge of the changes in *Vanity Fair*'s paper and format over the years, and a magnifying glass, to determine the real print from the copy. All lithographs have continuous colour, and a glance through a magnifying glass would immediately detect the dots that characterize the offset colour process. The paper and the format can be compared with the genuine article from a collection in a major library if there is serious doubt.[28]

As noted above, the magazine itself reprinted W. G. Grace (*Vanity Fair*, 9 June 1877) on 14 April 1898 in full size. Since then one of the authors has encountered another more recent copy offered for sale, as an original, in London. Its origins were unknown. Care should be taken with the popular Grace caricature to determine if it is the 1877 version, the 1898 reprint or a subsequent copy.

Reduced versions of *Vanity Fair* caricatures appeared several times in the magazine itself. Noteworthy are the twenty-eight sepia-toned, one-third size reproductions of several popular caricatures published in the issues of 6 July and 12 December 1880.[29] In the 1900s approximately quarter size reproductions were included to stimulate sales.

The popularity of the judges series led to the printing of *The Book of the Bench*, containing thirty-nine colour caricatures of legal personalities from *Vanity Fair* reduced to one third size. Published by J. MacKenzie in London in 1909, the cartoons were mounted on one page, with a facing text. There were two versions, one in a blue cloth cover which sold for 52s6d and the other in vellum which sold for five guineas. The reproductions are excellent. Complete editions of either are rare, though individual prints can still be found.

Another set of smaller copies was published, probably as a form of advertising by an American drug company, Petrolagar Laboratories, sometime after 1930. There were nine figures associated with medicine, about half size, matted, labelled with the subject's name and with an accompanying potted biography by Walter R. Betts of the Columbia University Medical School.[30] The continued demand for *Vanity Fair* caricatures associated with the Bench and Bar prompted a London bookdealer to reprint at least eleven best-selling figures in 1970. These reproductions, easily distinguishable from the original prints by their paper, are still available.[31]

More recently, Alfred Dunhill Ltd has begun to offer a series of full-size reproductions of *Vanity Fair* lithographs that they call 'smoking prints', as part of an advertising campaign for a brand of cigarettes said to be popularized by Ape.[32] The colour, detail and paper are all of high quality.[33]

Other reproductions have appeared. The authors and one of the owners of *Vanity Fair* Ltd have seen some gift items such as wastepaper baskets and ice buckets with copies of the cartoons pasted on.[34] The Irish Republic issued a 12p stamp in 1980 using Alick Ritchie's cartoon of Shaw (*Vanity Fair*, 16 August 1911). This discussion of reproductions of the caricatures is by no means exhaustive. The collector should always verify the offered print. Some of the reproductions, particularly these reduced versions, while not lithographs, are of good quality in their colour, reproduction of line and detail, and are relatively scarce.

Location of the Major Collections
PUBLIC COLLECTIONS IN GREAT BRITAIN AND NORTH AMERICA
At the *National Portrait Gallery* in London, a wide range of the *Vanity Fair* caricatures has been assembled. Over three hundred of the original watercolour cartoons, a substantial number of preliminary sketches by various *Vanity Fair* artists, a run of the albums that is nearly complete, and copies of the sale catalogues at Christie's, and Puttick and Simpson's are in their files. In 1976 Richard Ormond and Eileen Harris organized 'VANITY FAIR, an exhibition of original cartoons'. Harris's introduction and Ormond's catalogue were significant additions to scholarship about the cartoons and the milieu from which they emerged. As yet the Gallery has few proof copies. It is the most comprehensive public collection of original sources on the cartoons, and their files are an essential source for any further work. Other public libraries and museums in England have runs of the *Vanity Fair Albums*, but little else.

LIBRARIES, MUSEUMS AND UNIVERSITIES IN NORTH AMERICA
The *Library of Congress* has *Vanity Fair* available on microfilm. A few volumes are missing. The University of Minnesota Library has a broken set available on interlibrary loan. Other major university libraries have broken sets, including Bowdoin and Harvard Law. The scholar and collector in North America at least can consult the entire run of the magazine without travelling to England.

PRIVATE COLLECTIONS
Vanity Fair Ltd of Cincinnati, Ohio acquired from the estate of Paul Victorious his immense stock of *Vanity Fair* caricatures. They have published a sale catalogue listing all the cartoons in sixty-nine categories. In early 1981, the remaining stock of *Vanity Fair* Ltd was sold to Clive A. Burden of Rickmansworth, England.

The David Weir Collection (Inquiries: c/o The Hilton Galleries, Mrs I. J. Goold, 3 St Mary's Passage, Cambridge, England)
Mr Weir acquired the immense stock of the magazine sometime in the 1920s. When it was sold to Victorious in the 1930s some thousands of album prints, several hundred proof prints, a few original watercolour sketches and some preliminary printing sketches were kept by

Weir. This collection has not yet been catalogued. Many of the proof prints are in multiples, and include fine examples of the lithographs of Ape, Spy, Tissot, Chartran, Guth and others. The Spy proof prints, particularly of his early work for *Vanity Fair*, are much more incisive than the resulting album prints. The Tissot proofs are radiant with colour, strong in draftsmanship, and heighten one's sense of his ability as an artist and lithographer.

The John Franks Collection (London)
Since the early 1950s Mr Franks has collected volumes of *Vanity Fair Albums* as well as twenty-six original watercolours and some preliminary sketches. His watercolours include Hiram Maxim by Spy (*Vanity Fair*, 15 December 1904) and examples of Ape, Guth and the other major artists. He owns four complete proof print albums bound by *Vanity Fair* in green leather with gold edges for the years 1878, 1888, 1898 and 1899. He has ten privately bound albums of *Vanity Fair* lithographs including a red leather volume entitled "*Vanity Fair*, 1884, Pellegrini'. One of the other privately bound albums, with a Clarice Vivian bookplate, includes sixteen one-third size sepia toned reproductions of famous *Vanity Fair* caricatures, published on 6 July 1880. He also owns a complete run of the regular *Vanity Fair Albums* from 1869 to 1912, and parts of 1913. The originals and prints in the collection have been card indexed.

Dr Jerold Savory Collection (Inquiries: c/o Dept of English, Columbia College, Columbia, South Carolina)
Dr Savory has collected more than one thousand of the lithographs and has catalogued many of them.

DISPLAYS OF VANITY FAIR CARICATURES
In London, a number of clubs, restaurants and hotels have displays of *Vanity Fair* caricatures on their walls. Rules on Maiden Lane and Dick Brennan's Wig and Pen Club on The Strand both have a large number. The Wig and Pen Club also has a series of caricatures of newspapermen, by Sallon, in the *Vanity Fair* style created by Ape. The Royal Court Theatre bar has a number of theatrical *Vanity Fair* cartoons, as does Durrants Hotel and the Cavendish Hotel. In San Francisco, a new restaurant, The Rosebud, on Geary Street, has covered the walls of its bar with the caricatures. We have not seen all the caricatures which must hang in restaurants, pubs, hotels and clubs. However, the authors are locating, in scholarly, hedonistic fashion, all the collections.

1 'Vanity Fair Cartoons on Sale By the *Vanity Fair* Cartoon Co.' printed by R. Weir & Co. Proprietors E. M. Weir (his wife) and D. Weir (No date.)

2 Interview with C. R. Allinson, West Wickham, 19 July 1978.

3 He received royalties when they were reprinted from newspapers in the late 1920s or early 1930s.

4 He assembled sets in 'Cambridge Blue' folders, bound up with a ribbon. These folders, and his printed lists of sets, still turn up in Britain and North America.

5 Some time late in the 1920s or early 1930s part of Weir's stock of *Vanity Fair* prints was lost in a flood.

6 Interviews with Mrs I. J. Goold, Mrs Gladys Noble and Mrs Mary Barltrop, daughters of David Weir. 19, 21, 23 July 1978. Interview with Benjamin Weinreb, 12 May 1978.

7 Interview with Mr Ron Chapple, 19 April 1978.

8 Interview with Mr Andrew Block, 22 May 1978 and Mr Ron Chapple, 19 April 1978.

9 Interview with Eugene Okarma, 3–4 June 1978.

10 Interviews with Thomas S. Benjamin, 1976, 1977, 1978.

11 *Vanity Fair* Ltd Sale Catalogue, Cincinnati, 1976, 36 pp.

12 Richard Ormond, 'Catalogue of Original *Vanity Fair* Cartoons, in the National Portrait Gallery, London', National Portrait Gallery, 1976, p. 5.

13 'Original Drawings reproduced in *Vanity Fair*', Christie, Hanson & Woods, 5, 6, 7, 8 March 1912; Puttick and Simpson Catalogue, 17 March 1916, Sotheby's, 28 October 1912, National Portrait Gallery.

14 *The Vanity Fair Album: List of Cartoons and Volumes* (n.d., about 1902), p. 1.

15 *Vanity Fair*, Preface to 2 August 1911.

16 Vincent Brooks, Day & Son Ltd's records were almost all lost during the wars of 1914–18 and 1939–45. Letter from Sidney Reed, Managing Director, 25 May 1978.

17 The jockeys, Fred Archer and George Fordham, were the highest priced individual prints. *Vanity Fair*, 2 January 1907.

18 *The Vanity Fair Album List of Cartoons and Volumes* (no date, about 1903).

19 *Vanity Fair*, 29 June 1899.

20 *Vanity Fair*, 18 May 1878, and 7 June 1889.

21 *Vanity Fair*, 10 December 1885, Preface to the 17th Volume.

22 Examples are Spy's portrait of C. B. Fry, *Vanity Fair* 1894, and Ape's Lord Robert Montague, *Vanity Fair*, 1870, which were published with different colours and tones.

23 See Alick P. F. Ritchie's, Nibs's and Strickland's caricatures.

24 Beerbohm's caricatures are: Geoge Meredith, 24 September 1896; George Bernard Shaw, 28 December 1905; W. J. Galloway, 11 January 1906; Arthur Wing Pinero, 1 February 1906; Marquess of Soveral, 22 October 1907; Alfred E. Mason, 10 June 1908; Maurice Maeterlinck, 22 July 1908; George Alexander, 20 January 1909 and John Singer Sargent, 24 February 1909.

25 Preface to *The Vanity Fair Album*, 1883.

26 *Vanity Fair*, 14 April 1898.

27 In 1910 Spy drew for *The World*, in *Vanity Fair* style, a vigorous colourful Teddy Roosevelt, dressed in the red robes of an honorary degree from Oxford.

28 A reputable dealer or seller should be willing to guarantee these prints as originals and to buy them back if they are copies. In any case, *caveat emptor!*

29 The Bernhardt sepia reproduction has more character than the original published print by Chartran.

30 They were Dr Richard Owen (*Vanity Fair*, 1 March 1873); Charles Darwin (*Vanity Fair*, 30 September 1871); Thomas Henry Huxley (*Vanity Fair*, 28 January 1871); Rudolph Virchow (*Vanity Fair*, 25 May 1893); Oliver Wendell Holmes Senior (*Vanity Fair*, 19 June 1886); Louis Pasteur (*Vanity Fair*, 8 January 1889); Pierre and Marie Curie (*Vanity Fair*, 22 December 1904); Sir James Paget (*Vanity Fair*, 12 February 1876) and Sir William Crookes (*Vanity Fair*, 21 May 1903).

31 Those reproduced were: Mr Justice Chitty (*Vanity Fair*, 28 March 1885); Mr Justice Charles (*Vanity Fair*, 4 February 1888); Mr Justice Vaughan Williams (*Vanity Fair*, 13 December 1890); Lord Justice Lopes (25 March 1893); Mr Justice Kennedy (14 December 1893); Mr Justice Kekewich (*Vanity Fair*, 24 January 1895); Mr Justice Buckley (*Vanity Fair*, 5 April 1900); Mr Justice Bucknill (*Vanity Fair*, 10 May 1900); Lord Justice Rigby (*Vanity Fair*, 28 March 1901); Mr Justice Swinfin Eady (*Vanity Fair*, 13 February 1902); Mr F. E. Smith (*Vanity Fair*, 16 January 1907).

32 Interview with Robert Weir of Dunhill, 17 May 1978.

33 The smokers chosen in Dunhill's First Series – 1870s – were: Carlo Pellegrini (*Vanity Fair*, 27 April 1889); Viscount Ranleagh (*Vanity Fair*, 25 June 1870); The Hon. J. C. Vivian (*Vanity Fair*, 5 November 1870); Count Apponyi (*Vanity Fair*, 14 January 1871); Sir John Burgess Karslake (*Vanity Fair*, 22 February 1873); Sir Richard Wallace (*Vanity Fair*, 29 November 1873).

34 The tennis playing Grand Duke, Michael Michaelovitch of Russia (*Vanity Fair*, 4 January 1894) appeared recently on a wastepaper basket with the new caption 'Patience'.

'Vanity Fair' artists

During *Vanity Fair*'s existence, 1869–1914, many artists contributed cartoons. Some are well-known; other remain obscure. The following list was compiled by checking through the forty-five volumes, and by crosschecking in lists compiled by others over the years. A list of subjects and artists until 1889, with a few omissions, said to be compiled by Bowles as an index to the magazine's collection of original drawings, is held in typescript by the National Portrait Gallery. We are also indebted to Eileen Harris, Thomas S. Benjamin of Vanity Fair Ltd, and the late George Suckling for the use of their lists, which we have supplemented and amended.

The *nom de crayon* or acronym of the artist is bracketed. Numbers of caricatures attributable to each artist are given. Numbers in bold face in parentheses refer to an example of the artist's work in the book.

Adam, Emil (b. 1843) German sporting painter. 1 cartoon of a steeplechase horse LUTTEUR III, 1909 (**180**)
(AJM) see Marks
(Alick) see Ritchie
(ALS) 1 cartoon, 1910
(Ao) see L'Estrange
(Ape) see Pellegrini
(Ape Junior) 15 cartoons, 1911
(Armadillo) see L'Estrange
(Astz) 9 cartoons, 1913–1914 (**36**)
(Atń) see Thompson

(Bede) 2 cartoons, 1905–1906
Beerbohm, Sir Max (1872–1956) (Max, Ruth, or Bulbo) the famous caricaturist and essayist. 9 cartoons, 1896, 1905–1909 (**33, 35, 35, 35, 35, 84, 102**)
(Bint) possibly Mrs J. D. Rees. 2 cartoons, 1891, 1893
Braddell (KYO) 2 cartoons, 1891, 1892
Bradley, Cuthbert (CB) 6 cartoons, 1899, 1901, 1902
(Bulbo) see Beerbohm

(CB) see Bradley
(C. De-Grimm) see Grimm
Cecioni, Adriano (1838–1886) Italian caricaturist and sculptor. 26 cartoons, 1872 (**92**)
(CG) see Gould
(CGD) see Duff
(CHAM) see de Noe
Chartran, Théobald (T) ⚓ (1849–1907) Franch painter and caricaturist. 68 cartoons 1878–1884 (**66, 94, 100, 132**), 1887 (**154**)
(Cloister) see Duff
Cock, Eianley (?) (Eianley?) (Cock) 3 cartoons, 1913
(Coïdé) see Tissot
(Corbould, A.C.) 1 cartoon, 1879
⚓ see Chartran

Dalton, F.T. (F.T.D. or FTD) 9 cartoons, 1895–1900
De Grimm, see Grimm
Delfico, Melchiorre (1825–1895) Italian caricaturist. 8 cartoons, 1872–1873 (**169**)
de Noe, Count Amadée (CHAM) French caricaturist
D'Epinay, see Epinay
(Drawl) see Ward
Duff, Sir C. G. (?) (C.G.D. or Cloister) 7 cartoons, 1899–1900, 1903

Earl, Percy 10 drawings of horses 1909–1910
(E.B.N.) see Norton
(Eianley) see Cock
(ELF) 18 cartoons, 1908–1910 (**185**)
(EMU)
Epinay, Prosper, Comte d' (b. 1836) French sculptor and caricaturist. 1 cartoon, 1873

(FCG) see Gould
(FG) see Goedecker
Flagg, E. (Flagg) probably James Montgomery Flagg (1879–1960) noted American illustrator. 2 cartoons 1899, 1900. (**191**)
Fothergill, G. A. (GAF) 7 cartoons, 1898, 1899
(FR) 1 cartoon, 1897
(F.T.D.) see Dalton
Furniss, Harry (1854–1925) noted English caricaturist. 2 cartoons, 1881, 1898
(FV) 2 cartoons of Egyptian leaders, 1883

(GAF) see Fothergill
(G.A.W.) 1 cartoon, 1898
(G.D.G. or GD. G,) see Giles
(Geo. Hum.) 1 cartoon. 1901 (**163**)
Giles, Godfrey Douglas (b. 1857) (G.D.G. or GD. G.) soldier and painter. 4 cartoons 1899, 1900, 1903 (**178**)
Gleichen see (Glick)
(Glick) possibly daughter of Count Gleichen. 1 cartoon 1897
(Go) see Goedecker
Goedecker, F. (FG or Go) 4 cartoons, 1884 (**133**)
Gould, Sir Francis Carruthers (1844–1925) (CG or FCG) noted English caricaturist. 7 cartoons, 1879, 1890, 1897–1899
(Gownsman) see Wright
Grimm, Constantine de or von (C. de Grimm or Nemo) 6 cartoons, 1884 (**48**)
Guth, Jean Baptiste (fl. 1883–1921) (Guth or J. B. Guth) French painter and caricaturist. 43 cartoons, mainly of French personalities. 1889–1891 (**165**), 1893–1899 (**40, 138, 139**), 1901, 1902, 1905–1906, 1908, 1910

(Hadge) 1 cartoon, 1899
(Hay) 12 cartoons, 1886, 1888–1889, 1893
(H.C.O.) 15 cartoons, 1909–1911
Hester, Wallace (Wallace Hester, W. Hester or Hester) 12 cartoons, 1910, 1911, 1913
(Hic or Hit?) 1 cartoon, 1913
(HLO) 2 cartoons, 1910–1911
(How?) 1 cartoon 1902 (**147**) possibly Hal Hurst
Hurst, Hal (b. 1865) 1 cartoon, 1896

(Imp) see Price possibly JMP
(J:B:P.) see Partridge
(Jest) 1 cartoon, 1903
Jopling, Joseph Middleton (1831–1884) 2 cartoons, 1883
(JtJ) see Tissot
(K) initial on an ewer. 8 cartoons, 1912 (**69**)
(Kite) 2 cartoons, 1909
(Klúź?) 1 cartoon, 1877 listed as L. Ward in NPG list and Christie's catalogue.
(KYO) see Braddell

L'Estrange, Roland (1869–1919) (Ao, Armadillo) 9 cartoons, 1903–1904, 1907
(Lib) see Prosperi
Loye, Charles Auguste (1841–1905) (Montbard or MD) French caricaturist and illustrator. 7 cartoons, 1872 (**168**)
Lyall, 4 cartoons, 1872–1873

(m) see Tissot
Marks, A. J. or H.(?) (AJM) Arthur H. Marks was Pellegrini's pupil, 2 cartoons, 1889 (**27**)
(Max) see Beerbohm
(MD) see Loye
Mellor, John Page (Quiz or Qviz) lawyer who also worked for *Punch*. 7 cartoons, 1889–1890, 1893, 1898
(MIGS)
Miller, William Edwards (fl. 1873–1929) (W. E. Miller) 1 cartoon 1896
(Montbard) see Loye
(Mouse) contributed 1 cartoon 1913
(MR.) in monogramme. 2 cartoons, 1900–1901 (**182**)

(N.) 1 cartoon, 1899
Nast, Thomas, (1840–1902) noted American political cartoonist. 5 cartoons, 1872 (**189, 189**)
(Nemo) see Grimm
(Nibs) 7 cartoons, 1909, 1911 (**43, 64**)
Norton, Eardley (EBN or E.B.N.) 2 cartoons, 1895, 1902

(Owl) 22 cartoons, 1913 (**18, 85**)

(PAL) see Paleologue
Paleologue, Jean de (b. 1855) (PAL) of Rumanian origin. 3 cartoons, 1889–1890 (**28**)
Partridge, Sir Bernard (1861–1945) noted caricaturist especially in *Punch*. (J:B:P.) 1 cartoon, 1896
(Pat) 2 cartoons, 1885, 1894
Paton, Frank (1856–1909) 1 cartoon of a horse, 1910
Pellegrini, Carlo (1839–1889) (Ape, Singe) the style-setting Italian artist of the magazine. 333 cartoons, 1869–1871 (**52, 54, 56, 74, 78, 83, 123, 126, 151, 161**) 1874–1889 (**53, 79, 80, 89, 97, 101, 105, 108, 123, 134, 162, 171, 187, 195, 196**), 1898.
(Pip) 1 cartoon, 1910
Price, Julius Mendes (Imp) 6 cartoons, 1894, 1897, 1904 (**77. 155**), 1905.
Prosperi, Liberio (Lib) Italian caricaturist. 55 cartoons, 1885–1894 (**66**), (**184**), 1902–1903
(Pry) 4 cartoons, 1891, 1899, 1910

(Quip) 3 cartoons, 1909–1910
(Quiz or Qviz) see Mellor

(Ray) 9 cartoons, 1911–1912 (**18**)
Rees, Mrs J. D. possibly (Bint, MR)
Ritchie, Alick P. F. (Alick) 15 cartoons, 1911–1913 (**103, 173, 198, 199**)
(Ruth) see Beerbohm
(Ryg) 1 cartoon, 1907

(Sic) see Sickert
Sickert, Walter Richard (1860–1942) (Sic) noted English painter. 3 cartoons, 1897 (**34**)
(Singe) see Pellegrini
(SNAPP) 2 cartoons, 1901 (**87**)
(Spy) see Ward
(Strickland) 5 cartoons, 1912 (**62, 85**)
(Stuff or Stuff G.) see Wright
(Sue) 1 cartoon, 1877 (**47**)

(T., .T.) see Chartran
(Tec) 1 cartoon, 1911
(Tel, S.) 1 cartoon, 1891
Thompson, Alfred (fl. 1862–1876) (Atń) illustrator, designer and author. 18 cartoons, 1870 (**115**)
Tissot, James Jacques (1836–1902) (Coïdé, JtJ, m) skilled French painter and lithographer. 62 cartoons, 1869–1873 (**41, 45, 46, 49, 90, 127, 150**), 1876–1877

(unsigned) 7 cartoons: Le Vicomte Ferdinand de Lesseps, 27 November 1871 (**165**); The Gladstone Memorial, 7 December 1881 (**55**); 'In Vanity Fair' 29 November 1890; Alphonso VIII, King of Spain, 21 January 1893; Maharajah of Cuch Behar, 26 December 1901; Isidore de Lara, 23 December 1908; August Bebel, 27 August 1913
(VA) 2 cartoons, 1893–1894
(Vanitas) 1 cartoon, 1908
(VER) see Verheyden
Verheyden, (fl. 1878–1897) Sculptor 6 cartoons, 1883 (**117**)
Vine, W. (WV in monogram) 2 cartoons, 1873

(w.a.g. or wag) see Witherby
Ward, Sir Leslie (1851–1922) (Spy, Drawl, and L. Ward) English caricaturist and portraitist who contributed more than half the caricatures to *Vanity Fair*. 1325 cartoons, 1873 (**81, 93, 111, 112, 152**), 1876–1911 (**Frontispiece [2], 17, 25, 42, 50, 53, 56, 57, 58, 58, 59, 60, 61, 61, 63, 65, 65, 67, 67, 70, 71, 72, 72, 75, 76, 84, 88, 88, 94, 95, 96, 98, 98, 113, 114, 115, 116, 117, 119, 122, 124, 125, 125, 128, 129, 135, 136, 142, 143, 145, 146, 158, 159, 159, 164, 174, 175, 176, 183, 186, 192, 193, 193, 194, 197**)
(WGR) ? 1 cartoon, 1880
(WH- or WH) 41 cartoons, 1911–1913 (**23**)
(WH.O or WHO) perhaps (WH_ or WH) 26 cartoons, 1908–1911
Whistler, James A. M'Neil (1834–1903) noted American born artist who flourished in England. 1 sketch 2 July 1878
Witherby, A. G. (w.a.g. or wag) proprietor of *Vanity Fair* late in the nineteenth century. Also a clever caricaturist. 8 cartoons, 1894–1895 (**182**), 1899–1901
Wright, H. C. Sepping (?) (Gowsman, Stuff, and StuffGG.) 23 cartoons, 1891–1900 (**106–7**)
(WV in monogram) see Vine
(WW in monogram) 1 cartoon, 1894

(XIT) 4 cartoons, 1910

Complete list of
the caricatures

The lithographs have been listed by date printed, issue number, title (Statesmen, etc.) name of the sitter or subject, the caption, and the caricaturist. After the master list follows a list of Special Numbers, including the frontispieces, doubleprints, Summer and Winter Numbers and special supplementary cartoons. A name index follows.

DATE	ISSUE	TITLE	NAME, CAPTION, CARICATURIST
30.1.1869	13	S. No. 1	**Rt Hon Benjamin Disraeli** *He Educated the Tories.* Singe/Ape
6.2.1869	14	S. No. 2	**Rt Hon William E. Gladstone** *Were He a Worse Man.* Singe/Ape
13.2.1869	15	S. No. 3	**Rt Hon John Bright** *Will the Sentimental Orator be Lost in the Practical Minister, or Will Both be Extinguished?* Ape
20.2.1869	16	Pe. No. 1	**Mrs Star, Late Mother Superior of the Convent of Our Lady of Mercy at Hull** *I Felt Very Uncomfortable.* Ape
27.2.1869	17	S. No. 4	**Rt Hon Robert Lowe** *An Enemy to Democracy, yet a Professor of Liberal Principles, Which Tend to Democracy; The Combination Will One Day Make Him Prime Minister of England.* Ape
6.3.1869	18	S. No. 5	**Rt Hon William E. Forster** *If he is Not an Advanced Liberal, it is for Want of Advancing Himself.* Ape
13.3.1869	19	S. No. 6	**Earl Granville KG** *The Ablest Professor in the Cabinet of the Tact by Which Power is Kept: it is his Mission to Counteract the Talk by Which it is Won and Lost.* Ape
20.3.1869	20	S. No. 7	**Lord Hatherley, Lord High Chancellor** *When He Who Has Too Little Piety is Impossible, and He Who Has Too Much is Impracticable; He Who Has Equal Piety and Ability Becomes Lord Chancellor.* Ape
27.3.1869	21	S. No. 8	**The Marquis of Hartington** *His Ability and Industry Would Deserve Respect Even in a Man; in a Marquis They Command Admiration.* Ape
3.4.1869	22	S. No. 9	**Rt Hon Edward Cardwell** *If the State is Happy That Has No History, Thrice Happy is the Statesman Who Makes None.* Ape
10.4.1869	23	S. No. 10	**Rt Hon James Stansfeld** *Pour encourager les autres.* Ape
17.4.1869	24	S. No. 11	**Duke of Argyll** *God Bless the Duke of Argyll.* Ape
24.4.1869	25	S. No. 12	**Earl of Clarendon** *To Say That He is the Best Foreign Minister in The Country is Not Much as Foreign Ministers Go; But as Times Go it is a Great Deal.* Ape
1.5.1869	26	S. No. 13	**Viscount Sydney** *He Received the Royal Commands and Lengthened the Skirts of the Ballet.* Ape
8.5.1869	27	S. No. 14	**Earl Grey** *A Privileged Person.* Ape
15.5.1869	28	S. No. 15	**Lord Westbury** *An Eminent Christian Man.* Ape
22.5.1869	29	S. No. 16	**Earl de Grey and Ripon** *Qualis ab Inepto.* Ape
29.5.1869	30	S. No. 17	**Earl of Derby** *It is His Mission to Stem the Tide of Democracy.* Ape
5.6.1869	31	S. No. 18	**Earl Russell** *The Greatest Liberal Statesman of Modern Times.* Ape
12.6.1869	32	S. No. 19	**Rt Hon G. J. Goschen** *The Theory of Foreign Exchanges.* Ape
19.6.1869	33	S. No. 20	**Rt Hon Hugh C. E. Childers** *A Returned Colonist.* Ape
26.6.1869	34	S. No. 21	**Lord Stanley** *He Speaks With One Party and Acts With the Other.* Ape
3.7.1869	35	S. No. 22	**Bishop of Peterborough** *If Eloquence Could Justify Injustice He Would Have Saved the Irish Church.* Ape
10.7.1869	36	S. No. 23	**Marquis of Salisbury** *He is Too Honest a Tory for His Party and His Time.* Ape
16.7.1869	37	S. No. 24	**Earl Kimberley** *He Improves, if Possible, But He Accepts Always the Accomplished Fact.* Ape
24.7.1869	38	S. No. 25	**Bishop of Oxford** *Not a Brawler.* Ape
31.7.1869	39	S. No. 26	**Lord Cairns** *When Birth Cannot Lead Brains Must.* Ape
7.8.1869	40	S. No. 27	**Duke of Somerset** *Proud and Sincere, Yet Liberal and Just, He Refused to Serve Under the Most Humble of Premiers.* Ape
14.8.1869	41	S. No. 28	**Rt Hon Chichester S. P. Forestcue** *He Married Lady Waldegrave and Governed Ireland.* Ape
21.8.1869	42	S. No. 29	**Rt Hon Henry Austin Bruce** *He has Gained Credit.* Ape
28.8.1869	43	S. No. 30	**Rt Hon Austen Henry Layard** *He Combines the Love of Truths and Art with Equal Devotion and Success.* Ape
4.9.1869	44	Sov. No. 1	**Napoleon III** *Le Régime Parlementaire.* Coide
11.9.1869	45	S. No. 31	**Lord Carnarvon** *The Whole Life.* Ape
18.9.1869	46	Sov. No. 2	**Isabella II** *She Has Throughout Her Life Been Betrayed by Those Who Should Have Been Most Faithful to Her.* Coide
25.9.1869	47	S. No. 32	**Duke of Abercorn** *Promoted From a Viceroyalty to a Dukedom.* Ape
2.10.1869	48	S. No. 33	**M. E. Grant-Duff MP** *A Philosophic Liberal.* Ape
9.10.1869	49	Sov. No. 3	**Leopold II** *Un Roi Constitutionnel.* Coide
16.10.1869	50	Sov. No. 4	**Alexander II** *La Civilisation Russe.* Coide
23.10.1869	51	S. No. 34	**A. S. Ayrton MP** *Mind and Morality.* Coide
30.10.1869	52	Sov. No. 5	**Abdul Aziz** *Ote-toi de la que je m'y mette.* Coide
6.11.1869	53	M. No. 1	**Rev Frederick Temple DD, Bishop Designate of Exeter** *He Has Displayed Ability in the Free Handling of Religious Subjects, and Has Nevertheless Been Made a Bishop.* Coide
13.11.1869	54	S. No. 35	**Earl of Shaftesbury** *He is Not as Other Men Are, For He is Never Influenced by Party Motives.* Ape
20.11.1869	55	S. No. 36	**Rt Hon Lord J. R. Manners MP** *Let Arts and Commerce, Laws and Learning Die, But Leave us Our Old Nobility.* Ape
27.11.1869	56	M. No. 2	**Le Vicomte Ferdinand de Lesseps** *He Suppressed an Isthmus.* Unsigned
4.12.1869	57	S. No. 37	**Earl of Zetland** *The Most Worshipful Grand Master.* Coide
11.12.1869	58	J. No. 1	**Rt Hon Sir Alexander J. E. Cockburn, Bart** *The Lord Chief Justice of England.* Ape
18.12.1869	59	J. No. 2	**Lord Penzance** *A Judge and Peer.* Ape
25.12.1869	60	S. No. 38	**Archbishop of Canterbury** *An Honest and Liberal Primate.* Ape
1.1.1870	61	Sov. No. 6	**Pius IX** *The Infallible.* Coide

DATE	ISSUE	TITLE	NAME, CAPTION, CARICATURIST
8.1.1870	62	J. No. 3	**Chief Justice Bovill** *The Majesty of the Law.* Ape
15.1.1870	63	M. No. 3	**M Emille Ollivier** *The Parliamentary Empire.* Coide
22.1.1870	64	M. No. 4	**Henri Rochefort** *L'a Voyoucratie.* Coide
29.1.1870	65	Sov. No. 7	**Victor Emanuel I** *Il Rè Galantuòmo.* Coide
5.2.1870	66	S. No. 39	**Lord Chelmsford** *It is Hardly to be Believed That Two Political Leaders Should Fall Out Only Because Their Wives Cannot Agree.* Atn
12.2.1870	67	S. No. 40	**Sir John Pakington** *He Was Chairman of Quarter Sessions and Reconstructed the Navy.* Atn
19.2.1870	68	S. No. 41	**Sir Robert P. Collier** *Sir John Coleridge Serves Under Him.* Atn
26.2.1870	69	S. No. 42	**The Marquess Townshend** *The Beggar's Friend.* Atn
5.3.1870	70	M. No. 5	**Serjeant Ballantine** *He Resisted the Temptation to Cross-Examine a Prince of the Blood.* Atn
12.3.1870	71	S. No. 43	**Rt Hon the Speaker** *The First of the Commoners of England.* Atn
19.3.1870	72	S. No. 44	**Sir Robert Peel** *A Professor of Strong Languages.* Atn
26.3.1870	73	S. No. 45	**Duke of Richmond** *Highly Respectable.* Atn
2.4.1870	74	J. No. 4	**Rt Hon Sir Frederick Pollock** *A Souvenir.* Atn
9.4.1870	75	S. No. 46	**Lord Dufferin** *An Exceptional Irishman.* Atn
16.4.1870	76	Sov. No. 8	**The Nawab Nazim of Bengal, Behar and Orissa** *A Living Monument of English Injustice.* Atn
23.4.1870	77	S. No. 47	**HRH Duke of Cambridge** *A Military Difficulty.* Atn
30.4.1870	78	S. No. 48	**Sir John D. Coleridge** *A Risen Barrister.* Atn
7.5.1870	79	M. No. 6	**Admiral Rous** *As Straight as a Reed.* Atn
14.5.1870	80	M. No. 7	**Prince Teck** *The Most Popular of Princes he Has Married the Most Popular of Princesses.* Atn
21.5.1870	81	M. No. 8	**Sir Joseph Hawley** *A Purist of the Turf.* Atn
28.5.1870	82	S. No. 49	**Bernal Osborne** *The Smart Critic.* Atn
4.6.1870	83	S. No. 50	**W.G.G.V. Vernon-Harcourt MP** *He Was Considered an Able Man Till He Assumed His Own Name.* Atn
11.6.1870	84	S. No. 51	**E. H. Knatchbull-Hugessen MP** *A Promising Apprentice.* Ape
18.6.1870	85	S. No. 52	**Earl of Dudley** *Property.* Ape
25.6.1870	86	M. No. 9	**Viscount Ranelagh** *He Had Succeeded in Volunteering.* Ape
2.7.1870	87	S. No. 53	**Earl Spencer** *The Messenger of Peace.* Ape
9.7.1870	88	S. No. 54	**Duke of Sutherland** *Simple and Unassuming Himself, Yet Magnificent and Generous Toward His Fellow Men, He is the Very Prince of Dukes.* Ape
16.7.1870	89	S. No. 55	**Marquis of Westminster** *The Richest Man in England.* Ape
23.7.1870	90	S. No. 56	**Lord Elcho** *His Course Has Been if Not a Wise, Yet a Consistent One, and Dictated by Conscience Only.* Ape
30.7.1870	91	S. No. 57	**Lord Henry G. C. Gordon-Lennox** *A Man of Fashion and Politics.* Ape
6.8.1870	92	S. No. 58	**Lord Halifax** *He Fell off His Horse Into the Peerage.* Ape
13.8.1870	93	S. No. 59	**Mr C. N. Newdegate MP** *A Jesuit in Disguise.* Ape
20.8.1870	94	S. No. 60	**Lord Strathnairn** *He Was Made a Statesman Because He Was a Soldier.* Ape
27.8.1870	95	S. No. 61	**Sir Henry L. E. Bulwer** *A Superannuated Diplomat.* Ape
3.9.1870	96	S. No. 62	**Lord Houghton** *The Cool of the Evening.* Ape
10.9.1870	97	S. No. 63	**Alexander J. Beresford-Hope MP** *Batavian Grace.* Ape
17.9.1870	98	M. No. 10	**General Trochu** *The Hope of France.* Coide
24.9.1870	99	M. No. 11	**Crown Prince of Prussia** *Fritz.* Coide
1.10.1870	100	S. No. 64	**Lord Robert Montagu** *A Working Conservative.* Ape
8.10.1870	101	S. No. 65	**Sir Stafford Northcote** *He Does His Duty to His Party, and is Fortunate if it Happens to be Also His Duty to His Country.* Ape
15.10.1870	102	S. No. 66	**Count Von Bismarck-Schoenausen** *The Ablest Statesman in Europe.* Coide
22.10.1870	103	M. No. 12	**Thomas Carlyle** *The Diogenes of the Modern Corinthians without his tub.* Ape
29.10.1870	104	S. No. 67	**Lord Lytton** *The Representative of Romance.* Ape
5.11.1870	105	S. No. 68	**Hon J. C. Vivian** *Always Pleasant, Always Genial.* Ape
12.11.1870	106	S. No. 69	**Bishop of London** *One Who Has Grieved More Than Others Over 'The Sinfulness of Little Sins.'* Ape
19.11.1870	107	M. No. 13	**Marquis of Lorn** *If Everywhere is Successful as in Love, a Great Destiny Awaits Him.* Ape
26.11.1870	108	M. No. 14	**Sir Roderick Impey Murchison** *A Faithful Friend, an Eminent Savant and The Best Possible of Presidents.* Ape
3.12.1870	109	M. No. 15	**Baron De Brunnow** *One of the Most Precious Products of Political Miscegenation.* Ape
10.12.1870	110	M. No. 16	**Rev Charles Spurgeon** *No One Has Succeeded in Sketching the Comic Side of Repentance and Regeneration.* Ape
17.12.1870	111	M. No. 17	**Sir William Fergusson, Bart** *There is No Man of Greater Weight in His Profession.* Ape
24.12.1870	112	S. No. 70	**Sir H. K. Storks** *He is a Living Paradox; No One is Less Subject to Control, No One a Greater Slave of Control.* Ape
31.12.1870	113	M. No. 18	**Rev A. H. MacKonochie** *He Makes Religion a Tragedy, and the Movements of His Muscles a Solemn Ceremony.* Ape
7.1.1871	114	Sov. No. 8	**King of Prussia** *Les Mangeoit Pour Soi Refraischir Devant Souper.* Coide
14.1.1871	115	S. No. 71	**Count Apponyi** *One of the Lambs of the Political Fold.* Ape
21.1.1871	116	S. No. 72	**Lord Lawrence** *One of the Best Types of Administrative Ability in Modern Times.* Ape

DATE	ISSUE	TITLE	NAME, CAPTION, CARICATURIST
28.1.1871	117	M. No. 19	**Professor Huxley** *A Great Med'cine Man Among the Inquiring Redskins.* Ape
4.2.1871	118	S. No. 73	**H. E. Musurus Bey** *The Most Interesting of all Diplomatic Corps in London.* Ape
11.2.1871	119	S. No. 74	**Rt Hon William Monsell** *The Painstaking Irishman.* Ape
18.2.1871	120	S. No. 75	**George Hammond Whalley MP** *The Great Believer in Roman Catholicism.* Ape
25.2.1871	121	M. No. 20	**Archbishop Manning** *The Next Pope.* Ape
4.3.1871	122	S. No. 76	**The Chevalier Charles Cadorna** *A Liberal and an Enemy to Priests; He Fitly Represents the Power Which Has Seized Rome and Suppressed the Pope.* Ape
11.3.1871	123	S. No. 77	**Rt Hon George Ward Hunt** *The Fat of the Land.* Ape
18.3.1871	124	S. No. 78	**Hon Gerard James Noel MP** *A Nice Little Fellow.* Ape
25.3.1871	125	S. No. 79	**Richard Dowse MP** *An Irish Wit and Solicitor General.* Ape
1.4.1871	126	S. No. 80	**Lord Lyttelton** *A Man of Position.* Ape
8.4.1871	127	S. No. 81	**Earl of Harrowby KG** *The Last Generation.* Ape
15.4.1871	128	S. No. 82	**Lord Ebury** *A Common-Prayer Reformer.* Ape
22.4.1871	129	S. No. 83	**Marquis of Normanby** *By Birth a Man, by Inheritance a Marquis and a Governor by His Sovereign's Favour, He Fills All His Positions With Credit.* Ape
29.4.1871	130	M. No. 21	**Sir Francis Grant** *An Able Artist and an Excellent President.* Ape
6.5.1871	131	M. No. 22	**Sir Thomas Erskine May KCB** *Parliamentary Practice.* Ape
13.5.1871	132	M. No. 23	**John Everett Millais RA** *A Converted pre-Raphaelite.* Ape
20.5.1871	133	S. No. 84	**Michael Thomas Bass MP** *Beer.* Ape
27.5.1871	134	S. No. 85	**Baron Mayer Amschel De Rothschild MP** *The Winner of the Race.* Ape
3.6.1871	135	M. No. 24	**Captain Eyre Shaw** *He Well Deserves His Popularity.* Ape
10.6.1871	136	M. No. 25	**Sir Roger Doughty Tichborne, Bart** *Baronet or Butcher.* Ape
17.6.1871	137	M. No. 26	**Algernon Borthwick** *The Morning Post.* Ape
24.6.1871	138	S. No. 86	**Archbishop of York** *The Archbishop of Society.* Ape
1.7.1871	139	M. No. 27	**Sir John George Shaw-Lefevre KCB** *La Reyne le Veult.* Ape
8.7.1871	140	S. No. 87	**Duke of Marlborough** *A Conservative Religionist.* Ape
15.7.1871	141	S. No. 88	**Lord Skelmersdale** *A Conservative Whip.* Ape
22.7.1871	142	M. No. 28	**Alfred Tennyson** *The Poet Laureate.* Ape
29.7.1871	143	S. No. 89	**Edward Miall MP** *The Nonconformist.* Ape
5.8.1871	144	S. No. 90	**George Bentinck MP** *Big Ben.* Coide
12.8.1871	145	S. No. 91	**John Locke MP** *The Only Man Who is Ever Known to Make Gladstone Smile.* Coide
19.8.1871	146	M. No. 29	**Henry Cole CB** *King Cole.* Coide
26.8.1871	147	M. No. 30	**Don Manuel Rances Y Villanueva** *The Spanish Minister.* Coide
2.9.1871	148	M. No. 31	**Duke of Saldanha, the Portuguese Minister** *He Might Have Been a King.* Coide
9.9.1871	149	S. No. 92	**Rt Hon Russell Gurney MP** *A Commissioner.* Coide
16.9.1871	150	S. No. 93	**Duke of Rutland** *He Was Once Offered the Leadership of the Conservative Party.* Coide
23.9.1871	151	M. No. 32	**George John Whyte-Melville** *The Novelist of Society.* Coide
30.9.1871	152	M. No. 33	**Charles R. Darwin** *Natural Selection.* Coide
7.10.1871	153	S. No. 94	**Alderman Lusk MP** *Now I Want to Know.* Coide
14.10.1871	154	S. No. 95	**Henry William Eaton MP** *Silk.* Coide
21.10.1871	155	M. No. 34	**Rev Charles Voysey** *I Have Much to be Thankful For.* Coide
28.10.1871	156	M. No. 35	**John Pender** *Telegraphs.* Coide
4.11.1871	157	J. No. 5	**Rt Hon Sir Fitz Roy Edward Kelly** *The Lord Chief Baron.* Coide
11.11.1871	158	M. No. 36	**Matthew Arnold** *I Say the Critic.* Coide
18.11.1871	159	S. No. 96	**Lionel Seymour Dawson-Damer MP** *Hippy.* Coide
25.11.1871	160	S. No. 97	**Sir Charles Wentworth Dilke, Bart, MP** *A Far Advanced Radical.* Coide
2.12.1871	161	S. No. 98	**Alexander D.R.W. Baillie-Cochrane MP** *Judicious Amelioration.* Coide
9.12.1871	162	S. No. 99	**Anthony John Mundella MP** *Education and Arbitration.* Coide
16.12.1871	163	S. No. 100	**John George Dodson MP** *Ways and Means.* Coide
23.12.1871	164	S. No. 101	**Mr Cavendish-Bentinck MP** *Little Ben.* Coide
30.12.1871	165	S. No. 102	**William Henry Gregory MP** *An Art Critic.* Coide
6.1.1872	166	S. No. 103	**M Louis Adolphe Thiers** *Faute-de-mieux Premier.* Cecioni
13.1.1872	167	S. No. 104	**Earl of Cork and Orrery** *Master of Her Majesty's Buckhounds.* Cecioni
20.1.1872	168	M. No. 37	**Dr Quin** *Homeopathic Society.* Cecioni
27.1.1872	169	M. No. 38	**James Anthony Froude** *He Created Henry VIII, exploded Mary Stuart, and Demolished Elizabeth.* Cecioni
3.2.1872	170	M. No. 39	**Wilkie Collins** *The Novelist who Invented Sensation.* Cecioni
10.2.1872	171	S. No. 105	**Rt Hon Spencer Horatio Walpole MP** *He Defended Hyde Park.* Cecioni
17.2.1872	172	M. No. 40	**John Ruskin** *The Realization of the Ideal.* Cecioni
24.2.1872	173	S. No. 106	**Honourable George Grenfell Glyn** *The Whip.* Cecioni
2.3.1872	174	M. No. 41	**Alexander William Kinglake** *Not an M.P.* Cecioni
9.3.1872	175	S. No. 107	**William Henry Smith MP** *Newspapers.* Cecioni
16.3.1872	176	S. No. 108	**Sir Roundell Palmer** *He Refused the Woodstock, and Voted Against the Disestablishment of the Irish Church.* Cecioni
23.3.1872	177	S. No. 109	**Mr Maguire** *A Home Ruler.* Cecioni

DATE	ISSUE	TITLE	NAME, CAPTION, CARICATURIST
30.3.1872	178	M. No. 42	**Rev Canon Kingsley** *The Apostle of the Flesh*. Cecioni
6.4.1872	179	M. No. 43	**Professor John Tyndall FRS** *The Scientific Use of the Imagination*. Cecioni
13.4.1872	180	M. No. 44	**Rev John Cumming DD** *The End of the World*. Cecioni
20.4.1872	181	S. No. 110	**Rt Hon Gathorne Hardy MP DCL** *Conservative*. Cecioni
27.4.1872	182	M. No. 45	**William Hepworth Dixon** *He Discovered New America and Freed Russia*. Cecioni
4.5.1872	183	Sov. No. 9	**Amadeus, King of Spain** *He Would be a King*. Cecioni
11.5.1872	184	S. No. 111	**Sir Wilfrid Lawson, Bart, MP** *Permissive Prohibition*. Cecioni
18.5.1872	185	S. No. 112	**Hon Hamilton Fish, American Secretary of State for Foreign Affairs** *Consequential Damages*. Nast
25.5.1872	186	S. No. 113	**Hon Charles Sumner, Member of The United States Senate** *The Massive Grievance*. Nast
1.6.1872	187	Sov. No. 10	**General Ulysses S. Grant, President of the United States of America** *Captain, Tanner, Farmer, General, Imperator*. Nast
8.6.1872	188	S. No. 114	**Thomas Hughes MP** *Tom Brown*. Cecioni
15.6.1872	189	S. No. 115	**Samuel Morley MP** *Dissent*. Cecioni
22.6.1872	190	S. No. 116	**Sir Arthur Richard Wellesley, Duke of Wellington KG PC** *The Son of Waterloo*. Cecioni
29.6.1872	191	M. No. 46	**Frederick Leighton ARA** *A Sacrifice to the Graces*. Coide
6.7.1872	192	M. No. 47	**Sir Michael Costa** *Orchestration*. Lyall
13.7.1872	193	S. No. 117	**George Leeman MP** *A Yorkshire Solicitor*. Coide
20.7.1872	194	S. No. 118	**Horace Greeley** *Anything to Beat Grant*. Nast
27.7.1872	195	S. No. 119	**Rt Hon Edward Pleydell Bouverie MP** *He Did Not Decline the Speakership*. Lyall
3.8.1872	196	S. No. 120	**James Delahunty MP** *Currency*. Coide
10.8.1872	197	S. No. 121	**Rt Hon Edward Horsman MP** *The Eccentric Liberal*. Lyall
17.8.1872	198	S. No. 122	**Lord Radstock** *D.V.* Cecioni
24.8.1872	199	M. No. 48	**Dr Charles John Vaughan DD** *Nolo episcopari*. Montbard
31.8.1872	200	S. No. 123	**Rt Hon Charles Pelham Villiers MP** *He Advocated Free-trade Before it Was Safe to Attack Protection*. Coide
7.9.1872	201	M. No. 49	**Monsignor Capel** *The Apostle to the Genteel*. Montbard
14.9.1872	202	S. No. 124	**Viscount Enfield MP** *Answers Questions*. Cecioni
21.9.1872	203	M. No. 50	**Very Rev Arthur Penrhyn Stanley DD, Dean of Westminster** *Philosophic Belief*. Montbard
28.9.1872	204	S. No. 125	**Rt Hon Sir Colman Michael O'Loghlen, Bart, MP** *The Irish Baronet*. Cecioni
5.10.1872	205	S. No. 126	**Charles Francis Adams** *An Arbitrator*. Nast
12.10.1872	206	M. No. 51	**Rev Thomas Binney** *The Head of the Dissenters*. Montbard
19.10.1872	207	S. No. 127	**Léon Gambetta** *He Devoured France with Activity*. Montbard
26.10.1872	208	S. No. 128	**Joseph Cowen MP** *Newcastle-on-Tyne*. Coide
2.11.1872	209	M. No. 52	**H. M. Stanley** *He Found Livingstone*. Montbard
9.11.1872	210	M. No. 53	**Sir Sydney Hedley Waterlow** *The Lord Mayor*. Cecioni
16.11.1872	211	S. No. 129	**Rt Hon Henry Bouverie William Brand MP** *Mr. Speaker*. Coide
23.11.1872	212	M. No. 54	**Rev Hewman Hall** *Come to Jesus*. Montbard
30.11.1872	213	S. No. 130	**Roger Eykyn MP** *The Police Champion*. Coide
7.12.1872	214	S. No. 131	**Sir Francis Henry Goldsmid, Bart, MP** *Barrister and Baronet*. Coide
14.12.1872	215	M. No. 55	**Baron Paul Julius Reuter** *Telegrams*. Delfico
21.12.1872	216	S. No. 132	**Henry Fawcett MP** *A Radical Leader*. Delfico
28.12.1872	217	S. No. 133	**Gabriel Goldney MP** *Practical*. Delfico
4.1.1873	218	S. No. 134	**William Amelius, Aubrey De Vere Beauclerk, Duke of St Albans** *Hereditary Grand Falconer*. Delfico
11.1.1873	219	S. No. 135	**Robert Wigram Crawford MP** *A Man of Weight*. Delfico
18.1.1873	220	S. No. 136	**Charles Gilpin MP** *Capital Punishment*. Delfico
25.1.1873	221	S. No. 137	**Duke of Buccleuch and Queensberry** *The Governing Classes*. D'Epinay
1.2.1873	222	S. No. 138	**Earl of Galloway** *Army Reorganization*. Delfico
8.2.1873	223	J. No. 6	**Hon Sir James Bacon, Vice-Chancellor and Chief Judge in Bankruptcy** *Contempt of Court*. Vine
15.2.1873	224	S. No. 139	**Joseph D'Aguilar Samuda MP** *Iron Shipbuilding*. Lyall
22.2.1873	225	M. No. 56	**Sir John Burgess Karslake Knt** *Jack*. Lyall
1.3.1873	226	M. No. 57	**Professor Owen** *Old Bones*. Spy
8.3.1873	227	M. No. 58	**Mayne Reid** *Impossible Romance*. Coide
15.3.1873	228	S. No. 140	**Samuel Plimsoll MP** *The Sailor's Champion*. Vine
22.3.1873	229	M. No. 59	**Edward Levy** *The Daily Telegraph*. Spy
29.3.1873	230	S. No. 141	**John Stuart Mill** *A Feminine Philosopher*. Spy
5.4.1873	231	M. No. 60	**Anthony Trollope** *A Novelist*. Spy
12.4.1873	232	M. No. 61	**Lieutenant-Colonel Lord Charles James Fox Russell** *This Fell Sergeant—Strict in His Arrest*. Coide
19.4.1873	233	S. No. 142	**Rt Hon Thomas Emerson Headlam** *Has Kept His Seat for Six-and-twenty Years*. Spy
26.4.1873	234	M. No. 62	**Sir William Jenner, Bart, KCB** *Physic*. Spy
3.5.1873	235	S. No. 143	**Isaac Butt MP** *Home-Rule*. Spy
10.5.1873	236	M. No. 63	**William Powell Frith RA** *The Derby-Day*. Spy

DATE	ISSUE	TITLE	NAME, CAPTION, CARICATURIST
17.5.1873	237	S. No. 144	**John Laird MP** *He Built the 'Alabama' and the 'Captain.'* Spy
24.5.1873	238	J. No. 7	**Hon Sir John Mellor** *Judges the Claimant.* Spy
31.5.1873	239	J. No. 8	**Hon Sir Robert Lush** *A Little Lush.* Spy
7.6.1873	240	S. No. 145	**Robert Dalglish MP** *The Most Popular Man in The House of Commons.* Spy
14.6.1873	241	S. No. 146	**Sir Watkin Williams-Wynn, Bart, MP** *The King of Wales.* Spy
21.6.1873	242	M. No. 64	**Henry Hawkins QC** *The Tichborne Case.* Spy
28.6.1873	243	M. No. 65	**Washington Hibbert** *A Londoner.* Coide
5.7.1873	244	Sov. No. 11	**HIM The Shah of Persia** *He Endowed Persia with a National Debt.* Spy
12.7.1873	245	S. No. 147	**Sir Henry Creswicke Rawlinson KCB** *Our Eastern Policy.* Spy
19.7.1873	246	M. No. 66	**Sir Richard Airey GCB** *Adjutant-General of the Forces.* Spy
26.7.1873	247	S. No. 148	**Lord Colville of Culross** *A Good Fellow.* Spy
2.8.1873	248	S. No. 149	**George Otto Trevelyan MP** *A Competition Wallah.* Spy
9.8.1873	249	S. No. 150	**Rt Hon Lord Otho Augustus Fitzgerald MP** *A Message from the Queen.* Spy
16.8.1873	250	S. No. 151	**Samuel Laing MP** *The Infant Samuel.* Spy
23.8.1873	251	S. No. 152	**Earl of Wilton** *The Commodore.* Coide
30.8.1873	252	M. No. 67	**Field Marshal Sir William Gomm GCB** *The Constable of the Tower.* Spy
6.9.1873	253	S. No. 153	**Thomas Collins MP** *Noisy Tom.* Spy
13.9.1873	254	S. No. 154	**Lord Colonsay** *Scotch Law.* Spy
20.9.1873	255	M. No. 68	**Sir Henry Bartle Edward Frere KCB** *The Slave Trade.* Spy
27.9.1873	256	M. No. 69	**Sir Julius Benedict** *Sweet Sounds.* Spy
4.10.1873	257	S. No. 155	**Lord Campbell and Stratheden** *And Stratheden.* Spy
11.10.1873	258	M. No. 70	**Sir Augustus William James Clifford, Bart, CB** *Black Rod.* Spy
18.10.1873	259	S. No. 156	**William Alexander Louis Stephen Hamilton-Douglas, Duke of Hamilton** *Premier Peer of Scotland.* Coide
25.10.1873	260	S. No. 157	**Earl of Harrington** *An Unexpected Earl.* Coide
1.11.1873	261	M. No. 71	**Dr Edward Vaughan Kenealy** *The Claimant's Counsel.* Spy
8.11.1873	262	P. No. 1	**HRH The Prince of Wales** *The Prince.* Coide
15.11.1873	263	S. No. 158	**Colonel James MacNaghten Hogg MP** *Board of Works.* Spy
22.11.1873	264	S. No. 159	**Earl Bathurst** *A Relic.* Coide
29.11.1873	265	S. No. 160	**Sir Richard Wallace, Bart** *The Hertford Property.* Spy
6.12.1873	266	M. No. 72	**Dr John Doran FSH** *Notes and Queries.* Spy
13.12.1873	267	M. No. 73	**Serjeant Parry** *A Lawyer.* Spy
20.12.1873	268	M. No. 74	**Edward Matthew Ward RA** *Historic Art.* Spy
27.12.1873	269	M. No. 75	**Percy William Doyle CB** *Diplomacy.* Coide
3.1.1874	270	M. No. 76	**Augustus Sevile Lumley** *Cotillon.* Ape
10.1.1874	271	P. No. 2	**HRH The Duke of Edinburgh** *First Violin.* Ape
17.1.1874	272	M. No. 77	**Sir Anthony Panizzi KCB** *Books.* Ape
24.1.1874	273	M. No. 78	**Sir George Orby Wombwell, Bart** *Our Sir George.* Ape
31.1.1874	274	M. No. 79	**Earl of Desart** *Chesterfield Letters.* Ape
7.2.1874	275	S. No. 161	**Lord Carrington** *Charlie.* Ape
14.2.1874	276	M. No. 80	**James Johnstone** *The Standard.* Ape
21.2.1874	277	S. No. 162	**Albert Grant MP** *Leicester Square.* Ape
28.2.1874	278	S. No. 163	**John Walter Huddleston QC MP** *A Future Judge.* Ape
7.3.1874	279	S. No. 164	**Sir Henry James MP** *Nervous.* Ape
14.3.1874	280	M. No. 81	**Arthur Sullivan** *English Music.* Ape
21.3.1874	281	M. No. 82	**Captain Ralph Allen Gossett** *Popular Members.* Ape
28.3.1874	282	S. No. 165	**Sir Charles Forster, Bart, MP** *An Amateur Whip.* Ape
4.4.1874	283	S. No. 166	**Marquis of Lansdowne** *Family.* Ape
11.4.1874	284	S. No. 167	**John Arthur Roebuck MP** *Tear em.* Ape
18.4.1874	285	M. No. 83	**Sir Garnet J. Wolseley, Bart, KCB** *The Man Who Won't Stop.* Ape
25.4.1874	286	S. No. 168	**Rt Hon Joseph Warner Henley MP** *Common Sense.* Ape
2.5.1874	287	S. No. 169	**Rt Hon Sir William Robert Seymour Vesey Fitzgerald GCSI** *Bombay.* Ape
9.5.1874	288	S. No. 170	**Lord Hardwicke** *High Political Office.* Ape
16.5.1874	289	S. No. 171	**Rt Hon Richard Assheton Cross MP** *The New Man.* Ape
23.5.1874	290	S. No. 172	**Philip-Henry Stanhope, Earl Stanhope** *A Noble Writer.* Ape
30.5.1874	291	S. No. 173	**Rt Hon Lord Sandhurst GCB GCSI** *Military Advice.* Ape
6.6.1874	292	S. No. 174	**Duke of Devonshire KG** *Position.* Ape
13.6.1874	293	S. No. 175	**Marquis of Bath** *Ancient Lineage.* Ape
20.6.1874	294	M. No. 84	**Marquis D'Azeglio** *Il Marchese.* Ape
27.6.1874	295	S. No. 176	**Rt Hon William Patrick Adam MP** *The Past.* Ape
4.7.1874	296	S. No. 177	**Colonel Rt Hon Thomas Edward Taylor MP** *Lately Whipped.* Ape
11.7.1874	297	S. No. 178	**Duke of Bedford** *The Head of the Russells.* Ape
18.7.1874	298	S. No. 179	**Herbert Praed MP** *The Philanthropist.* Ape
25.7.1874	299	S. No. 180	**James Howard Harris, Earl of Malmesbury GCB PC DCL** *Diplomacy.* Ape
1.8.1874	300	M. No. 85	**Sir Henry Thompson** *Cremation.* Ape

DATE	ISSUE	TITLE	NAME, CAPTION, CARICATURIST
8.8.1874	301	S. No. 181	**Rt Hon George Sclater-Booth MP** *The Safe Man.* Ape
15.8.1874	302	M. No. 86	**Sir Arthur Helps KCB** *Council.* Ape
22.8.1874	303	S. No. 182	**Rt Hon Sir Michael Hicks Beach** *A Scagliola Apollo.* Ape
29.8.1874	304	S. No. 183	**Rowland Winn MP** *The Lash.* Ape
5.9.1874	305	S. No. 184	**Sir Henry Drummond Wolff KCMG MP** *Consular Chaplains.* Ape
12.9.1874	306	M. No. 87	**Oscar Clayton** *Fashionable Surgery.* Ape
19.9.1874	307	M. No. 88	**Count Edmund Batthyany** *Yachting.* Ape
26.9.1874	308	S. No. 185	**Sir James Hudson GCB** *Ill-used.* Ape
3.10.1874	309	S. No. 186	**Rt Hon Stephen Cave MP** *Amends.* Ape
10.10.1874	310	S. No. 187	**Rt Hon Edward Strathearn Gordon** *Lord Advocate.* Ape
17.10.1874	311	M. No. 89	**Rev James Augustus Hessey DCL** *Merchant Taylors.* Ape
24.10.1874	312	S. No. 188	**Earl of Bradford** *Master of the Horse.* Ape
31.10.1874	313	S. No. 189	**James Lloyd Ashbury MP** *The Ocean Race.* Ape
7.11.1874	314	M. No. 90	**Henry Du Pre Labouchère** *Modest Assurance.* Ape
14.11.1874	315	S. No. 190	**Christopher Sykes MP** *The Gull's Friend.* Ape
21.11.1874	316	M. No. 91	**Algernon Charles Swinburne** *Before Sunrise.* Ape
28.11.1874	317	M. No. 92	**Right Rev John Williams Colenso DD, Bishop of Natal** *The Pentateuch.* Ape
5.12.1874	318	S. No. 191	**Henry Chaplin MP** *A Turf Reformer.* Ape
12.12.1874	319	M. No. 93	**Lord William Hay** *The Director.* Ape
19.12.1874	320	An Actor	**Henry Irving** *The Bells.* Ape
26.12.1874	321	M. No. 94	**Rev Henry White MA** *Prayers.* Ape
2.1.1875	322	M. No. 95	**Rev Edward Bouverie Pusey DD** *High Church.* Ape
9.1.1875	323	S. No. 192	**Sir William Augustus Fraser, of Morar, Bart, MP** *The Sanitary.* Ape
16.1.1875	324	M. No. 96	**William Howard Russell LLD** *Our War Correspondence.* Ape
23.1.1875	325	S. No. 193	**General Robert Cumming Schenck USA** *The United States.* Ape
30.1.1875	326	M. No. 97	**Very Rev Henry George Liddell DD** *Christchurch.* Ape
6.2.1875	327	M. No. 98	**Frederick Maximilian Müller LLD** *The Science of Language.* Ape
13.2.1875	328	S. No. 194	**Count Schouvaloff** *Russia.* Ape
20.2.1875	329	S. No. 195	**Dr Lyon Playfair CB MP** *Chemistry.* Ape
27.2.1875	330	S. No. 196	**Lord Redesdale** *The Lord Dictator.* Ape
6.3.1875	331	M. No. 99	**Lieutenant-Colonel Edmund Yeamans Walcott Henderson CB** *Police.* Ape
13.3.1875	332	S. No. 197	**Major Purcell O'Gorman MP** *The Joker for Waterford.* Ape
20.3.1875	333	S. No. 198	**Edward James Reed CB** *Naval Construction.* Ape
27.3.1875	334	M. No. 100	**His Excellency Governor Pope Hennessy CMG** *Colonial Government.* Ape
3.4.1875	335	M. No. 101	**D. L. Moody** *Prayer & Praise.* Ape
10.4.1875	336	M. No. 102	**Ira D. Sankey** *Praise & Prayer.* Ape
17.4.1875	337	S. No. 199	**Henry Cecil Raikes MP** *Order Order.* Ape
24.4.1875	338	S. No. 200	**Sir George Samuel Jenkinson, Bart, MP** *The Colossus of Roads.* Ape
1.5.1875	339	M. No. 103	**Viscount Bury PC KCMG** *The Auxiliary Forces.* Ape
8.5.1875	340	S. No. 201	**M Michael Chevalier** *French Free Trade.* Ape
15.5.1875	341	S. No. 202	**Sir Massey Lopes, Bart, MP** *Local Taxation.* Ape
22.5.1875	342	M. No. 104	**Signor Tommaso Salvini** *Othello.* Ape
29.5.1875	343	S. No. 203	**Duke of Buckingham** *A Safe Duke.* Ape
5.6.1875	344	S. No. 204	**Clare Sewell Read MP** *A Tenant Farmer.* Ape
12.6.1875	345	S. No. 205	**Rt Hon Sir John Dalrymple Hay, Bart, MP** *The Retired List.* Ape
19.6.1875	346	S. No. 206	**Lord Hammond** *Foreign Policy.* Ape
26.6.1875	347	S. No. 207	**Earl of Abergavenny** *The Tory Bloodhound.* Ape
3.7.1875	348	M. No. 105	**Major-General Lord Alfred Henry Paget** *The Clerk Marshal.* Ape
10.7.1875	349	M. No. 106	**Sir Henry Josias Stracey, Bart** *A Country Gentleman.* Ape
17.7.1875	350	S. No. 208	**Frederick Accolm Milbank MP** *Yorkshire.* Ape
24.7.1875	351	M. No. 107	**Guilford James Hillier Mainwaring-Ellerker Onslow** *The Claimant's Friend.* Ape
31.7.1875	352	S. No. 209	**Earl of Stradbroke** *Suffolk.* Ape
7.8.1875	353	S. No. 210	**Philip Henry Muntz MP** *Birmingham.* Ape
14.8.1875	354	S. No. 211	**Lord Wharncliffe** *Conservative Conversions.* Ape
21.8.1875	355	S. No. 212	**Sir Thomas Bazley, Bart** *Manchester.* Ape
28.8.1875	356	M. No. 108	**Frederick Ferdinand, Count Beust** *Austria.* Ape
4.9.1875	357	S. No. 213	**William Hart Dyke MP** *A Whipper.* Ape
11.9.1875	358	S. No. 214	**Lord Barrington MP** *A Young Man.* Ape
18.9.1875	359	M. No. 109	**George Payne** *G.P.* Ape
25.9.1875	360	M. No. 110	**George Augustus Sala** *Journalism.* Ape
2.10.1875	361	M. No. 111	**Charles James Mathews** *Our Only Comedian.* Ape
9.10.1875	362	M. No. 112	**Matthew Webb** *Swam the Channel.* Ape
16.10.1875	363	S. No. 215	**Lord Forester** *The Ex-father of the House.* Ape
23.10.1875	364	M. No. 113	**Rear-Admiral Lord John Hay CB** *An Admiral.* Ape
30.10.1875	365	M. No. 114	**Prince Edward of Saxe-Weimar** *Guards.* Ape

DATE	ISSUE	TITLE	NAME, CAPTION, CARICATURIST
6.11.1875	366	S. No. 216	**Sir Edward William Watkin MP** *The Railway Interest.* Ape
13.11.1875	367	M. No. 115	**Sir George Biddell Airy KCB** *Astronomy.* Ape
20.11.1875	368	M. No. 116	**Robert Browning** *Modern Poetry.* Ape
27.11.1875	369	M. No. 117	**Abraham Hayward QC** *Anecdotes.* Ape
4.12.1875	370	M. No. 118	**Hon Spencer Lyttelton** *Marshal of the Ceremonies.* Ape
11.12.1875	371	J. No. 9	**Sir Richard Baggallay** *The Court of Appeal.* Ape
18.12.1875	372	M. No. 119	**Sir William Withey Gull, Bart, MD** *Physiological Physic.* Ape
25.12.1875	373	M. No. 120	**Admiral Rt Hon Lord Clarence Paget KCB** *Sailor, Politician and Sculptor.* Ape
1.1.1876	374	J. No. 10	**Sir William Baliol Brett** *Popular Judgment.* Ape
8.1.1876	375	S. No. 217	**Marquis of Tweeddale KT GCB** *A Peninsular Veteran.* Ape
15.1.1876	376	S. No. 218	**Hon Arthur Fitzgerald Kinnaird MP** *Piety and Banking.* Ape
22.1.1876	377	M. No. 121	**Rev Charles Old Goodford DD** *Old Goody.* Spy
29.1.1876	378	J. No. 11	**Hon Sir George William Wilshere Bramwell** *The Exchequer.* Spy
5.2.1876	379	J. No. 12	**Hon Sir Anthony Cleasby** *Formerly of the Carlton.* Spy
12.2.1876	380	M. No. 122	**Sir James Paget, Bart** *Surgery.* Spy
19.2.1876	381	M. No. 123	**Lionel Lawson** *Prosperity.* JTJ
26.2.1876	382	M. No. 124	**Rev Benjamin Jowett MA** *Greek.* Spy
4.3.1876	383	M. No. 125	**Henry Louis Bischoffsheim** *A Retired Financier.* JTJ
11.3.1876	384	M. No. 126	**Tom Taylor** *Punch.* Spy
18.3.1876	385	S. No. 219	**Lord Lytton** *The Vice-Empress.* Spy
25.3.1876	386	M. No. 127	**General Sir Frederick Paul Haines GCB** *Commander in Chief in India.* JTJ
1.4.1876	387	M. No. 128	**Major-General The Hon James MacDonald CB** *Jim.* JTJ
8.4.1876	388	M. No. 129	**Hon and Very Rev Gerald Valerian Wellesley** *The Old Dean.* Spy
15.4.1876	389	S. No. 220	**Viscount Torrington** *A Man of the World.* Spy
22.4.1876	390	M. No. 130	**Admiral Hon Sir Henry Keppel GCB** *Little Harry.* JTJ
29.4.1876	391	P. No. 3	**Carlo VII** *Legitimacy.* Spy
6.5.1876	392	S. No. 221	**Viscount Midleton** *Steward.* Spy
13.5.1876	393	S. No. 222	**Marcus Beresford MP** *Southwark.* Spy
20.5.1876	394	S. No. 223	**Earl of Roden** *In Waiting.* Spy
27.5.1876	395	S. No. 224	**Earl of Powis** *Mouldy.* Spy
3.6.1876	396	S. No. 225	**Earl of Rosebery** *Horse.* Spy
10.6.1876	397	S. No. 226	**Lord Eslington MP** *Shipping.* Spy
17.6.1876	398	P. No. 4	**HRH The Duke of Connaught KG** *A Future Commander in Chief.* Spy
24.6.1876	399	S. No. 227	**Henry Arthur Herbert of Muckross MP** *Of Muckross.* Spy
1.7.1876	400	S. No. 228	**Earl of Portsmouth** *Horse Flesh.* Spy
8.7.1876	401	S. No. 229	**Lord Alington** *Bunny.* Spy
15.7.1876	402	M. No. 131	**Lieutenant Cameron RN** *He Walked Across Africa.* Spy
22.7.1876	403	S. No. 230	**Lord Cottesloe** *Customs.* Spy
29.7.1876	404	M. No. 132	**John Laurence Toole** *A Spelling Bee.* Spy
5.8.1876	405	M. No. 133	**James Manby Gully MD** *Hydropathy.* Spy
12.8.1876	406	S. No. 231	**Lord Charles William De La Poer Beresford RN MP** *The Little Rascal.* Spy
19.8.1876	407	S. No. 232	**Lord Vivian** *Hook & Eye.* Spy
26.8.1876	408	M. No. 134	**Colonel James Farquharson of Invercauld** *The Queen's Landlord.* JTJ
2.9.1876	409	M. No. 135	**George Henry Lewis** *An Astute Lawyer.* Spy
9.9.1876	410	M. No. 136	**Admiral Frederick Beauchamp Paget-Seymour CB** *The Swell of the Ocean.* Spy
16.19.1876	411	M. No. 137	**Rev Henry Parry Liddon DD DCL** *High Church.* Spy
23.9.1876	412	M. No. 138	**Viscount Dupplin** *Petrarch.* Spy
30.9.1876	413	S. No. 233	**Duke of Beaufort KG** *The Duke of Sport.* Spy
7.10.1876	414	M. No. 139	**Viscount Cole** *Good Looks.* Spy
14.10.1876	415	S. No. 234	**Nawab Sir Salar Jung KCSI** *An Indian Statesman.* Spy
21.10.1876	416	Sov. No. 12	**HM Christian William Ferdinand Adolphus George, King of Greece** *Greece.* Spy
28.10.1876	417	M. No. 140	**Viscount Newry and Mourne** *Amateur Theatricals.* Spy
4.11.1876	418	S. No. 235	**Colonel Robert James Lloyd Lindsay VC MP** *The Victoria and Geneva Crosses.* Spy
11.11.1876	419	S. No. 236	**Marquess of Londonderry** *The Vice-Commodore.* Spy
18.11.1876	420	M. No. 141	**Major-General Sir Henry Percival De Bathe, Bart** *Henry.* Spy
25.11.1876	421	M. No. 142	**Colonel Charles Napier Sturt** *A Younger Son.* Spy
2.12.1876	422	M. No. 143	**Captain Frederick G. Burnaby** *Fred.* Spy
9.12.1876	423	S. No. 237	**Earl of Northbrook GCSI** *British Rule in India.* Spy
16.12.1876	424	S. No. 238	**Viscount MacDuff MP** *An Elder Son.* Spy
23.12.1876	425	S. No. 239	**Count George Herbert Munster** *The German Ambassador.* Spy
30.12.1876	426	J. No. 13	**Rt Hon Sir George Mellish DCL** *Appeals.* Spy
6.1.1877	427	S. No. 240	**Count Gyula Andrassy** *Hungary in Effigy.* Klúz
13.1.1877	428	M. No. 144	**Valentine C. Prinsep** *Val.* Spy
20.1.1877	429	M. No. 145	**Rev John Henry Newman DD** *Tracts for the Times.* Spy

DATE	ISSUE	TITLE	NAME, CAPTION, CARICATURIST
27.1.1877	430	S. No. 241	**Joseph Chamberlain MP** *Our Joe.* Spy
3.2.1877	431	M. No. 146	**Lieutenant-General Sir Alfred Hastings Horsford GCB** *The Beau Ideal.* Spy
10.2.1877	432	M. No. 147	**Rev Arthur Tooth** *The Christian Martyr.* Spy
17.2.1877	433	S. No. 242	**Robert Richardson-Gardner MP** *The Royal Borough.* Spy
24.2.1877	434	S. No. 243	**Marquis of Winchester** *The Premier Marquess.* Spy
3.3.1877	435	M. No. 148	**Montague William Corry** *The Pattern Private Secretary.* Spy
10.3.1877	436	S. No. 244	**Rt Hon Lord Claud Hamilton** *The Dowager.* Spy
17.3.1877	437	S. No. 245	**Rt Hon Sir Henry Elliot GCB** *Ambassador to the Porte.* Spy
24.3.1877	438	S. No. 246	**Lord Dorchester** *The Turf.* Spy
31.3.1877	439	S. No. 247	**Marquess of Headfort** *An Irish property.* Spy
7.4.1877	440	S. No. 248	**Marquess of Hertford** *The Lord Chamberlain.* Spy
14.4.1877	441	S. No. 249	**General Ignatieff** *Manipulator of Phrases.* Spy
21.4.1877	442	P. No. 5	**HRH Prince Leopold KG** *The Student Prince.* Spy
28.4.1877	443	S. No. 250	**Hon Robert Bourke MP** *Bobby.* Spy
5.5.1877	444	S. No. 251	**Jacob Bright MP** *The Apostle to the Women.* Spy
12.5.1877	445	S. No. 252	**William Bromley Davenport MP** *Clever.* Spy
19.5.1877	446	M. No. 149	**Richard Wagner** *The Music of the Future.* Spy
26.5.1877	447	S. No. 253	**Rt Hon Lord Henry Frederick Thynne MP** *Younger Son.* Spy
2.6.1877	448	S. No. 254	**Mr Thomas Bayley Potter MP** *The Manchester School.* Spy
9.6.1877	449	M. No. 150	**William Gilbert Grace** *Cricket.* Spy
16.6.1877	450	S. No. 255	**His Excellency Kuo Sung Tao** *China.* Spy
23.6.1877	451	M. No. 151	**Admiral Sir Hastings Reginald Yelverton GCB** *Spanish Ironclads.* JTJ
30.6.1877	452	S. No. 256	**His Highness Midhat Pasha** *The Turkish Constitution.* Spy
7.7.1877	453	M. No. 152	**Theodore Martin CB LLD** *The Royal Literary Assistant.* Spy
14.7.1877	454	P. No. 6	**HIR The Prince Imperial** *The Empire.* Spy
21.7.1877	455	S. No. 257	**Joseph Gillis Biggar MP** *Irish Obstruction.* Spy
28.7.1877	456	M. No. 153	**Rt Hon Lord Odo William Leopold Russell GCB** *Odo.* Spy
4.8.1877	457	S. No. 258	**Duke of Cleveland KC** *The Fourth Duke.* Spy
11.8.1877	458	M. No. 154	**Francis Seymour, Bart, KCB** *Albert's Seymour.* Ape
18.8.1877	459	M. No. 155	**Lord Ronald Charles Sutherland Leveson-Gower** *A Sculptor.* Spy
25.8.1877	460	M. No. 156	**General Rt Hon Sir William Thomas Knollys PC KCB** *Black Rod.* Ape
1.9.1877	461	S. No. 259	**Viscount Falmouth** *Never Bets.* Spy
8.9.1877	462	M. No. 157	**Henry Villebois** *The Squire.* Ape
15.9.1877	463	M. No. 158	**M Paul Gustave Doré** *Sensational Art.* Spy
22.9.1877	464	M. No. 159	**Baron Lionel Nathan de Rothschild** *Baron Lionel.* Ape
29.9.1877	465	M. No. 160	**Harry Benson** *The Turf Frauds.* Spy
6.10.1877	466	S. No. 260	**Thomas Brassey MP** *Round the World.* Ape
13.10.1877	467	M. No. 161	**General Lord George Augustus Frederick Paget KCB** *A Soldier.* Spy
20.10.1877	468	M. No. 162	**General Sir Charles Henry Ellice KCB** *The Adjutant General.* Ape
27.10.1877	469	M. No. 163	**Mr Steel** *The Leviathan.* Spy
3.11.1877	470	M. No. 164	**Hon Oliver George Paulett Montagu** *Oliver.* Ape
10.11.1877	471	S. No. 261	**Marquess of Queensberry** *A Good Light Weight.* Spy
17.11.1877	472	S. No. 262	**Sir John Dugdale Astley, Bart, MP** *The Mate.* Spy
24.11.1877	473	M. No. 165	**Sir Francis Hastings Charles Doyle, Bart** *Poetry.* Spy
1.12.1877	474	M. No. 166	**Sir John Lintorn Arabin Simmons KCB** *Fortifications.* Ape
8.12.1877	475	S. No. 263	**James Lowther MP** *Jim.* Spy
15.12.1877	476	M. No. 167	**Sir Allen Young** *Alleno.* Ape
22.12.1877	477	M. No. 168	**Sir John MacKenzie Grieve** *Haute Ecole.* Spy
29.12.1877	478	Sov. No. 13	**HI and RM The Emperor-King of Austro-Hungary** *Austria.* Sue
5.1.1878	479	M. No. 169	**Archibald Forbes** *Thorough.* Ape
12.1.1878	480	M. No. 170	**James Abbott M'Neill Whistler** *A Symphony.* Spy
19.1.1878	481	M. No. 171	**Colonel Owen Lewis Cope Williams** *The Prince.* Ape
26.1.1878	482	M. No. 172	**Hon Spencer Cecil Brabazon Ponsonby-Fane CB** *Spencer.* Spy
2.2.1878	483	S. No. 264	**Sir Charles Russell, Bart, VC MP** *Westminster.* Ape
9.2.1878	484	S. No. 265	**Sir John Holker** *Attorney-General.* Spy
16.2.1878	485	S. No. 266	**Lord Edmond George Fitzmaurice MP** *Calne.* Spy
23.2.1878	486	S. No. 267	**Sir John Lubbock, Bart, MP** *The Bank Holiday.* Spy
2.3.1878	487	S. No. 268	**Earl of Denbigh** *A Catholic.* Spy
9.3.1878	488	M. No. 173	**Lieutenant-General Valentine Baker Pasha** *Baker Pasha.* Ape
16.3.1878	489	M. No. 174	**General Frederick Marshall** *Handsome Fred.* Ape
23.3.1878	490	M. No. 175	**General Sir Charles Hastings Doyle KCMG** *A General.* Spy
30.3.1878	491	S. No. 269	**Earl of Feversham** *A Conservative.* Ape
6.4.1878	492	S. No. 270	**Lord Lyons** *Diplomacy.* Ape
13.4.1878	493	M. No. 176	**Major-General Sir Daniel Lysons KCB** *Dan.* Spy
20.4.1878	494	M. No. 177	**General Lord Napier of Magdala GCB BCSI** *The British Expedition.* Spy

DATE	ISSUE	TITLE	NAME, CAPTION, CARICATURIST
27.4.1878	495	S. No. 271	**Joseph Cowen MP** *Joe.* Ape
4.5.1878	496	S. No. 272	**Earl Dunraven and Mount-Earl KP** *Active.* Spy
11.5.1878	497	S. No. 273	**Lord Lindsay MP** *Astronomy.* Spy
18.5.1878	498	Sov. No. 14	**His Holiness Pope Leo XIII** *The Pope.* T
25.5.1878	499	M. No. 178	**Colonel Hon Frederick Arthur Wellesley** *Promotion by Merit.* Ape
1.6.1878	500	M. No. 179	**Admiral Hobart Pasha** *Hobart Pasha.* Spy
8.6.1878	501	M. No. 180	**Lt-General Sir Arnold Burrows Kemball KCSI CB** *Asia Minor.* Ape
15.6.1878	502	M. No. 181	**General Giuseppe Garibaldi** *Revolution.* T.
22.6.1878	503	S. No. 274	**Sir Hardinge Stanley Giffard** *The Solicitor General.* Spy
29.6.1878	504	M. No. 182	**George Lane-Fox Esq of Bramham** *George Fox.* Spy
2.7.1878	Season number		**Earl of Beaconsfield** *The Junior Ambassador.* Ape
2.7.1878	Season number		**St James Street–June 1878.** Whistler
6.7.1878	505	S. No. 275	**Sir James Dalrymple Horn Elphinstone MP** *The Admiral.* Spy
13.7.1878	506	M. No. 183	**Frederick Robert Spofforth** *The Demon Bowler.* Spy
20.7.1878	507	M. No. 184	**General Sir Thomas Montagu Steele KCB** *Aldershot.* Ape
27.7.1878	508	S. No. 276	**Lord Claud John Hamilton MP** *Bridegroom.* Spy
3.8.1878	509	Sov. No. 15	**HM The King of Italy** *Italy.* T
10.8.1878	510	S. No. 277	**Colonel John Sidney North MP** *A Tory.* Spy
17.8.1878	511	S. No. 278	**Lord Tenterden** *The Foreign Office.* Ape
24.8.1878	512	S. No. 279	**The Earl of Portarlington** *Port.* Spy
31.8.1878	513	S. No. 280	**Edward Jenkins MP** *Ginx's Baby.* Spy
7.9.1878	514	S. No. 281	**Lord Kensington MP** *A Whip.* Spy
14.9.1878	515	S. No. 282	**Earl Fitzwilliam KG** *Property and Principle.* Ape
21.9.1878	516	S. No. 283	**Sir George Campbell KCSI** *Indian Authority.* Spy
28.9.1878	517	S. No. 284	**M William Henry Waddington** *France at the Congress.* T
5.10.1878	518	S. No. 285	**Lord Gerard** *A New Peer.* Spy
12.10.1878	519	S. No. 286	**Marquess of Ormonde** *Kilkenny.* Spy
19.10.1878	520	S. No. 287	**Lord Londesborough** *A Whip.* Spy
26.10.1878	521	M. No. 185	**John Tenniel** *Punch.* Spy
2.11.1878	522	M. No. 186	**Alfred Montgomery** *Alfred.* Spy
9.11.1878	523	M. No. 187	**Rivers Wilson CB** *Egyptian Finance.* Ape
16.11.1878	524	M. No. 188	**Edmund Hodgson Yates** *The World.* Spy
23.11.1878	525	M. No. 189	**Sir Francis Philip Cunliffe Owen KCMG CB** *Paris Exhibition.* Spy
30.11.1878	526	M. No. 190	**John Morley** *The Fortnightly Review.* Ape
7.12.1878	527	S. No. 288	**Sir Frederick John William Johnstone MP** *Freddy.* Spy
14.12.1878	Season number		**HRH The Prince of Wales** *The Prince.* Spy
14.12.1878	528	S. No. 289	**The Earl of Dunmore** *Charlie.* Spy
21.12.1878	529	S. No. 290	**Charles Seely MP** *Pigs.* Spy
28.12.1878	530	S. No. 291	**Duke of Manchester KP** *The Colonies.* Spy
4.1.1879	531	M. No. 191	**Francis Bret Harte** *The Heathen Chinee.* Spy
11.1.1879	532	S. No. 292	**Lord Bateman** *Reciprocity.* Ape
18.1.1879	533	S. No. 293	**Sir George Bowyer, Bart, MP** *The Knight of Malta.* Spy
25.1.1879	534	S. No. 294	**Peter Rylands MP** *Foreign Policy.* Spy
1.2.1879	535	S. No. 192	**Francois Charles Gounod** *Emotional Music.* T
8.2.1879	536	S. No. 295	**Arthur John Otway MP** *He Killed the Cat.* Ape
15.2.1879	537	M. No. 193	**Giuseppe Verdi** *Italian Music.* T
22.2.1879	538	M. No. 194	**Joseph Ernest Renan** *La vie de Jésus.* T
1.3.1879	539	M. No. 195	**Rt Hon Sir George Jessel** *The Law.* Spy
8.3.1879	540	S. No. 296	**Admiral Sir William Edmonstone, Bart, CB MP** *Chorus.* Spy
15.3.1879	541	M. No. 196	**Major-General Henry Hope Crealock CB** *Second in Zululand.* Spy
22.3.1879	542	M. No. 197	**Laurence Alma-Tadema** *Ancient Painting.* Ape
29.3.1879	543	S. No. 297	**Major-General Sir Henry Marshman Havelock VC CB MP** *The Soldier Who Couldn't Draw His Sword.* Spy
5.4.1879	544	S. No. 298	**Rt Hon Lord George Francis Hamilton MP** *Georgie.* Spy
12.4.1879	545	S. No. 299	**Hon Edward Stanhope MP** *The Young Man.* Spy
19.4.1879	546	S. No. 300	**Mitchell Henry MP** *Home Rule.* Spy
26.4.1879	547	M. No. 198	**Herbert Spencer** *Philosophy.* CG
3.5.1879	548	S. No. 301	**Lord Suffield** *Charlie.* Ape
10.5.1879	549	M. No. 199	**Hon Mr Justice Straight** *The New Judge.* Spy
17.5.1879	550	S. No. 302	**George Osborne Morgan QC MP** *Burials.* Spy
24.5.1879	551	S. No. 303	**Rt Hon Frederick Arthur Stanley** *War.* Ape
31.5.1879	552	S. No. 304	**Sir Philip John Williams Miles, Bart, MP** *Philip.* Spy
7.6.1879	553	S. No. 305	**Viscount Castlereagh MP** *C.* Spy
14.6.1879	554	S. No. 306	**Earl of Lonsdale** *Self-Conquest.* Spy
21.6.1879	555	S. No. 307	**John Farley Leith MP** *Aberdeen.* Spy

DATE	ISSUE	TITLE	NAME, CAPTION, CARICATURIST
28.6.1879	556	S. No. 308	**Charles Watkin Williams-Wynn** *Montgomeryshire.* Spy
1.7.1879	Season number		**W. E. Gladstone** *The People's William.* Spy
1.7.1879	—		**The Row in the Season** *The Row in the Season.* Corbold
5.7.1879	557	W.G. No. 1	**Mademoiselle Sarah Bernhardt** *Sarah Bernhardt.* T
12.7.1879	558	S. No. 309	**M Jules Grévy** *The French Republic.* T
19.7.1879	559	M. No. 200	**William Holman Hunt** *The Pre-Raphaelite of the World.* Spy
26.7.1879	560	P. No. 8	**Prince Jerome Napoleon** *Plon-Plon.* T
2.8.1879	561	S. No. 310	**William Cunliffe Brooks MP** *The Golden Pippin.* Spy
9.8.1879	562	S. No. 311	**Marquis of Waterford KP** *The Great Man of Waterford.* Spy
16.8.1879	563	M. No. 201	**Sir Albert Abdallah David Sassoon CSI** *The Indian Rothschild.* Spy
23.8.1879	564	M. No. 202	**Sir Tatton Sykes, Bart** *Fifteen Churches.* Spy
30.8.1879	565	S. No. 312	**Earl De La Warr** *Jour de ma Vie.* Spy
6.9.1879	566	M. No. 203	**Major General Charles Craufurd Fraser VC** *Conspicuous & Cool.* Spy
13.9.1879	567	S. No. 313	**H. E. Phya Bhaskarawongse** *Siam.* Spy
20.9.1879	568	M. No. 204	**Victor Hugo** *A French Poet.* T.
27.9.1879	569	M. No. 205	**Lord William Leslie De La Poer Beresford VC** *Fighting Bill.* Spy
4.10.1879	570	M. No. 206	**Thomas Chenery** *The Times.* Spy
11.10.1879	571	S. No. 314	**Marshal MacMahon** *J'y suis J'y reste.* T.
18.10.1879	572	M. No. 207	**Hon and Rev Francis Edmund Cecil Byng MA** *Prayers.* Spy
25.10.1879	573	S. No. 315	**Earl of Donoughmore KCMG** *Eastern Roumelia.* Spy
1.11.1879	574	M. No. 208	**Montagu Williams** *In His Military Capacity.* Spy
8.11.1879	575	S. No. 316	**Duke of Athole KT** *The Seventh Duke.* Spy
15.11.1879	576	M. No. 209	**Brigadier-General Sir Evelyn Wood KCB VC** *The Flying Column.* Spy
22.11.1879	577	M. No. 210	**William Stuart Stirling-Crawfurd** *Gang Forward.* Spy
29.11.1879	578	S. No. 317	**Sir George Elliot, Bart, MP** *Geordie.* Spy
6.12.1879	579	S. No. 318	**M Paul De Granier De Cassagnac** *A French Duellist.* T
13.12.1879	580	M. No. 211	**Sir Percy Florence Shelley, Bart** *The Poet's Son.* Ape
16.12.1879	Season number		**Earl of Beaconsfield and Mr Montagu Corry** *Power and Place.* Spy
20.12.1879	581	S. No. 319	**M Jean Joseph Louis Blanc** *Social Revolution.* T
27.12.1879	582	M. No. 212	**M Alexandre Dumas Fils** *French Fiction.* T
3.1.1880	583	M. No. 213	**Henry Savile** *The Turf.* Spy
10.1.1880	584	M. No. 214	**Samuel Ward** *Uncle Sam.* Spy
17.1.1880	585	S. No. 320	**Captain Lord Gifford VC** *V.C.* Spy
24.1.1880	586	M. No. 215	**M Emile Zola** *French Realism.* T
31.1.1880	587	M. No. 216	**Sir Roger William Henry Palmer, Bart** *Roger.* Spy
7.2.1880	588	M. No. 217	**Vice-Admiral Sir Reginald John MacDonald KCSI** *Rim.* Spy
14.2.1880	589	S. No. 321	**Colonel Robert Nigel Fitzhardinge Kingscote MP** *The Court.* Spy
21.2.1880	590	S. No. 322	**M. E. Whitley MP** *Liverpool.* Spy
28.2.1880	591	M. No. 218	**Commander Lord Ramsay RN** *Liverpool.* Spy
6.3.1880	592	M. No. 219	**Colonel James Keith Fraser** *Keith.* Spy
13.3.1880	593	S. No. 323	**Edward Clarke MP** *Southwark.* Spy
20.3.1880	594	M. No. 220	**Markham Spofforth** *He Invented the Conservative Working Man.* Ape
27.3.1880	595	M. No. 221	**Lord Inverurie** *Candidate for Chelsea.* Spy
3.4.1880	596	M. No. 222	**Lord Headley** *A Loyal Irishman.* Ape
10.4.1880	597	M. No. 223	**General Sir F. Roberts KCB** *Bobs.* WGR
17.4.1880	598	S. No. 324	**George Burrow Gregory MP** *East Sussex.* Spy
24.4.1880	599	M. No. 224	**Lt-Colonel Henry Stracey** *Henry.* Ape
1.5.1880	600	M. No. 225	**M Jean Louis Ernest Meissonier** *A Great French Painter.* T
8.5.1880	601	S. No. 325	**Lord Ardilaun** *A Practical Patriot.* Spy
15.5.1880	602	M. No. 226	**Henry G. Calcraft** *Board of Trade.* Spy
22.5.1880	603	S. No. 326	**Baron Henry De Worms MP** *Intelligent Toryism.* Ape
29.5.1880	604	S. No. 327	**Rt Hon David Plunket MP** *Hereditary Eloquence.* Ape
5.6.1880	605	M. No. 227	**Sir William Alexander Gordon Cumming, Bart** *Bill.* Ape
12.6.1880	606	S. No. 328	**Charles Bradlaugh MP** *Iconoclast.* Spy
19.6.1880	607	M. No. 228	**Frederick Greenwood** *He Created 'The Pall Mall Gazette'.* Ape
26.6.1880	608	S. No. 329	**Rt Hon Sir Augustus Berkeley Paget KCB** *Promotion by Marriage.* T
3.7.1880	609	S. No. 330	**Viscount Folkestone MP** *South Wilts.* Ape
6.7.1880	Season number		**The Treasury Bench (Gladstone, Lord Hartington, and Chamberlain)** *Babble, Birth and Brummagen.* T
10.7.1880	610	S. No. 331	**Lord Randolph Henry Spencer-Churchill MP** *A Younger Son.* Spy
17.7.1880	611	S. No. 332	**Earl of Shrewsbury and Talbot** *The Premier Earl.* Spy
24.7.1880	612	M. No. 229	**Colonel Lewis Guy Phillips, Grenadier Guards** *Order at Wimbledon.* Ape
31.7.1880	613	S. No. 333	**John Eldon Gorst QC MP** *Tory Organisation.* Spy
7.8.1880	614	S. No. 334	**Montague John Guest MP** *Monty.* Spy
14.8.1880	615	M. No. 230	**Sir Charles John Forbes, Baronet, of Newe** *Of Newe.* Ape

DATE	ISSUE	TITLE	NAME, CAPTION, CARICATURIST
21.8.1880	616	S. No. 335	**James Russell Lowell LLD** *Hosea Riglow.* T
28.8.1880	617	S. No. 336	**Frank Hugh O'Cahan O'Donnell MP** *Roman Catholic Home-Rule.* T
4.9.1880	618	S. No. 337	**Henry Richard MP** *Peace.* Spy
11.9.1880	619	S. No. 338	**Charles Stewart Parnell MP** *Anti-Rent.* T
18.9.1880	620	S. No. 339	**Marquis of Anglesey** *The Head of the Pagets.* Ape
25.9.1880	621	S. No. 340	**Leonard Henry Courtney MP** *Proper Self-Sufficiency.* T
2.10.1880	622	S. No. 341	**Earl of Winchilsea and Nottingham** *Youth.* Spy
9.10.1880	623	S. No. 342	**Marquis of Ailesbury** *Three Dowagers.* T
16.10.1880	624	S. No. 343	**Sir John George Tollemache Sinclair, Bart, MP** *A Poet.* Ape
23.10.1880	625	S. No. 344	**O'Donoghue of the Glens MP** *The O'Donoghue.* Spy
30.10.1880	626	S. No. 345	**Hon Percy Scawen Wyndham MP** *Aesthetics.* Spy
6.11.1880	627	M. No. 231	**Sir Henry Bessemer CE** *Steel.* Spy
13.11.1880	628	S. No. 346	**Viscount Lymington MP** *Young Oxford.* Spy
20.11.1880	629	M. No. 232	**M Edmond Francois Valentin About** *French Fiction.* T
27.11.1880	630	M. No. 233	**Captain John Bastard** *Horses.* Spy
1.12.1880	Winter number		**'The Fourth Party'** (Lord Randolph Churchill, Sir Henry Drummond Wolff, A. J. Balfour, Mr Gorst) *The Fourth Party.* Spy
4.12.1880	631	S. No. 347	**M Jean Baptiste Léon Say** *President No. 3.* Ape
11.12.1880	632	S. No. 348	**Alderman Sir Robert Walter Carden KNT MP** *City Justice.* Spy
18.12.1880	633	M. No. 234	**Erasmus Wilson MRCS** *The Obelisk.* Spy
25.12.1880	634	M. No. 235	**M Victorien Sardou** *Ficelle dramatique.* T
1.1.1881	635	S. No. 349	**Marquis Conyngham** *Mount.* Spy
8.1.1881	636	M. No. 236	**Francis C. Burnand** *Punch.* Ape
15.1.1881	637	S. No. 350	**Sir Richard Temple, Bart, GCSI CIE** *Burra Dick.* Spy
22.1.1881	638	M. No. 237	**Joseph Edgar Boehm ARA** *The Queen's Sculptor.* Spy
29.1.1881	639	M. No. 238	**Charles Cunningham Boycott** *Boycott.* Spy
5.2.1881	640	M. No. 239	**Sir Bache Edward Cunard, Bart, MFH** *A Cunarder.* Spy
12.2.1881	641	M. No. 240	**Morgan Howard QC** *Energetic Toryism.* Spy
19.2.1881	642	M. No. 241	**Lieutenant-Colonel Charles George Gordon CB RE** *The Ever Victorious.* Ape
26.2.1881	643	S. No. 351	**Earl of Kenmare PC** *The Lord Chamberlain.* Spy
5.3.1881	644	S. No. 352	**Marquis of Hamilton** *Hamilie.* Spy
12.3.1881	645	M. No. 242	**William Lehman Ashmead Burdett-Coutts Bartlett** *The Baroness's Husband.* Spy
19.3.1881	646	S. No. 353	**Sir Farrer Herschell MP QC** *The Solicitor-General.* Spy
26.3.1881	647	S. No. 354	**Right Reverend John Ryle DD Bishop of Liverpool** *Liverpool.* Ape
2.4.1881	648	S. No. 355	**Lord Waveney** *Suffolk.* Spy
9.4.1881	649	S. No. 356	**Marquis of Exeter** *A Real English Gentleman.* Ape
16.4.1881	650	S. No. 357	**Earl Nelson** *The Noblest of English Names.* Spy
23.4.1881	651	S. No. 358	**General The Earl of Lucan GCB** *Balaklava.* Ape
30.4.1881	652	S. No. 359	**Lord Tollemache** *Cheshire.* Spy
7.5.1881	653	S. No. 360	**His Highness Ismail Pasha** *The Ex-Khedive.* T.
14.5.1881	654	M. No. 243	**Sir Philip Rose, Bart** *Lord Beaconsfield's Friend.* Spy
21.5.1881	655	M. No. 244	**William Schwenck Gilbert** *Patience.* Spy
28.5.1881	656	M. No. 245	**Fred Archer** *The Favorite Jockey.* Spy
4.6.1881	657	S. No. 361	**Earl Cadogan** *Chelsea & the Colonies.* Spy
11.6.1881	658	S. No. 362	**Lord Ribblesdale** *Mufti.* Spy
18.6.1881	659	M. No. 246	**Marquis of Blandford** *B.* T.
25.6.1881	660	S. No. 363	**Alderman Robert Nicholas Fowler MP** *The City.* T.
2.7.1881	661¹	M. No. 247	**Mr Charles Cox CB** *Colonial.* Spy
5.7.1881	Season number		**'Birth, Behavior and Business'** (Sir Stafford Northcote, Lord John Manners and Sir Richard Cross) *Her Majesty's Opposition.* T.
9.7.1881	661¹	M. No. 248	**Colonel Henry P. Ewart** *Croppy.* T
16.7.1881	662	S. No. 364	**Lord Harris** *Kent.* Spy
23.7.1881	663	S. No. 365	**Sir Matthew White Ridley, Bart, MP** *Ex-Official.* Ape
30.7.1881	664	S. No. 366	**Lord Aveland** *A Great Officer of State.* Spy
6.8.1881	665	S. No. 367	**Earl of Clonmell** *Earlie.* Ape
13.8.1881	666	S. No. 368	**Earl of Coventry** *Covey.* Ape
20.8.1881	667	M. No. 249	**'Honble' Alexander Grantham Yorke** *Alick.* Spy
27.8.1881	668	S. No. 369	**Rt Hon Earl Percy MP** *Northumberland.* T
3.9.1881	669	S. No. 370	**General Lord Chelmsford GCB** *Islandula.* Spy
10.9.1881	670	S. No. 371	**John Walter MP** *The Times.* Spy
17.9.1881	671	S. No. 372	**Earl Fortescue** *Sanitas.* T
24.9.1881	672	S. No. 373	**Lord Henry John Montagu-Douglas-Scott MP** *South Hants.* T
1.10.1881	673	S. No. 374	**Duke of Norfolk** *Our Little Duke.* Spy
8.10.1881	674	S. No. 375	**William M'Arthur MP, Lord Mayor of London** *The Lord Mayor.* Spy
15.10.1881	675	S. No. 376	**Lord Rendlesham MP** *Property in Suffolk.* T

DATE	ISSUE	TITLE	NAME, CAPTION, CARICATURIST
22.10.1881	676	S. No. 377	**Earl of Macclesfield** *A Coachman.* Spy
29.10.1881	677	S. No. 378	**Hon William Lowther MP** *Westmorland.* Spy
5.11.1881	678	S. No. 379	**Sir Rainald Knightley, Bart, MP** *A Fine Old Tory.* Spy
12.11.1881	679	S. No. 380	**Earl of Rosslyn** *The Kirk of Scotland.* T
19.11.1881	680	S. No. 381	**Rt Hon Lord Blackburn** *A Lord of Appeal.* Spy
26.11.1881	681	S. No. 382	**Viscount Hawarden** *Hereditary Whip.* T
3.12.1881	682	S. No. 383	**Mourdaunt Fenwick-Bissett** *The General.* Spy
7.12.1881	Winter number		**Mr Parnell and Mr Dillon & a policeman** *Force No Remedy.* Furniss
7.12.1881	—		**Mr Gladstone and Mr Bradlaugh** *The Gladstone Memorial.* Unsigned
10.12.1881	683	S. No. 384	**Hon Charles Robert Spencer MP** *Bradlaugh's Baby.* Spy
17.12.1881	684	S. No. 385	**Earl of Leven and Melville** *Amiability.* Spy
24.12.1881	685	M. No. 250	**Vice-Admiral Sir John Edmund Commerell KCB VC** *A Jingo.* T
31.12.1881	686	M. No. 251	**Hon Algernon William Fulke-Greville** *Racing & Politics.* Spy
7.1.1882	687	S. No. 388	**Lord Crewe** *Lay Episcopacy.* Spy
14.1.1882	688	M. No. 252	**Samuel Smiles LLD** *Self Help.* Spy
21.1.1882	689	M. No. 253	**Sir Daniel Cooper, Bart** *Sydney.* Spy
28.1.1882	690	S. No. 387	**Sir Thomas Bateson, Bart, MP** *Landed Estates in Ireland.* Spy
4.2.1882	691	S. No. 388	**Lord Robartes** *East Cornwall.* Spy
11.2.1882	692	S. No. 389	**Sir William Henry Gladstone MP** *His Father's Son.* Spy
18.2.1882	693	S. No. 390	**John Holms MP** *Military Changes.* Spy
25.2.1882	694	S. No. 391	**Earl of Munster** *Brighton.* Spy
4.3.1882	695	S. No. 392	**Lord Haldon** *Torquay.* Spy
11.3.1882	696	M. No. 254	**Sampson S. Lloyd** *Fair Trade.* Spy
18.3.1882	697	S. No. 393	**Duke of Montrose KT** *Scotland & Racing.* Spy
25.3.1882	698	S. No. 394	**Lord Penrhyn** *Slate.* Spy
1.4.1882	699	S. No. 395	**George Errington MP** *The Vatican.* T
8.4.1882	700	S. No. 396	**Rt Hon Sir John Robert Mowbray MP** *Committee of Selection.* Spy
15.4.1882	701	S. No. 397	**Arthur Loftus Tottenham MP** *Lofty.* Spy
22.4.1882	702	M. No. 255	**Viscount Mandeville** *Kim.* Spy
29.4.1882	703	S. No. 398	**Hon Thomas Charles Bruce MP** *Portsmouth.* Spy
6.5.1882	704	S. No. 399	**Herbert John Gladstone MP** *Young Hopeful.* Spy
13.5.1882	705	S. No. 400	**Lewis Llewellyn Dillwyn MP** *A Wet Quaker.* Spy
20.5.1882	706	S. No. 401	**Earl of Selkirk** *Created in 1646.* Spy
27.5.1882	707	M. No. 256	**William Edward Hartpole Lecky** *The Eighteenth Century.* Spy
3.6.1882	708	S. No. 402	**Duke of Portland** *The Young Duke.* Spy
10.6.1882	709	S. No. 403	**Montagu David Scott MP** *East Sussex.* Spy
17.6.1882	710	M. No. 257	**Mr Anstruther-Thomson** *Fife.* Spy
24.6.1882	711	M. No. 258	**Captain Arthur Gooch** *Goochie.* Spy
1.7.1882	713²	S. No. 404	**Lord Henniker** *A Man of Business.* T
5.7.1882	Season number		**'Purse, Pussy, Piety and Prevarication'** (Lord Northbrook, Lord Granville, Lord Selborne, and Lord Salisbury) *Purse, Pussy, Piety and Prevarication.* T
8.7.1882	713²	M. No. 259	**Sir John Bennet Lawes, Bart** *Agricultural Science.* T
15.7.1882	714	S. No. 405	**Sir Harry Verney, Bart, MP** *Bucks.* Spy
22.7.1882	715	S. No. 406	**Lord of Ilchester** *Fifth Earl.* Spy
29.7.1882	716	M. No. 260	**Sir Alexander Milne, Bart, GCB** *Admiral of the Fleet.* T
5.8.1882	717	M. No. 261	**Frederick Barne** *The Jockey Club.* Spy
12.8.1882	718	S. No. 407	**Hon Bernard Edward Barnaby Fitzpatrick MP** *Barnie.* Spy
19.8.1882	719	S. No. 408	**Mr Cyril Flower MP** *The Senator.* T
26.8.1882	720	Sov. No. 16	**Cetewayo** *Restored.* Spy
2.9.1882	721	M. No. 262	**George Fordham** *The Demon.* Spy
9.9.1882	722	S. No. 409	**Lord Walsingham** *A Naturalist.* T
16.9.1882	723	S. No. 410	**Rt Hon Lord Charles William Brudenell-Bruce MP** *Marlborough.* Spy
23.9.1882	724	S. No. 411	**Lord Wimborne** *Tennis.* T
30.9.1882	725	M. No. 263	**Hon Sir Adolph Frederick Octavius Liddell KCB AC** *Dodo.* Spy
7.10.1882	726	M. No. 264	**Colonel John J. MacDonnell** *Mac.* Spy
14.10.1882	727	S. No. 412	**J. H. Puleston MP** *Devonport.* Spy
21.10.1882	728	S. No. 413	**Ellis Ashmead-Bartlett MP** *The Patriotic League.* Spy
28.10.1882	729	S. No. 414	**George Armitstead MP** *Dundee.* Spy
4.11.1882	730	M. No. 265	**Sir John Whitaker Ellis, Bart, Lord Mayor of London** *The Lord Mayor.* Spy
11.11.1882	731	S. No. 415	**Henry Edwards MP** *Weymouth.* Spy
18.11.1882	732	M. No. 266	**His Highness the Maharajah Duleep Singh GCSI** *The Maharajah.* Spy
25.11.1882	733	M. No. 267	**'General' Booth** *The Salvation Army.* Spy
2.12.1882	734	S. No. 416	**Lord Foley** *A Liberal Peer.* Spy
5.12.1882	Winter number		**Her Royal Highness the Princess of Wales** *H.R.H. The Princess.* Chartran
9.12.1882	735	S. No. 417	**Sir Daniel Gooch, Bart, MP** *The Great Western.* Spy

DATE	ISSUE	TITLE	NAME, CAPTION, CARICATURIST
16.12.1882	736	M. No. 268	**Dion Boucicault** *The Sensation Drama.* Spy
23.12.1882	737	M. No. 269	**Colonel The Honourable Charles Hugh Lindsay CB** *Army, Court, & Volunteers.* Spy
30.12.1882	738	M. No. 270	**William Hurrell Mallock** *Is Life Worth Living?* Spy
6.1.1883	739	M. No. 271	**Ahmed Arabi** *Ahmed Arabi the Egyptian.* FV
13.1.1883	740	M. No. 272	**Sir John Bennett** *Clocks.* Spy
20.1.1883	741	M. No. 273	**HH Mehemed Tewfik Pasha, Khedive of Egypt** *The Khedive.* FV
27.1.1883	742	S. No. 418	**Viscount Baring MP** *Winchester.* Spy
3.2.1883	743	M. No. 274	**Sir Coutts Lindsay, of Balcarres, Bart** *The Grosvenor Gallery.* Jopling
10.2.1883	744	M. No. 275	**Captain Henry Montague Hozier** *Lloyds.* Jopling
17.2.1883	745	L. No. 1	**Her Grace the Duchess Dowager of Cleveland** *Her Grace the Duchess Dowager of Cleveland.* Chartran
24.2.1883	746	M. No. 276	**Sir Henry Ainslie Hoare** *A Reformed Radical.* Spy
3.3.1883	747	M. No. 277	**Richard Anthony Proctor BA FRAS** *Astronomy.* Spy
10.3.1883	748	S. No. 419	**Major-General Edwyn Sherard Burnaby** *A Crimean Hero.* T
17.3.1883	749	M. No. 278	**Rt Hon General Sir Henry Ponsonby KCB** *The Privy Purse.* T
24.3.1883	750	S. No. 420	**William Thackeray Marriott MP QC** *Brighton.* T
31.3.1883	751	M. No. 279	**Sir Charles Freake, Bart** *An Eminent Builder.* T
7.4.1883	752	M. No. 280	**Sir Julian Pauncefote KCMG CB** *The Foreign Office.* T
14.4.1883	753	M. No. 281	**Lieutenant-General Charles Baring** *An Old Coldstreamer.* T
21.4.1883	754	M. No. 282	**Lieutenant-Colonel Ralph Vivian** *Ralph.* T
28.4.1883	755	M. No. 283	**Rear-Admiral Sir Anthony Hiley-Hoskins KCB** *Naval Reserves.* Spy
5.5.1883	756	S. No. 421	**Charles Russell QC MP** *A Splendid Advocate.* Verheyden
12.5.1883	757	M. No. 284	**Charles Bennett Lawes** *Athlete and Sculptor.* Verheyden
19.5.1883	758	M. No. 285	**Lord Gerald Fitz Gerald** *A Wandering Minstrel.* Spy
26.5.1883	759	M. No. 286	**Richard Everard Webster QC** *Law and Conscience.* Verheyden
2.6.1883	760	S. No. 422	**Thomas Thornhill MP** *Tom.* Verheyden
9.6.1883	761	S. No. 423	**Charles Tennant MP** *Glasgow.* Verheyden
16.6.1883	762	S. No. 424	**Robert William Duff MP** *Fetteresso.* Verheyden
23.6.1883	763	S. No. 425	**Sir Edmund Anthony Harley Lechmere, Bart, MP** *St. John of Jerusalem.* T
30.6.1883	764	M. No. 287	**Captain William George Middleton** *Bay.* T
7.7.1883	765	M. No. 288	**Hon Charles Spencer Bateman Hanbury Kincaid-Lennox** *Charlie.* Spy
14.7.1883	766	S. No. 426	**General The Earl of Albemarle** *Waterloo.* T
21.7.1883	767	S. No. 427	**Lord Gardner** *Fox Hunting.* Spy
28.7.1883	768	S. No. 428	**John Hinde Palmer QC MP** *Lincoln.* Spy
4.8.1883	769	S. No. 429	**Earl of Leicester KG** *Agriculture.* Spy
11.8.1883	770	M. No. 289	**Earl of Rocksavage** *Rock.* Spy
18.8.1883	771	S. No. 430	**Earl of Onslow** *A Parliamentary Title.* Spy
25.8.1883	772	M. No. 290	**General The Hon St George Gerald Foley CB** *The Friend of Pelissier.* Spy
1.9.1883	773	L. No. 2	**Marchioness of Waterford** *The Marchioness of Waterford.* Chartran
8.9.1883	774	S. No. 431	**Earl of Mountcashell** *Ninety-one.* Spy
15.9.1883	775	S. No. 432	**Lord Digby** *Lord Leicester's Nephew.* Spy
22.9.1883	776	S. No. 433	**Earl of Stair KT** *White Dal.* Spy
29.9.1883	777	S. No. 434	**Earl of Seafield** *Sheep.* Spy
6.10.1883	778	L. No. 3	**Gladys, Countess of Lonsdale** *Gladys, Countess of Lonsdale.* Chartran
13.10.1883	779	S. No. 435	**Charles Cecil Cotes MP** *A Liberal Whip.* Spy
20.10.1883	780	M. No. 291	**Henry Reginald Corbet, of Adderley Hall** *Born in the Scarlet.* Spy
27.10.1883	781	S. No. 436	**Major Viscount Downe** *Smartness.* Spy
3.11.1883	782	L. No. 4	**Baroness Burdett-Coutts** *The Baroness Burdett-Coutts.* T
10.11.1883	783	S. No. 437	**Earl of Westmorland** *The Affable Earl.* Spy
17.11.1883	784	S. No. 438	**Hon Anthony Evelyn Melbourne Ashley MP** *Palmerston's secretary.* Spy
24.11.1883	785	S. No. 439	**Earl of Milltown** *A Persevering Politician.* Spy
27.11.1883	786	Winter number	**The Cabinet Council, 1883** *The Gladstone Cabinet.* T
1.12.1883	787	L. No. 5	**Countess of Dalhousie** *The Countess of Dalhousie.* T
8.12.1883	788	S. No. 440	**William Torrens McCullagh Torrens MP** *Finsbury.* Spy
15.12.1883	789	M. No. 292	**Richard Quain MD FRS** *Lord Beaconsfield's Physician.* Spy
22.12.1883	790	M. No. 293	**Charles Edward Howard Vincent** *Criminal Investigation.* Spy
29.12.1883	791	M. No. 294	**Lieutenant-Colonel Hon Henry Townshend Forester** *The Lad.* Spy
5.1.1884	792	L. No. 6	**Lady Florence Dixie** *The Lady Florence Dixie.* T
12.1.1884	793	M. No. 295	**Sir Edward Baldwin Malet KCB** *Justice! Justice! Justice!* Spy
19.1.1884	794	M. No. 296	**Seymour Portman** *Horse-race Management.* Spy
26.1.1884	795	M. No. 297	**Hubert Herkomer ARA** *Painter, Sculptor, Blacksmith Etc.* FG
2.2.1884	796	L. No. 7	**Lady Holland** *The Lady Holland.* T
9.2.1884	797	M. No. 298	**Sir Charles Lennox Wyke KCB GCMG** *The Baron.* Ape
16.2.1884	798	M. No. 299	**Captain Conway Seymour** *Despatches.* Spy
23.2.1884	799	M. No. 300	**Arthur Coventry** *The Baby.* Spy

DATE	ISSUE	TITLE	NAME, CAPTION, CARICATURIST
1.3.1884	800	L. No. 8	**Marchioness of Tweeddale** *The Marchioness of Tweeddale.* T
8.3.1884	801	M. No. 301	**Lord Cardross** *Horsey.* Spy
15.3.1884	802	S. No. 441	**Hon Henry Brand MP** *Ordnance.* Spy
22.3.1884	803	S. No. 442	**Lord Haldon** *A Legislator.* Spy
29.3.1884	804	S. No. 443	**James Edwin Thorold Rogers MP** *A Professor.* Spy
5.4.1884	805	L. No. 9	**Elizabeth, HIM The Empress of Austria** *H.I.M. The Empress of Austria.* C De Grimm
12.4.1884	806	M. No. 302	**Lieutenant-General George Wentworth Alexander Higginson CB** *A Good Soldier.* Spy
19.4.1884	807	M. No. 303	**Rev Joseph Parker** *Congregational Union?* Ape
26.4.1884	808	M. No. 304	**Carl Haag** *The Glorious East.* Go
3.5.1884	809	L. No. 10	**Georgina Weldon** *Mrs. Weldon.* Spy
10.5.1884	810	S. No. 444	**Charles Nicholas Warton MP** *Hear! Hear!! Hear!!! Hear!!!!* Ape
17.5.1884	811	S. No. 445	**Hon Frederick Stephen Archibald Hanbury-Tracy MP** *Gentle and Liberal.* Spy
24.5.1884	812	M. No. 305	**Oscar Wilde** *Oscar.* Ape
31.5.1884	813	M. No. 306	**Alfred De Rothschild** *Alfred.* Spy
7.6.1884	814	L. No. 11	**HIH The Crown Princess of Germany and of Prussia, Princess-Royal of Great Britain and Ireland** *The Princess Royal.* Nemo
14.6.1884	815	S. No. 446	**Duke of Northumberland** *The House of Percy.* Spy
21.6.1884	816	S. No. 447	**Sir Donald Currie KCMG MP** *The Knight of the Cruise of Mr. Gladstone.* Ape
28.6.1884	817	S. No. 448	**Sir John William Ramsden, Bart, MP** *Huddersfield.* Spy
5.7.1884	818	P. No. 8	**Vice-Admiral HSH Count Gleichen** *The Queen's Nephew.* Go
12.7.1884	819	M. No. 307	**John Coupland** *The Quorn.* Ape
19.7.1884	820	S. No. 449	**William Cornwallis Cartwright MP** *Oxfordshire.* Spy
26.7.1884	821	M. No. 308	**Sir Walter George Stirling, Bart** *Two-and-Eighty.* Spy
2.8.1884	822	S. No. 450	**John Slagg MP** *Manchester.* Ape
9.8.1884	823	S. No. 451	**Henry Broadhurst MP** *The Working-Man Member.* Spy
16.8.1884	824	M. No. 309	**Police-Inspector E. Denning** *Parliamentary Police.* Ape
23.8.1884	825	M. No. 310	**Field-Marshal Count Von Moltke** *Modern Strategy.* Go
30.8.1884	826	M. No. 311	**Hon George Charles Brodrick MA** *Merton College.* Spy
6.9.1884	827	M. No. 312	**Sir John Christopher Willoughby, Bart** *High Prices.* Spy
13.9.1884	828	M. No. 313	**George John Bonnor** *Australian Cricket.* Ape
20.9.1884	829	M. No. 314	**Hon Alfred Lyttleton** *English Cricket.* Ape
27.9.1884	830	P. No. 9	**HRH The Duc D'Aumale** *The Orleans Family.* Nemo
4.10.1884	831	S. No. 452	**Rt Hon John Jellibrand Hubbard MP** *Old Mother Hubbard.* Spy
11.10.1884	832	Sov. No. 17	**His Imperial Majesty Alexander III, Emperor and Autocrat of all the Russias.** *My August Master.* Nemo
18.10.1884	833	S. No. 453	**Charles Mark Palmer MP** *Shipping.* Ape
25.10.1884	834	M. No. 315	**Walter Coodall George** *The Champion of Champions.* Spy
1.11.1884	835	M. No. 316	**Thomas Firr** *The Huntsman.* Spy
8.11.1884	836	S. No. 454	**Frederick Winn Knight CB MP** *Has Sat for Three and Forty Years.* Spy
15.11.1884	837	M. No. 317	**James Gordon Bennett** *New York Herald.* Nemo
22.11.1884	838	S. No. 455	**Sir Thomas Chambers QC MP** *The Deceased Wife's Sister.* Spy
29.11.1884	839	M. No. 318	**Henry Hansard** *Hansard.* Ape
6.12.1884	840	M. No. 319	**Captain Arthur Smith** *Doggie.* Ape
13.12.1884	841	M. No. 320	**Leopold De Rothschild** *Racing and Sporting.* Spy
20.12.1884	842	M. No. 321	**Very Rev Edward Bickersteth DD, Dean of Lichfield** *Convocation.* Spy
27.12.1884	843	M. No. 322	**Monsieur De Giers** *The Russian Foreign Office.* Nemo
3.1.1885	844	S. No. 456	**His Grace the Duke of Wellington** *The Iron Duke's Grandson.* Ape
10.1.1885	845	S. No. 457	**Right-Rev Anthony Wilson Thorold, DD, Bishop of Rochester** *Rochester.* Spy
17.1.1885	846	S. No. 458	**Colonel James Patrick O'Gorman Mahon MP** *Mhagthamma.* Spy
24.1.1885	847	M. No. 323	**Sir Samuel Wilson** *A Squatter.* Spy
31.1.1885	848	M. No. 324	**Wilfrid Scawen Blunt** *A Prophet.* Ape
7.2.1885	849	M. No. 325	**Sir George Chetwynd, Bart** *Racing.* Spy
14.2.1885	850	M. No. 326	**Sir William Rose KCB** *The Clerk of Parliaments.* Spy
21.2.1885	851	S. No. 459	**Charles Henry Wilson MP** *Hall.* Ape
28.2.1885	852	S. No. 460	**Sir Thomas Edward Colebrooke, Bart, MP** *Lanarkshire.* Spy
7.3.1885	853	J. No. 14	**Hon Sir James Fitzjames Stephen KCSI** *The Criminal Code.* Spy
14.3.1885	854	M. No. 327	**John Delacour** *John.* Spy
21.3.1885	855	M. No. 328	**Luigi Arditi** *Il Bacio.* Ape
28.3.1885	856	J. No. 15	**Hon Sir Joseph William Chitty** *The Umpire.* Spy
4.4.1885	857	M. No. 329	**John Roberts, Junior** *The Champion Roberts.* Ape
11.4.1885	858	M. No. 330	**Robert W. Edis FRIBA FSA** *Architecture Militant.* Ape
18.4.1885	859	S. No. 461	**Edward Brydges-Willyams MP** *Cornwall.* Spy
25.4.1885	860	S. No. 462	**Rt Hon William Edward Baxter MP** *Montrose.* Spy
2.5.1885	861	M. No. 331	**T.H.S. Escott** *The Fortnightly Review.* Ape
9.5.1885	862	S. No. 463	**Sir John Eardley Eardley-Wilmot, Bart, MP** *South Warwickshire.* Spy

DATE	ISSUE	TITLE	NAME, CAPTION, CARICATURIST
16.5.1885	863	S. No. 464	**Hassan Fehmy Pasha** *The Turkish Alliance.* Spy
23.5.1885	864	S. No. 465	**Justin McCarthy MP** *Irish History.* Spy
30.5.1885	865	M. No. 332	**Major The Hon Augustus George Frederick Jocelyn** *The Father of the Rag.* Ape
6.6.1885	866	M. No. 333	**Venerable Benjamin Harrison MA** *The Revised Edition of the Bible.* Spy
13.6.1885	867	M. No. 334	**Sir Edward Robert Sullivan, Bart** *Common-sense in Politics.* Ape
20.6.1885	868	M. No. 335	**Rev Edmond Warre DD** *The Head.* Spy
27.6.1885	869	M. No. 336	**Sir Frederick George Milner, Bart, MP** *York.* Ape
4.7.1885	870	S. No. 466	**Rt Hon Edward Gibson PC QC LLD** *Dublin University.* Spy
11.7.1885	871	S. No. 467	**Earl of Limerick** *A Freemason.* Ape
18.7.1885	872	S. No. 468	**Rt Rev Charles John Ellicott DD, Bishop of Gloucester and Bristol** *Revision.* Spy
25.7.1885	873	S. No. 469	**Lord Calthorpe** *Fred.* Spy
1.8.1885	874	S. No. 470	**Samuel Charles Allsopp MP** *Burton Beer.* Spy
8.8.1885	875	M. No. 337	**Major-General Sir Peter Stark Lumsden GCB CSI** *Afghan Frontier.* Spy
15.8.1885	876	S. No. 471	**Edward Birkbeck MP** *The Fisherman's Friend.* Ape
22.8.1885	877	S. No. 338	**Corney Grain** *Corney Grain.* Spy
29.8.1885	878	S. No. 339	**Mr Opfer, of Blowitz** *The Times.* Ape
5.9.1885	879	S. No. 472	**William James Richmond Cotton MP** *The City.* Spy
12.9.1885	880	M. No. 340	**Tom Cannon** *Tom Cannon.* Spy
19.9.1885	881	M. No. 341	**M Paul Lessar** *The Afghan Frontier.* Ape
26.9.1885	882	S. No. 473	**Aretas Akers-Douglas MP** *The Kent Gang.* Ape
3.10.1885	883	S. No. 474	**William Henry Houldsworth MP** *Manchester.* Ape
10.10.1885	884	M. No. 342	**Richard Lloyd Price of Rhiwlas** *Pointers.* Spy
17.10.1885	885	S. No. 475	**John Passmore Edwards MP** *The Echo.* Ape
24.10.1885	886	M. No. 343	**Captain Richard Francis Burton** *The Arabian Nights.* Ape
31.10.1885	887	S. No. 476	**Charles Thomson Ritchie MP** *Sugar Bounties.* Ape
7.11.1885	888	S. No. 477	**Sir Robert Bateson-Harvey, Bart, MP** *Bucks.* Spy
14.11.1885	889	M. No. 344³	**Signor Paolo Tosti** *For Ever and For Ever.* Ape
21.11.1885	890	M. No. 344³	**Tom Nickalls** *Tom.* Pat
28.11.1885	891	S. No. 478	**Rt Hon The Earl of Harrowby** *The Sugar of Toryism.* Ape
30.11.1885	Winter number		**'The Paddock at Newmarket'** *The Paddock at Newmarket.* Lib
5.12.1885	892	S. No. 479	**M De Staal** *The Russian Ambassador.* Ape
12.12.1885	893	M. No. 346	**Samuel Pope QC** *Jumbo.* Spy
19.12.1885	894	M. No. 347	**Sir George Compton Archibald Arthur, Bart** *The Mite.* Spy
26.12.1885	895	S. No. 480	**Rt Rev George Howard Wilkinson DD, Bishop of Truro** *Truro.* Spy
2.1.1886	896	M. No. 348	**Rev Canon Robinson Duckworth DD** *A Court Parson.* Ape
9.1.1886	897	S. No. 481	**Colonel Edward Robert King-Harman MP** *The King.* Spy
16.1.1886	898	S. No. 482	**Earl Cairns** *The Woolsack.* Spy
23.1.1886	899	M. No. 349	**Frederic Harrison MA** *An Apostle of Positivism.* Ape
30.1.1886	900	M. No. 350	**Very Rev Richard William Church MA, Dean of St Paul's** *St. Paul's.* Lib
6.2.1886	901	M. No. 351	**Major-General Sir Charles Warren KCMB** *Bechuanaland.* Ape
13.2.1886	902	M. No. 352	**Hon Harry Tyrwhitt-Wilson** *Near the Rose.* Spy
20.2.1886	903	M. No. 353	**Sir James Taylor Ingham MA, Knight** *Bow Street.* Spy
27.2.1886	904	M. No. 354	**General Lord Mark Ralph George Kerr GCB** *Lord Mark.* Spy
6.3.1886	905	S. No. 483	**Count Nigra** *Italy.* Ape
13.3.1886	906	M. No. 355	**Henry Bodkin Poland** *For the Crown.* Spy
20.3.1886	907	M. No. 356	**Lieutenant-Colonel Lord Charles Innes Ker** *Charley.* Spy
27.3.1886	908	S. No. 484	**HE Rt Hon Sir Edward Thornton GCB** *A Safe Ambassador.* Ape
3.4.1886	909	S. No. 485	**Timothy Michael Healy MP** *Tim.* Spy
10.4.1886	910	S. No. 486	**Sir John Henry Kennaway, Bart, MP** *Devonshire.* Spy
17.4.1886	911	S. No. 487	**Herbert Gardner MP** *Amateur Theatricals.* Spy
24.4.1886	912	S. No. 488	**Lionel Louis Cohen MP** *The Stock Exchange.* Lib
1.5.1886	913	S. No. 489	**Rt Hon John Blair Balfour PC MP** *The Lord Advocate.* Spy
8.5.1886	914	M. No. 357	**Edmund Tattersall** *Tattersall's.* Lib
15.5.1886	915	M. No. 358	**The Abbé Liszt** *The Abbé.* Spy
22.5.1886	916	M. No. 359	**Charles Wood** *Charlie Wood.* Lib
29.5.1886	917	M. No. 360	**Lieut-Colonel John Palmer Brabazon** *Bwab.* Ape
5.6.1886	918	S. No. 490	**Sir Henry Hussey Vivian, Bart, MP** *Swansea.* Spy
12.6.1886	919	M. No. 361	**James Selby** *Old Times.* Ape
19.6.1886	920	M. No. 362	**Dr Oliver Wendell Holmes** *The Autocrat of the Breakfast Table.* Spy
26.6.1886	921	S. No. 491	**Joseph Arch MP** *The Agricultural Labourer.* Spy
3.7.1886	922	M. No. 363	**William George Craven** *Billy.* Lib
10.7.1886	923	S. No. 492	**Rt Hon Earl of Lonsdale** *Horses.* Spy
17.7.1886	924	S. No. 493	**Lieut-Colonel William Hood Walrond MP** *Whip.* Lib
24.7.1886	925	S. No. 494	**Rt Hon Lord Hastings** *Melton.* Lib
31.7.1886	926	S. No. 495	**Earl of Zetland** *A Gentleman.* Spy

DATE	ISSUE	TITLE	NAME, CAPTION, CARICATURIST
7.8.1886	927	S. No. 496	**Major-General The Duke of Grafton KG CB** *Charles II.* Spy
14.8.1886	928	M. No. 364	**George Granville Leveson-Gower** *My Dear George.* Spy
21.8.1886	929	S. No. 497	**Lord Arthur William Hill PC MP** *Orangeman.* Spy
28.8.1886	930	M. No. 365	**Andrew Fountayne-Wilson-Montagu** *The Squire.* Spy
4.9.1886	931	M. No. 366⁴	**Robert Peck** *Robert.* Lib
11.9.1886	932	S. No. 498	**Charles Beilby Stuart-Wortley MP** *Sheffield.* Spy
18.9.1886	933	S. No. 499	**Lord Ellenborough** *Law.* Spy
25.9.1886	934	S. No. 500	**Sir John Simon KNT MP, Serjeant-at-Law** *The Serjeant.* Spy
2.10.1886	935	S. No. 501	**Lord Edward Cavendish MP** *A Good Fellow.* Spy
9.10.1886	936	S. No. 502	**Sir Albert Kaye Rollit KNT LLD MP** *Municipal Corporations.* Spy
16.10.1886	937	S. No. 503	**Walter Hume Long MP** *Wiltshire.* Spy
23.10.1886	938	S. No. 504	**Sir Walter Barttelot Barttelot, Bart, MP CB** *One of Those.* Spy
30.10.1886	939	M. No. 366⁴	**John Perkins MA LLD** *Downing.* Hay
6.11.1886	940	S. No. 505	**Samuel Montagu MP** *Whitechapel.* Lib
13.11.1886	941	M. No. 367	**Rt Hon The Lord Mayor of London (Sir Reginald Hanson)** *The Lord Mayor.* Ape
20.11.1886	942	M. No. 368	**E. Sturge** *A Quaker.* Spy
27.11.1886	943	S. No. 506	**Lord Edgerton of Tatton** *Tatton.* Ape
30.11.1886	Winter number		**The Lobby of The House of Commons** *The Lobby of The House of Commons.* Lib
4.12.1886	944	M. No. 369	**Matthew Dawson** *Matt.* Lib
11.12.1886	945	S. No. 507	**Hon Sidney Herbert MP** *Croydon.* Ape
18.12.1886	946	S. No. 508	**Colonel Francis Charles Hugh-Hallett MP** *Rochester.* Ape
25.12.1886	947	M. No. 371⁴	**John O'Connor Power** *The Brains of Obstruction.* Spy
1.1.1887	948	S. No. 509	**Lord Truro** *Universal Knowledge.* Ape
8.1.1887	949	M. No. 372	**M Louis Pasteur** *Hydrophobia.* T
15.1.1887	950	M. No. 373	**General Sir Donald Martin Stewart, Bart, GCB GCSI CIE LLD** *Ahmed Khel.* Ape
22.1.1887	951	S. No. 510	**Earl of Ellesmere** *Bridgewater House.* Ape
29.1.1887	952	S. No. 511	**Rt Hon Sir Henry Thurstan Holland, Bart, MP** *The Colonies.* Ape
5.2.1887	953	M. No. 374	**Lieutenant-General Sir Samuel James Browne KCB DCSI VC** *Sir Sam.* Ape
12.2.1887	954	J. No. 16	**Sir Charles Parker Butt** *Divorce.* Ape
19.2.1887	955	S. No. 512	**Viscount Ebrington MP** *The Devon and Somerset.* Ape
26.2.1887	956	S. No. 513	**Colonel Edward James Saunderson MP** *Irish loyalty.* Ape
5.3.1887	957	J. No. 17	**Lord Coleridge, Lord Chief Justice of England** *The Lord Chief Justice.* Ape
12.3.1887	958	S. No. 514	**General George Boulanger** *La Revanche.* T
19.3.1887	959	S. No. 515	**Colonel Francis Duncan RA MP CB LLD DCL MA** *Finsbury.* Ape
26.3.1887	960	S. No. 516	**Captain John Charles Ready Colomb MP** *The Rule of the Road at Sea.* Ape
2.4.1887	961	S. No. 517	**Lieut-General Sir Edward Bruce Hamley KCB KCMG MP** *English Strategy.* Ape
9.4.1887	962	M. No. 375	**Rev Joseph Leycester Lyne (Father Ignatius)** *Father Ignatius.* Ape
16.4.1887	963	S. No. 518	**Lord Burghley MP** *North Northamptonshire.* Ape
23.4.1887	964	S. No. 519	**Sir Julian Goldsmid, Bart, MP** *St. Pancras.* Ape
30.4.1887	965	J. No. 18	**Justice Field** *Stay, please.* Spy
7.5.1887	966	S. No. 520	**John Dillon MP** *The Plan of Campaign.* Ape
14.5.1887	967	S. No. 521	**Sir James Porter Corry, Bart, MP** *A Temperate Ulster Man.* Ape
21.5.1887	968	M. No. 376	**Henry Rider Haggard** *She.* Spy
28.5.1887	969	S. No. 522	**George Pitt-Lewis QC MP** *Barnstaple.* Spy
4.6.1887	970	M. No. 377	**Sir Henry Meysey Meysey-Thompson, Bart** *Coaching.* Ape
11.6.1887	971	M. No. 378	**Colonel John Hargreaves MFH** *Mr. Hargreaves.* Spy
18.6.1887	972	M. No. 379	**General Sir Frederick Charles Arthur Stephenson GCB** *dear old Ben.* Spy
25.6.1887	973	M. No. 380	**John Watts** *Johnny Watts.* Lib
2.7.1887	974	S. No. 523	**Rt Hon Arthur Wellesley Peel PC MP** *The Speaker.* Spy
9.7.1887	975	M. No. 381	**Sir Henry Barkly KCB GCMG** *The Cape of Good Hope.* Spy
16.7.1887	976	M. No. 382	**Rev James Leigh Joynes MA** *Jimmy.* Spy
23.7.1887	977	M. No. 383	**Henry Ernest Schlesinger Benzon** *The Jubilee Plunger.* Spy
30.7.1887	978	S. No. 524	**Rt Hon and Most Rev Edward White Benson PC DD, Archbishop of Canterbury, Primate of all England & Metropolitan** *The Primate.* Spy
6.8.1887	979	S. No. 525	**Charles Isaac Elton QC MP** *Court Roll.* Spy
13.8.1887	980	M. No. 384	**Henry John Brinsley Manners** *Lord Salisbury's Manners.* Ape
20.8.1887	981	S. No. 526	**Frank Lockwood QC MP** *York.* Spy
27.8.1887	982	M. No. 385	**Mahraj Sir Pertab Sing KCSI** *Jodhpore.* Spy
3.9.1887	983	M. No. 386	**George Barrett** *George Barrett.* Lib
10.9.1887	984	S. No. 527	**Rt Hon Henry Matthews QC MP** *the Home Secretary.* Spy
17.9.1887	985	S. No. 528	**John Henniker Heaton MP** *International Penny Postage.* Spy
24.9.1887	986	S. No. 529	**Rt Hon Arthur James Balfour PC LLD MP** *the Irish Secretary.* Spy
1.10.1887	987	S. No. 530	**Sir Joseph Whitewall Pease, Bart, MP** *Peace.* Spy
8.10.1887	988	J. No. 19	**Hon Sir William Robert Grove** *galvanic electricity.* Spy
15.10.1887	989	M. No. 387	**Sir Morell MacKenzie KNT** *Disease of the Throat.* Ape

DATE	ISSUE	TITLE	NAME, CAPTION, CARICATURIST
22.10.1887	990	S. No. 531	**Thomas Sutherland MP** *P and O.* Ape
29.10.1887	991	M. No. 388	**Hon Sir Ford North** *gentle manners.* Spy
5.11.1887	992	S. No. 532	**William Ewart Gladstone MP** *The Grand Old Man.* Spy
12.11.1887	993	S. No. 533	**Rt Hon William Henry Smith MP** *First Lord of the Treasury.* Spy
19.11.1887	994	M. No. 388	**Major Lord Henry Arthur George Somerset** *Podge.* Spy
26.11.1887	995	M. No. 389	**Alderman Rt Hon Polydore De Keyser, Lord Mayor of London** *The Lord Mayor.* Spy
3.12.1887	996	M. No. 390	**Captain James Octavius Machell** *Jem.* Spy
6.12.1887	Winter number		**Tattersall's, Newmarket, 1887** *Tattersall's, 1887.* Lib
10.12.1887	997	M. No. 391	**John Osborne** *Johnny.* Lib
17.12.1887	998	S. No. 534	**Rt Hon Edward Heneage PC MP** *Grimsby.* Spy
24.12.1887	999	S. No. 535⁵	**Earl of Durham** *Coals.* Spy
31.12.1887	1000	S. No. 535⁵	**Earl of Suffolk and Berkshire** *dover.* Lib
7.1.1888	1001	J. No. 20	**Hon Sir Edward Ebenezer Kay** *costs disallowed.* Spy
14.1.1888	1002	M. No. 392	**Lord Alexander Victor Paget** *Dandy.* Spy
21.1.1888	1003	M. No. 393	**George Grossmith** *The Pinafore.* Spy
28.1.1888	1004	M. No. 394	**Rev Ernest John Heriz Smith MA** *Pembroke.* Hay
4.2.1888	1005	M. No. 395	**Hon Sir Arthur Charles** *The new Judge.* Spy
11.2.1888	1006	M. No. 396	**HE The Greek Minister, M John Gennadius** *Greece.* Spy
18.2.1888	1007	S. No. 536	**Charles Hall QC MP** *Charley.* Spy
25.2.1888	1008	S. No. 537	**Thomas Power O'Connor MA MP** *Tay Pay.* Spy
3.3.1888	1009	M. No. 397	**Reginald W. Chandos-Pole** *Shandy.* Spy
10.3.1888	1010	M. No. 398	**Lieutenant and Bandmaster Daniel Godfrey** *Dan Godfrey.* Spy
17.3.1888	1011	M. No. 399	**Rt Rev Harvey Goodwin DD Bishop of Carlisle** *Carlisle.* Spy
24.3.1888	1012	S. No. 538	**Thomas Wallace Russell MP** *loyal and patriotic.* Spy
31.3.1888	1013	S. No. 539	**Edward Hare Pickersgill MP** *Bethnal Green.* Spy
7.4.1888	1014	S. No. 540	**Marquis of Ailesbury** *the Marquis.* Lib
14.4.1888	1015	S. No. 541	**Earl Cathcart** *He has devoted his life to husbandry and has nine children.* Spy
21.4.1888	1016	J. No. 21	**Rt Hon Sir James Hannen KNT PC** *the great unmarrier.* Spy
28.4.1888	1017	M. No. 400	**John Francis Holcombe Read JP** *Father Time.* Lib
5.5.1888	1018	S. No. 542	**Viscount Combermere** *horses.* Spy
12.5.1888	1019	S. No. 543	**Sir Edward Bates, Bart, MP** *Plymouth.* Spy
19.5.1888	1020	J. No. 22	**Rt Hon Lord Justice Cotton** *guileless.* Spy
26.5.1888	1021	M. No. 401	**James Brand** *telephones.* Lib
2.6.1888	1022	M. No. 402	**J. H. Blackburne** *Chess.* Ape
9.6.1888	1023	S. No. 544	**Lord Rothschild** *Natty.* Lib
16.6.1888	1024	M. No. 403	**M Charles Floquet** *Vive la Pologne!* Ape
23.6.1888	1025	S. No. 545	**Rt Hon Colonel John Hay Athole MacDonald CB QC MP JP DL** *The Lord Advocate.* Spy
30.6.1888	1026	M. No. 404	**Walter Gilbey** *cart horses.* Spy
7.7.1888	1027	M. No. 405	**Frederick Charles Philips** *As in a Looking Glass.* Ape
14.7.1888	1028	S. No. 546	**Earl of Pembroke and Montgomery** *The Earl and the Doctor.* Ape
21.7.1888	1029	S. No. 547	**Rt Hon Marquis of Hartington MP** *The Right Hon. the Marquis of Hartington, M.P.* Spy
28.7.1888	1030	M. No. 406	**Walter William Read** *W.W.* Lib
4.8.1888	1031	S. No. 548	**Charles Kearns Deane Tanner BA MD FRCSI LKQCPI LRCSI MP** *the blister.* Spy
11.8.1888	1032	M. No. 407	**Colonel Cuthbert Larking** *Cuthbert.* Ape
18.8.1888	1033	M. No. 408	**General Viscount Templetown GCB** *Upty.* Ape
25.8.1888	1034	S. No. 549	**Mr R. Bontine-Cunninghame-Cunninghame-Graham MP JP DL** *Trafalgar Square.* Spy
1.9.1888	1035	S. No. 550	**William Bromley-Davenport MP** *Macclesfield.* Spy
8.9.1888	1036	M. No. 409	**James Payn** *The Heir of the Ages.* Ape
15.9.1888	1037	S. No. 551	**Lord Revelstoke** *Barings.* Lib
22.9.1888	1038	M. No. 410	**Rev Hugh Reginald Haweis MA** *The Parson, the Play and the Ballet.* Ape
29.9.1888	1039	M. No. 411	**Very Rev George Granville Bradley DD** *The Dean of Westminster.* Spy
6.10.1888	1040	M. No. 412	**G. A. Baird** *Mr. Abington.* Lib
13.10.1888	1041	P. No. 9	**Prince Albert Victor Christian Edward KG KP LLD** *Eddie.* Hay
20.10.1888	1042	S. No. 552	**Rt Hon The Earl of Bessborough** *Fred.* Spy
27.10.1888	1043	J. No. 23	**Hon Sir John Frederick Sigismund Charles Day** *2nd Commissioner.* Spy
3.11.1888	1044	J. No. 24	**Hon Sir Archibald Levin Smith** *3rd Commissioner.* Spy
10.11.1888	1045	M. No. 413	**Lord Rodney** *A pupil.* Lib
17.11.1888	1046	S. No. 553	**Sir Savile Brinton Crossley, Bart, MP JP** *Lowestoft.* Spy
24.11.1888	1047	M. No. 414	**Oscar Browning** *O.B.* Hay
1.12.1888	1048	S. No. 554	**Jesse Collings MP** *3 acres and a cow.* Spy
8.12.1888	1049	Winter number	**The Winning Post** *THE WINNING POST.* Lib
15.12.1888	1050	S. No. 555	**Robert Bannatyne Finlay QC MD MP** *hard head.* Ape
22.12.1888	1051	M. No. 415	**Sir William Bartlett Dalby, Knight, MP MA FRCS** *the ear.* Ape
29.12.1888	1052	S. No. 556	**Hon George Thomas Kenyon MP JP** *Denbigh Boroughs.* Spy
5.1.1889	1053	S. No. 557	**Rt Hon Lord Randolph Henry Spencer Churchill PC MP LLD** *in a new character.* Lib

DATE	ISSUE	TITLE	NAME, CAPTION, CARICATURIST
12.1.1889	1054	S. No. 558	**Viscount Dangan** *Viscount Dangan.* Spy
19.1.1889	1055	M. No. 416	**Rev Edmund Henry Morgan MA** *Red Morgan.* Hay
26.1.1889	1056	M. No. 417	**Rev Henry Arthur Morgan DD** *Black Morgan.* Hay
2.2.1889	1057	S. No. 559	**Rt Hon Lord Grimthorpe QC LLD** *bells.* Spy
9.2.1889	1058	S. No. 560	**William Cuthbert Quilter JP MP** *in Society and Member of Parliament.* Lib
16.2.1889	1059	S. No. 561	**Sir William Tindal Robertson, Knight, MD FRCP MRCS JP MP** *Brighton.* Spy
23.2.1889	1060	S. No. 562	**Marquis of Carmarthen MP** *Dolly.* Hay
2.3.1889	1061	S. No. 563	**Sir George Russell MP** *Wokingham.* Spy
9.3.1889	1062	M. No. 418	**Richard Pigott** *Richard Pigott.* Spy
16.3.1889	1063	M. No. 419	**Rt Hon James Whitehead JP DL, Lord Mayor of London** *Bonnie Westmoreland.* Hay
23.3.1889	1064	M. No. 420	**J. T. MacKenzie of Kintail** *the Universal Benefactor.* Lib
30.3.1889	1065	S. No. 564	**Marquess of Drogheda KP PC JP DL** *Punchestown.* Hay
6.4.1889	1066	S. No. 565	**John Bright** *John Bright.* Ape
13.4.1889	1067	M. No. 421	**Colonel George E. Gouraud** *Little Menlo.* Ape
20.4.1889	1068	S. No. 566	**Hon George Higginson Allsopp MP** *beer.* Lib
27.4.1889	1069	M. No. 422	**Carlo Pellegrini** *Ape.* AJM
4.5.1889	1070	M. No. 423	**John Patrick Murphy QC** *For the 'Times'.* Spy
11.5.1889	1071	M. No. 424	**M Alexandre Gustave Eiffel** *Gustave Eiffel.* Guth
18.5.1889	1072	M. No. 425	**Rev Henry Montague Butler DD** *the Master of Trinity.* Hay
25.5.1889	1073	M. No. 426	**Senor Pablo Martin Meliton Sarasate** *Sarasate.* Ape
1.6.1889	1074	M. No. 427	**Fred Barrett** *Fred Barrett.* Lib
8.6.1889	1075	M. No. 428	**Harry Marks** *Financial News.* AJM
15.6.1889	1076	S. No. 567	**Baron Ferdinand James De Rothschild MP** *Ferdy.* Hay
22.6.1889	1077	S. No. 568	**Rt Hon Lord Sandhurst** *A Soldier's Son.* Spy
29.6.1889	1078	M. No. 429	**Hylton Philipson** *Oxford Cricket.* Spy
6.7.1889	1079	M. No. 430	**HSH Prince Demtrey Soltykoff** *Prince Soltykoff.* Spy
13.7.1889	1080	M. No. 431	**Thomas Gibson Bowles** *Tommy.* Spy
20.7.1889	1081	M. No. 432	**Guy Nickalls** *Wingfield Sculls.* Spy
27.7.1889	1082	M. No. 433	**Earl of Fife KT** *A Princess's Husband.* Spy
3.8.1889	1083	M. No. 434	**Admiral Sir John Edmund Commerell GCB VC** *Admiral Sir John Edmund Commerell, V.C.* Spy
10.8.1889	1084	M. No. 435	**Fred Webb** *Fred Webb.* Lib
17.8.1889	1085	M. No. 436	**Rt Hon Lord Hothfield** *Lord Hothfield.* Spy
24.8.1889	1086	M. No. 437	**Major E. H. Egerton** *Major E. H. Egerton/Official Handicapper to the Jockey Club.* Lib
31.8.1889	1087	M. No. 438	**James Coates** *Mr. James Coates.* Spy
7.9.1889	1088	M. No. 439	**Henry Searle** *H. Searle/Professional Champion Sculler of the World.* Spy
14.9.1889	1089	M. No. 440	**John Corlett** *The Pink 'Un.* Lib
21.9.1889	1090	S. No. 569	**M Marie Francois Sadi Carnot** *M. Carnot/President of the French Republic.* PAL
28.9.1889	1091	M. No. 441	**Augustus Henry Glossop Harris** *Drury Lane.* Spy
5.10.1889	1092	M. No. 442	**Harry McCalmont** *Mr. H.L.B. McCalmont.* Spy
12.10.1889	1093	M. No. 443	**John Porter** *Mr. John Porter.* Lib
19.10.1889	1094	M. No. 444	**Major-General Sir Francis Grenfell KCB** *General Sir Francis Grenfell, K.C.B.* Spy
26.10.1889	1095	M. No. 445	**Hon Chauncey Mitchell Depew LLD** *Mr. Chauncey M. Depew/President of the New York Central Road.* Spy
2.11.1889	1096	M. No. 446	**Colonel John Thomas North** *The Nitrate King.* Spy
9.11.1889	1097	M. No. 447	**Sir Henry Aaron Isaacs** *A New Lord Mayor.* Spy
16.11.1889	1098	M. No. 448	**Phineas Taylor Barnum** *Barnum.* Spy
23.11.1889	1099	M. No. 449	**Leslie Ward** *Spy.* PAL
30.11.1889	1100	M. No. 450	**Sir Henry Manisty** *Mr. Justice Manisty.* Qviz[6]
7.12.1889	1101	M. No. 451	**Monsieur De Blowitz** *'The Times' in Paris.* Guth
14.12.1889	1102	M. No. 452	**Alexander Meyrick Broadley** *He defended Arabi.* Spy
21.12.1889	1103	M. No. 453	**Lord Justice Barry** *Lord Justice Barry.* Lib
28.12.1889	1104	M. No. 454	**Arthur Cecil** *Mr. Arthur Cecil.* Spy
4.1.1890	1105	M. No. 455	**Sir Myles Fenton KB** *A Railway Knight.* Spy
11.1.1890	1106	M. No. 456	**Edward Frederick Smyth Pigott MA** *Mr. Edward F. Smyth Pigott/Examiner of Plays.* PAL
18.1.1890	1107	M. No. 457	**Archibald John Stuart-Wortley** *Mr. Archibald Stuart-Wortley/'Sports & Arts'.* Spy
25.1.1890	1108	M. No. 458	**Stewart Pixley JP DL** *Bullion.* Spy
1.2.1890	1109	M. No. 459	**G. Rowland Hill** *Rugby Union.* Spy
8.2.1890	1110	J. No. 27	**Lord Justice Lindley** *Partnership.* Spy
15.2.1890	1111	M. No. 460	**Earl De Grey** *The Best Game Shot in England.* Spy
22.2.1890	1112	M. No. 461	**Francis Carruthers Gould** *Mr. F. Carruthers Gould.* Lib
1.3.1890	1113	M. No. 462	**John Hare** *Mr. John Hare.* Spy
8.3.1890	1114	M. No. 463	**Sir William Christopher Leng** *The Sheffield Daily Telegraph.* Spy
15.3.1890	1115	M. No. 464	**Hon Sir William Grantham** *Mr. Justice Grantham.* Spy
22.3.1890	1116	M. No. 465	**S. D. Muttlebury** *One of the Presidents.* Spy

DATE	ISSUE	TITLE	NAME, CAPTION, CARICATURIST
29.3.1890	1117	S. No. 570[7]	**Sir Charles Russell QC MP** *Cross Examination.* Quiz
5.4.1890	1118	M. No. 466	**Bernard John Angle** *Jack in the Box.* F.C.G.
12.4.1890	1119	P. No. 11	**HRH The Duke of Orleans** *Ier Conscrit de France.* Guth
19.4.1890	1120	M. No. 467	**John Jaffray JP DL** *The Birmingham Daily Post.* Spy
26.4.1890	1121	M. No. 468	**Lord Marcus Beresford** *Starting.* Lib
3.5.1890	1122	S. No. 570[7]	**Rt Hon Lord Brooke DL JP MP** *He sits for Colchester.* Spy
10.5.1890	1123	M. No. 469	**John Sims Reeves** *'The' English Tenor.* Spy
17.5.1890	1124	M. No. 470	**James Weatherby** *Mr. James Weatherby.* Lib
24.5.1890	1125	P. No. 12	**Prince George Frederick Ernest Albert KG** *Our Sailor Prince.* Spy
31.5.1890	1126	M. No. 471	**Frank Crisp** *Mr. Frank Crisp.* Spy
7.6.1890	1127	M. No. 472	**Sir Andrew Barclay Walker, Bart, DL JP** *Sir Andrew Barclay Walker.* Lib
14.6.1890	1128	M. No. 473	**James Munro CB** *Metropolitan Police.* Spy
21.6.1890	1129	M. No. 474	**James Woodburn** *James Woodburn.* Spy
28.6.1890	1130	M. No. 475	**Albert Deacon** *Tea.* Spy
5.7.1890	1131	M. No. 476	**Sir Henry Mitchell JP** *Bradford goods.* Spy
12.7.1890	1132	M. No. 477	**Herbert Beerbohm Tree** *Mr. Herbert Beerbohm Tree.* Spy
19.7.1890	1133	M. No. 478	**Horace G. Hutchinson** *Mr. Horace Hutchinson.* Spy
26.7.1890	1134	M. No. 479	**Baron Hirsch** *Baron Hirsch.* Lib
2.8.1890	1135	P. No. 13	**HRH The Duke of Connaught and Strathearn KB KT KP** *Our Soldier Prince.* Spy
9.8.1890	1136	J. No. 29	**Hon Sir Charles Edward Pollock** *One of the Family.* Quiz
16.8.1890	1137	S. No. 571	**Arthur Bower Forwood MP** *Mr. A. B. Forwood.* Lib
23.8.1890	1138	S. No. 572	**Sir Robert Jardine, Bart, MP DL** *Sir Robert Jardine.* Spy
30.8.1890	1139	M. No. 480	**Hon Henry Lorton Bourke DL JP** *The Lord Harry.* FCG
6.9.1890	1140	M. No. 481	**Sir James Percy Miller, Bart** *Sir James Miller.* Lib
13.9.1890	1141	M. No. 482	**Rt Rev Edward King DD, Bishop of Lincoln** *a persecuted Bishop.* Spy
20.9.1890	1142	M. No. 483	**Reuben David Sassoon** *Mr. Reuben Sassoon.* Spy
27.9.1890	1143	M. No. 484	**Jonathan Hutchinson FRS** *Mr. Jonathan Hutchinson.* Spy
4.10.1890	1144	M. No. 485	**Tom Loates** *Tom Loates.* Spy
11.10.1890	1145	S. No. 573	**Rt Hon The Earl of Jersey** *New South Wales.* Spy
18.10.1890	1146	M. No. 486	**Marcus Henry Milner** *Mr. Marcus Henry Milner.* Lib
25.10.1890	1147	M. No. 487	**James Vaughan** *Bow Street.* Spy
1.11.1890	1148	M. No. 488	**Alderman Savory JP** *a new Lord Mayor.* Spy
8.11.1890	1149	S. No. 574	**Lord Halsbury** *From the Old Bailey.* Spy
15.11.1890	1150	M. No. 489	**Sir Edward Bradford KCSI** *Scotland Yard.* Spy
22.11.1890	1151	M. No. 490	**Joseph Fletcher Green** *Shipping.* Spy
29.11.1890	1152	Supplement	**'In Vanity Fair'** *In Vanity Fair.* Unsigned
6.12.1890	1153	M. No. 491	**Howard John Kennard** *Beggar-General to the Metal Trades.* Lib
13.12.1890	1154	J. No. 30	**Hon Sir Roland Vaughan Williams** *The Mandarin.* Quiz
20.12.1890	1155	M. No. 492	**William Henry Grenfell JP DL** *Taplow Court.* Spy
27.12.1890	1156	M. No. 493[8]	**Joseph Henry Houldsworth** *The New Steward.* Spy
3.1.1891	1157	M. No. 493[8]	**Sir Philip Magnus** *Technical Education.* S. Tel
10.1.1891	1158	M. No. 494	**Christopher Wyndham Wilson** *Mr. Christopher W. Wilson.* Spy
17.1.1891	1159	M. No. 495	**Alfred Cock QC** *He has leathern lungs and a voice of brass.* Stuff
24.1.1891	1160	M. No. 496	**General Sir James Charlemagne Dormer KCB** *Madras.* Bint
31.1.1891	1161	M. No. 497	**Sir George Grove DCL LLD** *G.* Spy
7.2.1891	1162	S. No. 576	**Cornelius Marshall Warmington QC MP** *Directors' Liability.* Stuff
14.2.1891	1163	M. No. 498	**Richard D'Oyly Carte** *Royal English Opera.* Spy
21.2.1891	1164	M. No. 499	**William Black** *Mr. William Black.* Spy
28.2.1891	1165	P. No. 14	**Prince Henri Eugene Philippe Louis d'Orleans, Duc d'Aumale** *The Duc D'Aumale.* Guth
7.3.1891	1166	M. No. 500	**Arthur Wing Pinero** *Lady Bountiful.* Spy
14.3.1891	1167	M. No. 501	**Sir Francis Knollys KCMG CB** *Sir Francis Knollys.* Spy
21.3.1891	1168	M. No. 502	**Lord Ampthill** *O.U.B.C.* Spy
28.3.1891	1169	M. No. 503	**Hon Cecil Rhodes** *The Cape.* Spy
4.4.1891	1170	M. No. 504	**Charles Scotter** *London & South Western Railway.* Spy
11.4.1891	1171	J. No. 31	**Sir Francis Henry Jeune** *Matrimonial Causes.* Stuff
18.4.1891	1172	S. No. 577	**M Charles Louis de Saulces de Freycinet** *French Warfare.* Guth
25.4.1891	1173	M. No. 505	**Sir John Bridge** *Chief Magistrate.* Spy
2.5.1891	1174	M. No. 506	**M Victorien Sardou** *Thermidor.* Guth
9.5.1891	1175	M. No. 507	**Charles Frederick Gill** *Gill Brass.* Spy
16.5.1891	1176	M. No. 508	**Captain Francis Pavy** *Railway Trusts.* Spy
23.5.1891	1177	M. No. 509	**Thomas Beard** *Under Sheriff.* Spy
30.5.1891	1178	J. No. 32	**Rt Hon Sir Edward Fry** *Specific Performance.* Spy
6.6.1891	1179	S. No. 578	**John Blundell Maple MP** *Cheap Fares.* Spy
13.6.1891	1180	M. No. 510	**Squire Bancroft Bancroft** *B.* Spy
20.6.1891	1181	S. No. 579	**John Aird MP** *North Paddington.* Spy

DATE	ISSUE	TITLE	NAME, CAPTION, CARICATURIST
27.6.1891	1182	J. No. 33	**Mr Justice Wright** *He declined Knighthood, but thought better of it.* Stuff
4.7.1891	1183	Sov. No. 18	**Emperor of Morocco** *The Emperor of Morocco.* Pry
11.7.1891	1184	M. No. 511	**Lord Iveagh** *Guinness Trust.* Spy
18.7.1891	1185	S. No. 580	**Rear-Admiral Edward Field RN JP MP** *The Yellow Admiral.* Spy
25.7.1891	1186	S. No. 581	**Michael Biddulph MP** *South Herefordshire.* Spy
1.8.1891	1187	S. No. 582	**Herbert Henry Asquith QC MP** *East Fife.* Spy
8.8.1891	1188	M. No. 512	**M Jean de Reszke** *Polish Tenor.* Spy
15.8.1891	1189	M. No. 513	**Albert Neilson Hornby** *Monkey.* Stuff
22.8.1891	1190	M. No. 514	**Major-General Charles Taylor du Plat CB** *Senior Equerry.* Spy
29.8.1891	1191	M. No. 515	**Sir John Stainer MA MusDoc** *Oxford Music.* Spy
5.9.1891	1192	M. No. 516	**Archbishop of York** *From the Army to the Church.* Spy
12.9.1891	1193	M. No. 517	**M Jan Van Beers** *The Modern Wiertz.* Spy
19.9.1891	1194	S. No. 583	**Earl of Harrington** *Yeoman-like Polo.* Lib
26.9.1891	1195	M. No. 518	**Harry Seymour Foster** *An Undersheriff.* Spy
3.10.1891	1196	M. No. 519	**Colonel the Honourable Herbert Francis Eaton** *Brown.* Spy
10.10.1891	1197	M. No. 520	**Venerable Frederick William Farrar DD FRS** *Chaplain to the Commons.* Spy
17.10.1891	1198	Sov. No. 19	**HH Tunkoo Abubeker Ben Ibrahim GCMG KCSI, Sultan of Johore** *Johore.* KYO
24.10.1891	1199	M. No. 521	**H. Mornington Cannon** *Morny.* Spy
31.10.1891	1200	J. No. 34	**Sir Peter Henry Edlin QC JP DL** *London Sessions.* Spy
7.11.1891	1201	M. No. 522	**Hwfa Williams** *Sandown Park.* Spy
14.11.1891	1202	M. No. 523	**Professor John Hall Gladstone PhD FRS** *Chemistry & Optics.* Spy
21.11.1891	1203	M. No. 524	**General Sir Michael Anthony Shrapnel Biddulph KCB** *The Regalia.* Spy
28.11.1891	1204	M. No. 525	**Captain Edward Rodney Owen** *Roddy.* Spy
5.12.1891	1205	Winter number	**'Bench and Bar'** *Bench and Bar.* Stuff
12.12.1891	1206	J. No. 35	**Hon Sir Robert Romer** *Bob.* Stuff
19.12.1891	1207	S. No. 584	**James William Lowther LLM DL MP** *Foreign Affairs.* Spy
26.12.1891	1208	M. No. 526	**George Frederick Watts RA DCL LLD** *He paints portraits & ideas.* Spy
2.1.1892	1209	M. No. 527	**Edward Temple Gurdon** *Rugby Union.* Stuff
9.1.1892	1210	S. No. 585	**Lord Lurgan** *Billy.* Spy
16.1.1892	1211	M. No. 528	**Edward Linley Sambourne** *Sammy.* Spy
23.1.1892	1212	M. No. 529	**Sir Cecil Clementi Smith KCMG** *Straits Settlements.* KYO
30.1.1892	1213	M. No. 530	**Rev Edward Hale MA FRCS FGS** *Badger.* Spy
6.2.1892	1214	M. No. 531	**Charles Willie Mathews** *He can marshal evidence.* Spy
13.2.1892	1215	M. No. 532	**Canon Alfred Ainger LLD** *Temple Reader.* Spy
20.2.1892	1216	M. No. 533	**William Hamo Thornycroft RA** *Bronze Statuary.* Spy
27.2.1892	1217	S. No. 586	**Lord Walter Charles Gordon-Lennox PC MP** *Treasurer of the Household.* Spy
5.3.1892	1218	M. No. 534	**John Ball Junior** *Mr. John Ball jun.* Lib
12.3.1892	1219	J. No. 36	**Rt Hon Sir Charles Synge Christopher Bowen PC DCK LLD FRS** *Judicial Politeness.* Spy
19.3.1892	1220	S. No. 587	**Jabez Spencer Balfour MP** *Burnley.* Spy
26.3.1892	1221	S. No. 588	**Lord Elcho MP** *Derby Day.* Spy
2.4.1892	1222	M. No. 535	**Henry Arthur Jones** *Author-Manager.* Spy
9.4.1892	1223	M. No. 536	**Robert Brudenell Carter FRCS** *a Literary Ocultist.* Stuff
16.4.1892	1224	S. No. 589	**Henry Wiggin MP** *Wiggin!* Stuff
23.4.1892	1225	M. No. 537	**Colonel Vivian Dering Majendie CB** *Explosives.* Spy
30.4.1892	1226	S. No. 590	**Sir James Fergusson, Bart, PC GCSI KCMC CIE** *A Postmaster General.* Spy
7.5.1892	1227	S. No. 591	**Hon Humphrey Napier Sturt MP** *East Dorsetshire.* Spy
14.5.1892	1228	M. No. 538	**Colonel Hon Henry William John Byng JP** *Byngo.* Stuff
21.5.1892	1229	M. No. 539	**Charles Hawtrey** *From Eton to the Stage.* Spy
28.5.1892	1230	S. No. 592	**Gainsford Bruce QC DCL MP** *Holborn.* Spy
4.6.1892	1231	M. No. 540	**Thomas Hardy** *Tess.* Spy
11.6.1892	1232	S. No. 593	**Robert Trotter Hermon-Hodge MA JP MP** *Accrington.* Spy
18.6.1892	1233	S. No. 594	**Hon George Nathaniel Curzon MP JP DL** *Persia and India.* Spy
25.6.1892	1234	M. No. 541	**Edward Lloyd** *English tenor.* Lib
2.7.1892	1235	M. No. 542	**Francis Schnadhorst** *The Caucus.* Stuff
9.7.1892	1236	M. No. 543	**Andrew Ernest Stoddart** *A Big Hitter.* Stuff
16.7.1892	1237	S. No. 595	**Colonel William Cornwallis West MP** *Denbighshire.* Spy
23.7.1892	1238	S. No. 596	**Philip Albert Muntz MP** *Metal.* Spy
30.7.1892	1239	S. No. 597	**Charles Wallwyn Radcliffe Cooke JP DL** *The Constitutional Union.* Spy
6.8.1892	1240	M. No. 544	**Samuel Moses James Woods** *Sammy.* Stuff
13.8.1892	1241	M. No. 545	**Sir Algernon Edward West** *Algy.* Spy
20.8.1892	1242	S. No. 598	**Lord Lamington** *A Traveller.* Spy
27.8.1892	1243	M. No. 546	**Sir Frederick Joseph Bramwell, Bart** *An Arbitrator.* Spy
3.9.1892	1244	M. No. 547	**Clement Nugent Jackson MA** *Jacky.* Spy
10.9.1892	1245	S. No. 599	**Sir Charles Dalrymple, Bart, of Newhailes** *Ipswich senior.* Spy
17.9.1892	1246	S. No. 600	**Rt Hon Lord Norton PC KCMG** *Colonial Self-Government.* Spy

DATE	ISSUE	TITLE	NAME, CAPTION, CARICATURIST
24.9.1892	1247	S. No. 601	**Lord Hawke** *Yorkshire Cricket.* Spy
1.10.1892	1248	M. No. 548	**Dr Samuel Wilks FRS** *Philosophical Pathology.* Spy
8.10.1892	1249	S. No. 602	**Seymour Keay MP** *Prosy Facts & Figures.* Spy
15.10.1892	1250	S. No. 603	**John Burns MP** *Battersea.* Spy
22.10.1892	1251	S. No. 604	**John William Maclure MP JP DL** *The Whitehead Torpedo.* Spy
29.10.1892	1252	M. No. 549	**Sir George Findlay** *North Western.* Spy
5.11.1892	1253	M. No. 550	**Hon Kenneth Howard** *Dear Boy.* Spy
12.11.1892	1254	S. No. 605	**John Edward Redmond MP** *Elisha.* Spy
19.11.1892	1255	J. No. 37	**Hon George Denman** *He was an ornament on the Bench.* Stuff
26.11.1892	1256	M. No. 551	**William Ernest Henley** *The National Observer.* Spy
3.12.1892	1257	Winter number	**'Mixed Political Wares'** *Mixed Political Wares.* Spy
10.12.1892	1258	S. No. 606	**Lord Houghton** *a young Viceroy.* Spy
17.12.1892	1259	S. No. 607	**Major-General Lord Methuen CB CMG** *The Home District.* Spy
24.12.1892	1260	M. No. 552	**Luke Fildes RA** *He painted 'the Doctor'.* Spy
31.12.1892	1261	M. No. 553	**Walter Herries Pollock** *The Saturday Review.* Spy
7.1.1893	1262	M. No. 554	**Archbishop of Westminster** *Westminster.* Spy
14.1.1893	1263	J. No. 38	**Hon Sir Richard Henn Collins** *Smith's Leading Cases.* Quiz
21.1.1893	1264	Sov. No. 20	**Alphonzo VIII, The King of Spain** *A born King.* Unsigned
28.1.1893	1265	S. No. 608	**Lord Wenlock** *Madras.* Bint
4.2.1893	1266	M. No. 555	**Monsieur Quesnay De Beaurepaire** *As Procureur Général.* Guth
11.2.1893	1267	M. No. 556	**Joseph William Comyns Carr** *An Art Critic.* Spy
18.2.1893	1268	J. No. 39	**Hon Sir John Gorell Barnes** *Admirality Jurisdiction.* Spy
25.2.1893	1269	S. No. 609	**Rt Hon James Bryce MP** *Privy Councillor, Professor and Politician.* Stuff
4.3.1893	1270	M. No. 557	**Colonel The Hon William Henry Peregrine Carington** *Bill.* Spy
11.3.1893	1271	M. No. 558	**M Alphonse Daudet** *He Wrote Sappho.* Guth
18.3.1893	1272	M. No. 559	**William Alfred Littledale Fletcher** *Flea.* Spy
25.3.1893	1273	J. No. 40	**Lord Justice Lopes** *An Old-Fashioned Judge.* Quiz
1.4.1893	1274	M. No. 560	**President of St John's College, Oxford** *St. John's, Oxford.* Spy
8.4.1893	1275	M. No. 561	**President of Magdalen College, Oxford** *Magdalen College, Oxford.* Spy
13.4.1893	1276	M. No. 562[9]	**Herbert Hardy Cozens-Hardy QC MP** *North Norfolk.* Spy
20.4.1893	1277	M. No. 563	**William Hunter Kendal** *Mr. W. H. Kendal.* Spy
27.4.1893	1278	S. No. 610	**Duke of Somerset** *An Old-Fashioned Duke.* Spy
4.5.1893	1279	M. No. 564	**Count Della Catena** *Count Strickland.* Hay
11.5.1893	1280	S. No. 611	**Harry Robert Graham MP** *West St. Pancras.* Spy
18.5.1893	1281	S. No. 612	**Sir Frederick Seager Hunt, Bart** *West Marylebone.* Spy
25.5.1893	1282	M. No. 565	**Professor Rudolf Virchow** *Cellular Pathology.* Spy
1.6.1893	1283	M. No. 566	**Sir James Sivewright MA LLD KCMG** *Imperialist Afrikander.* Spy
8.6.1893	1284	M. No. 567	**Fred Crisp** *He Owns 'Chancellor'.* Spy
15.6.1893	1285	S. No. 613	**Alpheus Cleophas Morton MP** *Peterborough.* Spy
22.6.1893	1286	M. No. 568	**William Sydney Penley** *Charley's Aunt.* Spy
29.6.1893	1287	S. No. 614	**Lord Thring** *He has written on companies.* Spy
6.7.1893	1288	L. No. 12	**Her Serene Highness The Princess Victoria Mary of Teck** *Victoria Mary of Teck.* Leslie Ward
13.7.1893	1289	S. No. 615	**Charles Frederick Hamond MP** *Newcastle-upon-Tyne.* Spy
20.7.1893	1290	M. No. 569	**Arthur Hepburn Hastie** *he is a smart fellow & an honest lawyer.* Spy
27.7.1893	1291	M. No. 570	**Sir John Richard Somers Vine CMG** *The Imperial Institute.* Spy
3.8.1893	1292	M. No. 571	**M Benoit Constant Coquelin** *Coquelin Aine.* Guth
10.8.1893	1293	M. No. 572	**Sir Ralph William Payne-Gallwey, Bart** *Letters to young Shooters.* Spy
17.8.1893	1294	M. No. 573	**Walter Winans** *The Record Revolver Shot.* VA
24.8.1893	1295	M. No. 574	**Signor Pietro Mascagni** *Cavalleria Rusticana.* Lib
31.8.1893	1296	S. No. 616	**Sir John Rigby QC MP** *Mr. Solicitor.* Stuff
7.9.1893	1297	S. No. 617	**Duke of Beaufort KG PC** *Badminton.* Spy
14.9.1893	1298	S. No. 618	**Lord Morris of Spiddal** *An Irish Lawyer.* Spy
21.9.1893	1299	M. No. 576	**Arthur John Edward Newton** *The Marlborough Street Solicitor.* Spy
28.9.1893	1300	S. No. 619	**Sir Herbert Eustace Maxwell, Bart, MP** *Wigtownshire.* Spy
5.10.1893	1301	S. No. 620	**William Grey Ellison-Macartney MP** *Fighting Ulster.* Spy
12.10.1893	1302	S. No. 621	**Thomas Henry Bolton MP** *Buonaparte B.* Spy
19.10.1893	1303	S. No. 622	**Robert Armstrong Yerburgh MP** *Chester.* Spy
26.10.1893	1304	S. No. 623	**William Allan MP** *The Gateshead Giant.* Spy
2.11.1893	1305	S. No. 624[9]	**Hon Frederic Morgan MP** *Fred.* Spy
9.11.1893	1306	S. No. 625	**Edward Henry Carson MP** *Dublin University.* Lib
16.11.1893	1307	S. No. 626	**Harry Lawson Webster Lawson MP** *Cirencester.* Spy
23.11.1893	1308	M. No. 575	**Sir William-Henry Wills, Bart** *Birdseye.* Spy
30.11.1893	1309	Winter number	**'On the Terrace'** *On the Terrace/A Political Spectacle:* —*'The Ayes have it—the Noes have it'.* Spy
7.12.1893	1310	J. No. 42	**Hon Sir Lewis William Cave** *That won't do, you know!* Spy
14.12.1893	1311	J. No. 43	**Hon Sir William Rann Kennedy** *Our Weakest Judge.* Spy

DATE	ISSUE	TITLE	NAME, CAPTION, CARICATURIST
21.12.1893	1312	S. No. 627	**Earl of Darnley** *Cobham Hall.* Spy
28.12.1893	1313	M. No. 576[10]	**M Pierre Louis Albert Decrais** *M. Decrais.* Guth
4.1.1894	1314	P. No. 15	**Grand Duke Michael Michailovitch of Russia** *Michael Michailovitch.* WAG
11.1.1894	1315	S. No. 628	**Edward Blake MP** *South Longford.* Spy
18.1.1894	1316	M. No. 577[10]	**Frederick Harrison** *L. & N.W.R.* Spy
25.1.1894	1317	S. No. 629	**Lord Monk Bretton** *Lord Monk Bretton.* Spy
1.2.1894	1318	S. No. 630	**Lord Congleton** *Lord Congleton.* Spy
8.2.1894	1319	S. No. 631	**John Cumming Macdona MP** *St. Bernards.* Spy
15.2.1894	1320	S. No. 632	**Henry John Cockayne Cockayne-Cust MP** *The Pall Mall Gazette.* Spy
22.2.1894	1321	M. No. 578	**George Alexander** *Aubrey Tanqueray.* Spy
1.3.1894	1322	S. No. 633	**Rochfort Maguire MP** *West Clare.* Spy
8.3.1894	1323	M. No. 579	**Alderman William Treloar** *Ludgate Hill.* Spy
15.3.1894	1324	M. No. 580	**Hugh Benjamin Cotton** *Benjie.* Spy
22.3.1894	1325	M. No. 581	**Mr Charles Thurston Fogg-Elliott** *Fogg.* Spy
29.3.1894	1326	S. No. 634	**Lord Stanley** *Westhoughton.* Spy
5.4.1894	1327	M. No. 582	**Warden of New College, Oxford** *The Shirt.* Spy
12.4.1894	1328	M. No. 583	**Henry David Erskine** *Serjeant-at-Arms.* Spy
19.4.1894	1329	M. No. 584	**Charles Burgess Fry** *Oxford Athletics.* Spy
26.4.1894	1330	M. No. 585	**Frederick Courtney Selous** *Big Game.* VA
3.5.1894	1331	S. No. 635	**Earl of Sefton** *The Earl of Sefton.* Lib
10.5.1894	1332	M. No. 586	**John Willis Clark MA** *Cambridge Registrary.* Spy
17.5.1894	1333	M. No. 587	**Dr John Scott Burdon Sanderson** *Oxford Physiology.* Spy
24.5.1894	1334	M. No. 588	**Robinson Ellis** *Latin Literature.* Spy
31.5.1894	1335	S. No. 636	**George Newnes MP** *East Cambridgeshire.* Spy
7.6.1894	1336	M. No. 589	**Rudyard Kipling** *Soldiers Three.* Spy
14.6.1894	1337	M. No. 590	**Charles Grey Mott** *a Railway Director.* Spy
21.6.1894	1338	M. No. 591	**William Montagu Tharp** *Chippenham Park.* Spy
28.6.1894	1339	M. No. 592	**Hon Thomas Francis Bayard** *The United States.* Spy
5.7.1894	1340	M. No. 593	**Sir Henry Brougham Loch GCMG GCB** *The Cape High Commissioner.* Spy
12.7.1894	1341	S. No. 637	**Lord Tweedmouth** *A Late Whip.* Spy
19.7.1894	1342	S. No. 638	**Hon Arthur George Brand MP** *North Cambridgeshire.* Spy
26.7.1894	1343	M. No. 594	**Sir John Dugdale Astley, Bart** *The Literary Mate.* Spy
2.8.1894	1344	M. No. 595	**Warren William De La Rue** *Old Warren.* Spy
9.8.1894	1345	S. No. 639	**Captain Herbert Scarisbrick Naylor Leyland MP** *Colchester.* Spy
16.8.1894	1346	S. No. 640	**Earl of Portarlington** *The Dasher.* Spy
23.8.1894	1347	S. No. 641	**Earl of Denbigh** *H.A.C.* Spy
30.8.1894	1348	M. No. 596	**M Pierre Paul Casimir-Perier** *The French Republic.* Guth
6.9.1894	1349	S. No. 642	**Colonel Amelius Richard Mark Lockwood MP** *West Essex.* Spy
13.9.1894	1350	S. No. 643	**Marquis of Breadalbane KG** *The Queen's Lord Steward.* Spy
20.9.1894	1351	M. No. 597	**Baron Alphonse de Rothschild** *Alphonse.* Guth
27.9.1894	1352	M. No. 598	**George Jay Gould** *Vigilant.* Spy
4.10.1894	1353	S. No. 644	**Earl of Albemarle** *Arnold.* Spy
11.10.1894	1354	S. No. 645	**Sir Balthazar Walter Foster MP MD DCL** *The Ilkeston Division.* Spy
18.10.1894	1355	M. No. 599	**Hon Schomberg Kerr McDonnell C** *He was Lord Salisbury's Private Secretary.* Spy
25.10.1894	1356	M. No. 600	**Charles Gibson Millar** *Saide, R.Y.S.* Spy
1.11.1894	1357	M. No. 601	**Sir Joseph Barnby** *Albert Hall.* Spy
8.11.1894	1358	M. No. 602	**Sir George Carlyon Hughes Armstrong** *The Globe.* Spy
15.11.1894	1359	M. No. 603	**Thomas Henry Ismay** *White Star.* Lib
22.11.1894	1360	M. No. 604	**Very Rev Francis Paget DD** *The House.* Spy
29.11.1894	1361	M. No. 605	**Vice-Admiral The Hon Sir Edmund Robert Fremantle KCB CMG** *on 1 China Station.* Pat
6.12.1894	1362	Winter Supplement	**'At Cowes'** *At Cowes/The R.Y.S.* Spy
13.12.1894	1363	M. No. 606	**William Luson Thomas RI** *The Graphics.* Spy
20.12.1894	1364	M. No. 607	**Clement King Shorter** *Three Editors.* Spy
27.12.1894	1365	M. No. 608	**Sir Robert Hart, Bart, GCMG MA LLD** *Chinese Customs.* Imp
3.1.1895	1366	M. No. 609	**Captain Lord Charles De La Poer Beresford RN CB** *Steam Reserve.* Spy
10.1.1895	1367	S. No. 646	**Sir Robert Threshie Reid QC MP** *Mr. Attorney.* Spy
17.1.1895	1368	M. No. 610	**Rudolf Chambers Lehmann** *Rudy.* Spy
24.1.1895	1369	J. No. 44	**Hon Sir Arthur Kekewich** *A hasty Judge.* Spy
31.1.1895	1370	M. No. 611	**Baron Chaudron De Courcel** *The French Ambassador.* Guth
7.2.1895	1371	S. No. 647	**Lord Frederic Spencer Hamilton MP** *The Pall Mall Magazine.* Spy
14.2.1895	1372	M. No. 612	**Barnett I. Barnato** *Barney.* Spy
21.2.1895	1373	M. No. 613	**Phil May** *Phil.* Spy
28.2.1895	1374	S. No. 648	**Robert Uniacke Penrose-Fitzgerald MP** *Cambridge Borough.* Spy
7.3.1895	1375	M. No. 614	**Count Paul Wolff Metternich** *Count Paul Metternich.* Spy
14.3.1895	1376	S. No. 649	**Earl of Camperdown** *The Earl of Camperdown.* Spy
21.3.1895	1377	M. No. 615	**Frederick York Powell** *Oxford Modern History.* Spy

DATE	ISSUE	TITLE	NAME, CAPTION, CARICATURIST
28.3.1895	1378	M. No. 616	**Charles Murray Pitman** *O.U.B.C.* Spy
4.4.1895	1379	M. No. 617	**The Master of Balliol** *Balliol.* Spy
11.4.1895	1380	M. No. 618	**Dr Richard Garnett CB** *Printed Books.* Spy
18.4.1895	1381	S. No. 650	**M Francois Felix Fauré** *The eminently respectable.* Guth
25.4.1895	1382	P. No. 16	**The Prince Royal of Siam** *A Prince Royal.* Spy
2.5.1895	1383	M. No. 619	**Johnston Forbes-Robertson** *Forbie.* Spy
9.5.1895	1384	S. No. 651	**Victor Cavendish MP** *Heir presumptive to a Dukedom.* Spy
16.5.1895	1385	M. No. 620	**Alfred Charles Harmsworth** *He is Conservative Candidate for Portsmouth.* Spy
23.5.1895	1386	S. No. 652	**Lord Hatherton** *Lord Hatherton.* Stuff
30.5.1895	1387	S. No. 653	**Dr Robert Farquharson MP** *West Aberdeenshire.* Spy
6.6.1895	1388	M. No. 621	**Pierre Loti** *Pierre Loti.* Guth
13.6.1895	1389	M. No. 622	**August Manns** *Crystal Palace.* Spy
20.6.1895	1390	S. No. 654	**Lord Wrottesley** *A Staffordshire Peer.* Stuff
27.6.1895	1391	S. No. 655	**William Wither Bramston Beach MP** *West Hampshire.* Spy
4.7.1895	1392	M. No. 623	**Montague Shearman** *AAA.* Wag
11.7.1895	1393	S. No. 656	**Sir Henry Hoyle Howorth KCIE DCL FRS** *a Lancashire Lad.* Spy
18.7.1895	1394	M. No. 624	**Dean Hole** *Roses.* FTD
25.7.1895	1395	M. No. 625	**Alfred James Bethell** *Go, Gas & Gold.* Spy
1.8.1895	1396	P. No. 17	**Le Prince De Sagan** *Le Prince du Chic.* Guth
8.8.1895	1397	M. No. 626	**Samuel Whitbread** *Parliamentary Procedure.* Spy
15.8.1895	1398	M. No. 627	**James Thompson** *Caledonian Railway.* Spy
22.8.1895	1399	M. No. 628	**Tom Simpson** *Jay J.* Spy
29.8.1895	1400	M. No. 629	**Herr Eduard Strauss** *Eduard Strauss.* E.B.N.
5.9.1895	1401	M. No. 630	**John Loraine Baldwin** *I Zingari.* Spy
12.9.1895	1402	M. No. 631	**Albert George Sandeman** *The Bank of England.* Spy
19.9.1895	1403	M. No. 632	**Hon Seymour John Fortescue RN** *An Equerry in Waiting.* Spy
26.9.1895	1404	S. No. 657	**Mr Lewis Vernon Harcourt** *Lulu.* Spy
3.10.1895	1405	M. No. 633	**Colonel Sir Henry Edward Colville KCMG CB** *Odger.* Spy
10.10.1895	1406	S. No. 658	**Earl of Dartmouth** *The Earl of Dartmouth.* Stuff
17.10.1895	1407	M. No. 634	**Hon Derek William George Keppel** *Derek.* Spy
24.10.1895	1408	S. No. 659	**James Mellor Paulton MP** *Harry.* Spy
31.10.1895	1409	S. No. 660	**Baron Macnaghten PC** *He succeeded Lord Blackburn.* Spy
7.11.1895	1410	M. No. 635	**Albert Frederick Calvert** *Westralia.* Spy
14.11.1895	1411	M. No. 636	**General Duchesne** *Madagascar.* Guth
21.11.1895	1412	M. No. 637	**Bishop of Derry** *Derry.* Spy
28.11.1895	1413	Winter Supplement	**A Masters' Meet** *A Masters' Meet.* Spy
5.12.1895	1414	M. No. 638	**Harry Kent Paxton** *Pakky.* Spy
12.12.1895	1415	P. No. 18	**HRH The Crown Prince of Denmark** *H.R.H. The Crown Pince of Denmark.* Spy
19.12.1895	1416	M. No. 639	**Captain Frederick John Dealtry Lugard DSO CB** *an earnest African.* Spy
26.12.1895	1417	M. No. 640	**Anthony Hope Hawkins** *Anthony Hope.* Spy
2.1.1896	1418	S. No. 661	**Earl of Yarborough** *Brocklesby.* Spy
9.1.1896	1419	S. No. 662	**Harry Leslie Blundell McCalmont MP** *Giralda.* Spy
16.1.1896	1420	S. No. 663	**Earl of Eglinton and Winton** *A good sportsman.* Spy
23.1.1896	1421	M. No. 641	**George Louis Palmella Busson Du Maurier** *Trilby.* Spy
30.1.1896	1422	S. No. 664	**Edmund Widdrington Byrne QC MP** *Chitty's Leader.* Spy
6.2.1896	1423	S. No. 665	**Marquis of Londonderry KG PC LLD** *The London School Board.* FTD
13.2.1896	1424	S. No. 666	**Richard Burdon Haldane QC MP** *A Hegelian Politician.* Spy
20.2.1896	1425	M. No. 642	**Alfred Austin** *the Laureate.* Spy
27.2.1896	1426	M. No. 643	**Captain Oswald Henry Ames** *Ossie.* Spy
5.3.1896	1427	M. No. 644	**Arthur Bourchier** *A.B.* Spy
12.3.1896	1428	J. No. 45	**Justice Mathew** *Commercial Court.* Spy
19.3.1896	1429	M. No. 645	**President of the Oxford University Boat Club** *'Crumbo' (Walter E. Crum).* Spy
26.3.1896	1430	M. No. 646	**W. FitzHerbert** *Fitz.* Spy
2.4.1896	1431	S. No. 667	**Major Frederic Carne Rasch MP** *South-East Essex.* Spy
9.4.1896	1432	M. No. 647	**Dr Leander Starr Jameson CB** *Dr. Jim.* Spy
16.4.1896	1433	M. No. 648	**Colonel Laurence James Oliphant** *Bully.* Spy
23.4.1896	1434	S. No. 668	**Marquess of Bath** *Frome.* Spy
30.4.1896	1435	S. No. 669	**Augustus Helder MP** *Whitehaven.* Spy
7.5.1896	1436	S. No. 670	**Sir Francis Henry Evans KCMB MP** *Union Steamship.* Spy
14.5.1896	1437	M. No. 649	**Arthur Richard Jelf QC** *Oxford Circuit.* Spy
21.5.1896	1438	M. No. 650	**Andrew Barclay Walker** *Ailsa.* W. E. Miller
28.5.1896	1439	S. No. 671	**Rt Hon Robert William Hanbury MP** *A Financial Secretary.* Spy
4.6.1896	1440	S. No. 672	**Viscount Curzon MP** *South Bucks.* Spy
11.6.1896	1441	Summer number	**Cycling in Hyde Park** *Cycling in Hyde Park.* Hal Hurst
18.6.1896	1442	S. No. 673	**Earl De La Warr** *Bexhill & Dunlop.* Spy

DATE	ISSUE	TITLE	NAME, CAPTION, CARICATURIST
25.6.1896	1443	J. No. 46	**Hon Sir Alfred Wills** *Benevolence on the Bench.* Spy
2.7.1896	1444	M. No. 651	**Thomas Henry Hall Caine** *The Manxman.* J.B.P.
9.7.1896	1445	M. No. 652	**Captain Edgeworth Johnstone** *Hard Hitter.* Spy
16.7.1896	1446	M. No. 653	**R.A.H. Mitchell** *Mike.* Spy
23.7.1896	1447	S. No. 674	**Sir Lewis McIver, Bart, MP** *The Member For Scotland.* Spy
30.7.1896	1448	M. No. 654	**Frederic Andrew Inderwick QC** *Divorce Court.* Spy
6.8.1896	1449	S. No. 675	**Hon Ailwyn Fellowes MP** *North Huntingdonshire.* Spy
13.8.1896	1450	M. No. 655	**Viceroy of China 'Li'** *(Li Hung Chang).* Guth
20.8.1896	1451	M. No. 656	**Earl of March** *Goodwood.* Spy
27.8.1896	1452	M. No. 657	**Arthur Edward Guest** *A South Western Director.* Spy
3.9.1896	1453	M. No. 658	**Colonel George Malcolm Fox** *Swordsmanship.* Spy
10.9.1896	1454	S. No. 676	**Duke of Bedford** *Rousseau.* Spy
17.9.1896	1455	S. No. 677	**The Speaker** *Mr. Speaker.* Spy
24.9.1896	1456	M. No. 659	**George Meredith** *Our first novelist.* Max
1.10.1896	1457	M. No. 660	**Sir William McCormac PRCS** *Gun Shot Wounds.* Spy
8.10.1896	1458	S. No. 678	**Hon John Walter Douglas-Scott-Montagu MP** *A Southern Scott.* Spy
15.10.1896	1459	S. No. 679	**William Woodall MP** *Hanley.* Spy
22.10.1896	1460	S. No. 680	**The Lord Advocate** *Lord Advocate.* Spy
29.10.1896	1461	M. No. 661	**Thomas Colleton Garth** *A Very Old Master.* Spy
5.11.1896	1462	M. No. 662	**Sam Loates** *Sam Loates.* Spy
12.11.1896	1463	M. No. 663	**M Gabriel Hanotaux** *Affaires étrangères.* Guth
19.11.1896	1464	M. No. 664	**Charles Carlos Clarke** *The Consol Market.* Spy
26.11.1896	1465	Winter number	**'On the Heath'** *On the Heath.* Spy
3.12.1896	1466	S. No. 681	**Lord Willoughby de Broke** *The Warwickshire.* Spy
10.12.1896	1467	S. No. 682	**Gerald Balfour MP** *A Chief Secretary.* Spy
17.12.1896	1468	M. No. 665	**Ernest Terah Hooley** *Papworth.* Spy
24.12.1896	1469	M. No. 666	**General Frederick Marshall CMG** *Fred.* Spy
31.12.1896	1470	M. No. 667	**Colonel Sir George Archibald Leach** *An agriculturalist.* F.T.D.
7.1.1897	1471	M. No. 668	**James Rennell Rodd CMG** *Diplomacy & Poetry.* Spy
14.1.1897	1472	M. No. 669	**Alfred Edward Thomas Watson** *The Badminton.* Spy
21.1.1897	1473	M. No. 670	**George Moore** *Esther Waters.* Sic
28.1.1897	1474	J. No. 47	**Hon Sir James Stirling** *Equity.* Spy
4.2.1897	1475	M. No. 671	**Max Pemberton** *A Puritan's Wife.* Spy
11.2.1897	1476	M. No. 672	**Sir Vincent Henry Penalver Caillard** *Ottoman Public Debt.* Spy
18.2.1897	1477	M. No. 673	**John Lawson Johnston** *Dietetics.* Spy
25.2.1897	1478	M. No. 674	**Israel Zangwill** *A Child of the Ghetto.* Sic
4.3.1897	1479	M. No. 675	**President of the Royal Academy** *P.R.A.* Spy
11.3.1897	1480	M. No. 676	**Cyril Francis Maude** *Squirrel.* Spy
18.3.1897	1481	J. No. 48	**Hon Sir John Compton Lawrance** *Long Lawrance.* Spy
25.3.1897	1482	M. No. 677	**Captain Wentworth William Hope Johnstone** *Wenty.* Spy
1.4.1897	1483	M. No. 678	**Gilbert Jordan** *O.U.A.C.* Spy
8.4.1897	1484	M. No. 679	**Douglas Hamilton McLean** *Ducker.* Spy
15.4.1897	1485	M. No. 680	**Sir Alfred Milner KCB** *High Commissioner.* Spy
22.4.1897	1486	S. No. 683	**Bishop of London** *Ecclesiastical History.* F.T.D.
29.4.1897	1487	S. No. 684	**Lord Kelvin** *Natural Philosophy.* Spy
6.5.1897	1488	M. No. 685	**Charles Ernest Tritton MP** *The Norwood Division.* Spy
13.5.1897	1489	M. No. 681	**Henry Fielding Dickens QC** *His father invented Pickwick.* Spy
20.5.1897	1490	M. No. 682	**Captain Sir Alfred Jephson** *The Imperial Institute.* Spy
27.5.1897	1491	S. No. 686	**Bishop of Lichfield** *Lichfield.* Stuff
3.6.1897	1492	Summer number	**Au Bois De Boulogne** *Au Bois De Boulogne.* Guth
10.6.1897	1493	M. No. 683	**The Lord Mayor (The Right Honourable George Faudel Faudel-Phillips)** *Mansion House.* Spy
17.6.1897	1494	Diamond Jubilee Number	**Her Majesty The Queen Empress** *À CIMIEZ/Promenade Matinale.* Guth
24.6.1897	1495	M. No. 684	**United States Ambassador, John Hay** *U.S.A.* Spy
1.7.1897	1496	J. No. 49	**Justice Ridley** *The New Judge.* F.T.D.
8.7.1897	1497	S. No. 687	**John Gilbert Talbot MP DCL** *Oxford University.* Spy
15.7.1897	1498	S. No. 688	**Charles John Darling QC MP** *Little Darling.* Spy
22.7.1897	1499	M. No. 685	**Major-General The Hon Reginald Talbot CB** *Aldershot Cavalry.* Spy
29.7.1897	1500	Sov. No. 21	**The Emperor of Abyssinia** *Abyssinia.* Glick
5.8.1897	1501	M. No. 686	**Samuel Rutherford Crockett** *The Stickit Minister.* F.R.
12.8.1897	1502	M. No. 687	**Captain George Colborne Nugent** *A Sub Editor.* Spy
19.8.1897	1503	M. No. 688	**Rt Hon Sir Wilfrid Laurier** *Canada.* Spy
26.8.1897	1504	M. No. 689	**Kumar Shri Ranjitsinhji** *Ranji.* Spy
2.9.1897	1505	S. No. 689	**Lord Warkworth MP** *South Kensington.* Spy
9.9.1897	1506	M. No. 690	**Colonel Francis Reginald Wingate CB** *In the Mahdi's Camp.* Spy

DATE	ISSUE	TITLE	NAME, CAPTION, CARICATURIST
16.9.1897	1507	M. No. 691	**Rt Hon Sir John Gordon Sprigg KC MG** *The Cape.* Spy
23.9.1897	1508	M. No. 692	**Hon Gerald William Lascelles** *The New Forest.* Spy
30.9.1897	1509	P. No. 19	**Prince Henry of Orleans** *Prince Henry of Orleans.* Guth
7.10.1897	1510	M. No. 693	**Rt Hon Sir John Forrest KCMG** *W.A.* Imp.
14.10.1897	1511	S. No. 690	**Henry Torrens Anstruther MP** *St. Andrews District.* Spy
21.10.1897	1512	Sov. No. 23[11]	**HIM The Czar Nicholas II, KG** *The Little Father.* Guth
28.10.1897	1513	M. No. 694	**Lord Dungarvan** *Sol.* Spy
4.11.1897	1514	J. No. 50	**Judge Bacon** *A Judicial Joker.* Spy
11.11.1897	1515	M. No. 695[12]	**Thomas Merthyr Guest MFH** *Blackmore Vale.* CG
18.11.1897	1516	S. No. 691	**Sir Mancherjee Merwanjee Bhownaggree KCIE MP** *North East Bethnal Green.* Spy
25.11.1897	1517	Winter number	**'Of Empire Makers and Breakers'** *A Scene at the South Africa Committee, 1897.* Stuff
2.12.1897	1518	M. No. 695[12]	**Joseph Hollman** *A Great Cellist.* CG
9.12.1897	1519	M. No. 696	**Max Beerbohm** *Max.* Sic
16.12.1897	1520	M. No. 697	**Frederick George Jackson** *Franz Joseph Land.* Spy
23.12.1897	1521	M. No. 698	**Rev Arthur Robins** *The Soldier's Bishop.* Spy
30.12.1897	1522	M. No. 699	**Alfred Cooper FRCS** *Alfred.* Spy
6.1.1898	1523	M. No. 700	**Viscount Falmouth** *The Star.* Spy
13.1.1898	1524	M. No. 701	**Count Albert Edward Wilfrid Gleichen** *Glick.* Spy
20.1.1898	1525	M. No. 702	**Hon Algernon Henry Bourke** *Algy.* Spy
27.1.1898	1526	M. No. 703	**M Félix Jules Méline** *A Premier of France.* Guth
3.2.1898	1527	J. No. 51	**Justice Bigham** *We Shall See.* Spy
10.2.1898	1528	M. No. 704	**Senhor Luiz De Soveral GCMG** *Portugal.* Spy
17.2.1898	1529	J. No. 52	**Justice Channell** *An amiable Judge.* Spy
24.2.1898	1530	M. No. 705	**Count Franz Deym** *Austro-Hungary.* Spy
3.3.1898	1531	M. No. 706	**The Head Master of Westminster School** *Westminster.* Spy
10.3.1898	1532	M. No. 707	**Ralph Sneyd** *Ralph.* Stuff
17.3.1898	1533	M. No. 708	**John George Witt** *A Sporting Lawyer.* Spy
24.3.1898	1534	M. No. 709	**William Quiller Orchardson RA** *Artist and R.A.* Spy
31.3.1898	1535	M. No. 710	**Captain David Longfield Beatty** *A Hard Rider.* Gaf
7.4.1898	1536	S. No. 692	**Dunbar Plunket Barton QC MP** *Mid Armagh.* Spy
14.4.1898	1537	Supplement[13]	**W. G. Grace** *Cricket.* Spy
21.4.1898	1538	M. No. 711	**W. A. Spooner MA** *Spooner.* Spy
28.4.1898	1539	S. No. 693	**Earl Grey** *A Chartered Administrator.* Spy
5.5.1898	1540	M. No. 712	**M Benoit Constant Coquelin** *Coquelin aîné.* Guth
12.5.1898	1541	S. No. 694	**Ian Zachary Malcolm MP** *North-West Suffolk.* Spy
19.5.1898	1542	M. No. 713	**Canon Eyton** *A Fashionable Canon.* F.T.D.
26.5.1898	1543	M. No. 714	**Major Esterhazy** *Major Esterhazy.* Guth
26.5.1898			**Rt Hon William E. Gladstone.** Ape
2.6.1898	1544	S. No. 695	**Lord Farquhar** *Horace.* Spy
9.6.1898	1545	S. No. 696	**Earl of Moray** *a Fifteenth Earl.* Spy
16.6.1898	1546	M. No. 715	**Henry Vincent Higgins** *Grand Opera.* Spy
23.6.1898	1547	M. No. 716	**Mr Danckwerts** *Danky.* Spy
30.6.1898	1548	S. No. 697	**Henry Cosmo Orme Bonsor MP** *The Wimbledon Division.* Spy
7.7.1898	1549	M. No. 717	**Hon Sir Walter Francis Hely-Hutchinson GCMG** *Natal.* Spy
14.7.1898	1550	M. No. 718	**Sir Henry Charles Burdett KCB** *Hospitals.* Quiz
21.7.1898	1551	M. No. 719	**Baron Hermann Von Eckardstein** *A German Attaché.* Spy
28.7.1898	1552	M. No. 720	**Neil Haig** *I Say.* GAF
4.8.1898	1553	M. No. 721	**Henry Bargrave Finnelly Deane QC** *Bargrave.* Spy
11.8.1898	1554	S. No. 698	**Lord Revelstoke** *Barings.* Spy
18.8.1898	1555	M. No. 722	**The Chevalier De Souze Correa** *Brazil.* Spy
25.8.1898	1556	M. No. 723	**Captain Edward Wynyard** *Hampshire.* C.G.
1.9.1898	1557	M. No. 724	**Sir Oswald Mosley, Bart** *John Bull.* Spy
8.9.1898	1558	M. No. 725	**General Sir William Stephen Alexander Lockhart KCB KCSI** *Tirah.* Spy
15.9.1898	1559	M. No. 726	**General Julian Hamilton Hall** *Julian.* Spy
22.9.1898	1560	S. No. 699	**Duke of Marlborough** *Blenheim Palace.* Spy
29.9.1898	1561	S. No. 700	**Colonel Brookfield MP** *East Sussex.* Spy
6.10.1898	1562	M. No. 727	**M Henri Brisson** *Justice to Dreyfus.* Guth
13.10.1898	1563	M. No. 728	**Major Michael Rimington** *Descended from Edward Longshanks.* GAF
20.10.1898	1564	M. No. 729	**M Victor Maurel** *A Fine Baritone.* Spy
27.10.1898	1565	S. No. 701	**Sir Henry Fletcher, Bart, MP** *Mid Sussex.* Spy
3.11.1898	1566	S. No. 702	**Viscount Portman** *An Old Master.* Spy
10.11.1898	1567	S. No. 703	**Sir Thomas Henry Sanderson KCB KCMG** *Foreign Affairs.* Spy
17.11.1898	1568	M. No. 730	**Bishop-Designate of Calcutta** *Calcutta.* Spy
24.11.1898	1569	J. No. 53	**Hon Sir Walter George Frank Phillimore, Bart, DCL** *A Judicial Churchman.* Spy
1.12.1898	1570	Winter Supplement	**The Lord Protect Us.** Furniss
8.12.1898	1571	M. No. 731	**Walpole Greenwell** *Walpole.* Spy

DATE	ISSUE	TITLE	NAME, CAPTION, CARICATURIST
11.12.1898			**'The Pilgrim Resting on His Way'.** G.A.W.
15.12.1898	1572	S. No. 704	**Lord Barnard** *Raby Castle.* GAF
22.12.1898	1573	M. No. 732	**James Lennox Hannay** *Marlborough Street.* Spy
29.12.1898	1574	M. No. 733	**Edwin Austin Abbey RA** *Fairford Abbey.* Spy
5.1.1899	1575	S. No. 705	**Viscount Galway** *Serlby.* Spy
12.1.1899	1576	M. No. 734	**Jonathan Edmund Backhouse** *Jed.* GAF
19.1.1899	1577	M. No. 735	**Sir Charles Anthony Brooke GCMG** *Sarawak.* Spy
26.1.1899	1578	M. No. 736	**Sir James John Trevor Lawrence, Bart** *Horticulture.* Spy
2.2.1899	1579	M. No. 737	**The President of the United States of America** *An American Protector.* E. Flagg
9.2.1899	1580	M. No. 738	**M Theophile Delcassé** *French Foreign Affairs.* Guth
16.2.1899	1581	M. No. 739	**Marquis of Hamilton** *He Will be the Third Duke.* Hadge
23.2.1899	1582	S. No. 706	**Lord Kitchener of Khartoum GCB KCMG** *Khartoum.* Spy
2.3.1899	1583	J. No. 54	**Lord Justice Williams** *A Rustic Judge.* CGD
9.3.1899	1584	M. No. 740	**M Paul Cambon** *French Ambassador.* Guth
16.3.1899	1585	M. No. 741	**Henry White** *A Diplomatic Cousin.* Spy
23.3.1899	1586	M. No. 742	**Harcourt Gelbey Gold** *Tarka.* Spy
30.3.1899	1587	M. No. 743	**John Hargreaves MFH** *Cattistock.* CG
6.4.1899	1588	M. No. 744	**William Ward Tailby** *A Leicester Man.* GAF
13.4.1899	1589	M. No. 745	**John Balfour** *J.B.* Spy
20.4.1899	1590	M. No. 746	**Sir Edgar Vincent KCMG** *Eastern finance.* Spy
27.4.1899	1591	M. No. 747	**Major-General Sir Archibald Hunter KCB DSO** *our youngest General.* Spy
4.5.1899	1592	M. No. 748	**Sir Gilbert Greenall, Bart** *Belvoir.* CB
11.5.1899	1593	S. No. 707	**Sir William George Granville Venables Vernon Harcourt PC MP QC** *a retired Leader.* Cloister
18.5.1899	1594	M. No. 749	**The President of the French Republic** *the new French President.* Guth
25.5.1899	1595	M. No. 750	**Tod Sloan** *An American Jockey.* G.D.G.
1.6.1899	1596	P. No. 20	**Prince Victor Jerome Frederic Napoleon** *Victor.* Guth
8.6.1899	1597	M. No. 751	**Colonel Francis William Rhodes DSO** *Soldier and Correspondent.* Spy
15.6.1899	1598	M. No. 752	**Colonel Sir Rudolf Carl Slatin KCMG CB MVO** *Salatin.* Spy
22.6.1899	1599	S. No. 708	**Lord Balcarres MP** *Bal.* Spy
29.6.1899	1600	M. No. 753	**Canon Fleming** *Chester Square.* Spy
6.7.1899	1601	S. No. 709	**Lord Charles Beresford MP** *The Commercial Traveller.* Cloister
13.7.1899	1602	M. No. 754	**Reginald Ward** *Copper.* Spy
20.7.1899	1603	S. No. 710	**Earl Beauchamp** *New South Wales.* Spy
27.7.1899	1604	M. No. 755	**Dr Carl Muck** *Wagnerian Opera.* WAG
3.8.1899	1605	S. No. 711	**Austen Chamberlain MP** *East Worcestershire.* Spy
10.8.1899	1606	M. No. 756	**Rt Hon Sir Henry Campbell-Bannerman** *The Opposition.* Spy
17.8.1899	1607	M. No. 757	**Franklin Lushington** *He Believe in the Police.* Spy
24.8.1899	1608	M. No. 758	**Edward Tyas Cook** *The Daily News.* Spy
31.8.1899	1609	S. No. 712	**Rt Hon William Lawies Jackson MP** *North Leeds.* Spy
7.9.1899	1610	M. No. 759	**Capt Alfred Dreyfus** *At Rennes.* Guth
14.9.1899	1611	S. No. 713	**Viscount Valentia** *Oxford City.* Spy
21.9.1899	1612	M. No. 760[14]	**Rev Joseph Wood DD** *Harrow.* GAF
28.9.1899	1613	M. No. 760[14]	**The American Ambassador, Joseph H. Choate** *United States Embassy.* Spy
5.10.1899	1614	S. No. 715[15]	**Dr James Stuart MP** *Hoxton Division.* Stuff
12.10.1899	1615	M. No. 761	**The Comte De Dion** *Automobile.* Guth
19.10.1899	1616	Sov. No. 24	**Emperor of Corea** *Emperor of Corea.* Pry
26.10.1899	1617	M. No. 762	**Major Edward James Montagu Stuart-Wortley** *Eddie.* Spy
2.11.1899	1618	M. No. 763	**Vice-Chancellor of Oxford (The Rev Thomas Fowler)** *Corpus.* FTD
9.11.1899	1619	M. No. 764	**Lord Edward Herbert Cecil** *At Mafeking.* Spy
16.11.1899	1620	M. No. 765	**Capt George Lindsay Holford** *An Equerry.* Spy
23.11.1899	1621	Winter number	**'At Rennes'** *At Rennes.* Guth
30.11.1899	1622	M. No. 766	**Dr Thomas Stevenson** *Medical Jurisprudence.* WAG
7.12.1899	1623	M. No. 767	**Sir Ernest Cassel** *Egyptian Finance.* Spy
14.12.1899	1624	M. No. 768	**John Seymour Lucas RA** *A Connoisseur.* N.
21.12.1899	1625	S. No. 716	**Lord Rayleigh** *Argon.* FTD
28.12.1899	1626	M. No. 769	**M Ignace Jan Paderewski** *Easy Execution.* Spy
4.1.1900	1627	P. No. 21	**HH The Maharaja of Patiala GCSI** *Patiala.* MR
11.1.1900	1628	M. No. 770	**Arthur Yates** *Arthur.* Cloister
18.1.1900	1629	M. No. 771	**Gen Sir Redvers Henry Buller PC VC GCB KCMG** *Redrag.* Spy
25.1.1900	1630	M. No. 772	**Col Audley Dallan Neeld** *Composite Regiment.* Cloister
1.2.1900	1631	S. No. 717	**Sir Albert Edward Sassoon, Bart** *Hythe.* Spy
8.2.1900	1632	M. No. 773	**George Denison Faber** *ex opera* Stuff
15.2.1900	1633	M. No. 774	**Sir Thomas Salter Pyne CSI** *Afghan engineering.* Spy
22.2.1900	1634	M. No. 775	**James Staats Forbes** *L.C.D.R.* Spy
1.3.1900	1635	S. No. 718	**Rt Hon James Lowther MP** *Thanet.* Spy

DATE	ISSUE	TITLE	NAME, CAPTION, CARICATURIST
8.3.1900	1636	M. No. 776	**Stephanus Johannes Paulus Kruger** *Oom Paul.* Drawl
15.3.1900	1637	S. No. 719	**Lord Chesham** *Imperial Yeomanry.* Spy
22.3.1900	1638	S. No. 720	**Percy Melville Thornton MP** *Clapham.* Spy
29.3.1900	1639	M. No. 777	**The President of the CUBC** *C.U.B.C.* Spy
5.4.1900	1640	J. No. 55	**Justice Buckley** *Company Law.* Spy
12.4.1900	1641	M. No. 778	**Dr Nathaniel Edward Yorke-Davies** *Dietetics.* Spy
19.4.1900	1642	S. No. 721	**Lord Strathcona and Mount Royal** *Canada in London.* Spy
26.4.1900	1643	S. No. 722	**Richard Frederick Cavendish MP** *North Lancashire.* Spy
3.5.1900	1644	S. No. 723	**William Hayes Fisher MP** *Fulham.* Spy
10.5.1900	1645	J. No. 56	**Justice Bucknill** *Tommy.* Spy
17.5.1900	1646	S. No. 724	**Earl of Hopetoun** *The Lord Chamberlain.* Spy
24.5.1900	1647	S. No. 725	**Marquis of Clanricarde** *old wares.* Spy
31.5.1900	1648	M. No. 779	**Hon Sidney Robert Greville** *A Private Secretary.* Spy
7.6.1900	1649	P. No. 22	**The Prince of Monaco** *The Prince of Monaco.* Spy
14.6.1900	1650	M. No. 780	**General Sir George Stuart White VC** *Ladysmith.* Spy
21.6.1900	1651	S. No. 726	**Field Marshal Lord Roberts VC KP** *Bobs.* Spy
28.6.1900	1652	M. No. 781	**Captain the Honourable Hedworth Lambton RN** *H.M.S. Powerful.* Spy
5.7.1900	1653	M. No. 782	**General Robert Stephenson Smyth Baden-Powell** *Mafeking.* Drawl
12.7.1900	1654	M. No. 783	**General John Denton Pinkstone French** *the Cavalry Division.* G.D.G.
19.7.1900	1655	M. No. 784	**Mr Frederick Treves FRCS** *Freddie.* Spy
26.7.1900	1656	M. No. 785	**Otto Madden** *Otto Madden.* G.D.G.
2.8.1900	1657	M. No. 786	**Arthur De Rothschild** *Eros.* Spy
9.8.1900	1658	M. No. 787	**Martinus Theunis Steyn** *Ex-President Steyn.* W.A.G.
16.8.1900	1659	M. No. 788	**Albert De Rutzen** *A Model Magistrate.* W.A.G.
23.8.1900	1660	M. No. 789	**John Reiff** *Johnny.* Spy
30.8.1900	1661	M. No. 790	**Lester Reiff** *Lester.* Spy
6.9.1900	1662	M. No. 791	**Colonel Sir Arthur John Bigge** *Her Majesty's Private Secretary.* Spy
13.9.1900	1663	S. No. 727	**Hon Walter Lionel Rothschild MP** *the Aylesbury Division.* Spy
20.9.1900	1664	S. No. 728	**George Wyndham MP** *Dover and War.* Spy
27.9.1900	1665	M. No. 792	**Winston Leonard Spencer Churchill** *Winston.* Spy
4.10.1900	1666	M. No. 793	**John Fletcher Moulton QC FRS** *Patents.* Spy
11.10.1900	1667	M. No. 794	**Sir John Talbot Dillwyn-Llewelyn, Bart** *Swansea.* Spy
18.10.1900	1668	S. No. 729	**Lord Hugh Cecil MP** *Greenwich.* Spy
25.10.1900	1669	M. No. 795	**The Master of the Quorn** *Long Burns.* C.B.
1.11.1900	1670	J. No. 57	**Lord Justice of England** *Dick.* Spy
8.11.1900	1671	M. No. 796	**Admiral Lord Walter Talbot Kerr KCB** *A Sea Lord.* Spy
15.11.1900	1672	J. No. 58	**Justice George Farwell** *Powers.* FTD
22.11.1900	1673	J. No. 59	**Mr Commissioner Kerr** *The City of London.* Spy
29.11.1900	1674	Winter number	**'A General Group'** *A General Group.* Spy
6.12.1900	1675	J. No. 60	**Justice Gainsford Bruce** *Slow and Steady.* Spy
13.12.1900	1676	M. No. 797	**Colonel Vesey Dawson** *Irish Guards.* Spy
20.12.1900	1677	S. No. 730[16]	**The Prime Minister. Robert Arthur Talbot Gascoyne-Cecil, Third Marquis of Salisbury KG** *The Prime Minister.* Spy
27.12.1900	1678	M. No. 798	**John Earle Welby** *A Father of the Belvoir.* C.B.
3.1.1901	1679	P. No. 23	**The Gaekwar of Baroda** *The Gaekwar.* MR
10.1.1901	1680	S. No. 730[16]	**Earl of Clarendon** *The Lord Chamberlain.* Spy
17.1.1901	1681	M. No. 799	**Admiral Sir Algernon Charles Fieschi Heneage KCB** *Pompo.* Spy
24.1.1901	1682	J. No. 61	**Hon Mr Justice Cozens-Hardy** *Fair, if not beautiful.* Spy
31.1.1901	1683	M. No. 800	**The Provost of Eton** *The Head.* Spy
31.1.1901			**Her Majesty The Queen Empress.** Guth
7.2.1901	1684	M. No. 801	**General William Henry MacKinnon** *C.I.V.* Spy
14.2.1901	1685	S. No. 731	**Lord Raglan** *Under-Secretary for War.* Spy
21.2.1901	1686	M. No. 802	**General Reginald Pole-Carew CB** *Polly.* Spy
28.2.1901	1687	M. No. 803	**A. C. Ainger** *M'tutor.* Spy
7.3.1901	1688	S. No. 732	**Joseph Chamberlain** *The Colonies.* Spy
14.3.1901	1689	S. No. 733	**Earl of Rosebery** *Little Bo-Peep.* Spy
21.3.1901	1690	M. No. 804	**Rev William Baker DD** *M.T.S.* W.A.G.
28.3.1901	1691	J. No. 62	**Lord Justice Rigby** *a blunt Lord Justice.* Spy
4.4.1901	1692	S. No. 734	**The Earl of Hardwicke** *Tommy Dodd.* Spy
11.4.1901	1693	M. No. 805	**Alfred Chichele Plowden** *Marylebone.* W.A.G.
18.4.1901	1694	M. No. 806	**Richard William Evelyn Middleton** *the Conservative Party.* Spy
25.4.1901	1695	M. No. 807	**Vice-Admiral Sir Harry Holdsworth Rawson KCB** *Fresh from the Channel Fleet.* Spy
2.5.1901	1696	M. No. 808	**General Sir Ian Standish Monteith Hamilton CB DSO** *Mixed Forces.* Spy
9.5.1901	1697	M. No. 809	**Rev and Hon Canon Edward Lyttelton MA** *Haileybury.* Spy
16.5.1901	1698	S. No. 735	**Charles Algernon Whitmore MP** *Chelsea.* Spy

DATE	ISSUE	TITLE	NAME, CAPTION, CARICATURIST
23.5.1901	1699	S. No. 736	**Bishop of London** *London.* Spy
30.5.1901	1700	M. No. 810	**Colonel Sir Edward Willis Duncan Ward** *a Permanent Warrior.* Spy
6.6.1901	1701	M. No. 811	**E. C. Austen Leigh MA** *The Flea.* Spy
13.6.1901	1702	S. No. 737	**Sir William Reynell Anson, Bart, MP** *All Souls.* Spy
20.6.1901	1703	M. No. 812	**M Edmond Rostand** *Cyrano.* Guth
27.6.1901	1704	M. No. 813	**The High Master of St Paul's School** *St. Paul's School.* Spy
4.7.1901	1705	M. No. 814	**Reginald Saumarez De Havilland** *Harry.* Spy
11.7.1901	1706	M. No. 815	**Rev Cecil Legard** *A Judge.* C.B.
18.7.1901	1707	S. No. 738	**The Secretary of State for War** *War.* Spy
25.7.1901	1708	M. No. 816	**Gilbert Laird Jessop** *the Croucher.* Spy
1.8.1901	1709	M. No. 817	**Surgeon-General Jameson** *Army Medical.* Spy
8.8.1901	1710	M. No. 818	**The Knight of Kerry** *Knight of Kerry.* Spy
15.8.1901	1711	M. No. 819	**Bishop of Southwell** *Southwell.* Spy
22.8.1901	1712	M. No. 820	**Sir Godfrey Yeatman Lagden KCMG** *Basutoland.* Spy
29.8.1901	1713	M. No. 821	**General Kelly-Kenny CB** *6th Division.* Spy
5.9.1901	1714	M. No. 822	**General The Hon Neville Gerald Lyttelton CB** *4th Division.* Spy
12.9.1901	1715	M. No. 823	**Fred Rickaby** *Rick.* Spy
19.9.1901	1716	M. No. 824	**Sir Thomas Johnstone Lipton KCVO** *Shamrock.* Spy
26.9.1901	1717	M. No. 825[17]	**The Vice-Provost of Eton** *The Vice-Provost.* Spy
3.10.1901	1718	S. No. 741	**Earl of Selborne PC** *Admirality.* Spy
10.10.1901	1719	M. No. 825[17]	**Sir Claude Maxwell MacDonald** *Tokio.* Spy
17.10.1901	1720	M. No. 826	**Edward Weatherby** *The Match-Book.* Spy
24.10.1901	1721	M. No. 827	**Count Lyof Nikolaivitch Tolstoi** *War and Peace.* Snapp
31.10.1901	1722	M. No. 828	**Sir Edward Hobart Seymour GCB KCB** *China.* Spy
7.11.1901	1723	M. No. 829[18]	**John George Butcher KC MP** *York City.* Spy
14.11.1901	1724	M. No. 829[18]	**M Alberto Santos Dumont** *the Deutsch Prize.* Geo. Hum
21.11.1901	1725	J. No. 63	**The Common Serjeant of London** *Bosey.* Spy
28.11.1901	1726	Winter number	**'Kirby Gate'.** C.B.
5.12.1901	1727	M. No. 830	**General Smith-Dorrien DSO** *Doreen.* Spy
12.12.1901	1728	M. No. 831	**Henrik Ibsen** *The Master Builder.* Snapp
19.12.1901	1729	S. No. 743	**Bishop of Winchester** *Prelate of the Garter.* Spy
26.12.1901	1730	P. No. 24	**Maharajah of Cuch Behar** *Cuch Behar.* unsigned
2.1.1902	1731	S. No. 744	**Earl of Cromer** *Egypt.* Spy
9.1.1902	1732	M. No. 832	**Major-General Sir Henry Trotter KCVO** *Home District.* Spy
16.1.1902	1733	M. No. 833	**Earl of Desart** *Public Prosecutions.* Spy
23.1.1902	1734	J. No. 64	**Hon Sir Matthew Inglé Joyce** *Steady-going.* Spy
30.1.1902	1735	M. No. 834	**J. Otho Paget** *Otho.* C.B.
6.2.1902	1736	S. No. 745	**Earl of Aberdeen** *Aberdeenshire.* Spy
13.2.1902	1737	J. No. 65	**Hon Mr Justice Swinfen Eady** *plausible.* Spy
20.2.1902	1738	S. No. 746	**Sir John Benjamin Stone MP** *East Birmingham.* Spy
27.2.1902	1739	M. No. 835	**Charles Santley** *Student & Singer.* Spy
6.2.1902	1740	S. No. 747	**John Lawson Walton KC MP** *a Radical Lawyer.* Spy
13.3.1902	1741	S. No. 748	**John Gordon Swift MacNeill KC MP** *South Donegal.* Spy
20.3.1902	1742	M. No. 836	**Dr Robert Henry Scanes Spicer** *rhinology.* Spy
27.3.1902	1743	M. No. 837	**Sir Frank Cavendish Lascelles** *Berlin.* Spy
3.4.1902	1744	S. No. 749	**Lord Alwyne Frederick Compton DSO DL MP** *North Bedfordshire.* Spy
10.4.1902	1745	S. No. 750	**Charles Alfred Cripps KC MP** *Vicar General.* Spy
17.4.1902	1746	M. No. 838	**Rt Hon Richard John Seddon PC LLD** *King Dick.* How
24.4.1902	1747	M. No. 839	**Viscount Tadasu Hayashi** *Japan.* Spy
1.5.1902	1748	M. No. 840	**Sir Felix Semon MD FRCP** *Laryngology.* Spy
8.5.1902	1749	S. No. 751	**Earl of Dundonald** *a Cavalry Reformer.* Spy
15.5.1902	1750	S. No. 752	**Duke of Devonshire KG** *Education & Defense.* Spy
22.5.1902	1751	M. No. 841	**Digby Loder Armroid Jephson** *The Lobster.* Spy
29.5.1902	1752	P. No. 25	**HSH The Duke of Teck GCVO** *The Duke of Teck.* Spy
5.6.1902	1753	M. No. 842	**Robert Abel** *Bobby.* Spy
12.6.1902	1754	P. No. 26	**HRH Prince Charles of Denmark** *a Prince of Denmark.* Spy
19.6.1902	1755	Sov. No. 25	**His Majesty King Edward VII** *His Majesty The King.* Spy
26.6.1902	1756	Sov. No. 26	**King of Italy** *Italia.* Lib
3.7.1902	1757	M. No. 843	**Admiral Sir Archibald Lucius Douglas** *North America and West Indies.* Spy
10.7.1902	1758	M. No. 844	**The Master of Marlborough College** *Marlborough College.* Spy
17.7.1902	1759	P. No. 27	**Major HSH Prince Francis Joseph Leopold Frederick of Teck** *Frank.* Spy
24.7.1902	1760	J. No. 66	**Hon Sir Joseph Walton** *a Lawyer on the Bench.* Spy
31.7.1902	1761	M. No. 845	**General Christian De Wet** *De Wet.* EBN
7.8.1902	1762	M. No. 846	**Admiral Gervais** *l'Amiral.* Guth
14.8.1902	1763	S. No. 753	**Lord Balfour of Burleigh KT** *Secretary for Scotland.* Spy

DATE	ISSUE	TITLE	NAME, CAPTION, CARICATURIST
21.8.1902	1764	M. No. 847	**Rev Henry Montagu Villiers MA** *St. Paul's Knightsbridge.* Spy
28.8.1902	1765	M. No. 848	**Hon Frank Stanley Jackson BC** *A Flannelled Fighter.* Spy
4.9.1902	1766	M. No. 849	**The President of the United States** *U.S.A.* Flagg
11.9.1902	1767	S. No. 754	**Archbishop of Canterbury** *Just.* Spy
18.9.1902	1768	M. No. 860[19]	**General Sir Edwin Markham** *R.M.C.* Spy
25.9.1902	1769	M. No. 861	**Whitelaw Reid** *The New York Tribune.* Spy
2.10.1902	1770	M. No. 862	**Arthur Diósy** *the Japan Society.* Spy
9.10.1902	1771	M. No. 863	**The Master of Wellington College** *Wellington College.* Spy
16.10.1902	1772	M. No. 854	**Sir Edmund Barton PC KC** *Australia.* Spy
23.10.1902	1773	S. No. 755	**The Lord Mayor of London** *The Lord Mayor.* Spy
30.10.1902	1774	M. No. 855	**Sir William Henry Broadbent** *orthodoxy.* Spy
6.11.1902	1775	M. No. 856	**Admiral Sir John Arbuthnot Fisher GCB** *Jacky.* Spy
13.11.1902	1776	M. No. 857	**General Plumer** *Self-reliant.* Spy
20.11.1902	1777	M. No. 858	**Sir Joseph Loftus Wilkinson** *G.W.R.* Spy
27.11.1902	1778	Winter number	**'Heads of the Law'** *Heads of the Law.* Spy
4.12.1902	1779	M. No. 859	**Walter Durnford** *Walter D.* Spy
11.12.1902	1780	M. No. 860	**William McEwan** *McEwan & Co.* Spy
18.12.1902	1781	M. No. 861	**Sir Alexander Condie Stephen KCMG KCVO CB** *Russian, Persian and Turkish.* Spy
25.12.1902	1782	M. No. 862	**General Sir Frederick William Edward Forestier Forestier-Walker GCMG CB** *Shookey.* Spy
1.1.1903	1783	M. No. 863	**Colonel Douglas Frederick Rawdon Dawson CMG** *A Military Secretary.* Spy
8.1.1903	1784	M. No. 864	**Rt Hon William James Pirrie PC LLD** *Harland & Wolff.* Spy
15.1.1903	1785	M. No. 865	**Rt Hon Sir Machael Henry Herbert PC KC MG** *Washington.* Spy
22.1.1903	1786	S. No. 755	**Admiral of the Fleet The Earl of Clanwilliam GCB KCMG** *An Admiral of the Fleet.* Spy
29.1.1903	1787	Sov. No. 27	**Shah of Persia** *Persia.* Spy
5.2.1903	1788	S. No. 756	**Rt Hon Sir Edward Grey, Bart, MP** *A Liberal Imperialist.* Spy
12.2.1903	1789	M. No. 866	**HH Ras Makunan KCMG** *An Abysinnian General.* Spy
19.2.1903	1790	M. No. 867	**Sir Francis Henry Laking, Bart, GCVO** *The King's Physician.* Spy
26.2.1903	1791	M. No. 868	**Bishop of Kensington** *Kensington.* Spy
5.3.1903	1792	S. No. 757	**Duke of Wellington** *Strathfieldsaye.* Spy
12.3.1903	1793	M. No. 869	**Chang Ta-Jen** *China in London.* Spy
19.3.1903	1794	M. No. 870	**Sir Charles John Owens** *South Western Transport.* Spy
26.3.1903	1795	M. No. 871	**Rear-Admiral William Henry May MVO** *Navy control.* Spy
2.4.1903	1796	M. No. 872	**Captain Wilfrid Hubert Chapman** *C.U.B.C.* Spy
9.4.1903	1797	M. No. 873	**Sir William Huggins** *Spectroscopic Astronomy.* Spy
16.4.1903	1798	M. No. 874	**Aubrey Coventry** *Orleans.* Cloister
23.4.1903	1799	M. No. 875	**Sir Ernest Satow GCMG** *Peking.* Spy
30.4.1903	1800	M. No. 876	**Seymour Berkeley Portman-Dalton DL JP** *Kempton.* Cloister
7.5.1903	1801	M. No. 877	**Jan Kubelik** *Kubelik.* Spy
14.5.1903	1802	M. No. 878	**Baron Adolph Wilhelm Deichmann** *Four-in-Hand.* Spy
21.5.1903	1803	M. No. 879	**Sir William Crookes FRS** *ubi Crookes ibi lux.* Spy
28.5.1903	1804	M. No. 880	**Rev Henry Montagu Butler DD** *Trinity.* Spy
4.6.1903	1805	M. No. 881	**Arthur Christopher Benson MA** *Fasti Etonenses.* Spy
11.6.1903	1806	M. No. 882	**Sir Edward George Clarke KC** *Sir Edward.* Spy
18.6.1903	1807	M. No. 883	**Samuel Mure Fergusson** *Muir.* Spy
25.6.1903	1808	M. No. 884	**Field Marshal Sir Henry Wylie Norman GCB** *Chelsea Hospital.* Spy
2.7.1903	1809	M. No. 885	**The Head Master of Winchester** *Winchester.* Spy
9.7.1903	1810	J. No. 60[20]	**The Recorder of London** *The Recorder.* Spy
16.7.1903	1811	M. No. 886	**Horace Harold Hilton** *Hoylake.* Spy
23.7.1903	1812	J. No. 61[20]	**Baron Shand** *A Scots Lawyer.* Spy
30.7.1903	1813	S. No. 758	**Earl of Shrewsbury and Talbot** *Cabs.* Spy
6.8.1903	1814	M. No. 887	**Lionel Charles Hamilton Palairet** *Repton, Oxford & Somerset.* Spy
13.8.1903	1815	M. No. 888	**Captain Alfred Hutton FSA** *Cold Steel.* Jest
20.8.1903	1816	M. No. 889	**George Hirst** *Yorkshire.* Spy
27.8.1903	1817	M. No. 890	**Colonel Robert George Broadwood** *Natal.* Spy
3.9.1903	1818	M. No. 891	**Pelham F. Warner** *Plum.* Spy
10.9.1903	1819	M. No. 892	**'Danny' Maher** *Danny.* Ao
17.9.1903	1820	M. No. 893	**Captain Percy Scott RN ADC CVD LLD** *Gunnery.* Spy
24.9.1903	1821	S. No. 759	**Edward Marshall Hall KC MP** *Southport Division.* Spy
1.10.1903	1822	M. No. 894	**John Evelyn Watts** *J. E. Watts.* Ao
8.10.1903	1823	M. No. 895	**The Danish Minister** *Denmark in England.* Spy
15.10.1903	1824	M. No. 896	**Admiral of the Fleet the Honourable Sir Henry Keppel GCB OM DCL** *94.* Ao
22.10.1903	1825	M. No. 897	**Sir Edward Letchworth FSA** *The Grand Secretary.* Spy
29.10.1903	1826	M. No. 898	**Andrew Carnegie** *Free Libraries.* Spy
5.11.1903	1827	M. No. 899	**Sir Robert Rodney Wilmot, Bart** *Berks and Bucks.* Ao
12.11.1903	1828	P. No. 28	**HRH The Duke of Aosta KG** *The Duke of Aosta.* Lib

DATE	ISSUE	TITLE	NAME, CAPTION, CARICATURIST
19.11.1903	1829	M. No. 900	**Robert Albert McCall KC** *Ulsterman K.C.* Spy
26.11.1903	1830	S. No. 760	**Sir Alexander Fuller-Acland-Hood MP** *The First Conservative Whip.* Spy
3.12.1903	1831	M. No. 901	**Admiral Sir Frederick George Denham Redford GCB** *Western Australia.* Spy
10.12.1903	1832	Sov. No. 28	**His Holiness Pius X** *His Holiness Pius X.* Lib
17.12.1903	1833	M. No. 902	**Sir Frederick Peel, Bart, PC** *A Railway Commissioner.* Spy
24.12.1903	1834	M. No. 903	**The Russian Ambassador** *Russia in England.* Spy
31.12.1903	1835	M. No. 904	**Captain Charles Harold Longfield Beatty DSO** *Charlie.* G.D.G.
7.1.1904	1836	S. No. 761	**Ernest William Beckett MP** *Whitby.* Spy
14.1.1904	1837	M. No. 905	**Sir Alexander Campbell MacKenzie MusDoc LLD DCL** *R.H.M.* Spy
21.1.1904	1838	S. No. 762	**Viscount Churchill GCVO** *Conservative Whip.* Spy
28.1.1904	1839	M. No. 906	**Charles Sydney Goldmann** *A Self-Made African.* Spy
4.2.1904	1840	M. No. 907	**Sir Oliver Joseph Lodge FRS DSc LLD** *Birmingham University.* Spy
11.2.1904	1841	S. No. 763	**Marquis of Northampton** *the Lordship of Compton.* Spy
18.2.1904	1842	M. No. 908	**Rufus Daniel Isaacs KC** *Rufus.* Spy
25.2.1904	1843	M. No. 909	**General Sir Harry Aubrey De Maclean, Kaid** *The Kaid.* Spy
3.3.1904	1844	S. No. 764	**Lord Northcote** *The Australian Commonwealth.* Spy
10.3.1904	1845	S. No. 765	**Earl Amherst** *The Pro Grand Master.* Spy
17.3.1904	1846	M. No. 910	**Hon George Lambton** *Stanley House.* Spy
24.3.1904	1847	M. No. 911	**Rev Edgar Sheppard DD CVO** *A Great Marrier.* Spy
31.3.1904	1848	M. No. 912	**Very Rev Hermann Adler DD LLD PhD** *The Chief Rabbi.* Spy
7.4.1904	1849	S. No. 766	**Earl of Darnley** *Ivo.* Spy
14.4.1904	1850	M. No. 913	**Sir John Frederick Bridge MVO MusDoc** *Westminister Bridge.* Spy
21.4.1904	1851	M. No. 914	**Bishop of Rochester** *Rochester.* Spy
28.4.1904	1852	M. No. 915	**Sir Richard Douglas Powell, Bart, KCVO MD FRCP MRCS** *Chests.* Spy
5.5.1904	1853	S. No. 767	**Viscount Cobham** *Cricket, Railways & Agriculture.* Spy
12.5.1904	1854	M. No. 916	**Rt Hon Sir Henry Mortimer Durand GCMG ICSI KCIE** *Washington Post.* Spy
19.5.1904	1855	J. No. 62[20]	**Hon Sir Arthur Richard Jelf KC** *ermined urbanity.* Spy
26.5.1904	1856	M. No. 917	**Arthur James** *a hard rider.* Spy
2.6.1904	1857	M. No. 918	**Horace Avory KC** *slim.* Spy
9.6.1904	1858	M. No. 919	**Sir Charles W. Cayzer** *Chief of the 'clans'.* Spy
16.6.1904	1859	M. No. 920	**Lord Redesdale** *The Nobleman of the Garden.* Spy
23.6.1904	1860	M. No. 921	**William Crawfurd Stirling-Stuart** *the Hatter.* Spy
30.6.1904	1861	M. No. 922	**Charles Day Rose** *Newmarket.* Spy
7.7.1904	1862	S. No. 768	**John Edward Redmond** *the Irish petrel.* Spy
14.7.1904	1863	S. No. 769	**Rt Hon Herbert Henry Asquith MP** *brains.* Spy
21.7.1904	1864	M. No. 923	**Count Charles De Lalaing** *The Belgian Minister.* Spy
28.7.1904	1865	M. No. 924	**Lord Inverclyde** *Cunarder.* Spy
4.8.1904	1866	M. No. 925	**Samuel Smith MP** *Sammy.* Spy
11.8.1904	1867	M. No. 926	**Charles Hare Hemphill KC MP** *The Irish Serjeant.* Spy
18.8.1904	1868	S. No. 770	**Rt Hon Lord Shuttleworth of Gawthorpe** *Shuttleworth.* Spy
25.8.1904	1869	M. No. 927	**Hon Sydney Holland** *How much?* Spy
1.9.1904	1870	M. No. 928	**H. L. Doherty** *Thrice Champion.* Spy
8.9.1904	1871	M. No. 929	**Major-General H. D. Hutchinson CSI** *Patronage.* Spy
15.9.1904	1872	M. No. 930	**B.J.T. Bosanquet** *an artful bowler.* Spy
22.9.1904	1873	M. No. 931	**Lord Dalmeny** *In his father's steps.* Spy
29.9.1904	1874	M. No. 932	**Herbert Jones** *a King's jockey.* Ao
6.10.1904	1875	M. No. 933	**Lord Duncannon** *Duncannon.* Spy
13.10.1904	1876	M. No. 934	**Lewis Waller** *Romantic Drama.* Imp
20.10.1904	1877	M. No. 935	**Sir Richard Jebb** *Ajax M.P.* Spy
27.10.1904	1878	M. No. 936	**Major Eustace-Jameson MP** *the Major from Clare.* Spy
3.11.1904	1879	M. No. 937	**Marquess of Winchester** *The Premier Marquess.* Spy
10.11.1904	1880	M. No. 938	**The Aga Khan** *The Aga Khan.* Spy
17.11.1904	1881	M. No. 939	**Mr Cyril Arthur Pearson** *Joe's Stage Manager.* Spy
24.11.1904	1882	M. No. 940	**Reverend R. J. Campbell** *Fearless but intemperate.* Spy
1.12.1904	1883	M. No. 941	**Sir Alfred Scott-Gatty** *The Minstrel Boy.* Spy
8.12.1904	1884	M. No. 942	**Hon W.F.D. Smith MP** *head of the greatest publishing house in Christendom.* Spy
15.12.1904	1885	M. No. 943	**Sir Hiram Stevens Maxim** *In the Clouds.* Spy
22.12.1904	1886	Pe. No. 1	**Monsieur and Madame Curie** *Radium.* Imp
29.12.1904	1887	M. No. 944	**M Auguste Rodin** *he thinks in marble.* Imp
5.1.1905	1888	M. No. 945	**Joseph Joachim** *The last of a classic school.* Spy
12.1.1905	1889	M. No. 946	**Professor Ray Lankester FRS** *His religion is the worship of all sorts of winged and funny freaks.* Spy
19.1.1905	1890	M. No. 947	**Sir John Isaac Thornycroft** *Destroyers.* Spy
26.1.1905	1891	M. No. 948	**Sir John Wolfe-Barry** *He has engineered nothing better than his own fortunes.* Spy
2.2.1905	1892	M. No. 949	**Sir Charles Villiers Stanford MA DCL** *He found harmony in Ireland.* Spy
9.2.1905	1893	M. No. 940[21]	**Earl of Donoughmore** *A most discreet under secretary, drawn for the first time.* Spy

DATE	ISSUE	TITLE	NAME, CAPTION, CARICATURIST
16.2.1905	1894	M. No. 941	**Prince Louis of Battenberg** *He was born a Serene Highness but he has lived it down.* Spy
23.2.1905	1895	M. No. 942	**Major John Edward Bernard Seely DSO MP** *Extinction, Distinction—which one will it be? Something of both at present, say the spiteful.* Spy
2.3.1905	1896	M. No. 943	**Andrew Bonar Law MP** *A gentle shepherd who would lead his flock into the protectionists fold.* Spy
9.3.1905	1897	M. No. 944	**Egerton Castle** *He insists that his pen is mightier than his sword.* Spy
16.3.1905	1898	M. No. 945	**Giuglielmo Marconi** *Wires without wires.* Spy
23.3.1905	1899	M. No. 946	**Marquess of Tullibardine** *Scottish horse.* Spy
30.3.1905	1900	M. No. 947	**Lionel Brough** *a fellow of infinite jest.* Spy
6.4.1905	1901	M. No. 948	**William Crooks MP** *The Labourer is worthy of his hire.* Spy
13.4.1905	1902	M. No. 949	**Sir Robert Ball** *Popular Astronomy.* Spy
20.4.1905	1903	M. No. 960[22]	**Earl of Onslow** *Chairman of Committees in the Lords.* Spy
27.4.1905	1904	M. No. 961	**Earl of Elgin** *He has decided where Churches disagreed.* Spy
4.5.1905	1905	M. No. 962	**Major-General Sir James Wolfe Murray** *The Master General.* Spy
11.5.1905	1906	M. No. 963	**Major William Eden Evans Gordon** *The Alien Immigrant.* Spy
18.5.1905	1907	M. No. 964	**Sir Anderson Critchett** *The King's Oculist.* Spy
25.5.1905	1908	M. No. 965	**John Roberts and H. W. Stevenson** (2 cartoons) *He might be Champion if there were a Championship. The Champion of 1885.* Spy
1.6.1905	1909	M. No. 966	**HIH The German Crown Prince** *Oh child mayst thou be less talkative than thy father, but in all else like him.* Guth
8.6.1905	1910	M. No. 967	**Sir Peter Carlaw Walker** *Peter.* Spy
15.6.1905	1911	M. No. 968	**Sir Walter Roper Lawrence** *The Prince's cicerone.* Spy
22.6.1905	1912	M. No. 969	**Sir John Dickson-Poynder** *To abandon Conservative ideals is to destroy the Empire.* Spy
29.6.1905	1913	M. No. 970	**Earl of Minto** *Roley.* Spy
6.7.1905	1914	M. No. 971	**Thomas Rawle** *The President of the Law Society.* Spy
13.7.1905	1915	M. No. 972	**Ernest Baggallay** *A popular magistrate.* Spy
20.7.1905	1916	M. No. 973	**Admiral Caillard** *Vice-Admiral Caillard.* Guth
27.7.1905	1917	M. No. 974	**Finley Peter Dunne** *Mr. Dooley.* Spy
3.8.1905	1918	M. No. 975	**Sir Anthony MacDonnell** *Sir Antony MacDonnell.* Spy
10.8.1905	1919	M. No. 976	**Edward O'Connor Terry** *Edward O'Connor Terry.* Spy
17.8.1905	1920	M. No. 977	**Samuel Hope Morley** *Dissent.* Spy
24.8.1905	1921	M. No. 978	**Rt Hon H. O. Arnold-Forster MP** *The Heritage of Woe.* Spy
31.8.1905	1922	M. No. 979	**H. W. Lucy** *Toby M.P.* Spy
7.9.1905	1923	M. No. 980	**General Kuropatkin** *I regret to report.* IMP
14.9.1905	1924	M. No. 981	**William Arthur Hamar Bass** *Billy.* Spy
21.9.1905	1925	M. No. 982	**Thomas Brock RA** *The Queen's Memorial.* Spy
28.9.1905	1926	M. No. 983	**R.H.R. Rimington-Wilson** *Driven Grouse.* Spy
5.10.1905	1927	M. No. 984	**Edward Richard Henry CSI** *Finger Prints.* Spy
12.10.1905	1928	M. No. 985	**Robert Henry Bullock-Marsham RH** *Bow Street.* Spy
19.10.1905	1929	M. No. 986	**Thomas Gibson-Bowles MP** *An Encyclopedia.* Spy
26.10.1905	1930	M. No. 987	**Hon Alexander Nelson Hood** *The Princess's Private Secretary.* Spy
2.11.1905	1931	M. No. 988	**Leo Trevor** *Leo.* Spy
9.11.1905	1932	M. No. 989	**Hon Rupert Guinness** *Rupert.* Spy
16.11.1905	1933	M. No. 990	**Weedon Grossmith** *The Duffen.* Spy
23.11.1905	1934	M. No. 991	**Lord Willoughby De Broke** *An M.F.H. with a sense of humour.* Spy
30.11.1905	1935	M. No. 992	**Colonel Barrington Foote** *Military Music.* Spy
7.12.1905	1936	The Winter Supplement	**A Fox Hunting Constellation.** Bede
14.12.1905	1937	M. No. 993	**The Dean of Westminster (Dr J. Armitage Robinson)** *An erudite dean.* Spy
21.12.1905	1938	M. No. 994	**Count Albert Mensdorff** *Austria in England.* Spy
28.12.1905	1939	M. No. 995	**George Bernard Shaw** *Magnetic.* Ruth
4.1.1906	1940	M. No. 996	**Edgar Lubbock** *The Master of the Blankney.* Bede
11.1.1906	1941	M. No. 997	**W. J. Galloway MP** *He is very affluent.* Ruth
18.1.1906	1942	M. No. 998	**Rt Hon Augustine Birrell** *The Passive Resister's last hope.* Spy
25.1.1906	1943	M. No. 999	**Sir W. S. Robson KC MP** *The Solicitor General.* Spy
1.2.1906	1944	M. No. 1000	**Arthur Wing Pinero** *Though It Is.* Bulbo
8.2.1906	1945	M. No. 1001	**J. Keir Hardie** *Queer Hardie.* Spy
15.2.1906	1946	M. No. 1002	**General Sir Hugh Gough VC GCB** *Keeper of the Crown Jewels.* Spy
22.2.1906	1947	M. No. 1003	**Lord Robert Cecil MP KC** *So voluable an advocate should become a successful Parliamentarian.* Spy
1.3.1906	1948	M. No. 1004	**George Charles Fitzwilliam** *Billy.* Spy
8.3.1906	1949	M. No. 1005	**Bishop of Ripon** *A Man Right Reverend and Well-Beloved.* Spy
15.3.1906	1950	M. No. 1006	**Albert Brassey** *The Master of the Heythrop.* Spy
22.3.1906	1951	M. No. 1007	**Major-General Sir R. B. Lane** *Rowdy.* Spy
29.3.1906	1952	M. No. 1008	**John Eldon Bankes KC** *Good Form.* Spy
5.4.1906	1953	M. No. 1009	**Earl of Plymouth** *Good Works.* Spy

DATE	ISSUE	TITLE	NAME, CAPTION, CARICATURIST
12.4.1906	1954	M. No. 1010	**Sir Thomas Barlow** *Physician to His Majesty's Household.* Spy
19.4.1906	1955	M. No. 1011	**Bishop of Stepney** *A Bishop of Decision.* Spy
26.4.1906	1956	M. No. 1012	**John Henry Taylor** *John Henry.* Spy
3.5.1906	1957	M. No. 1013	**Lieut-Col Anstruther Thomson** *Commanding 2nd Life Guards.* Spy
10.5.1906	1958	M. No. 1014	**Maj-Gen Sir Hugh McCalmont** *Sir Hugh.* Spy
17.5.1906	1959	M. No. 1015	**Lord Howard De Walden** *He patronises literature and the Turf, but does not waste his money.* Spy
24.5.1906	1960	M. No. 1016	**Alfonso XIII** *S. M. Alfonso XIII.* Guth
31.5.1906	1961	Supplement	**HRH Victoria Eugenie of Battenberg** *H.R.H. Victoria Eugenie of Battenberg.* Leslie Ward
7.6.1906	1962	M. No. 1017	**Rt Hon R. K. Causton MP** *A Cheery Paymaster.* Spy
14.6.1906	1963	M. No. 1018	**Lord Fitzmaurice** *He does not under-estimate his own ability.* Spy
21.6.1906	1964	M. No. 1019	**W. Hall Walker** *A Lucky Owner.* Spy
28.6.1906	1965	M. No. 1020	**Felix Schuster** *Free Trade and Finance.* Spy
4.7.1906	1966	M. No. 1021	**George Duncan Rowe** *A celebrated oarsman who prefers cricket to rowing and golf to both.* Spy
11.7.1906	1967	M. No. 1022	**Thomas Hayward** *Tom.* Spy
18.7.1906	1968	M. No. 1023	**Reginald Herbert Spooner** *Reggie.* Spy
25.7.1906	1969	M. No. 1024	**Lord Weardale** *A cynical Radical.* Spy
1.8.1906	1970	M. No. 1025	**Duke of Leeds** *Vice-Commodore.* Spy
8.8.1906	1971	M. No. 1026	**J. T. Tyldesley** *Forty-six centuries in eleven years.* Spy
15.8.1906	1972	M. No. 1027	**Rev F. H. Gillingham** *Cricketing Christianity.* Spy
22.8.1906	1973	M. No. 1028	**Robert Maxwell** *North Berwick.* Spy
29.8.1906	1974	M. No. 1029	**E. P. Mathers** *South Africa.* Spy
5.9.1906	1975	M. No. 1030	**Major Eustace Loder** *Spearmint.* Spy
12.9.1906	1976	M. No. 1031	**Bernard Dillon** *Bernard.* Spy
19.9.1906	1977	M. No. 1032	**Earl of Lytton** *Victor.* Spy
26.9.1906	1978	M. No. 1033	**Bishop of St. Albans** *Tolerance.* Spy
3.10.1906	1979	M. No. 1034	**Colonel Calley CB MVO** *1st Life Guards.* Spy
10.10.1906	1980	M. No. 1035	**Admiral Sir Compton Domvile** *40 H.P. in a dinghy.* Spy
17.10.1906	1981	M. No. 1036	**Justice Bray** *A Man of Law and Broad Acres.* Spy
24.10.1906	1982	M. No. 1037	**The Speaker** *Mr. Speaker.* Spy
31.10.1906	1983	M. No. 1038	**Reginald McKenna MP** *In the winning crew.* Spy
7.11.1906	1984	M. No. 1039	**Arthur Templeman** *A rising star.* Spy
14.11.1906	1985	M. No. 1040	**Silas Kitto Hocking** *Silas Hocking.* Spy
21.11.1906	1986	M. No. 1041	**William Higgs** *Top of the List.* Spy
28.11.1906	1987	M. No. 1042	**William Griggs** *He rides for Lord Durham.* Spy
5.12.1906	1988	M. No. 1043	**Evan Hanbury** *Cottesmore.* Spy
12.12.1906	1989	M. No. 1044	**Reginald Corbet** *To the manner born.* Spy
19.12.1906	1990	M. No. 1045	**Lord Joicey** *Colleries.* Spy
26.12.1906	1991	M. No. 1046	**Captain John Rushworth Jellicoe RN** *Naval Ordinance.* Spy
2.1.1907	1992	M. No. 1047	**Rt Hon Sydney Charles Buxton MP** *The Post-Master General.* Spy
9.1.1907	1993	M. No. 1048	**Gen Sir William Francis Butler GCB** *A Radical General.* Spy
16.1.1907	1994	M. No. 1049	**F. E. Smith MP** *A Successful First Speech: 'Moab is my washpot'.* Spy
23.1.1907	1995	M. No. 1050	**Arthur Lee MP** *our army critic.* Spy
30.1.1907	1996	M. No. 1051	**Father Bernard Vaughan SJ** *A Modern Savonarola.* Spy
6.2.1907	1997	M. No. 1052	**The Lord Bishop of Truro** *A most select preacher.* Spy
13.2.1907	1998	M. No. 1053	**Lord Althorp** *an expert in ceremony.* Spy
20.2.1907	1999	M. No. 1054	**J. D. Rees MP** *Montgomery District.* Spy
27.2.1907	2000	M. No. 1055	**William Gillette** *Sherlock Holmes.* Spy
6.3.1907	2001	M. No. 1056	**Lord Southampton** *The Sinner.* Spy
13.3.1907	2002	M. No. 1057	**Douglas Stewart** *Duggie.* Spy
20.3.1907	2003	M. No. 1058	**Lord De Ros** *The Premier Baron.* Spy
27.3.1907	2004	M. No. 1059	**H. C. Biron** *Worship Street.* Spy
3.4.1907	2005	M. No. 1060	**Sir William Bull MP** *Hammersmith.* Spy
10.4.1907	2006	M. No. 1061	**Hon Charles Russell** *A son of his father.* Spy
17.4.1907	2007	M. No. 1062	**Henry J. Wood** *Queen's Hall.* Spy
24.4.1907	2008	M. No. 1063	**Henry Kemble** *Hereditary Actor.* Spy
1.5.1907	2009	M. No. 1064	**Rt Hon Sir Nicholas O'Conor GCMG KCB** *Diplomacy.* Spy
8.5.1907	2010	M. No. 1065	**Hon Mr Justice Darling** *Judicial Light Weight.* Spy
15.5.1907	2011	M. No. 1066	**William O'Brien MP** *United Ireland.* Spy
22.5.1907	2012	M. No. 1067	**Rev Canon Frederick Hervey CVO MA** *Domestic Chaplain.* Ao
29.5.1907	2013	M. No. 1068	**General Louis Botha** *Uncle Louis.* Ryg
5.6.1907	2014	M. No. 1069	**J. H. Martin** *Skeets.* Ao
12.6.1907	2015	M. No. 1070	**Rt Hon Edmund Robertson MP** *Admiralty.* Spy
19.6.1907	2016	M. No. 1071	**G. A. Prentice** *The Portly One.* Spy
26.6.1907	2017	M. No. 1072	**James Braid** *Jimmy.* Spy
3.7.1907	2018	M. No. 1073	**B. C. Johnstone** *Bush.* Spy

DATE	ISSUE	TITLE	NAME, CAPTION, CARICATURIST
10.7.1907	2019	M. No. 1074	**C. M. Wells** *Father.* Spy
17.7.1907	2020	M. No. 1075	**Lord Suffield PC GCVO KCB** *Suffield.* Ao
24.7.1907	2021	M. No. 1076	**H. S. Foster** *The Fisherman's Friend.* Spy
31.7.1907	2022	M. No. 1077	**Alfred Gwynne Vanderbilt** *Mr. Alfred Gwynne Vanderbilt.* Spy
7.8.1907	2023	M. No. 1078	**Sir Richard Bulkeley** *Tiggy.* Spy
14.8.1907	2024	M. No. 1079	**K. L. Hutchings** *A Century Maker.* Spy
21.8.1907	2025	M. No. 1080	**Earl of Portsmouth** *The Demon.* Spy
28.8.1907	2026	M. No. 1081	**Sir John Omerod Scarlett Thursby** *J.O.S.* Spy
4.9.1907	2027	M. No. 1082	**Walter S. Buckmaster** *Buck.* Spy
11.9.1907	2028	M. No. 1083	**Lord Carrington LG** *Small Holding.* Spy
18.9.1907	2029	M. No. 1084	**Sir Alfred Fripp** *A Master of the Knife.* Spy
25.9.1907	2030	M. No. 1085	**Earl of Aylesford** *Charlie Aylesford.* Ao
2.10.1907	2031	M. No. 1086	**Marquess de Soveral GCMG GCVO** *Unlike Wilkes, who was only half-an-hour behind the handsomest man in Europe, M. de Soveral is usually a minute or two ahead of him.* Ruth
9.10.1907	2032	M. No. 1087	**Thomas James MacNamara MA LLD MP** *The School Master.* Spy
16.10.1907	2033	M. No. 1088	**Hon Sir Alfred Tristam Lawrence** *Lorry.* Spy
23.10.1907	2034	M. No. 1089	**Hugh Cecil Lea MP** *East St. Pancras.* Spy
30.10.1907	2035	M. No. 1090	**Samuel Fay** *Great Central.* Spy
6.11.1907	2036	M. No. 1091	**Frederic Abernathy Coleman** *Steam.* Spy
13.11.1907	2037	M. No. 1092	**Rt Hon David Lloyd George** *A Nonconformist Genius.* Spy
20.11.1907	2038	M. No. 1093	**James Buchanan** *Whiskey and Horses.* Spy
27.11.1907	2039	M. No. 1094	**Hon Mr Justice Warrington** *A Very Sound Judge.* Spy
4.12.1907	2040	M. No. 1095	**Lieutenant-General Sir George Luck KCB** *A Keeper of the Tower.* Spy
11.12.1907	2041	M. No. 1096	**Frank Hedges Butler FRGS** *The Air.* Spy
18.12.1907	2042	M. No. 1097	**George Thursby** *Mr. George.* Spy
25.12.1907	2043	M. No. 1098	**Gerald du Maurier** *Gerald.* Spy
1.1.1908	2044	M. No. 1099	**Peter Purcell Gilpin** *Condition.* Spy
8.1.1908	2045	M. No. 1100	**John Frederick Deel Rawlinson KC LLM MP** *Eton and Cambridge.* Spy
15.1.1908	2046	M. No. 1101	**Edward Snow Fordham** *North London.* Spy
22.1.1908	2047	M. No. 1102	**The Grand Duke Michael Michaelovitch of Russia** *Michael.* Spy
29.1.1908	2048	M. No. 1103	**Rt Hon Joseph Chamberlain MP** *War-worn.* Who
5.2.1908	2049	M. No. 1104	**Sir Edward Robert Pearch Edgcumbe LLD DL JP** *Small Freeholds.* Spy
12.2.1908	2050	M. No. 1105	**Sir Samuel Thomas Evans KC JP** *Sam.* Spy
19.2.1908	2051	M. No. 1106	**His Excellency the Marquis Di San Guiliano** *The Italian Ambassador.* Spy
26.2.1908	2052	M. No. 1107	**George Elliot** *George.* Spy
4.3.1908	2053	M. No. 1108	**Lord Armstrong** *The Ogre.* Spy
11.3.1908	2054	M. No. 1109	**James Inglis** *Great Western.* Spy
18.3.1908	2055	M. No. 1110	**G. P. Huntley** *G.P.* Spy
25.3.1908	2056	M. No. 1111	**Sir Boverton Redwood DSc FRSE** *Petroleum.* Spy
1.4.1908	2057	M. No. 1112	**Oliver R. H. Bury** *Great Northern.* Spy
8.4.1908	2058	M. No. 1113	**Peter Jeffrey Mackie** *Restless Peter.* Spy
15.4.1908	2059	M. No. 1114	**Lord Savile** *Rufford Abbey.* Spy
22.4.1908	2060	M. No. 1115	**David Jardine Jardine** *Davie.* Spy
29.4.1908	2061	M. No. 1116	**Mark Hambourg** *Impromptu.* Spy
6.5.1908	2062	M. No. 1117	**Sir Thomas Wrightson, Bart** *Tariff Reform.* Spy
13.5.1908	2063	M. No. 1118	**Samuel Langhorne Clemens** *'Mark Twain' or 'Below The Mark'.* Spy
20.5.1908	2064	M. No. 1119	**Allan Aynesworth** *Tony.* Spy
27.5.1908	2065	M. No. 1120	**George Benjamin Clemenceau** *The Little Great Premier.* Vanitas
3.6.1908	2066	M. No. 1121	**Sir Daniel Cooper** *Dan.* Spy
10.6.1908	2067	M. No. 1122	**Alfred Edward Woodley Mason MP** *Four Feathers.* Max
17.6.1908	2068	M. No. 1123	**Sir David Salomons** *Electricity.* Spy
24.6.1908	2069	M. No. 1124	**Frank Curzon** *The Gaffer.* Spy
1.7.1908	2070	M. No. 1125	**Earl of Granard** *Master of the Horse.* Spy
8.7.1908	2071	M. No. 1126	**A. G. Hales** *Peace and War.* Spy
15.7.1908	2072	M. No. 1127	**Gen Sir Arthur Henry Paget** *Soudan.* Spy
22.7.1908	2073	M. No. 1128	**Maurice Maeterlinck** *The Belgian Poet.* Max
29.7.1908	2074	M. No. 1129	**Benjamin Tillett—John Ward MP** *Labour Men.* Spy
5.8.1908	2075	M. No. 1130	**Raymond Broadley Etherington-Smith BA MB BC** *Ethel.* Spy
12.8.1908	2076	M. No. 1131	**Earl of Crawford** *The Transit of Venus.* Spy
19.8.1908	2077	M. No. 1132	**Sir Melville MacNaghten** *Scotland Yard.* Spy
26.8.1908	2078	M. No. 1133	**Sir Thomas Shaughnessy** *The Canadian Pacific.* Spy
2.9.1908	2079	M. No. 1134	**Alfred Deakin** *Australia.* Spy
9.9.1908	2080	M. No. 1135	**Hon Abe Bailey** *Rhodes the Second.* Spy
16.9.1908	2081	M. No. 1136	**Earl Winterton** *A Sticker.* Spy
23.9.1908	2082	M. No. 1137	**Charles Bright FRSE** *Submarine Telegraphs.* Spy

DATE	ISSUE	TITLE	NAME, CAPTION, CARICATURIST
30.9.1908	2083	M. No. 1138	**Alfred F. Bird** *A Midland Imperialist.* Spy
7.10.1908	2084	M. No. 1139	**Jean Leon Jaurès** *A Great French Orator.* Spy
14.10.1908	2085	M. No. 1140	**Lord Newton** *An Imperialist without Guile.* Spy
21.10.1908	2086	M. No. 1141	**Sir Christopher Furness MP JP** *The Furness Line.* Spy
28.10.1908	2087	M. No. 1142	**Harry Leo Sydney Richardson LLD** *The Official Assignee.* Who
4.11.1908	2088	M. No. 1143	**Alderman Sir George Wyatt Truscott** *The Lord Mayor.* Spy
11.11.1908	2089	M. No. 1144	**W. Guy Granet** *The Midland.* Spy
18.11.1908	2090	M. No. 1145	**Elemir Bourges** *An Artist in Words.* Guth
18.11.1908	—	M. No. 1146	**Lady Dorothy Neville.** Who
25.11.1908	2091	M. No. 1147	**Lord Burton** *Burton.* Spy
2.12.1908	2092	M. No. 1148	**Sir William Ramsay KCB** *Chemistry.* Spy
9.12.1908	2093	M. No. 1149	**HSH Prince Alexander of Teck.** Spy
16.12.1908	2094	M. No. 1150	**Alfred Chichele Plowden** *Wit & Wisdom.* Spy
23.12.1908	2095	M. No. 1151	**Isidore de Lara** *A Great English Composer.* unsigned
30.12.1908	2096	M. No. 1152	**Paul Nelka** *Options.* Elf
6.1.1909	2097	M. No. 1153	**Archdeacon Wilberforce** *The Chaplain.* Spy
13.1.1909	2098	M. No. 1154	**Lord Coleridge** *The Silver Voiced.* Spy
20.1.1909	2099	M. No. 1155	**George Alexander** *The St. James's.* Max
27.1.1909	2100	M. No. 1156	**Earl of Chesterfield** *A Dandy.* Spy
3.2.1909	2101	M. No. 1157	**Sir Clifton Robinson** *Electric Traction.* Spy
10.2.1909	2102	M. No. 1158	**Col Frank Shuttleworth** *Charlie.* Spy
17.2.1909	2103	M. No. 1159	**Sir Horace Regnart** *Sir Horace, J.P.* Spy
24.2.1909	2104	M. No. 1160	**John Singer Sargent RA** *A Great Realist.* Max
3.3.1909	2105	M. No. 1161	**Sir Colin Richard Keppel** *Commodore H.M.'s Yachts.* Spy
10.3.1909	2106	M. No. 1162	**James Horlick JP DL** *Malted Milk.* Spy
17.3.1909	2107	M. No. 1163	**Carl Meyer** *C.M.* Spy
24.3.1909	2108	M. No. 1164	**Frederick J. Benson** *Swansea Harbour.* Who
31.1.1909	2109	M. No. 1165	**Sir Theodore Fry** *Not a Small Fry.* Spy
7.4.1909	2110	M. No. 1166	**H. Mallaby-Deeley** *The Prince of Princes.* Spy
14.4.1909	2111	M. No. 1167	**Sir John Edward Arthur Murray Scott** *The Wallace Collection.* Who
21.4.1909	2112	M. No. 1168	**Lord Inverclyde** *Jim.* Spy
28.4.1909	2113	M. No. 1169	**Lord Barrington** *Lord Barrington.* Spy
5.5.1909	2114	M. No. 1170	**Lord Newlands** *Jim.* Spy
12.5.1909	2115	M. No. 1171	**M. J. Reid Walker** *John.* Spy
19.5.1909	2116	M. No. 1172	**Edward G. Hemmerde KC** *The New Recorder.* Spy
26.5.1909	2117	M. No. 1173	**Maurice Fitzgerald** *Knight of Kerry.* Spy
2.6.1909	2118	M. No. 1174	**Sir Arthur Lucas** *Arthur.* Elf
9.6.1909	2119	M. No. 1175	**Walter Winans** *Tracks and Triggers.* Who
16.6.1909	2120	M. No. 1176	**Hon Robert Garnett Tatlow** *Finance and Fruit.* Spy
23.6.1909	2121	M. No. 1177	**Sir Gilbert Parker** *The Member for Greater Britain.* Spy
30.6.1909	2122	M. No. 1178	**Alfred James Curnick** *Alfred.* Spy
7.7.1909	2123	M. No. 1179	**Baron George de Reuter** *The Wicked Baron.* Spy
14.7.1909	2124	M. No. 1180	**Sir John Irving Courtenay** *A City Liberal.* Spy
21.7.1909	2125	M. No. 1181	**W. Gardner Sinclair** *Beer, Budget & Brains. W.G.* Spy
28.7.1909	2126	M. No. 1182	**S. Ernest Palmer** *Patrons' Fund.* Elf
4.8.1909	2127	M. No. 1183	**Lord Leith of Fyvie** *Fyvie.* Spy
11.8.1909	2128	M. No. 1184	**Anatole France** *The Greatest Living Frenchman.* Guth
18.8.1909	2129	M. No. 1185	**Captain Malcolm Kincaid-Smith** *National Military Training.* Spy
25.8.1909	2130	M. No. 1186	**Rt Hon James H. M. Campbell** *The Rt. Hon. James.* Spy
1.9.1909	2131	M. No. 1187	**Harding De Fonblanque Cox** *Cockie.* Kite
8.9.1909	2132	M. No. 1188	**Frank Wooton** *Frank Wooton.* Spy
		F.R. No. I	**Minoru** *Minoru.* Percy Earl
15.9.1909	2133	M. No. 1189	**John Cathcart Wason** *Orkney and Shetland.* Who
		F.R. No. II	**Bayardo** *Bayardo.* Percy Earl
22.9.1909	2134	M. No. 1190	**Raymond Blathwayt** *A Good Listener.* Spy
		F.R. No. III	**Cyllene** *Cyllene.* Percy Earl
29.9.1909	2135	M. No. 1191	**Sir John Jackson LLD** *Docks and Harbours.* Spy
		F.R. No. IV	**Dean Swift** *Dean Swift.* Percy Earl
6.10.1909	2136	M. No. 1192	**Ernest Shackleton** *The South Pole.* Kite
(2 cartoons)		M. No. 1193	**Dr H. S. Lunn** *The King of Clubs.* Elf
13.10.1909	2137	M. No. 1194	**Sir Edward Daniel Walker** *E.D.* Quip
		F.R. No. V	**Lutteur III** *Lutteur III.* Emil Adam
20.10.1909	2138	M. No. 1195	**Sir R. W. Buchanan Jardine** *Willie.* Elf
		F.R. No. VI	**Sceptre** *Sceptre.* Percy Earl

DATE	ISSUE	TITLE	NAME, CAPTION, CARICATURIST
27.10.1909	2139	M. No. 1196	**Lord Monk Bretton** *The Private Secretary.* Spy
		F.R. No. VII	**Pretty Polly** *Pretty Polly.* Percy Earl
3.11.1909	2140	M. No. 1197	**Hon W. S. Fielding MP** *Canadian Finance.* Who
		F.R. No. VIII	**St Simon** *St. Simon.* Who
10.11.1909	2141	M. No. 1198	**The King of Portugal** *Europe's Youngest Monarch.* Nibs
17.11.1909	2142	M. No. 1199	**Colonel W. J. Bosworth** *The Colonel.* Elf
		F.R. No. IX	**Rock Sand** *Rock Sand.* Percy Earl
24.11.1909	2143	M. No. 1200	**Sir Charles Friswell** *Frizzy.* HCO
		F.R. No. X	**Persimmon** *Persimmon.* Percy Earl
1.12.1909	2144	M. No. 1201	**Osmond Williams, Bart, MP** *The Champion of the Ladies.* HCO
		F.R. No. XI	**Flying Fox** *Flying Fox.* Percy Earl
8.12.1909	2145	M. No. 1202	**H. A. Barker** *Bones.* HCO
16.12.1909	2146	M. No. 1203	**Sir Archibald Williams** *Moray and Nairn.* HCO
23.12.1909	2147	M. No. 1204	**Mr Harold John Tennant MP** *Dangerous Trades.* Spy
(2 cartoons)		M. No. 1205	**Col E. Hildred Carlile MP** *Mid-Herts.* Elf
30.12.1909	2148	M. No. 1206	**Frederick Leverton Harris** *Leverton.* Spy
(2 cartoons)		M. No. 1207	**Douglas Vickers** *Brightside D.V.* Spy
6.1.1910	2149	M. No. 1208	**George Younger MP** *Ayr Bunghe.* HCO
(4 cartoons)		M. No. 1209	**Sir John Barker** *Falmouth.* HCO
		M. No. 1210	**R. E. Belilios** *Billy.* Pip
		M. No. 1211	**Arthur DuCros JP MP** *Hastings and Aviation.* HCO
13.1.1910	2150	M. No. 1212	**Archer Baker** *C.P.R. In Europe.* Elf
20.1.1910	2151	M. No. 1213	**S. B. Joel** *Sollie.* HCO
27.1.1910	2152	M. No. 1214	**Rt Hon A. J. Balfour** *Dialectics.* XIT
		F.R. No. XII	**Santry** *Santry.* Frank Paton
3.2.1910	2153	M. No. 1215	**John Bland-Sutton FRCS** *A Great Surgeon.* Elf
10.2.1910	2154	M. No. 1216	**Sir Evelyn John Ruggles-Brise** *Borstal System.* Spy
		F.R. No. XIII	**Torpoint** *Torpoint.* Percy Earl
17.2.1910	2155	M. No. 1217	**Herbert Haynes Twining** *Herbs.* HCO
24.2.1910	2156	M. No. 1218	**James Richard Hennessey** *Lutteur ★ ★ ★.* HCO
3.3.1910	2157	M. No. 1219	**Joseph Lyons** *Joe.* HCO
10.3.1910	2158	M. No. 1220	**Lord Welby** *The Treasury.* HCO
17.3.1910	2159	M. No. 1221	**Rt Hon H. H. Asquith** *A Great Orator.* XIT
24.3.1910	2160	M. No. 1222	**P. H. Pridham-Wippell** *Pridham.* Elf
31.3.1910	2161	M. No. 1223	**C. Herbert Workman** *Through every passion ranging.* Elf
7.4.1910	2162	M. No. 1224	**Sir Phillip Watts KCB** *Naval Construction.* Spy
14.4.1910	2163	M. No. 1225	**Marquess of Bute** *The Bute.* Who
21.4.1910	2164	M. No. 1226	**Sir Theodore Francis Brinckman** *Theodore.* Elf
28.4.1910	2165	M. No. 1227	**Robert Armstrong Yerburgh** *Chester.* Who
5.5.1910	2166	M. No. 1228	**Anthony J. Drexel** *Tony.* Elf
12.5.1910	2167	Special Cartoon	**HM Edward VII** *The Pacification of Europe.* XIT
19.5.1910	2168	M. No. 1229	**Sir John G. Nutting** *J.G.* Pry
26.5.1910	2169	M. No. 1230	**Sir Charles Philip Huntington** *Tubby.* Quip
1.6.1910	2170	M. No. 1231	**John Porter** *John Porter.* XIT
8.6.1910	2171	M. No. 1232	**Gen Sir Arthur Turner KCB** *Versatility.* Who
15.6.1910	2172	A Woman of the Day	**Miss Christabel Pankhurst LLB** *Women's Suffrage.* Spy
22.6.1910	2173	M. No. 1233	**Guy Owen** *Tea cum Rubber.* Elf
29.6.1910	2174	M. No. 1234	**A. W. Cox** *Fairie.* Spy
6.7.1910	2175	M. No. 1235	**Robert Henry Forster MA LLB** *Bill.* Elf
13.7.1910	2176	M. No. 1236	**Lord Niniah Crichton-Stuart** *Cardiff.* Who
20.7.1910	2177	M. No. 1237	**Richard Vassar Vassar Smith** *Lloyd's Bank.* HCO
27.7.1910	2178	M. No. 1238	**Hon Stephen Coleridge** *Anti-Vivisection.* Elf
3.8.1910	2179	M. No. 1239	**Colin Blythe** *Charlie.* A.L.S.
10.8.1910	2180	M. No. 1240	**Col John McAusland Denny** *Philip.* Who
17.8.1910	2181	M. No. 1241	**William Balle Huntington** *Endowed Lectures.* Pry
24.8.1910	2182	M. No. 1242	**Sir James King** *King of Campsie.* HCO
31.8.1910	2183	M. No. 1243	**Lord Barrymore** *An Irish Landowner.* Spy
7.9.1910	2184	M. No. 1243a	**John Hamilton-Buchanan** *Long John.* Quip
14.9.1910	2185	M. No. 1244	**Marshall Stevens** *Manchester Ship Canal.* Elf
21.9.1910	2186	M. No. 1245	**Godfrey Baring MP** *Isle of Wight.* Spy
28.9.1910	2187	M. No. 1246	**William Speirs Simpson** *Science and Invention.* Spy
5.10.1910	2188	M. No. 1247	**Joseph Ernest Renan** *The Greatest of the Fathers.* Guth
12.10.1910	2189	M. No. 1248	**Viscount Ridley** *Tariff Reform League.* Who
19.10.1910	2190	M. No. 1249	**Rt Hon Alfred Emmott MP** *The Deputy Speaker.* Who

DATE	ISSUE	TITLE	NAME, CAPTION, CARICATURIST
26.10.1910	2191	M. No. 1250	**Lord Herschell** *A Lord-in-Waiting*. Who
2.11.1910	2192	M. No. 1251	**Sir Edward Tennant** *Glen*. Who
9.11.1910	2193	M. No. 1252	**Emile Garcke** *Electrical Energy*. HCO
16.11.1910	2194	M. No. 1253	**Lord Glantawe** *Swansea*. Who
23.11.1910	2195	M. No. 1254	**Mr Martinez DeHoz** *An Argentine Sportsman*. Who
30.11.1910	2196	M. No. 1255	**Sir Philip Hickson Waterlow** *Philip*. Who
7.12.1910	2197	M. No. 1256	**J. Stirling Ainsworth** *Johnnie*. Who
14.12.1910	2198	M. No. 1257	**Col Sir Philip W. Chetwode, Bart, DSO** *19th Hussars*. Who
21.12.1910	2199	M. No. 1258	**Alfred Butt** *The Palace*. HCO
29.12.1910	2200	M. No. 1259	**Arthur Collins** *The Guv'nor*. Wallace Hester
4.1.1911	2201	M. No. 1260	**Oswald Stoll** *The Coliseum*. Ape Junior
11.1.1911	2202	M. No. 1261	**Clarence F. Ravenscroft** *The Birkbeck*. Ape Junior
18.1.1911	2203	M. No. 1262	**Justice Lush** *Like Father Like Son*. Ape Junior
25.1.1911	2204	M. No. 1263	**Hon Price Ellison** *British Columbia*. Wallace Hester
1.2.1911	2205	M. No. 1264	**William Lowndes Toller Foy** *A well-Known Face in the Timber World*. HCO
8.2.1911	2206	M. No. 1265	**Rt Hon Edward H. Carson KC MP** *Dublin University*. Wallace Hester
15.2.1911	2207	M. No. 1266	**Col D. P. Driscoll DSO** *An Old War Horse*. Ape Junior
22.2.1911	2208	M. No. 1267	**Marshall O. Roberts** *Easton Hall*. Spy
1.3.1911	2209	M. No. 1268	**Mr Ernest Collins MICE** *A Great Engineer*. Ape Junior
8.3.1911	2210	M. No. 1269	**Rt Hon Winston L. S. Churchill MP** *Winnie*. Nibs
15.3.1911	2211	M. No. 1270	**Hon Mr Justice Eve** *A Cool Judge*. Ape
22.3.1911	2212	M. No. 1271	**Julian W. Orde** *A Popular Secretary*. Ape Junior
29.3.1911	2213	M. No. 1272	**R. C. Bourne, The Oxford Stroke** *A good stroke*. Ape Junior
5.4.1911	2214	M. No. 1273	**Sir Herbert Beerbohm Tree** *His Majesty's*. Who
12.4.1911	2215	M. No. 1274	**Rev Canon Edgar Sheppard DD CVO** *the Sub-Dean*. Ape Junior
19.4.1911	2216	M. No. 1275	**Lieut-Gen Sir Robert Baden-Powell** *Boy Scouts*. Ape Junior
26.4.1911	2217	M. No. 1276	**George Edwardes** *The Guv'nor*. Nibs
3.5.1911	2218	M. No. 1277	**C. C. Hutchinson KC** *Hutchy*. Ape Junior
10.5.1911	2219	M. No. 1278	**Claude Grahams-White** *Claudie*. Tec
17.5.1911	2220	M. No. 1279	**Montagu A. Pyke** *Cinematographs*. Ape Junior
24.5.1911	2221	M. No. 1280	**Sir John Robinson JP** *Worksop Manor*. Spy
31.5.1911	2222	M. No. 1281	**Rt Hon Lord Elphinstone** *Carberry Tower*. Ape Junior
7.6.1911	2223	O.C. No. 1282	**HM Queen Alexandra** *Her Majesty Queen Alexandra*. Spy
14.6.1911	2224	O.C. No. 1283	**R. P. Houston MP** *The Britisher's Friend*. Spy
21.6.1911	2225	M. No. 1284	**H. J. Brown** *Oil*. Spy
		Special Number 2226	**His Majesty The King (George V)** *His Majesty The King*. Ape Junior
28.6.1911	2226	M. No. 1285	**Justice Scrutton** *Copyright*. Ape Junior
5.7.1911	2227	M. No. 1286	**Frank Matcham** *Architect Matcham*. Nibs
12.7.1911	2228	O.C. No. 1287	**HRH The Prince of Wales (Edward VIII)** *H.R.H.* Nibs
19.7.1911	2229	M. No. 1288	**Captain James Craig MP JP** *Orangeman*. Who
26.7.1911	2230	M. No. 1289	**Sir George William Kekewich KCB** *A Sturdy Educationist*. Who
2.8.1911	2231	M. No. 1290	**Hon Thomas H.A.E. Cochrane DL JP** *North Ayrshire*. Spy
9.8.1911	2232	M. No. 1291	**F. E. Smith** *No Surrender*. Nibs
16.8.1911	2233	M. No. 1292	**George Bernard Shaw** *G.B.S.* Alick P. F. Ritchie
23.8.1911	2234	M. No. 1293	**Lord Ellenborough** *Nautical Freshness*. Who
30.8.1911	2235	M. No. 1294	**Col Rookes Evelyn Bell Crompton BB** *The Road Builder*. Who
6.9.1911	2236	M. No. 1295	**Sir Charles Holcroft** *Brumagem Varsity*. HCO
13.9.1911	2237	M. No. 1296	**James Louis Garvin** *? - !* Alick P. F. Ritchie
20.9.1911	2238	M. No. 1297	**Captain Sir W. Nott-Bower CVO** *City Police*. Ray
27.9.1911	2239	M. No. 1298	**Sir Alfred Pearce Gould KCVO MS FRCS** *Surgical Diagnosis*. WH
4.10.1911	2240	M. No. 1299	**Dr Thomas Richard Allinson** *Wholemeal Bread*. Ray
11.10.1911	2241	M. No. 1300	**Rt Rev Edward Stuart Talbot DD** *Winton*. Ray
18.10.1911	2242	M. No. 1301	**Sir John Allsebrook Simon Kt KC, Solicitor-General** *Simple Simon*. WH
25.10.1911	2243	M. No. 1302	**Sir George Ranken Askwith KC KCB** *The Conciliator*. WH
1.11.1911	2244	M. No. 1303	**S. F. Cody** *All British*. Alick P. F. Ritchie
8.11.1911	2245	M. No. 1304	**Sir Thomas Boor Crosby KT MD FRCS JP** *His Lordship of London, M.D.* WH
15.11.1911	2246	M. No. 1305	**Oscar Hammerstein** *Opera de Luxe*. Ray
22.11.1911	2247	M. No. 1306	**Arthur Frederick Bettinson** *Peggy*. WH
29.11.1911	2248	M. No. 1307	**Oscar Asche** *kismet*. Alick P. F. Ritchie
6.12.1911	2249	M. No. 1308	**H. Gordon Selfridge** *Self—*. Alick P. F. Ritchie
13.12.1911	2250	M. No. 1309	**William McAuliffe** *Stonehenge, 1911*. Alick P. F. Ritchie
20.12.1911	2251	M. No. 1310	**Lucien Wolfe** *Diplomaticus*. Alick P. F. Ritchie
27.12.1911	2252	M. No. 1311	**Phillip Whitwell Wilson** *P.W.W.* Alick P. F. Ritchie
3.1.1912	2253	M. No. 1312	**Vice Admiral Sir Frederick William Fisher** *Uncle Bill*. Ray

DATE	ISSUE	TITLE	NAME, CAPTION, CARICATURIST
10.1.1912	2254	M. No. 1313	**Robert Loraine** *The Flying Stag.* Alick P. F. Ritchie
17.1.1912	2255	M. No. 1314	**Rt Hon Sir Edward Henry Carson Kt PC MP LLD** *I never ask Anyone.* WH
24.1.1912	2256	M. No. 1315	**Llewellyn Archer Atherley-Jones KC MP** *Jonesy.* WH
31.1.1912	2257	M. No. 1316	**Very Rev William Ralph Inge DD** *The Genial Dean.* WH
7.2.1912	2258	M. No. 1317	**Sir George Henry Savage MD FRCP** *Mens Sana.* Ray
14.2.1912	2259	M. No. 1318	**Eugene Corri** *a typical Englishman.* Alick P. F. Ritchie
21.2.1912	2260	M. No. 1319	**Gilbert Keith Chesterton** *G.K.C.* Strickland
28.2.1912	2261	M. No. 1320	**W. Morgan Shuster** *The Yankee from Persia.* WH
6.3.1912	2262	M. No. 1321	**Ralph Norman Angell Lane** *an Angel of Peace.* Strickland
13.3.1912	2263	M. No. 1322	**Sir Charles Wright Macara, Bart** *A Leading Figure in Cotton.* Alick P. F. Ritchie
20.3.1912	2264	M. No. 1323	**Sir Charles Edward Cradock-Hartopp, Bart** *Topps.* WH
27.3.1912	2265	M. No. 1324	**Rt Rev Herbert Edward Ryle DD CVO** *The Dean.* WH
3.4.1912	2266	M. No. 1325	**Sydney Ernest Swann ('Cygnet')** *The Light Blue Stroke.* WH
10.4.1912	2267	M. No. 1326	**Rt Hon Andrew Bonar Law MP PC JP** *The Opposition.* Strickland
17.4.1912	2268	M. No. 1327	**Signor Pietro Mascagni** *The Intermezzo.* WH
24.4.1912	2269	M. No. 1328	**Rev Herbert Hensley Henson DD** *St. Margaret's.* WH
1.5.1912	2270	M. No. 2270[23]	**Rev Lionel George Bridges Justice Ford** *New Harrow.* Strickland
8.5.1912	2271	M. No. 2271	**Evan Spicer DL JP** *Paper.* Ray
15.5.1912	2272	M. No. 2272	**Samuel Osborn FRCS JP** *Sam.* WH
22.5.1912	2273	M. No. 2273	**Bishop of London** *In his lighter moments.* WH
29.5.1912	2274	M. No. 2274	**Charles W. Coop** *Prospectuses.* WH
5.6.1912	2275	M. No. 2275	**Frank Ree** *L. and N.W.* WH
12.6.1912	2276	M. No. 2276	**R. A. Stewart Hollebone** *big things in Oil.* WH
19.6.1912	2277	M. No. 2277	**Earl of Lonsdale** *The Horse has no better friend.* WH
26.6.1912	2278	M. No. 2278	**Lt Col Mark Sykes JP FRGS MP** *Our Mark.* WH
3.7.1912	2279	M. No. 2279	**John Corrie Carter, Esquire** *Steered three winning crews.* WH
10.7.1912	2280	M. No. 2280	**Lt Col Charles Robert Crosse MVO** *Bisley Camp.* WH
17.7.1912	2281	M. No. 2281	**Major General the Lord Cheylesmore KCVO** *Arms and Sport.* Ray
24.7.1912	2282	M. No. 2282	**Captain Swinton** *East & West.* WH
31.7.1912	2283	M. No. 2283	**Gustav Hamel** *Flight.* WH
7.8.1912	2284	M. No. 2284	**J. B. Hobbs** *'Test Cricket.' or 'A Tested Centurion.'* WH
14.8.1912	2285	M. No. 2285	**Sir Arthur Sackville Trevor Griffith-Boscawen** *Housing.* Ray
21.8.1912	2286	M. No. 2286	**John Hassall RI** *Posters.* Strickland
28.8.1912	2287	M. No. 2287	**Charles Edward Jerningham** *Marmaduke.* WH
4.9.1912	2288	M. No. 2288	**Sir Robert A. Hadfield Kt FRS** *Steel.* WH
11.9.1912	2289	M. No. 2289	**Lord Kinnaird FRGS DL JP** *Soccer.* WH
18.9.1912	2290	M. No. 2290	**Frederick Vincent Brooks** *A Master Craftsman.* WH
25.9.1912	2291	M. No. 2291	**Harry Tate** *The King's Jester.* WH
2.10.1912	2292	M. No. 2292	**His Excellency The French Ambassador** *His Excellency The French Ambassador.* K
9.10.1912	2293	M. No. 2293	**Earl Waldegrave** *Earl Waldegrave.* WH
16.10.1912	2294	M. No. 2294	**Sir Henry Austin Lee KCMG CB** *Sir Henry Austin Lee, K.C.M.G., C.B.* K
23.10.1912	2295	M. No. 2295	**Sir Frank Lascelles GCB GCMG** *Sir Frank Lascelles, G.C.B., G.C.M.G.* K
30.10.1912	2296	M. No. 2296	**Madame Sarah Bernhardt** *Madame Sarah Bernhardt.* K
6.11.1912	2297	Women of the Day	**Lady Dorothy Neville** *The Lady Dorothy Neville.* K
13.11.1912	2298	M. No. 2298	**Marquis De Soveral KCMG** *The Marquis De Soveral, K.C.M.G.* K
20.11.1912	2299	Women of the Day	**Mrs George Cornwallis-West** *Mrs. George Cornwallis-West.* K
27.11.1912	2300	M. No. 2300	**Lord Annaly** *The Lord Annaly.* K
4.12.1912	2301	M. No. 2301	**Captain Hon Henry Denison** *Captain the Hon. Henry Denison.* K
11.12.1912	2302	M. No. 2302	**His Grace The Duke of Wellington KG GCVO** *His Grace The Duke of Wellington, K.G., G.C.V.O.* WH
18.12.1912	2303	M. No. 2303	**Laurence Sydney Brodribb Irving** *Mr. Laurence Irving.* WH
25.12.1912	2304	M. No. 2304	**Col William Hall Walker MP** *Col. William Hall Walker, M.P.* WH
1.1.1913	2305	M. No. 2305	**Earl Brownlow PC** *Earl Brownlow, P.C.* WH
8.1.1913	2306	M. No. 2306	**Lt Col Sir Robert William Inglis** *Lt. Col. Sir Robert William Inglis.* WH
15.1.1913	2307	M. No. 2307	**Sir Richard Webster, Baron Alverstone** *The Lord Chief Justice of England.* WH
22.1.1913	2308	M. No. 2308	**Malcolm Burr DSc (Oxon)** *Science and Sport.* WH
29.1.1913	2309	M. No. 2309	**Rt Hon Sir Ralph Henry Knox PC DCB** *Knox.* WH
5.2.1913	2310	M. No. 2310	**John Hickory Wood** *Modern Pantomime.* Hester
12.2.1913	2311	No Cartoon	Notice printed that due to change in ownership and editorship, no caricature was to be published the week of 12 February 1913
19.2.1913	2312	M. No. 2311[24]	**Captain Robert Falcon Scott RN CVO FRGS** *The South Pole.* Hester
26.2.1913	2313	M. No. 2312	**Dennis Eadie** *Mr. Eadie.* Hester
5.3.1913	2314	M. No. 2313	**Maurice Henry Hewlett** *an Artist in verbal pigments.* Hester
12.3.1913	2315	M. No. 2314	**Thomas Woodrow Wilson, President of the US** *The New President of the United States.* Hester
19.3.1913	2316	M. No. 2315	**Rt Hon Richard Burdon Haldane FRS PC LLD** <u>Government Marked.</u> Owl

DATE	ISSUE	TITLE	NAME, CAPTION, CARICATURIST
26.3.1913	2317	M. No. 2316	**Rt Hon Sir Edward Grey KG PC PCL** *The general colour of the Secretary Bird is bluish grey.* Owl
2.4.1913	2318	M. No. 2317	**Enoch Arnold Bennett** *The Business Man of Letters.* Owl
9.4.1913	2319	M. No. 2318	**Herbert Alfred Humphrey MICE MIME MIEE** *The Chingford Pump.* Hester
16.4.1913	2320	M. No. 2319	**Sir Frederick George Banbury, Bart** *The Blocker.* Eianley Cock
23.4.1913	2321	M. No. 2320	**Rt Hon Reginald M'Kenna** *The Universal Puzzle is: Find Mr. M'Kenna.* Owl
30.4.1913	2322	M. No. 2321	**Mr Charles Hallam Elton Brookfield** *He never attacks morality.* Alick P. F. Ritchie
7.5.1913	2323	M. No. 2322	**Mr John Lavery RSA RHA ARA HROI** *He paints various Royalties.* Alick P. F. Ritchie
14.5.1913	2324	M. No. 2323	**Henry V. Esmond** *Uncle Sandy.* Wallace Hester
21.5.1913	2325	M. No. 2324	**William Arbuthnot Lane MB MS IRCS** *Willie.* Eianley Cock
28.5.1913	2326	M. No. 2325	**Herr Arthur Nikisch** *Nikisch.* Owl
4.6.1913	2327	M. No. 2326	**Sir Johnston Forbes-Robertson Kt** *Mr. Forbes-Robertson.* Alick P. F. Ritchie
11.6.1913	2328	M. No. 2327	**Eden Phillpotts** *The Prophet of Dantymoor.* Alick P. F. Ritchie
18.6.1913	2329	M. No. 2328	**Sir Rufus Daniel Isaacs, Attorney-General** *Why Man he Doth.* Owl
25.6.1913	2330	M. No. 2329	**M Raymond Poincare** *Messieurs!* Owl
2.7.1913	2331	M. No. 2330	**A. W. Gore** *Baby.* Eianley-Cock
9.7.1913	2332	M. No. 2331	**Col Montague George Johnstone DSO** *Monty.* Wallace Hester
16.7.1913	2333	M. No. 2332	**HRH Prince Arthur William Patrick Albert** *H.R.H.* Wallace Hester
23.7.1913	2334	M. No. 2333	**M Cheri Raymond Halbronn** *The French Tattersall.* Owl
30.7.1913	2335	M. No. 2334	**Rt Hon Sir Charles Tupper, Bart, etc** *The Rt. Hon. Sir Charles Tupper, Bart., etc.* Owl
6.8.1913	2336	M. No. 2335	**Sir Charles Allom** *Istria.* Owl
13.8.1913	2337	M. No. 2336	**Charles E. Nicholson** *He is the one designer.* Owl
20.8.1913	2338	M. No. 2337	**John Merry LeSage** *The Daily Telegraph.* Owl
27.8.1913	2339	M. No. 2338	**Ferdinand August Bebel** *August Bebel.* Unsigned
3.9.1913	2340	M. No. 2339	**Edward Wentworth Dillon** *The Champion County.* Owl
10.9.1913	2341	M. No. 2340	**Monsieur Lou Tellegen** *Dorian Gray.* Owl
17.9.1913	2342	M. No. 2341	**Sir James Rankin Bt JP DL MA** *M.F.H. of Herefordshire.* Owl
24.9.1913	2343	M. No. 2342	**Lord Loreburn** *Loreburn.* Owl
1.10.1913	2344	M. No. 2343	**Captain Quintin Dick DL** *Dandy Dick.* Astz
8.10.1913	2345	M. No. 2344	**Oswald Stoll** *The Coliseum.* Owl
15.10.1913	2346	M. No. 2345	**HRH Prince Arthur Frederick Patrick Albert** *Prince Arthur.* Owl
22.10.1913	2347	M. No. 2346	**James Stevens** *Jimmy.* Astz
29.10.1913	2348	M. No. 2347	**R.H.Y.S. Williams, Esquire KC** *Rhys, K.C.* Owl
5.11.1913	2349	M. No. 2348	**Dr Emile Joseph Dillon** *The Semi-official Ambassador.* Owl
12.11.1913	2350	M. No. 2349	**Frank Harris** *Unpath'd Waters.* Owl
19.11.1913	2351	M. No. 2350	**Rt Hon Sir Stanley Owen Buckmaster KC MP** *The Solicitor General.* Owl
26.11.1913	2352	M. No. 2351	**A. Henry Savage Landor** *The Cutter of Continents.* Astz
3.12.1913	2353	M. No. 2352	**Landon Ronald** *Guildhall Music.* Astz
10.12.1913	2354	M. No. 2353	**Raymond Roze** *Opera In English.* Astz
		Special Supplement	**Collapse of the Conference** *Born June 17 died November 10.* Mouse
17.12.1913	2355	M. No. 2354	**Kenelm Foss** *Magic.* Astz
24.12.1913	2356	M. No. 2355	**Courtenay Foote** *The Man on the Film.* Astz
31.12.1913	2357	M. No. 2356	**Earl of Plymouth** *Crystal Palace.* Hit
7.1.1914	2358	M. No. 2357	**Sir Charles Wyndham** *Le Doyen.* Astz
14.1.1914	2359	M. No. 2358	**Joseph Chamberlain** *The Great Imperialist.* Astz
21.1.1914	2360	No cartoon	
28.1.1914	2361	No cartoon	
5.2.1914	2362		*Vanity Fair* and *Hearth and Home*

1 *Vanity Fair* numbered their 2 July 1881 and 9 July 1881 issue 661. This list has been recorded as originally numbered by *Vanity Fair* and corresponds to the magazine's numbers.

2 *Vanity Fair* numbered their 1 July 1882 and 8 July 1882 issues 713. This list has been recorded as originally numbered by *Vanity Fair* and corresponds to the magazine's numbers.

3 *Vanity Fair* numbered Tosti (14 November 1885) and Nickalls (21 November 1885) Men of the Day No. 344. Pope (12 December 1885) Number 346 continued the correct sequence of numbers.

4 The Men of the Day numbers in sequence record number 366 repeated (4 September 1886 and 30 October 1886). Number 370 was omitted. Number 371 (25 December 1886) resumed the correct numbering process.

5 The Statesmen number 535 was repeated in the 24 December 1887 and 31 December 1887 issues.

6 The caricaturist signed his name Qviz and Quiz.

7 *Vanity Fair* numbered Russell (29 March 1890) and Brooke (3 May 1890) Statesmen No. 570. Forwood (16 August 1890) Number 571 continued the correct sequence of numbers.

8 The Men of the Day number 493 was repeated in the 27 December 1890 and 3 January 1891 issues.

9 Beginning with Cozens-Hardy (13 April 1893), the numbers of the Statesmen were changed in the album to 610 through 624 when with Morgan (2 November 1893) the magazine and the album sequence agree again. The magazine numbering is given here.

10 The Men of the Day numbers were misnumbered for the 21 September 1893, 23 November 1893 and 28 December 1893 issue. The correct sequence began again with 577 on 18 January 1894.

11 The Sovereigns number 22 was omitted.

12 The Men of the Day number 695 was repeated in the 11 November 1897 and 2 December 1897 issues.

13 Caricature for 14 April 1898 was a reproduction of the 9 June 1877 caricature which was substituted for the regular caricature destroyed in a fire at Vincent Brooks, Day & Son. In 21 April 1898 issue new caricatures appeared again.

14 The Men of the Day number 760 was repeated in the 21 September 1899 and 28 September 1899 issues.

15 The Statesmen number 714 was omitted.

16 The Statesmen number 730 was repeated in the 20 December 1900 and 10 January 1901 issues.

17 The Men of the Day number 825 was repeated in the 26 September 1901 and 10 October 1901 issues.

18 The Men of the Day number 829 was repeated in the 7 November 1901 and 14 November 1901 issues. Butcher (7 November 1901) was numbered 742 in the album.

19 *Vanity Fair* misnumbered Men of the Day, numbers 850–853 as 860–863.

20 Judges 60, (9 July 1903), 61 (23 July 1903) and 62 (19 May 1904) were misnumbered. They should have been number 67, 68 and 69 to maintain the correct sequence in *Vanity Fair*.

21 Men of the Day number 940 (9 February 1905) is misnumbered. The 940's are repeated.

22 *Vanity Fair* dropped the Men of the Day sequence 950–959, and began with Onslow (20 April 1905) numbering 960.

23 Beginning with Justice Ford (1 May 1912) *Vanity Fair* began to number the Men of the Day the same as the issue number.

24 On 19 February 1913, Men of the Day was numbered 2311, and continued in sequence.

Special Numbers

Including frontispieces, doubleprints (doublesized, or larger prints, marked by an asterisk★),
Summer and Winter Numbers, and special supplement cartoons found in *Vanity Fair*, 1869–
1914.

DATE	TITLE/CAPTION/SUBJECTS, CARICATURIST
2.7.1878	*St James Street, June 1878.* J. M. Whistler
2.7.1878	*Earl of Beaconsfield/ 'The Junior Ambassador'/ (Disraeli).* Ape
14.12.1878	*HRH The Prince of Wales/ 'The Prince' (later Edward VII).* Spy
1.7.1879	*The Rt Hon W. E. Gladstone/ 'The People's William'.* Spy
	The Row in the Season★ (English Society in Hyde Park) (Sir Francis Seymour, Miss Van de Weyer, Mr Montague Corry, Captain Fred Burnaby, Miss Whitshed, Mr W. Wynans, Mr Mocatta; Sir Watkin Wynn, Mr Christopher Sykes, Mr Frederick Cooper, Colonel Wolfe, Mrs Langtry, Admiral Edmonstone, Lady Cardigan, Sir Wilfrid Lawson, Sir Henry Edwards, Miss Lawson, Mr Pulsford; Count Münster, Lady Lonsdale, Sir George Wombwell, HRH the Princess of Wales, HRH the Prince of Wales, Mr Mackenzie Grieves, Lord Gerard, Lord Forrester, Lord Folkestone; Lady Rivers, Mr Bowles, Lord Albemarle, Count Schouvaloff, Colonel Farquharson, Miss Graham, Lord Fitzwilliam, Mr Bass, Mr Edmund Yates, the Duchess of Cleveland, and others.) Corbould
16.12.1879	*Earl of Beaconsfield and Mr M. Corry/ 'Power & Place'.* Spy
6.7.1880	*The Treasury Bench/ 'Babble, Birth and Brummagen' (Mr Gladstone, Lord Hartington, & Mr Chamberlain).* T.
1.12.1880	*'The Fourth Party' (Lord Randolph Churchill, A. J. Balfour, Sir Henry Drummond Wolff, & John Gorst).* Spy
5.7.1881	*'Birth, Behaviour, and Business' Her Majesty's Opposition (Lord John Manners, Sir Stafford Northcote, and Sir Richard Cross).* T.
7.12.1881	*'The Gladstone Memorial' (Gladstone & Charles Bradlaugh).* Unsigned
7.12.1881	*'Force No Remedy' (Parnell and Dillon and a policeman in gaol).* Furniss
5.7.1882	*'Purse, Pussy, Piety and Prevarication' (Lord Northbrook, Lord Granville, Lord Selborne, and Lord Salisbury).* T.
5.12.1882	*HRH The Princess of Wales.* Chartran
27.11.1883	*The Cabinet Council, 1883/ The Gladstone Cabinet (W. E. Gladstone, Earl of Selborne, Earl Granville, Earl of Derby, Earl Spencer, Earl of Kimberley, Earl of Northbrook, Marquis of Hartington, Lord Carlingford, W. V. Harcourt, H.C.E. Childers, J. G. Dodson, J. Chamberlain, Charles Dilke).* Chartran
30.11.1885	*'The Paddock at Newmarket' (The Prince of Wales, the Dowager Duchess of Montrose, Duchess of Manchester, Duke of Portland, Duke of Hamilton, Marquis of Londonderry, Marquis of Hartington, Earl Spencer, Lord Hastings, Sir John Astley, Henry Chaplin, Leopold de Rothschild, W. G. Craven, Capt Machell, Mr Tattersall, Robert Peck, Mat Dawson and Fred Archer).* Lib
30.11.1886 Winter Number	*The Lobby of the House of Commons★ (Mr Gladstone, Lord Randolph Churchill, J. Chamberlain, Lord Hartington, Mr Parnell, John Bright, W. V. Harcourt, Mr H. Labouchère, Mr Bradlaugh, C. R. Spencer, Mr Chaplin, Lord Arthur Hill, George Leveson-Gower, Mr Gossett, Inspector Denning & others).* Lib
6.12.1887	*Tattersall's Newmarket, 1887/'Tattersall's, 1887'★ (The Prince of Wales, Prince Soltykoff, Duke of Beaufort, Duke of Hamilton, Duke of Westminster, Duke of Wellington, Lord Falmouth, Lord Zetland, Lord Cadogan, Lord Rosslyn, Lord Hastings, Lord Calthorpe, Lord Ailesbury, Hon H. W. Fitzwilliam, Sir George Chetwynd, James Lowther, Col Forester, Capt Machell, Mr Benzon, Mr Tattersall, Mr Weatherby, Mr J. Hammond, John Porter, C. Wood, & others).* Lib
8.12.1888	*The Winning Post★ ('Judge' Clark, J. Osborne, Tom Cannon, J. Watts, F. Webb, F. Barrett, G. Barrett, W. Robinson, F. Rickaby, Sir John Astley).* Lib
29.11.1890	*'In Vanity Fair'★ (Mr Leslie Ward, James Weatherby, Sir R. Jardine, Louis Pasteur, Lord Hartington, Major Egerton, Edmund Tattersall, Senor Sarasate, John Sims Reeves, George Grossmith, HRH The Prince George of Wales, Duke of Orleans, Henry Irving, Arthur Cecil, John Hare, Duke of Connaught, Herbert Beerbohm Tree, Dr Tanner, T. P. O'Connor, Augustus Harris, Rt Hon Mr W. H. Smith, Justice Smith).* Unsigned

5.12.1891   'Bench and Bar'★ (Mr Cozens-Hardy QC, Mr Jelf QC, Mr Justice Smith, Sir Horace Davey QC, Baron Pollock, Mr Finlay QC, Mr Grahm, Mr Bosanquet QC, Mr Justice Day, Mr Coward, Sir Henry James QC, Lord Esher, Lord Justice Bowen, Lord Justice Fry, Mr Justice Charles, Mr Waddy QC, Mr Poland QC, Mr Dugale QC, Mr Charles Mathews, Mr Justice Hawkins, Mr Gill, The Attorney General, Lord Coleridge, The Solicitor General, Sir Charles Russell QC, Mr R. T. Reid QC, Mr Justice Williams, The Lord Chancellor, Mr Justice Lindley, Mr Murphy QC, Mr Justice Collins, Mr Justice Jeune, Mr Inderwick QC). Stuff

3.12.1892   'Mixed Political Wares'★ (Campbell-Bannerman, Henry Harley Fowler, Gladstone, Sir William Harcourt, Lord Spencer, Lord Ripon). Spy

30.11.1893   'On the Terrace'★ (A. J. Balfour, J. Chamberlain, Sir John Gorst, Sir Richard Temple, Sir William Harcourt, Anthony John Mundella, Justin McCarthy). Spy

6.12.1894   At Cowes/At Cowes/The RYS★ (HRH The Prince of Wales, HIM The German Emperor, Marquis of Ormonde, Earl of Dunraven, Earl of Lonsdale, Rear Admiral Hon Victor Montagu). Spy

28.11.1895   'A Master Meet'★ (Lord Lonsdale, Lord Portman, Lord Willoughby de Broke, Captain Park Yates, Mr Garth). Spy

11.6.1896   Cycling in Hyde Park★ (W. H. Grenfell, Marchioness of Londonderry, Mrs Sanford, Lord William Nevill, Countess of Minto, Mrs Adrian Hope, Lady William Nevill, Mrs W. H. Grenfell, Lady Griffin, Lady Alexander Kennedy, Lady Norreys, The Countess Cairns). Hal Hurst

26.11.1896   'On the Heath'★ (James Jewitt, Richard Marsh, Tom Jennings Senior, John Dawson, Matthew Dawson, John Porter, James Ryan). Spy

3.6.1897   Au Bois De Boulogne★ (Princess Ghika, Comtesse Liane de-Pougy, Caran d'Ache, La Belle Otéro, Comtesse de Kersaint, Colonel Gibert, Baronne de Fleury, Duchesse & Duc de Rohan, Cléo de Mérode, Comtesse Martel (Gyp), Princesse & Prince de Broglie, Princesse de Sagan, Coquelin Cadet, Duchesse Doudeauville, Princesse Brancovan, Duc de Lesparre). Guth

25.11.1897   'Empire Makers and Breakers'/A Scene at the South Africa Committee, 1897★ (Sir Richard Webster, Mr H. Labouchère, Cecil Rhodes, Sir William Harcourt, Joseph Chamberlain). Stuff

26.5.1898   The Right Honourable William E. Gladstone. Ape

1.12.1898   'The Lord Protect Us'★ (Sir William Harcourt, A. J. Balfour, Joseph Chamberlain, W.E.H. Lecky, L. H. Courtney, and Chief Inspector Horsley). Furniss

11.12.1898   'The Pilgrim Resting on His Way'. G.A.W.

23.11.1899   'At Rennes'★ (Colonel Jacaust, Captain Dreyfus, Mes. Labori and Demange, Generals Billot, Mercier, Zurlinden, Roget, Gonse, and Boisdeffre, Colonel Picquart, MM Hanotaux and Cavaignac and others connected with the trial of Captain Dreyfus at Rennes). Guth

29.11.1900   'A General Group'★ (Lord Roberts, Sir Redvers Buller, Lord Kitchener, General Archibald Hunter, General French, General Pole-Carew, Sir George White, Lord Dundonald, General Baden-Powell, Colonel Plumer, Sir Frederick Carrington, General Hector MacDonald). Spy

28.11.1901   'Kirby Gate'★ (The Duke of Marlborough, Hugh Owen, H. T. Barclay, Mr & Mrs Molyneux, Arthur Coventry, Mrs Burns-Hartopp, Lord Belper, E. H. Baldock, Captain Burns Hartopp, Lancelot Lowther, Walter Kyte, J. D. Craddock, Mrs W. Lawson, Henry Chaplin, Lady Angela Forbes, The Countess Warwick, Earl of Lonsdale, General Brocklehurst, A. Pryor, Foxhall Keene, Mrs Asquith, Princess Henry of Pless, Lord Henry Bentinck, Mrs Lancelot Lowther, Tempest Wade, Tom Firr, Captain Boyce and others). C.B.

27.11.1902   'Heads of the Law'★ (The Lord Chief Justice, (Lord Alverstone) the Master of the Rolls, (Sir Richard Henn Collins) Lord Justice Sterling, Lord Justice Cozens-Hardy, Lord Justice Romer, Lord Justice Williams, Lord Justice Mathew, Mr Justice Barnes, Mr Justice Bigham, Mr Justice Wright). Spy

7.12.1905   'A Fox Hunting Constellation'★ (Duke of Beaufort, (The Duke of Beaufort's) Ben Capell (Belvoir), G. W. Fitzwilliam (Mr G. W. Fitzwilliam's), Sir Gilbert Greenall (Belvoir), The Earl of Yarborough (Brocklesby), Duke of Rutland (Belvoir), Earl of Lonsdale (Quorn), Henry Chaplin (Blankney) and others). Bede

21.6.1911   His Majesty the King (George V). Ape Junior

undated   Collapse of the Conference/Born June 17,—Died November 10 'If so shortly I was done for, What
Special Supplementary Cartoon   was I begun for?' Old Epitaph for an infant. (Lloyd George, Mr Asquith, Mr Balfour, Austen
Listed after 10.12.1913   Chamberlain, Bonar Law and others). Mouse

Bibliography

Alexander, Michael *The True Blue, the Life and Adventures of Fred Burnaby 1842–1884*, New York: St Martin's Press, 1958.

Altholz, Josef (ed.) *The Mind and Art of Victorian England*, Minneapolis: University of Minnesota Press, 1976.

Arlott, John 'Ape, Spy and Jehu Junior' in *Late Extra* edited by John Milwane, London: Associated Newspapers Ltd. n.d.

Beerbohm, Max *A Variety of Things*, New York: Knopf, 1928

Behrman, S. N. *Portrait of Max: An Intimate Memoir of Sir Max Beerbohm*, New York: Random House, 1960.

Bentley, Nicholas *The Victorian Scene 1837–1901*, London: George Weidenfeld & Nicolson, 1968.

Bowles, Thomas Gibson *The Defense of Paris*, London: Sampson, Low, Son, 1871.
————. *Flotsam and Jetsam: A Yachtsman's Experience at Sea and Ashore*, New York: Funk and Wagnalls, 1883.
————. *Maritime Warfare* (Second Edition), London: W. Ridgway, 1878.
————. *Sea Law and Sea Power*, London: John Murray, 1910.

Cecil, David *Max: A Biography*, London: Constable, 1964.

Davies, Randall, R. H. 'Caricature of Today' *The Studio* (Special Number), 1928.

Escott, Thomas Hay Sweet *Masters of English Journalism: A Study of Personal Forces*, London: T. Fisher Unwin, 1911.

George, Dorothy *English Political Caricature* (2 volumes), Oxford: Oxford University Press, 1959.

Gombrich, Ernst H. and Kris, Ernst *Caricature*, London: Penguin Books, 1940.
————. 'The Principles of Caricature,' *British Journal of Medical Psychology*, Vol. XVII, 1938.

Harris, Eileen 'Carlo Pellegrini 'Man and Ape', *Apollo*, Vol. 103, No. 167, January 1976.

Harris, Eileen and Ormond, Richard *Vanity Fair: An Exhibition of Original Cartoons: Introduction to Catalogue*, London: National Portrait Gallery, 1976.

Hillier, Bevis *Cartoons and Caricatures*, London: Studio Vista/Dulton Picturebook, 1970.

Hofmann, Werner *Caricature from Leonardo to Picasso*, London: John Calder, 1957.

Kemnitz, Thomas M. 'Matt Morgan of *Tomahawk* and English Cartooning, 1867–1870,' *Victorian Studies*, Vol. XIX, September 1975.

Knoblock, E. 'James Tissot and the Seventies' *Apollo*, Vol. 17, June 1933.

Kris, Ernst 'The Psychology of Caricature' *International Journal of Psycho-Analysis*, Vol. XVII, 1936.

Laver, James *Vulgar Society: The Romantic Career of James Tissot, 1836–1902*, London: Constable and Co Ltd, 1938.

Longden, Alfred Appleby *Cartoon Wit and Caricature in Britain*, London: Print Collector's Club, 1944.

Low, David *British Cartoonists, Caricaturists and Comic Artists*, London: William Collins, 1942.
————. *Ye Madde Designer*, London: The Studio Ltd, 1935.

Lynch, Bohun *A History of Caricature*, Boston: Little, Brown & Co, 1927.

MacKay, William *Bohemian Days in Fleet Street*, London: John Long Ltd, 1913.

Man, Felix H. *Artists' Lithographs: A World History from Senefelder to the Present Day*, London: Studio Vista, 1970.

Manvell, Brian 'Cartoons of Theatrical Interest Appearing in *Vanity Fair.*' *Theatre Notebook*, Vol. XIX, No. 4 Summer 1965.

Matthews, Roy 'Spy,' *British History Illustrated*, Vol. III, June–July 1976.

Meyer, Susan E. *Flagg*, New York: Watson-Guptill Publications, 1974.

Naylor, Leonard E. *The Irrepressible Victorian: The Story of Thomas Gibson Bowles, Journalist, Parliamentarian and Founder Editor of the Original Vanity Fair*, London: MacDonald, 1965.

Pearsall, Ronald *Collapse of Stout Party: Victorian Art and Humour*. London: Weidenfeld & Nicolson, 1975.
————. *Edwardian Life and Leisure*, New York: St Martin's Press, 1973.

Pullar, Philippe *Frank Harris*, London: Hamish Hamilton, 1975.

Robinson, B. Fletcher 'Chronicles in Cartoons: A Record of our Times', *The Windsor Magazine*, 1905–1906.

Rogers, W. G. *Mightier than the Sword: Cartoon, Caricature & Social Comment*, New York: Harcourt, Brace & World, 1969.

Ross, Marita 'The Truth About Tissot', *Everybody's Weekly*, June 1946.

Savory, Jerold J. *The Vanity Fair Lithographs: An Illustrated Checklist*, New York: Garland Publishing, Inc., 1978.
————. *The Vanity Fair Gallery*. New York: A. S. Barnes and Co., 1979.

Vanity Fair Ltd, Cincinnati: Privately published, 1974, 1976

Ward, Leslie (Sir) *Forty Years of Spy*, London: Chatto and Windus, 1915.

Wynn Jones, Michael *The Cartoon History of Britain*, New York: The Macmillan Company, 1971.

Zerner, Henri 'James Jacques Joseph Tissot, 1836–1902. A Retrospective Exhibition,' Providence, R.I.: Introductory Essay, Museum of Art, Rhode Island School of Design, 1968.
201

Index to the 'Vanity Fair' caricatures

The characters and the cartoons are alphabeticized by *Vanity Fair*'s spelling. Each name is followed by the date, or dates, when the subject appeared. Where names or titles were the same, different individuals can be identified by their respective date. Included in this index are the names of all those who appeared in the Special Numbers, who could be identified. They are designated by (sn). Page references to caricatures in the book are in parentheses.

General index